Microsoft® Excel for Accounting

Eric A. Weinstein, CPA

Suffolk County Community College

LABYRINTH

LEARNING™

Microsoft Excel for Accounting
by Eric A. Weinstein, CPA

Copyright © 2017 by Labyrinth Learning

LABYRINTH
LEARNING™

Labyrinth Learning
2560 9th Street, Suite 320
Berkeley, California 94710
800.522.9746
On the web at: lablearning.com

President:
Brian Favro

Product Manager:
Jason Favro

Development Manager:
Laura Popelka

Senior Editor:
Alexandra Mummery

Junior Editor:
Alexandria Henderson

Production Manager:
Debra Grose

Compositor:
Happenstance Type-O-Rama

Indexer:
Valerie Perry

EBOOK ITEM: 1-59136-973-8
EBOOK ISBN-13:   978-159136-973-8

PRINT ITEM: 1-59136-697-6
ISBN-13:   978-159136-697-3

Manufactured in the United States of America

GPP   10 9 8 7 6 5 4

Contents in Brief

CHAPTER 1
The Accounting Equation and Recording Journal Entries   1

CHAPTER 2
Financial Statements   31

CHAPTER 3
Statement of Cash Flows   67

CHAPTER 4
Inventory Costing and Analysis   93

CHAPTER 5
Bank Reconciliation   127

CHAPTER 6
Depreciation Schedule   157

CHAPTER 7
Payroll Register   191

CHAPTER 8
Bond Amortization   225

CHAPTER 9
Financial Statement Analysis   259

CHAPTER 10
Budgeting and Cost Analysis   297

Table of Contents

Preface   ix

CHAPTER 1
The Accounting Equation and Recording Journal Entries   1

PROJECT: City Music World   2
   Accounting Refresher: The Accounting Equation   3
Entering Data to Display the Accounting Equation   3
   Data Types   4
   Completing Cell Entries   4
   Deleting and Replacing Entries   4
   Number Formats   4
   Decimals and Negative Numbers   5
   Formatting Changes   5
   Accounting Refresher: Recording Journal Entries   7
Using Cut, Copy, and Paste to
   Record Journal Entries   8
   Paste Options   9
   Moving and Copying Cells   10
   Long Text Entries   10
   Modifying Column Width and Row Height   11
Using Undo and Redo   13
   Undoing Multiple Actions   14
Printing Worksheets   16
   Print Preview   16
   Print the Full Worksheet   17
   Print Selections   17
   Orientation   18
   Real-World Accounting: What Are the
     Benefits of Using Excel to Record
     Journal Entries?   20
Self-Assessment   21
Reinforce Your Skills   23
Apply Your Skills   26
Extend Your Skills   28
Critical Thinking   30

CHAPTER 2
Financial Statements   31

PROJECT: City Music World   32
   Accounting Refresher: Financial Statements   33
Modifying Columns and Rows   34
   Modifying Cells   35
Hiding Columns and Rows   35
Managing Worksheets   38
Changing Vertical Alignment
   and Rotating Text   39
   Rotating Text   39
Using Alignment, Indent, and Text
   Control Options   41
   Aligning Entries   41
   Indenting Cell Entries   42
   Merging Cells   42
   Wrapping Text and Entering Line Breaks   42
Applying Borders and Fills   43
   Borders   43
   Fill Colors   44
   Real-World Accounting: What Are the
     Benefits of Using Excel to Create
     Financial Statements?   49
Self-Assessment   50
Reinforce Your Skills   52
Apply Your Skills   58
Extend Your Skills   63
Critical Thinking   65

CHAPTER 3

Statement of Cash Flows   67

PROJECT: City Music World	**68**
Accounting Refresher: Statement of Cash Flows	69
Working with Formulas	**70**
Cell and Range References	70
The Language of Excel Formulas	70
Using Cell References in Formulas	**72**
Relative Cell References	72
What-If Analysis	72
Modifying and Copying Formulas	**73**
Circular References	73
Copying Formulas	74
Using Excel's Find and Replace Commands	**76**
Replacing Cell Contents	76
Replacing Cell Formats	77
Real-World Accounting: What Are the Benefits of Using Excel to Create the Statement of Cash Flows?	80
Self-Assessment	**81**
Reinforce Your Skills	**83**
Apply Your Skills	**87**
Extend Your Skills	**90**
Critical Thinking	**92**

CHAPTER 4

Inventory Costing and Analysis   93

PROJECT: City Music World	**94**
Accounting Refresher: Inventory Costing Methods	95
Working with Functions	**96**
Using AutoSum to Create a SUM Formula	96
Status Bar Functions	97
Formula AutoComplete	97
Function Syntax	97
Insert Function	98
Using Functions to Format Text	**100**
LEFT, MID, and RIGHT to Extract Text	100
Flash Fill and the CONCATENATE Function	101
Applying Conditional Formatting	**103**

Creating PivotTables	**105**
Arranging the Source Data	105
PivotTable Example 1	105
PivotTable Example 2	106
How PivotTables Work	107
Filtering a PivotTable with AutoFilter	108
Filtering PivotTables with Slicers	109
Creating PivotCharts	**111**
Filtering PivotCharts	112
Real-World Accounting: What Are the Benefits of Using Excel to Examine and Analyze an Inventory Listing?	114
Self-Assessment	**115**
Reinforce Your Skills	**117**
Apply Your Skills	**121**
Extend Your Skills	**124**
Critical Thinking	**126**

CHAPTER 5

Bank Reconciliation   127

PROJECT: City Music World	**128**
Accounting Refresher: Bank Reconciliations	129
Importing External Data	**130**
Importing Data from QuickBooks with Copy and Paste	131
Importing Data with Drag and Drop	131
Importing Data from a Text File	131
Using the Format Painter and Quick Styles	**134**
Format Painter	134
Applying Quick Styles to Cells	135
Using Preset and Customized Conditional Formatting	**137**
Presets and Multiple Conditions	137
Conditional Formatting Rules	138
The Conditional Formatting Rules Manager	138
Creating and Formatting Headers and Footers	**141**
Real-World Accounting: What Are the Benefits of Using Excel to Create a Bank Reconciliation?	142
Self-Assessment	**143**
Reinforce Your Skills	**145**
Apply Your Skills	**151**
Extend Your Skills	**154**
Critical Thinking	**156**

CHAPTER 6

Depreciation Schedule 157

PROJECT: City Music World 158
Accounting Refresher: Depreciation Expense 159
Working with Tables 161
Creating a Table 161
Converting a Range to a Table 161
Table Rows and Columns 162
Populating and Formatting a Table 163
Formatting a Table 164
Adding and Deleting Rows and Columns 165
Selecting Table Rows and Columns 165
Printing and Deleting a Table 166
Applying Depreciation Functions with Structured References 167
Structured References 168
Formulas with Structured References 169
Using Enhanced Sorting and Filtering 171
Sorts 171
Filters 172
Custom Filters 173
Using Quick Analysis 174
Real-World Accounting: What Are the Benefits of Using Excel to Populate a Depreciation Schedule? 175
Self-Assessment 176
Reinforce Your Skills 178
Apply Your Skills 183
Extend Your Skills 186
Critical Thinking 189

CHAPTER 7

Payroll Register 191

PROJECT: City Music World 192
Accounting Refresher: Payroll Register 193
Creating Formulas with ROUND and IF Functions 195
ROUND Function 195
IF Function 195
How the IF Function Works 196
Using Nested IF Functions and Absolute/Mixed Cell References 199
Nested IF Function 199
Absolute Cell References 200
Mixed Cell References 201

Using VLOOKUP and HLOOKUP Functions 203
Lookup Function Syntax 203
How the VLOOKUP Function Works 203
Ensuring Effective Worksheet Layout 207
Enhancing Worksheet Readability 207
Highlighting Key Headers and Data 208
Real-World Accounting: What Are the Benefits of Using Excel to Create a Payroll Register? 210
Self-Assessment 211
Reinforce Your Skills 213
Apply Your Skills 217
Extend Your Skills 220
Critical Thinking 223

CHAPTER 8

Bond Amortization 225

PROJECT: City Music World 226
Accounting Refresher: Bond Amortization Schedule 227
Working with Financial Functions 228
PMT Function 228
PV Function and FV Function 229
Financial Function Syntax 230
Protecting Workbooks and Worksheets 233
Protecting the Workbook Structure 233
Protecting the Worksheet Elements 234
Protecting Individual Cells 236
The Protection Tab of the Format Cells Dialog Box 236
Unlocking Cells in a Protected Worksheet 237
To Lock or Not to Lock? 237
Using Macros 238
Security Levels 238
Recording Macros 239
Running Macros 241
Real-World Accounting: What Are the Benefits of Using Excel to Create a Bond Amortization Schedule? 242
Self-Assessment 243
Reinforce Your Skills 245
Apply Your Skills 252
Extend Your Skills 256
Critical Thinking 258

CHAPTER 9

Financial Statement Analysis   259

PROJECT: City Music World | 260
Accounting Refresher: Financial Statement Analysis | 261
Creating Charts in Excel | **262**
Choosing the Proper Data Source and Chart Type | 263
Chart and Axis Titles | 264
Chart Formatting Control | 265
Moving, Sizing, and Deleting Charts | 266
Changing the Chart Type and Source Data | 267
Modifying and Formatting Chart Elements | 268
Working with Line and Pie Charts | **270**
Exploding, Rotating, and Elevating Pie Slices | 271
Applying Chart Layouts and Styles and Creating Sparklines | **272**
Sparklines | 273
Inserting and Modifying Cell Comments | **275**
Inserting and Deleting Comments | 275
Adding to and Formatting Comments | 276
Real-World Accounting: What Are the Benefits of Using Excel to Perform a Financial Statement Analysis? | 279
Self-Assessment | **280**
Reinforce Your Skills | **282**
Apply Your Skills | **288**
Extend Your Skills | **292**
Critical Thinking | **295**

CHAPTER 10

Budgeting and Cost Analysis   297

PROJECT: City Music World | 298
Accounting Refresher: Budgeting and Cost Analysis | 299
Using Flexible Worksheet Views | **300**
Freezing Rows and Columns | 300
Splitting the Worksheet Window | 300
Viewing Worksheets in Multiple Windows | 301
Printing Multipage Worksheets | **305**
Sizing Options | 305
Setting Additional Printing Options | **308**
Title Rows and Columns | 308
Sheet Options | 308
Managing Multiple Worksheets | 309
Using Data Analysis Tools | **311**
Goal Seek | 311
Solver | 312
Real-World Accounting: What Are the Benefits of Using Excel to Complete Budgeting and Cost Analyses? | 315
Self-Assessment | **316**
Reinforce Your Skills | **318**
Apply Your Skills | **325**
Extend Your Skills | **329**
Critical Thinking | **333**

Self-Assessment Answer Key | **335**
Glossary | **341**
Index | **345**

Preface

Microsoft Excel for Accounting provides the ideal blend of accounting principles coverage and detailed, step-by-step instruction on using Microsoft Excel. This is the only solution on the market that offers both a sequential progression of material for accounting *and* Excel topics.

Key points:

- **Accounting Refresher:** Each chapter applies the Excel skills being taught to a specific accounting principle, which is covered in the Accounting Refresher section at the beginning of the chapter and that is typically introduced in an Accounting 1 or Accounting 2 course.
- **Real-World Accounting Application:** The ability to apply what is learned to a real-world scenario is critical to success in this and any course. Located immediately before the end-of-chapter content, the Real-World Accounting Application helps students understand how their new Excel skills can be applied to accounting problems.
- **Logical sequencing of content:** This textbook introduces the accounting principles in a logical sequence, progressing from the more basic to advanced. Excel topics are introduced with the accounting principle to which they are most relevant, also progressing from more basic to advanced. Chapters may be taught in sequence or as standalone chapters.
- **Detailed, step-by-step instruction:** Labyrinth Learning's highly effective approach to teaching hands-on computer applications, featuring detailed, step-by-step instruction, enables students to more easily learn and then apply the Excel skills being covered.
- **Supplemental resources:** This course is associated with a robust set of student and educator resources to both assist in student learning and educator course preparation. Each textbook includes a license key for Labyrinth eLab, our online assessment and learning platform.

Learning Resource Center

The exercise files that accompany this textbook can be found within eLab and on the Learning Resource center, which may be accessed at:
www.labyrinthlab.com/lrc

Visual Conventions

This book uses visual conventions and typographic cues to guide students through the chapters. Some of the cues are indicated here.

Cue	What It Does
`Type this text`	Text to type at the keyboard is shown in this typeface.
Action words	Important action words in exercise steps are shown in bold.
accounting equation	Glossary terms are set in bold within concepts sections.
↱ Home→Editing→Find & Select→Find | Ctrl + F	Reference steps present shortcut steps for executing certain tasks.
TIP! NOTE! WARNING!	Tips, notes, and warnings are called out with special icons.
Accounting Refresher ↻	Accounting Refresher sections are called out with this icon and set within a light blue box.
REAL-WORLD Accounting	Real-World Accounting Applications are called out with this icon and are also set within a light blue box.

About the Author

Eric A. Weinstein (MBA, CPA) is an Associate Professor of Business Administration at Suffolk County Community College on Long Island, NY. Eric graduated Summa Cum Laude from Georgetown University in 1999, where he earned a BS in Business Administration and majored in Accounting. In 2004, he earned an MBA from the Fuqua School of Business at Duke University. Eric has received many awards in his career, including the State University of New York Chancellor's Award for Excellence in Teaching. Eric has also been a practicing Certified Public Accountant in New York for more than ten years, where he provides accounting services for small businesses and individuals. Eric and his beautiful wife, Cara, are the proud parents of twin sons, Tyler and Lucas. The family lives in Huntington, NY, where they enjoy being bossed around by their two mini-dachshunds, Nathan and Molly.

Acknowledgements

Many individuals contribute to the development and completion of a textbook. We appreciate the careful attention and informed contributions of our Advisory Group members for their assistance in the development of this book. We would like to express our appreciation for the significant contributions of these educators in the development of this text:

Maggie Hilgart, *Mid-State Technical College*

Lynne Kemp, *North Country Community College*

Barbara Larew, *Coe College*

Laura Lee, *Minnesota School of Business*

Jennifer Moriarty, *Hudson Valley Community College*

Erik Richter, *Colorado Community College System*

We are also grateful to the instructors and professionals who provided feedback and suggested improvements. This book has benefited from the feedback and suggestions of the following reviewers:

Jennifer Adkins, *North Central State College*

Lisa Banks, *Mott Community College*

Cherie Brown, *Tyler Junior College*

Lindy Byrd, *Augusta Technical College*

Brenda Canning, *Springfield College*

Tracey Colville, *Lively Technical Center*

Harry Dewolf, *Mt. Hood Community College*

Carol Dutchover, *Eastern New Mexico University-Roswell*

Shmuel Fink, *Touro College*

Ken Gaines, *East West University*

Patrick Geer, *Hawkeye Community College*

Mark Gershman, *Oakton Community College*

Greg Goussak, *Ashford University*

Diann Hammon, *JF Drake State Community and Technical College*

Donna Hickling, *Monroe Community College*

Carol Hughes, *Asheville-Buncombe Technical College*

Kim Hurt, *Central Community College*

Gina Jones, *Aims Community College*

Heather Lynch, *Northeast Iowa Community College*

Kevin McFarlane, *Front Range Community College*

Terry Mullin, *Cabrillo College*

Patti Norris, *Central Oregon Community College*

Robert Pacheco, *Massasoit Community College*

Veronica Paz, *Indiana University of Pennsylvania*

Roxanne Phillips, *Colorado Community Colleges Online*

Erik Richter, *Colorado Community College System*

Anita Ricker, *Walters State Community College*

Jennifer Robinson, *Trident Technical College*

Cle Royal, *Tarrant County College Small Business Development Center*

Debra Schmidt, *Cerritos College*

Achraf Seyam, *Borough of Manhattan Community College-CUNY*

Linda Snidere, *Grossmont College*

Shanna Stein, *Sacramento City College*

Ted Stryk, *Roane State Community College*

Cathy Van Loon, *Cabrillo College*

Lori Yecoshenko, *Lake Superior College*

Peter Young, *San Jose State University*

Mellissa Youngman, *National Technical Institute for the Deaf at RIT*

Ranae Ziwiski, *Elgin Community College*

The Accounting Equation and Recording Journal Entries

LEARNING OBJECTIVES

- Display the accounting equation
- Record journal entries
- Enter data and numbers in Excel
- Use Undo and Redo in Excel
- Print worksheets

Microsoft Excel is a worksheet application that can be used to facilitate accounting tasks. You will find that even the most basic elements of accounting can be completed more efficiently in the Excel environment. In this chapter, you will examine two fundamental accounting concepts: the accounting equation and the transaction recording process. These accounting concepts will provide the foundation for all subsequent topics. As you examine these topics, you will be introduced to a number of basic Excel features.

| PROJECT | City Music World |

City Music World is a retail store located in Niskayuna, NY. The store sells musical equipment and offers lessons for beginning and experienced musicians. The company has used pen and paper to track accounting activity since its inception in 1979 and has now decided to work with Excel to increase its efficiency. You are spearheading this process.

In this chapter, you will examine how the accounting equation and journal entries can be expressed within Excel. You will then examine how this data can be managed within Excel and then conclude by reviewing printing methods.

Date	Account	Debit	Credit	Assets	=	Liabilities	+	Equity
4/1/2016	Cash	$ 30,000		$ 30,000				
	Harold Cameron, Capital		$ 30,000					$ 30,000
	Investment by Owner			$ 30,000	=	$ -	+	$ 30,000
4/3/2016	Supplies	$ 2,000		$ 2,000				
	Accounts Payable		$ 2,000			$ 2,000		
	Purchase of Supplies			$ 32,000	=	$ 2,000	+	$ 30,000
4/8/2016	Utilities Expense	$ 250						$ (250)
	Cash		$ 250	$ (250)				
	Payment of Utilities Expense			$ 31,750	=	$ 2,000	+	$ 29,750
4/9/2016	Accounts Receivable	$ 1,500		$ 1,500				
	Service Revenue		$ 1,500					$ 1,500
	Services Provided on Account			$ 33,250	=	$ 2,000	+	$ 31,250

Journal entries for City Music World (left) and their corresponding impact on the accounting equation (right) can be easily entered in Excel.

Accounting *Refresher* ↻   The Accounting Equation

The accounting equation is a simple formula that must remain in balance at all times. The equation is as follows:

Assets = Liabilities + Owner's Equity

Assets are items of value within the business. Types of assets include Cash, Accounts Receivable (monies owed to the business from a customer), Supplies, Inventory, Equipment, and Land. These resources are used to generate income for the business.

Liabilities are the portions of assets owed to entities outside the business. Examples include Accounts Payable (monies owed by the business to other companies), outstanding loans, mortgages, and monies received in advance of services rendered (such as a sports team receiving season ticket revenue before the actual games are played).

Owner's Equity is the portion of the assets not owed to entities outside the organization. This portion of the assets represents that to which the owner(s) can lay claim, hence the term *owner's equity*.

Stated in different terms, the accounting equation dictates that all items of value (assets) equal the portion of the assets owed to others (liabilities) plus the portion of the assets not owed to others (owner's equity). Remember that the accounting equation must always be in balance. If you find that total assets do not equal total liabilities plus total owner's equity, you must identify and correct the error.

Entering Data to Display the Accounting Equation

Within Excel, data is entered into the active cell, which is surrounded by a thick border known as the *highlight*. Data may be entered as text (used for headings and entries containing alphabetic characters) or numbers (can be entered directly or can be calculated using formulas). Excel recognizes whether the data you enter is text, a number, or a formula.

Data Types

Entries are defined as one of two main classifications: constant values or formulas. Depending on the method used, the accounting equation can use entries from each classification. Constant values can be text, numeric, or a combination of both. Formula entries display the results of dynamic calculations.

| 2000 |

This entry is a constant value.

| =2000+31250 |

This entry is a formula that results in the sum of 33,250 being displayed.

Completing Cell Entries

Text and numbers are entered by positioning the highlight in the desired cell, typing the text or number, and completing the entry. You can use [Enter], [Tab], or any of the arrow keys to complete an entry. The method you use determines where the active cell moves.

Entry Completion Method	Where the Active Cell Will Appear
[Enter]	It will move down to the next cell.
[Tab]	It will move to the next cell to the right.
[↓][↑][→][←]	It will move to the next cell in the direction of the arrow key.
[Esc]	The entry will be deleted and the current cell will remain active.

When [Tab] is used to populate multiple cells in a row and [Enter] is used to complete the entry, the highlight is returned to the beginning of the next row. This simplifies the process of entering multiple rows of data.

The Enter and Cancel buttons appear on the Formula Bar whenever you enter or edit an entry. The Enter button completes the entry and keeps the highlight in the current cell. Similar to the [Esc] key, the Cancel button discards changes made before completing the entry.

Cancel button

Enter button

TIP!   Simply clicking within a different cell after typing a cell entry also confirms the typed entry.

Deleting and Replacing Entries

You can delete an entire entry after it has been completed by clicking in the cell and tapping [Delete]. Likewise, you can replace an entry by clicking in the cell and typing a new entry.

Number Formats

When entering numbers, it isn't necessary to type commas, dollar signs, and other number formats. Instead, you can use Excel's formatting commands (located on the Home tab of the Ribbon) to add the desired number formats.

Decimals and Negative Numbers

You should always type a decimal point if the number you are entering requires one. Likewise, you should precede a negative number entry with a minus (–) sign or enclose it in parentheses ( ).

Formatting Changes

Other formatting changes can be made from the Font group on the Home tab, including bold, italics, and underline. In order to apply these changes to non-adjacent cells, the Ctrl key can be used while highlighting the desired cells with the mouse.

↗ Home→Font→Bold B │ Ctrl + B

↗ Home→Font→Italic I │ Ctrl + I

↗ Home→Font→Underline U │ Ctrl + U

Develop Your Skills EA1-D1

In this exercise, you will create a workbook in Excel and enter the headers and amounts that comprise the accounting equation for City Music World.

Before You Begin: *Be sure to visit the Learning Resource Center at labyrinthelab.com/lrc to retrieve the student files for this course before beginning this exercise.*

1. Start Excel and open a **Blank Workbook** template file.
2. Save the file in your **Chapter 01** folder as: **EA1-D1-AcctEquation-[YourName]**

Enter Headers for the Accounting Equation

3. Make **cell A1** active by clicking the **mouse pointer** ⊕ in it.
4. Type **Assets** and tap Tab.

   The text is entered in the cell and the highlight moves right to cell B1.
5. Type **=** and tap Tab.

   Because nothing was typed after the equals sign, it is displayed within cell B1.
6. Type **Liabilities** and tap Tab, type **+** and tap Tab, type **Equity** and tap Enter.

   The highlight returns to column A on the next row (cell A2).
7. Click **cell A1**, drag to the right, and release the mouse on **cell E1**.

   You have now highlighted the range A1:E1, which includes cells A1, B1, C1, D1, and E1.
8. Choose **Home→Font→Bold** B.

   Bold formatting is applied to each cell within the highlighted range.

9. Choose **Home→Alignment→Center** ☰ to center the headers.

Enter Figures Within the Accounting Equation

10. Follow these steps to enter data:

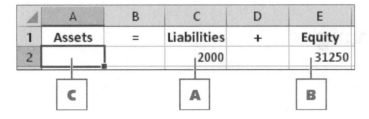

A. Select **cell C2**, type **2000**, and tap Enter .

B. Select **cell E2**, type **31250**, and tap Enter .

C. Select **cell A2**, type **33250**, and tap Esc .

The entry in cell A2 is deleted, while the highlight remains within the cell. You have deleted this entry so that you may type a formula within this cell instead.

11. Type **=2000+31250** and tap Enter .

The result of the formula is now displayed in cell A2.

12. Select **cell B2**, type **=** and tap Enter , select **cell D2**, and then type **+** and tap Enter .

13. Select **cell B2**, hold Ctrl , and select **cell D2**.

Cells B2 and D2 are now highlighted. The Ctrl *key can be used in this manner to highlight non-adjacent cells.*

14. Choose **Home→Alignment→Center** ☰ .

Format Figures Within the Accounting Equation

15. Select **cell A2**, hold Ctrl , and then select **cells C2** and **E2**.

Now that you have selected the three figures within the accounting equation, you will format them as currency.

16. Choose **Home→Number→Accounting** $.

Notice that the dollar sign has been placed in front of each figure, two decimal places have been added, and the width of the columns has increased to accommodate the increased length of the entries. As every figure is a whole dollar amount, you will now reduce the number of visible decimal places.

17. Choose **Home→Number→Decrease Decimal** twice to remove the two decimal places for each figure.

	A	B	C	D	E
1	Assets	=	Liabilities	+	Equity
2	$ 33,250	=	$ 2,000	+	$ 31,250

The headers and the figures of the accounting equation are now appropriately displayed.

18. Save and close the file.

Accounting Refresher — Recording Journal Entries

A **transaction** represents a single event that has occurred within a business. When these events take place, they must be recorded in a manner that can be understood by an outsider. We use **journal entries** to accomplish this goal. A journal entry is a visual display of a transaction in which debits are listed on top and credits are listed on the bottom and indented.

Impact of Debits and Credits on Account Types

Account Type	Debit	Credit
Asset	Increase	Decrease
Liability	Decrease	Increase
Capital	Decrease	Increase
Withdrawal	Increase	Decrease
Revenue	Decrease	Increase
Expense	Increase	Decrease

You can determine whether the balance within an account is increasing or decreasing based on whether it is being debited or credited within a journal entry. The format for a journal entry is as follows.

8/4/2016 Supplies	1,400	
Accounts Payable		1,400
Purchase of Supplies on Account		

Supplies (asset) is being debited (displayed at the top of the journal entry) and Accounts Payable (liability) is being credited (displayed on the bottom of the journal entry, indented). This journal entry indicates that the balance within each of these accounts is increasing, as a debit increases an asset account and a credit increases a liability account.

Although it is good form to include an explanation beneath each journal entry (the final, italicized row in the journal entry above), for the sake of efficiency you will exclude these explanations throughout this chapter. Also keep in mind that a journal entry can have multiple debits (each of which would be listed on a single row at the top of the journal entry) and multiple credits (each of which would be listed on a single row at the bottom of the journal entry and indented once), but the total debits must always equal the total credits.

Using Cut, Copy, and Paste to Record Journal Entries

With Cut, Copy, and Paste, you can move or copy cells. As certain accounts are used frequently within journal entries, using Copy and Paste can increase efficiency. The Copy command can copy a range from one worksheet, and the Paste command will paste the range within or between worksheets.

WARNING! When copying and pasting to a cell that already contains an entry, the existing entry is deleted and replaced with the copied entry.

When an item is either copied or cut, it is placed on the **Office Clipboard**. It can then be pasted from the Clipboard, which can be opened via the dialog box launcher on the Clipboard group of the Home tab.

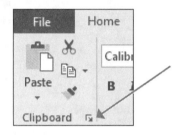

The Office Clipboard with several items available to paste

> ↗ Home→Clipboard→Copy 📋 | Ctrl + C

> ↗ Home→Clipboard→Cut ✂ | Ctrl + X

> ↗ Home→Clipboard→Paste 📋 | Ctrl + V

Paste Options

The Paste Options button displays at the lower-right corner of the destination cell(s) after a paste action. Its drop-down list provides options that let you modify the effect of the Paste command.

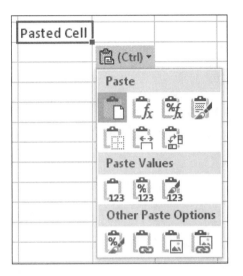

The button disappears upon the next action you take. The Paste Options menu can also be accessed from the Home tab within the Clipboard section.

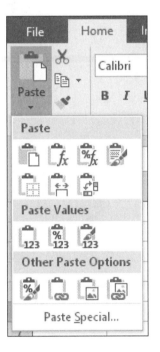

Moving and Copying Cells

Drag and drop, in which you drag a cell's contents to a new location, produces the same result as Cut and Paste. However, drag and drop is preferable if the original location and new destination are both visible in the current window. The mouse pointer changes to a four-pointed arrow as you point at the highlight around the selected cell or range.

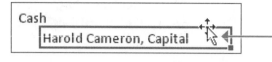

Right-dragging is a variation of drag and drop. With the right-drag method, you use the right mouse button to drag the selected cell or range. When the button is released, you choose to move, copy, or link. This approach provides more control because there is no need to use the Ctrl key when copying and you have the option of canceling the action.

> Move Here
> Copy Here
> Copy Here as Values Only
> Copy Here as Formats Only
> Link Here
> Create Hyperlink Here
> Shift Down and Copy
> Shift Right and Copy
> Shift Down and Move
> Shift Right and Move
> Cancel

Pop-up menu that appears when using the right-drag method

Long Text Entries

Text entries that do not fit in a cell are known as long entries. Excel will display a long entry over the adjacent cell, if it is empty, or shorten (truncate) the display of the long entry if the cell to the right is in use. In the latter instance, the entire long entry remains within the cell but is not fully visible. You can widen a column to accommodate a long entry.

	A	B	C
1	Harold Cameron, Capital		

This long entry is entered in cell A1, although it displays over the range A1:C1.

Modifying Column Width and Row Height

Modifying column width and/or row height can improve the appearance of a worksheet. You should strive to make data fully visible, while ensuring that no unnecessary space is displayed within the rows or columns. There are a variety of methods for changing column widths and row heights. One efficient way is with AutoFit, which adjusts column width to fit the widest entry in a column and row height to the tallest entry in a row. Note that you can adjust column widths and row heights on one or multiple columns or rows.

NOTE! The default column width is 8.43 characters and the default row height is 15 points.

Develop Your Skills EA1-D2

In this exercise, you will use Cut, Copy, and Paste to record two journal entries for City Music World.

1. Open a **Blank Workbook** template and save the file in your **Chapter 01** folder as: **EA1-D2-JournalEntries-[YourName]**

2. Make **cell A1** active by clicking the **mouse pointer** ⊕ in it.

3. Type **4/1/16** and tap Tab.

   By default, the date is entered in the Short Date format of 4/1/2016.

4. Use the right arrow to move to **cell C1**, type **Cash**, and tap Enter.

   Although you intended to enter all debited accounts in column B, you accidentally entered the Cash account in cell C1. You will now cut this entry from cell C1 and paste it on cell B1.

5. Select **cell C1** and choose **Home→Clipboard→Cut**.

   Notice the marquee (moving lines) surrounding cell C1. This indicates that the Cut command has been applied to the cell.

6. Select **cell B1** and choose **Home→Clipboard→Paste**.

7. Use the right arrow to move to **cell D1** and then type **30,000** and tap Enter.

   You have now entered the date, debited account, and debited amount in row 1.

8. Select **cell C2**, type **Harold Cameron, Capital**, and tap Enter.

   This long text entry extends beyond the right border of the cell.

9. Select **cell D1**, hold down Ctrl, and tap C.

   Notice the marquee around cell D1 indicating that the Copy command has been applied.

10. Select **cell E2**, hold down Ctrl, and tap V.

    This keyboard shortcut has pasted the contents of cell D1 to cell E2.

11. Tap Enter.

    By tapping Enter you have confirmed the entry in cell E2 and terminated the Copy command. Notice that the marquee is no longer around cell D1.

12. Select **cell B3**, type **Investment by Owner**, and tap Enter.

13. Right-click the **column B** header and choose **Column Width**, type **3**, and click **OK**.

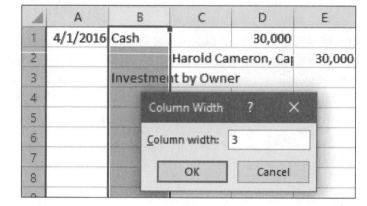

14. Set the column width of **column C** to **27**.

15. Highlight the **columns D–E** headers, right-click and choose **Column Width**, type **11**, and click **OK**.

    By highlighting two column headers before applying the new column width, you have changed the width of both columns simultaneously.

16. Select **cell B3** and choose **Home→Font→Italic**.

    Italicizing the journal entry explanation ensures that it will stand out and not be confused with the account names listed above.

Create a Journal Entry for the Purchase of Supplies on Account

17. Enter the data for the journal entry as indicated:

Cell A4	4/3/2016
Cell B4	Supplies
Cell D4	2,000
Cell B5	Accounts Payable
Cell D5	2,000

    Because these items are being credited in the second journal entry, they should be indented. Now you will change their location.

18. Select **cell B5** and then click the border around that cell and drag and drop the contents to **cell C5**.

19. Follow these steps to use the right mouse button with drag and drop:

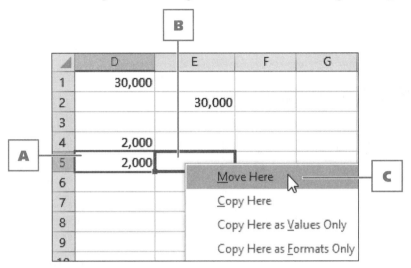

A. Select **cell D5** and then right-click the border around that cell (do not release the mouse button).

B. Drag the contents to **cell E5** and release the mouse button.

C. Choose **Move Here** from the menu.

20. Select **cell B6** and type: `Purchase of Supplies`

21. Select **cell B3** and choose **Home→Clipboard→Copy**.

22. Select **cell B6**, choose **Home→Clipboard→Paste ▾→Formatting**, and then tap Esc.

This Paste option applied the formatting from cell B3 to cell B6 without changing the contents of the cell. Pressing Esc *cancelled the Copy command.*

23. Save your file.

Unless otherwise directed, always keep your file open at the end of each exercise.

Using Undo and Redo

The Undo ⤺ command reverses actions taken within a worksheet. Most actions can be undone, but those that cannot include printing and saving workbooks.

The Redo ⤻ command reverses an Undo command. The Redo button is visible on the Quick Access toolbar only after you have undone an action.

➐ Ctrl + Z to undo

➐ Ctrl + Y to redo

Undoing Multiple Actions

Clicking the arrow ▼ on the Undo button displays a list of actions that can be undone. You can undo multiple actions by dragging the mouse over the desired actions. You must undo actions in the order they appear on the list.

Borders
Italic
Typing 'Total Revenue' in I14
Typing '' in J16
Bold
Typing '4500' in J14

When you click the arrow on the Undo button, you will see a list of previous actions with the most recent at the top.

Limitations to Undoing

There are times when Undo will not work, such as when you select any command from the File tab. When an action cannot be undone, Excel will change the Undo ScreenTip to *Can't Undo*. (ScreenTips appear when the mouse pointer hovers over a worksheet element for a short period of time.)

Develop Your Skills EA1-D3

In this exercise, you will use Undo and Redo while recording two journal entries for City Music World.

1. Save your file as: **EA1-D3-JournalEntries-[YourName]**

2. Follow these steps to begin recording the journal entries:

	A	B	C	D
7	4/8/2016	Utilities Expense		250
8				

   A. Select **cell A7**, type **4/8/2016**, and tap Tab.

   B. Type **Utilities Expense** in **cell B7** and tap Tab twice.

   C. Type **250** in **cell D7** and tap Enter.

You confirmed the 250 entry in cell D7 by tapping Enter *after using* Tab *for the preceding entries. The active cell is now in column A on the subsequent row.*

3. Select **cell C8**, type **Accounts Payable**, and tap Enter.

   You have incorrectly entered Accounts Payable as the credited account. Because the utility bill was paid, the Cash account should be credited. You will now correct this error.

4. Click **Undo** on the Quick Access toolbar.

   Accounts Payable has now been removed and the highlight has returned to cell C8.

5. Type **Cash**, tap Tab twice, type **250**, and tap Enter.

6. Select **cell B9** and choose **Home→Font→Italic**.

   Although you have not yet written the explanation for the third journal entry, you can still apply italics to this cell. When you ultimately type the explanation, it will be italicized.

7. Type **Payment of Utilities Expense**, tap Enter, and then tap the left arrow key.

8. Type **4/9/2016** and tap Tab, type **Accounts Receivable** and tap Tab twice, and finally type **1,500** and tap Enter.

9. Select **cell C11**, type **Service Revenue** and tap Tab twice, and then type **1,500** and tap Enter.

10. Select **cell B12**, type **Services Provided on Account**, and tap Enter.

    After typing this entry you decide that your explanation is inaccurate; therefore, you will now undo your previous action.

11. Choose **Undo** from the Quick Access toolbar.

    The explanation in cell B12 has been removed. Upon further consideration you decide that the explanation was sufficient, so you will now return it to cell B12.

12. Choose **Redo** from the Quick Access toolbar.

    The explanation has now been returned to its original location.

13. Choose **Home→Font→Italic**.

14. Highlight the **range D1:E11** and choose **Home→Number→Accounting**.

15. Click **Decrease Decimal** twice.

16. Save your file.

Printing Worksheets

Excel gives you options for printing your work. Among these are the Quick Print button, Print Selection, and Print Area. These options provide flexibility so that printing can be adapted to accommodate all workbooks.

NOTE! The light gridlines displayed around cells in Normal and Page Layout views do not print.

Print Preview

Print Preview shows how a worksheet will look when printed. It's wise to preview a large or complex worksheet before sending it to the printer. The Print tab of Backstage view (available via the File tab) displays a preview along with print options. You cannot edit worksheets in Backstage view.

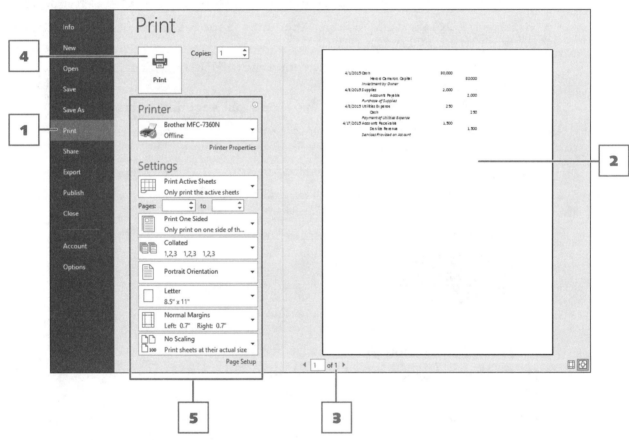

1. Print tab

2. Print preview

3. Page Navigation indicating the total number of pages that will print

4. Button that sends the document to the printer using the print options in effect

5. Print settings

Print the Full Worksheet

You can customize the Quick Access toolbar to include the Quick Print button, which sends the entire worksheet to the current printer using the print options in effect.

TIP! In general, customizing the Quick Access toolbar to display your most commonly used buttons can greatly increase your efficiency.

Although the Quick Print button is useful for standard printing, you must use the Print tab in Backstage view if you want to change printers, adjust the number of copies to be printed, print only certain pages, or set other printing options such as printing only selected cells.

↗ File→Print │ Ctrl+P

Print Selections

You may want to print only a single range of cells or multiple nonadjacent ranges within a worksheet. Note that if you highlight nonadjacent selections, they will print on separate pages.

Print Area

An alternative to using the Print Selection option is to set the print area, which is done via the Page Setup group on the Page Layout tab. There are two primary benefits of using this method instead of Print Selection:

- The portion of the worksheet designated as the print area does not change when the worksheet is altered. This differs from Print Selection, which prints only the highlighted area within the worksheet.

- When printing a designated print area, no additional options must be selected from Backstage view, whereas Print Selection requires you to select a Settings option from Backstage view prior to printing.

↗ Page Layout→Page Setup→Print Area→Set Print Area

Orientation

When printing a worksheet, you can use portrait or landscape orientation. Depending on whether the worksheet primarily extends vertically or horizontally, you will find that each of these options will be useful.

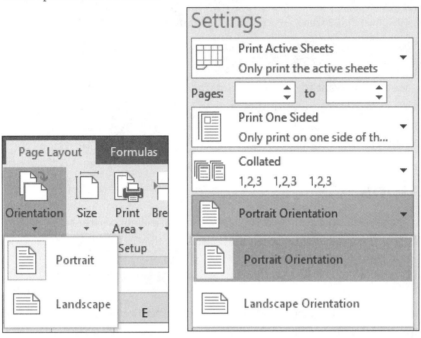

Worksheet orientation can be changed from the Ribbon (left) or the Print tab of Backstage view (right).

➚ Page Layout→Page Setup→Orientation→Portrait *or* Landscape *or* File→Print→ Settings→Portrait Orientation *or* Landscape Orientation

Develop Your Skills EA1-D4

In this exercise, you will print four journal entries for City Music World.

1. Save your file as: **EA1-D4-JournalEntries-[YourName]**
2. Highlight the **range A1:E6** and choose **File→Print**.

3. In the Settings section, click **Print Active Sheets** and choose **Print Selection** from the menu that appears.

Settings

Print Active Sheets
Only print the active sheets

Print Active Sheets
Only print the active sheets

Print Entire Workbook
Print the entire workbook

Print Selection
Only print the current selection

Ignore Print Area

The preview displays the first two journal entries, which is your selected area.

4. If directed, choose **Print**; otherwise, click the back arrow at the top-left corner of Backstage view.

You are returned to your worksheet.

5. Highlight the **range A1:E9**, choose **Page Layout→Page Setup→Print Area→ Set Print Area**, and then choose **File→Print**.

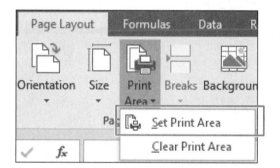

The preview displays the first three journal entries, as these are the ones in your print area.

6. In the Settings section, click **Portrait Orientation** and choose **Landscape Orientation** from the menu.

The page within the preview has now turned such that the longer sides of the page are on the top/bottom.

7. If directed, choose **Print**; otherwise, click the back arrow at the top-left corner of Backstage view.

8. Save and close your file.

REAL-WORLD Accounting

What Are the Benefits of Using Excel to Record Journal Entries?

As you have learned, Excel can increase your efficiency when recording journal entries. Years ago, all journal entries were handwritten on large (typically either green or yellow) journal paper. It is not difficult to see how using Excel for this purpose is not only a quicker method, but also one that is far less prone to errors.

Today, many businesses use computerized accounting systems that automatically generate journal entries. While some companies praise the simplicity of these systems, others have difficulty using the software and, therefore, generate inaccurate results.

Small-business owners can maintain a close watch on a company's performance by using Excel to complete the journal entry recording process. While this method increases the business owner's speed (in comparison to using journal paper), it also minimizes the possibility of user error (in comparison to an untrained employee working with computerized software). The business owner is, therefore, given more time to devote to improving the business and possesses accurate records that will enable this improvement.

Self-Assessment

Check your knowledge of this chapter's key concepts and skills using the Self-Assessment here or in your eLab course.

1. Using `Tab` to complete a cell entry moves the active cell one column to the right.   *True   False*

2. When you use the Enter button on the Formula Bar to complete a cell entry, the highlight moves one row down.   *True   False*

3. A negative number can be indicated through the use of a minus sign or parentheses.   *True   False*

4. The Paste option can be executed from the Ribbon or via a keyboard shortcut.   *True   False*

5. When using drag and drop, a menu of options appears.   *True   False*

6. If the cell to the right of a long text entry is in use, the long text entry will cover the contents of this adjacent cell.   *True   False*

7. The Undo button can be used to reverse every action in Excel.   *True   False*

8. Print Preview can be accessed via the Home tab.   *True   False*

9. The Quick Access toolbar can be customized to include options such as Quick Print.   *True   False*

10. The two orientation options are portrait and landscape.   *True   False*

11. Which key CANNOT be used to complete an entry and move to a new cell?
    A. `Enter`
    B. `Tab`
    C. `→`
    D. `Esc`

12. Which action CANNOT be taken from the Home tab?
    A. Bold
    B. Right-dragging
    C. Italic
    D. Underline

13. How can you open the Office Clipboard?
    A. Copy a cell or range.
    B. Paste a cell or range.
    C. Click the dialog box launcher in the Clipboard group.
    D. Click the dialog box launcher in the Font group.

14. Which of these CANNOT be used to move the contents of one cell to another location?
    A. Undo and Redo
    B. Cut and Paste
    C. Drag and drop
    D. Right-dragging

15. Long text entries:
   A. cannot be made to fit within a single column.
   B. initially extend beyond the right border of the cell in which they are entered.
   C. will always cover the contents of the cell to the right.
   D. must be shortened before completing the entry.

16. Which of these actions CANNOT be reversed with Undo?
   A. Italic
   B. Paste
   C. Save
   D. Bold

17. The Redo button becomes visible only after doing what?
   A. Pasting cell contents
   B. Using Undo
   C. Copying cell contents
   D. Typing a number within a cell

18. The Quick Print button can be added to:
   A. the Quick Access toolbar.
   B. the Home tab.
   C. Backstage view.
   D. an individual cell within the worksheet.

19. Which of these will NOT result in only a portion of a worksheet being printed?
   A. Setting the print area from the Ribbon
   B. Choosing Print Selection in Backstage view
   C. Selecting only certain pages to print in Backstage view
   D. Changing the orientation from the Ribbon

20. Which of these is NOT displayed in Backstage view?
   A. Print Preview
   B. The Ribbon
   C. The Print button
   D. Print Settings

Reinforce Your Skills

EA1-R1 Display the Accounting Equation

In this exercise, you will enter the beginning and ending accounting equations in Excel. The beginning assets equal $62,000 and the beginning liabilities equal $19,000. During the year, liabilities increased by $13,000 and equity increased by $4,000.

1. Create a **Blank Workbook** and save the file in your **Chapter 01** folder as: **EA1-R1-AcctEquation-[YourName]**

   You will begin by formatting the cells into which you'll enter the accounting equation.

2. Highlight the **range A1:E1**, choose **Home→Font→Bold**, and then click **Center** ≣.

3. Using Tab to navigate and Enter to complete the final entry, type the beginning accounting equation into the **range A1:E1**.

◢	A	B	C	D	E
1	**Assets**	**=**	**Liabilities**	**+**	**Equity**

   The accounting equation headers appear in row 1 with the bold formatting and center alignment you applied in the previous step.

4. In **cell A2**, type the beginning asset dollar amount and tap Tab.

   Hint: Here and throughout, refer to the exercise instructions for the dollar amounts to enter within the accounting equations.

5. Type **=** and tap Tab, type the beginning liability dollar amount and tap Tab, type **+** and tap Tab, and then type the beginning equity dollar amount and tap Tab.

   As this is the beginning accounting equation, the spreadsheet should indicate this fact. To accomplish this, you will now enter a description in cell F2.

6. In **cell F2**, type **Beginning Accounting Equation** and tap Enter.

7. Select **cell A2**, hold Ctrl, select **cells C2** and **E2**, and release Ctrl.

   You have highlighted the three dollar amounts in the beginning accounting equation. You will now apply a number format to these dollar amounts simultaneously.

8. Choose **Home→Number→Accounting** then click **Decrease Decimal** 🔢 twice.

9. In **cell A3**, enter the ending asset dollar amount and tap Tab.

10. Type **=** and tap Tab, type the ending liability dollar amount and tap Tab, type **+** and tap Tab, and then type the ending equity dollar amount and tap Tab.

11. In **cell F3**, type **Ending Accounting Equation** and tap Enter.

12. Select **cell F3**, choose **Home→Cells→Format→Column Width**, type **30**, and click **OK**.

13. Select **cell A3**, hold Ctrl, select **cells C3** and **E3**, and release Ctrl.

14. Choose **Home→Number→Accounting** and then click **Decrease Decimal** twice.

15. Highlight the **range B2:B3**, hold Ctrl, highlight the **range D2:D3**, release Ctrl, and choose **Home→Alignment→Center**.

16. Highlight the **range A1:F3** and choose **File→Print**.

17. In the Settings section, click **Print Active Sheets** and choose **Print Selection**.

18. Open the **Portrait Orientation** menu and choose **Landscape Orientation**.

19. If directed, choose **Print**; otherwise, click the back arrow at the top left of Backstage view.

20. Save and close your file.

EA1-R2 Record Journal Entries

In this exercise, you will record journal entries in Excel. The four transactions you use, all of which took place during 2016, are as follows:

- *August 2: Purchased twelve months of insurance coverage in advance for $3,600*

- *August 9: Billed clients $6,000 for services rendered*

- *August 21: Received $4,200 from clients for previously billed services*

- *August 31: Recorded an adjusting journal entry for the portion of insurance coverage from the August 2 purchase that has now expired*

1. Create a **Blank Workbook** template and save the file in your **Chapter 01** folder as:
   EA1-R2-JournalEntries-[YourName]

2. In **cell A1**, type **8/2/2016** and then enter the debited account for the first journal entry in **cell B1** and its amount in **cell D1**. Tap Enter to complete your final cell entry.

3. In **cell C2**, type the credited account for the first journal entry and tap Enter.

4. Select **cell D1** and choose **Home→Clipboard→Copy**.

5. Select **cell E2** and press Ctrl+V.

   The debited amount is pasted into cell E2 as the credited amount in the first journal entry.

6. Type **Purchased Insurance Coverage in Advance** in **cell B3** and click **Enter** on the Formula Bar.

   Clicking the Enter checkmark on the Formula Bar confirms the entry within cell B3 while keeping that cell active.

7. Choose **Home→Font→Italic**.

8. In **cell A4**, type **8/9/2016** and then enter the debited account for the second journal entry in **cell B4** and its amount in **cell D4**. Tap Enter to complete your final cell entry.

9. In **cell C5**, type the credited account and tap Tab two times, type the credited amount in **cell E5**, and tap Enter.

10. In **cell B6**, type **Billed Clients for Services** and tap Enter.

11. Tap the up arrow and then press Ctrl+I to apply italic formatting.

12. In **cell A7**, type **8/21/2016** and then enter the debited account for the third journal entry in **cell B7** and its amount in **cell D7**. Tap Enter to complete your final cell entry.

13. In **cell C8**, type the credited account and tap Tab twice, type the credited amount in **cell E8**, and tap Enter.

14. In **cell B9**, type **Received Payment on Account** and tap Enter.

15. Select **cell B9** and choose **Home→Font→Italic**.

16. In **cell A10**, type **8/31/2016** and then enter the debited account for the fourth journal entry in **cell B10** and its amount in **cell D10**. Tap Enter to complete your final cell entry.

17. In **cell C11**, type the credited account and tap Tab twice, type the credited amount in **cell E11**, and tap Enter.

18. In **cell B12**, type **Adjusting Entry for Expired Insurance** and tap Enter.

19. Select **cell B9**, choose **Home→Clipboard→Copy**, select **cell B12**, and choose **Home→Clipboard→Paste ▼→Formatting**.

20. Highlight the **range D1:E11**, choose **Home→Number→Number Format→ Accounting**, and then click **Decrease Decimal** twice.

21. Click the **columns A–E** headers and then double-click between the **columns A–B** headers.

    Double-clicking widened the columns to fit the text within them.

22. Click **cell A1**, right-click the **column B** header, choose **Column Width**, and then type **5** and click **OK**.

23. Highlight the range **A1:E12**, choose **Page Layout→Page Setup→Print Area→ Set Print Area**, and choose **File→Print**.

24. If directed, choose **Print**; otherwise, click the back arrow at the top-left of Backstage view.

25. Save and close your file.

Apply Your Skills

EA1-A1 Display the Accounting Equation

In this exercise, you will enter the beginning and ending accounting equations in Excel. The beginning assets equal $97,000 and the beginning liabilities equal $59,000. During the year, liabilities increased by $9,000 and equity decreased by $11,000.

1. Create a **Blank Workbook** and save the file in your **Chapter 01** folder as:
   EA1-A1-AcctEquation-[YourName]

2. In the **range A1:E1** type appropriate headers for the accounting equation. Ensure that you enter the equals sign and plus sign in the proper locations.

3. Apply bold formatting to and center all entries in **row 1**.

4. In **row 2**, enter the beginning accounting equation amounts and any necessary mathematical symbols in the appropriate locations.

5. In **cell F2**, enter an appropriate description of the figures displayed in row 2.

6. In **row 3**, enter the ending accounting equation amounts and any necessary mathematical symbols in the appropriate locations.

7. In **cell F3**, enter an appropriate description of the figures displayed within row 3.

8. In **rows 2–3**, format all dollar amounts in the accounting number format with zero decimal places; center all mathematical symbols.

9. Change the worksheet orientation to be landscape.

10. Review the print preview and then save and close the file.

EA1-A2 Record Journal Entries

In this exercise, you will record four journal entries in Excel. The four transactions you will use, all of which took place during 2016, are as follows:

- *February 4: Purchased $1,100 of supplies on account*

- *February 12: Received $2,600 of Service Revenue*

- *February 17: Paid $3,100 for Rent Expense*

- *February 27: Recorded an adjusting journal entry for Supplies Expense after determining that the value of remaining supplies is $350 (the company had no supplies prior to February)*

1. Create a **Blank Workbook** and save the file in your **Chapter 01** folder as:
   EA1-A2-JournalEntries-[YourName]

2. In **row 1**, for the first transaction enter the date (including the year) in **column A**, the debited account in **column B**, and the debited amount in **column D**.

3. Ensure that the format for the date in cell A1 is **Short Date**.

4. In **row 2**, for the first transaction enter the credited account in **column C** and its amount in **column E**.

5. Enter an explanation for the first transaction in **cell B3**.

6. Record the second journal entry on **rows 4–6** and the third on **rows 7–9**.

7. Enter the fourth transaction as described:

In this cell:	Enter the data for the:
Cell A10	Date of the fourth transaction
Cell B10	Debited account
Cell D10	Debited amount
Cell C11	Credited account
Cell E11	Credited amount
Cell B12	Explanation for the fourth transaction

8. Highlight all amounts within the four journal entries and apply the accounting number format with zero decimal places.

9. Adjust the width of **columns A–E** by double-clicking the right border of **column E**.

10. Adjust the column width of **column B** to equal **5**.

11. Use a keyboard shortcut to italicize the explanations for the first and second journal entries and use the Ribbon to italicize the explanation for the third journal entry.

12. Copy the formatting in **cell B9** and paste it to **cell B12**.

13. Set the print area to encompass only the first two journal entries.

14. Save and close the file.

Extend Your Skills

EA1-E1 Enter the Accounting Equation

In this exercise, you will enter the accounting equation in Excel. First enter appropriate headers and then enter each accounting equation on subsequent rows. Use proper spacing and include the entire accounting equation based on the figures provided.

Assets = $53,000, Liabilities = $31,000, Equity = ???

Assets = $91,000, Liabilities = ???, Equity = $77,000

Assets = ???, Liabilities = $18,000, Equity = $27,000

Assets = $116,000, Liabilities = $41,000, Equity = ???

Assets = $72,000, Liabilities = ???, Equity = $50,000

EA1-E2 Record Journal Entries for A-Man Corp.

In this exercise, you will record journal entries in Excel for A-Man Corp. Ensure that each journal entry is recorded in proper form, including date and explanation. The transactions that you will journalize, all of which took place during 2016, are as follows:

April 1: Aidan Frank deposited $45,000 in a bank account to start a new business, A-Man Corp.

April 3: Purchased office furniture for $8,000

April 4: Purchased $1,200 of supplies on account

April 8: Received $2,200 for services provided to clients

April 13: Billed clients for $3,000 of services rendered

April 18: Paid $800 for the supplies purchased on April 4

April 19: Paid telephone expense of $130

April 23: Received $1,300 from clients who were billed on April 13

April 27: Paid utilities expense of $370

April 29: Aidan Frank withdrew $2,500 for personal use

EA1-E3 Record Journal Entries for Piracy, Inc.

In this exercise, you will record journal entries in Excel. Ensure that each journal entry is recorded in proper form, including date and explanation. The transactions to journalize, all of which took place during 2016, are as follows.

October 1: Sean Brendan deposited $30,000 in a bank account to start a new business, Piracy, Inc.

October 2: Received $5,100 for services provided to clients

October 6: Purchased office equipment for $5,500

October 9: Purchased $900 of supplies on account

October 11: Paid $400 for the supplies purchased on October 9

October 15: Paid telephone expense of $90

October 16: Billed clients for $1,900 of services rendered

October 20: Received $1,600 from clients who were billed on October 16

October 25: Paid miscellaneous expense of $460

October 30: Sean Brendan withdrew $900 for personal use

Critical Thinking

EA1-C1 Discuss Using Excel Formatting Tools in an Accounting Context

Excel features many formatting tools. Among these are bold, italics, underline, borders, font types, font colors, number types, etc. When properly used, these formatting tools can significantly enhance the readability of an accounting worksheet. For example, earlier in this chapter the italics option was used to distinguish journal entry explanations from the account names within each entry. As we often complete Excel worksheets to summarize information for others, enhancing their readability will allow the end user to more quickly identify important information within the worksheet.

Write a paragraph of at least five sentences in which you identify five ways formatting tools can be used to make accounting worksheets more easily understandable. Discuss how your selected formatting tools are applied to a worksheet. Write a second paragraph of at least five sentences to discuss ways in which each of these tools can be used to enhance the readability of a worksheet.

EA1-C2 Discuss Increasing Efficiency with Cut, Copy, and Paste

The Cut, Copy, and Paste features can be used in a variety of circumstances. And they can be particularly helpful when working on a worksheet that contains significant repetition or requires the consistent relocation of multiple items. A number of accounting-related worksheets fit this description; therefore, Cut, Copy, and Paste can be particularly useful in an accounting context.

Identify four accounting-related worksheets for which these options would be particularly beneficial. Write a paragraph of at least six sentences to discuss how the use of Cut, Copy, and/or Paste would be beneficial when creating each worksheet.

Financial Statements

LEARNING OBJECTIVES

- Create an income statement

- Create a statement of owner's equity

- Create a balance sheet

- Alter columns, rows, and text alignment

- Add, remove, and adjust worksheets

Certain elements of the accounting cycle are completed in the same manner each period. Among these are the financial statements which, for a given business, will have a consistent appearance from one period to another. In this chapter, you will examine three of the four financial statements: the income statement, the statement of owner's equity, and the balance sheet. Because these statements tend to have the same appearance from one period to the next, creating an Excel file as a base can significantly increase efficiency. You will review various Excel features regarding row and column manipulation, text alignment/control, and worksheet management. Doing so will allow you to create a uniform appearance across multiple versions of financial statements, as well as other accounting cycle components.

PROJECT   City Music World

City Music World is a retail store that sells musical equipment and offers lessons for beginning and experienced musicians. Now that the company is using Excel to increase its efficiency, it must establish templates for its financial statements that can be used every period (City Music World creates monthly financial statements). You are responsible for creating the current period's financial statements such that they can be easily updated for subsequent periods.

In this chapter, you will create financial statements in Microsoft Excel. You will examine techniques for adjusting columns and rows, altering the appearance of text, and altering the appearance of individual cells. You will finish with an examination of worksheet management.

City Music World
Income Statement
For the Month Ended December 31, 2016

Sales Revenue	$42,000
Expenses:	
Rent Expense	$12,000
Insurance Expense	$ 4,900
Telephone Expense	$ 3,100
Miscellaneous Expens	$ 2,600
Total Expenses	$22,600
Net Income	$19,400

Many Excel features can be used to improve the appearance of an income statement.

Accounting Refresher

Financial Statements

Four financial statements are completed near the end of the accounting cycle to summarize activity for the period and indicate the company's current financial position. The order in which the financial statements are completed is as follows:

- Income statement

- Statement of owner's equity

- Balance sheet

- Statement of cash flows

We will examine the first three financial statements here.

Income Statement

The income statement displays revenues and expenses for the period. The final line within the income statement calculates revenues minus expenses and is referred to as either net income (if revenues exceed expenses) or net loss (if expenses exceed revenues).

Net Income = Revenues - Expenses

At the top of the income statement, the three-line header displaying the company name on the top line and *Income Statement* on the second line does not simply list the final date of the period. Rather, it shows: *for the month/year/period ended xx/xx/xxxx*. This phrasing indicates that the income statement conveys activity for an entire period of time, which in this case is a month.

> **Nonners Corp.**
> **Income Statement**
> **For the Month Ended 8/31/2016**

This income statement covers the period from 8/1/2016 through 8/31/2016.

Statement of Owner's Equity

The **statement of owner's equity** is a reconciliation that combines the beginning owner's equity with account changes that occurred during the period in order to arrive at the ending owner's equity. Items added to the beginning owner's equity include net income and investments made by the owner. Items deducted from beginning owner's equity include net loss and owner withdrawals.

TIP! The Withdrawals account is used by a sole-proprietorship. For a corporation, the equivalent account is Dividends.

As the statement of owner's equity displays activity for an entire period of time (similar to the income statement), the third line of the header displays: *for the month/year/period ended xx/xx/xxxx*.

(continued)

Balance Sheet

The balance sheet displays the balances within all Asset, Liability, and Owner's Equity accounts. It shows that the accounting equation is in balance as of the end of the period. The balance sheet is a *snapshot* of the financial status of a company.

Assets = Liabilities + Owner's Equity

The balance sheet displays account balances as of the final day of the period; that is, it does not convey information regarding the activity during the period (it shows only the ending balances). Unlike the previous two financial statements, the third line of the balance sheet header shows the final date of the period.

Modifying Columns and Rows

You can insert and delete columns, rows, and cells in your worksheets. This can be particularly beneficial when completing financial statements. For example, if you determine that an account has been omitted, a row can be added in the proper location. The ability to add and delete rows ensures that a template can be created for each financial statement and then modified for different accounts when updating from one period to the next.

You can insert or delete columns and rows by first selecting the desired columns or rows in one of several ways:

- Clicking a single column or row heading
- Dragging to select adjacent headings
- Holding Ctrl while clicking nonadjacent headings

TIP!   You can also right-click a column or row header to initiate the insertion or deletion.

Once you have selected the desired rows or columns, you can either insert columns or rows beside those that are highlighted (to the left of selected columns or above selected rows) or delete the highlighted columns or rows.

➤ Home→Cells→Insert Cells ▼→Insert Sheet Columns ⊞ *or* Insert Sheet Rows ⊞

➤ Home→Cells→Delete Cells ▼→Delete Sheet Columns ⊞ *or* Delete Sheet Rows ⊞

Modifying Cells

When deleting a cell or a range, you must indicate how to shift the surrounding cells to either make room for the addition or fill the space from the deletion. Doing so can impact the cells both below and to the right of the insertion or deletion. Therefore, take care when altering a worksheet in this manner.

There are four *shift cells* options available when you insert cells.

↗ Home→Cells→Insert Cells ▼→Insert Cells ⊞ | Ctrl + Shift + =

↗ Home→Cells→Delete Cells ▼→Delete Cells ⊞ | Ctrl + -

Hiding Columns and Rows

To hide columns or rows, you must first highlight them in the same manner used to insert/ delete columns or rows. And, you can hide columns or rows by right-clicking those that are highlighted. Alternatively, when using the Ribbon or keyboard shortcuts, you can highlight any cells within the columns or rows you wish to hide.

Hidden rows and columns are not visible and do not print, but they do remain part of the worksheet. You can use the Unhide command to make hidden rows and columns visible once again.

Column C and row 2 are hidden.

The Hide command is useful when financial statements are used for managerial purposes. For example, commentary regarding a company's performance can be entered below the income statement so that management can review these performance indicators. This commentary can then be hidden from view when sharing the income statement with parties to whom it does not apply.

To Unhide a hidden column or row, you first highlight the headers of the columns or rows surrounding the hidden ones. For example, to unhide column E, first highlight the columns D and F headers.

NOTE!   If column A (or row 1) is hidden, you can unhide it by first highlighting the column B (or row 2) header and the Select All button and then choosing Unhide.

Home→Cells→Format→Hide & Unhide→Hide Rows | Ctrl + 9

Home→Cells→Format→Hide & Unhide→Unhide Rows | Ctrl + Shift + (

Home→Cells→Format→Hide & Unhide→Hide Columns | Ctrl + 0

Home→Cells→Format→Hide & Unhide→Unhide Columns | Ctrl + Shift +)

Develop Your Skills EA2-D1

In this exercise, you will complete City Music World's income statement for the month ending December 31, 2016. Month-end revenue and expense account balances are as follows: Sales Revenue equals $42,000, Rent Expense equals $12,000, Insurance Expense equals $4,900, Telephone Expense equals $3,100, and Miscellaneous Expense equals $2,600.

1. Start Excel. Open a **Blank Workbook** and save the file in your **Chapter 02** folder as: **EA2-D1-FinancialStatements-[YourName]**

2. Enter this data:

cell A1	City Music World
cell A2	Income Statement
cell A3	For the Month Ended December 31, 2016

3. Select **cell A5**, type **Sales Revenue** and tap Tab three times, and then type **42,000** and tap Enter.

   When multiple revenue accounts exist, the header Revenues is entered above the account names. Here we have only one revenue account, so no header is necessary.

Enter Expenses

4. Type **Expenses:** in **cell A6**.

5. Right-click the **row 6** header and choose **Insert**.

   It is customary to include a blank line between revenues and expenses.

6. Enter this data:

Cell B8	Rent Expense
Cell B9	Insurance Expense
Cell B10	Telephone Expense
Cell B11	Miscellaneous Expense
Cell C8	12,000
Cell C9	4,900
Cell C10	3,100
Cell C11	2,600

The amounts are entered in column C so that when they are later totaled in cell D12, the total will appear directly below total revenues (in cell D5). The result is that only total revenues, total expenses, and ultimately net income are displayed in column D.

7. Select **cell A12**, type **Total Expenses** and tap Tab three times, and then type **22,600** and tap Enter.

This total represents the sum of the four figures in the range C8:C11.

Complete the Income Statement

8. Select **cell A13**, type **Net Income** and tap Tab three times, and then type **19,400** and tap Enter.

Net Income is entered here because total revenues exceed total expenses. The amount is determined by subtracting total expenses of $22,600 from total revenues of $42,000. (When total expenses are higher than total revenues, Net Loss is used.)

9. Highlight the **range C5:D13**, choose **Home→Number→Accounting**, and then click **Decrease Decimal** twice.

Every dollar amount within the income statement now appears with a dollar sign and zero decimal places. Alternatively, financial statements can also be displayed such that the first and last figures include a dollar sign, while all other figures exclude them.

10. Select the **columns B–D** headers and then double-click the border between the **columns B–C** headers.

Because multiple columns were highlighted here, AutoFit was applied to all of them simultaneously when you double-clicked the border.

11. Right-click the **column A** header, choose **Column Width**, and then type **4** and tap Enter.

12. In **cell A16,** type this text: **Review Miscellaneous Expenses - Potential Savings?**

13. Select **cell A16** and choose **Home→Cells→ Format→Hide & Unhide→Hide Rows**.

Although you have included the note in cell A16 as a reminder for yourself, you don't want it displayed when you distribute the income statement to others. Therefore, you have now hidden row 16.

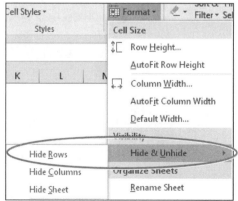

14. Save your file.

Unless otherwise directed, keep your file open at the end of each exercise.

Managing Worksheets

As you work with more complex workbooks, workbook management will increase in importance. You can organize a workbook by inserting, deleting, and rearranging worksheets. You also can rename worksheet tabs and apply colors to them. These options can be accessed via the Ribbon, by right-clicking, and by using keyboard controls.

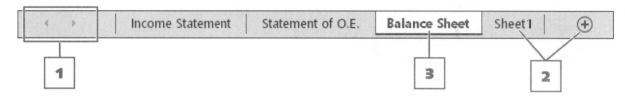

1. Navigation buttons allow you to scroll left and right between worksheet tabs.

2. The New Sheet button inserts a new sheet to the right of the active sheet tab.

3. The active worksheet is displayed prominently.

WARNING! You cannot undo the Delete Worksheet command. If you issue the command by mistake, you can close the workbook without saving and then reopen it to recover the lost worksheet.

When completing period-end financial statements, it is beneficial to maintain all statements in a single Excel workbook, each on a separate worksheet. Alternatively, multiple versions of the same financial statement (representing different periods) can be maintained within a single workbook.

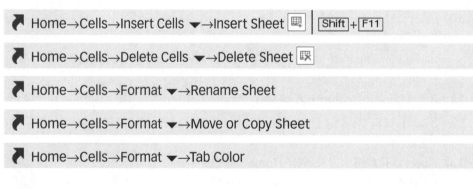

Changing Vertical Alignment and Rotating Text

Vertical alignment positions cell contents between the top and bottom of the cell. Vertical alignment options include Top, Bottom, Center, and Justify. The default alignment is bottom. The Justify option (which can be selected only via the Alignment dialog box launcher) evenly distributes unused space between lines in a multiple-line entry so text fills the cell from the top edge to the bottom edge. Within financial statements, vertical alignment is primarily used to ensure that headers and account names stand out.

> Home→Alignment→Top Align

> Home→Alignment→Middle Align

> Home→Alignment→Bottom Align

Rotating Text

The Orientation feature has several rotation options. When you change the orientation, Excel increases the row height to accommodate the rotated text. While rotating text can make titles more aesthetically pleasing, make sure the rotation doesn't increase row height so worksheet data becomes difficult to view.

Although standard financial statements do not typically contain rotated text, the use of a rotation option can make separate commentary (that is positioned below the financial statement) stand out to the end user.

> Home→Alignment→Orientation

> Home→Alignment→Orientation→Format Cell Alignment

Develop Your Skills EA2-D2

In this exercise, you will modify the income statement and create the statement of owner's equity for City Music World. Note that the beginning balance within the Harold Cameron, Capital account was $184,000, and the owner withdrew $14,000 during the month.

1. Save your file as: **EA2-D2-FinancialStatements-[YourName]**

2. Right-click the active worksheet tab, choose **Rename**, and then type **Income Statement** and tap Enter.

3. Type **Monthly Net Income is Acceptable** in **cell A17**.

   This note is placed below the income statement to direct the user to examine the net income. By next changing the orientation of this note, it will further stand out when the financial statement is viewed.

4. Select **cell A17** and choose **Home→Alignment→Orientation→Format Cell Alignment** to open the Format Cells dialog box.

5. Follow these steps to change the text orientation:

A

Format Cells   ?   ×

| Number | Alignment | Font | Border | Fill | Protection |

Text alignment

Horizontal:

General ∨   Indent: 0 ⊞

Vertical:

Bottom ∨

☐ Justify distributed

Text control

☐ Wrap text

☐ Shrink to fit

☐ Merge cells

Right-to-left

Text direction:

Context ∨

Orientation

T e x t   Text

10 ⊞ Degrees ——— **B**

C

    A. Click the **Alignment** tab, if necessary.

    B. Type **10** in the **Degrees** box.

    C. Click **OK**.

Complete the Statement of Owner's Equity

6. If a second worksheet tab is visible to the right of the Income Statement tab, select that second tab. If a second worksheet tab is not visible, click **New Sheet**.

7. Choose **Home→Cells→Format→Rename Sheet** and then type `Statement of O.E.` and tap ⌷Enter⌷.

   The abbreviation O.E. is used for Owner's Equity.

8. On the **Income Statement** tab, select and then right-click the **range A1:A3** and choose **Copy**.

9. On the **Statement of O.E.** tab, click **cell A1** and choose **Home→Clipboard→Paste**.

10. Type `Statement of Owner's Equity` in **cell A2**.

   The three-line header for the statement of owner's equity is the same as the header for the income statement (with the exception of the second line). Therefore, it is efficient to copy and paste the income statement header here.

11. Enter this data:

Cell A5	Harold Cameron, Capital – 12/1/2016
Cell C5	184,000
Cell A6	Net Income
Cell C6	19,400
Cell C7	203,400

The net income is taken from the income statement, which you completed first, so the $19,400 can now be inserted into the statement of owner's equity. The $203,400 is a subtotal that represents the sum of the beginning capital balance and net income.

12. Enter this data:

Cell A8	Harold Cameron, Drawing
Cell C8	14,000
Cell A9	Harold Cameron, Capital – 12/31/2016
Cell C9	189,400

13. Highlight the **range C5:C9**, choose **Home→Number→Accounting**, and then click **Decrease Decimal** twice.

14. Highlight the headers for **columns A–C** and then double-click the border between the **columns A–B** headers.

15. In **cell B1**, choose **Home→Cells→Format→Column Width** and then type **2** and click **OK**.

16. Save your file.

Using Alignment, Indent, and Text Control Options

Excel allows you to alter how text is aligned within cells. In addition to the standard left, center, and right horizontal alignments, you can indent cell contents from either edge. Additionally, you can change a worksheet's appearance by merging cells, wrapping lengthy text within a cell, and entering a line break within a cell.

Aligning Entries

To align an entry within a cell is to shift that entry either to the left, center, or right of the cell. By default, text entries are left aligned and number entries are right aligned. Often the appearance of a financial statement can be greatly improved through the effective use of alignment options.

Home→Alignment→Align Left ≣

Home→Alignment→Center ≣

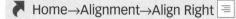

> Home→Alignment→Align Right ▤

Indenting Cell Entries

Indenting a cell entry offsets the entry from either the left or right edge of the cell, depending on the manner in which it is aligned. If a cell entry is left aligned, it will indent from the left edge, and if it is right aligned, it will indent from the right edge.

Indenting can be used in a variety of instances, such as when entering a credit within a journal entry or listing multiple expenses within an income statement.

> Home→Alignment→Decrease Indent ▤

> Home→Alignment→Increase Indent ▤

Merging Cells

Merging cells means to combine cells. You can merge cells both vertically and horizontally, and merged cells will behave as one large cell. The merged cell takes on the name of the top-left cell in the merged range. For example, if you merge cells A1:E1, the resulting merged cell will be named cell A1.

WARNING! If you merge two or more cells, each of which contains data, some data will be lost.

The Merge & Center command merges selected cells and sets center alignment to it. This technique can be used to center a heading across columns, but it can only be used on one row at a time. You can split the merged and centered cell by clicking the Merge & Center button again.

The Merge Across command merges the contents of multiple rows simultaneously. For example, if you use Merge & Center on the range A1:D2, the result would be one large merged cell over this range. However, if you use Merge Across on this same range, the result would be two merged cells (neither of which is centered) within the ranges A1:D1 and A2:D2.

Either Merge & Center or a combination of Merge Across and Center alignment should be used for the three-line header at the top of every financial statement.

> Home→Alignment→Merge & Center ▦

> Home→Alignment→Merge & Center ▾→Merge Across ▦

> Home→Alignment→Merge & Center ▾→Unmerge Cells ▦

Wrapping Text and Entering Line Breaks

The Wrap Text option forces text to wrap within a cell, ensuring that no text is cut off. When entering headers at the top of a table (such as *Owner's Equity* as part of the accounting equation), this command can be particularly useful. An alternative to Wrap Text is to manually insert a line break. Doing so moves all text after the line break to the next line within the same cell.

With both techniques, row height increases to accommodate the additional lines of wrapped text. However, you may still need to adjust the column width and/or row height after either of these commands is applied.

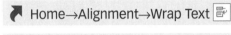

◢	A	B	C	D	E
1	**Assets**	**=**	**Liabilities**	**+**	**Owner's Equity**
2	$ 33,250	=	$ 2,000	+	$ 31,250

A line break has been entered after *Owner's* that forces *Equity* to a second line. The line break can be removed by clicking after the "s" in *Owner's* and tapping Delete .

↱ Home→Alignment→Wrap Text 🗇

↱ Alt + Enter to insert a line break

Applying Borders and Fills

Borders are lines around the cell edges that both print and display in the worksheet. Fills are background shading and pattern effects that fill entire cells. While borders serve an essential purpose within each financial statement, the fill color option should be used sparingly.

Borders

The Borders button lets you add borders to cell edges. When you click the Borders ▼, a list of options appears.

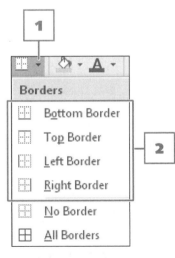

1. The Borders ▼ displays the image of the last border applied.

2. These border options are applied one edge at a time to each cell in the selected range.

While borders can be used to distinguish elements within many accounting-related work-sheets, they are particularly important in financial statements. A single underline within a financial statement indicates that a calculation (typically addition or subtraction) is being performed on the above figures; a double underline indicates that a figure is the final one for an entire statement or a portion of the statement.

For example, when multiple expenses are listed within an income statement, a single underline is displayed below the final expense amount to indicate that all are being added to arrive at the total expense figure. Then a double underline below the net income or loss within the income statement indicates that this is the final figure.

➦ Home→Font→Borders ⊞ ▾

Fill Colors

The Fill Color button fills the background of selected cells with color. When you click the Fill Color ▾, a palette of colors appears. You can apply a color to all selected cells by choosing it from the palette and remove a color with the No Fill option.

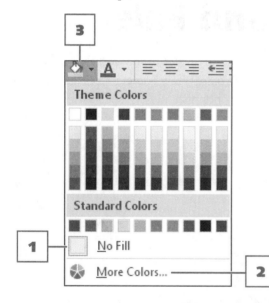

1. Remove a color fill from cells

2. Access a palette of standard colors or create a custom color

3. Shows the most recently used color

TIP! Printing a test version of a worksheet allows you to see how your color choices will print, which is especially important for grayscale printers.

While fill color can help to ensure that, in particular, financial statement headers stand out, they can also be distracting within business reports. A good rule of thumb is to use fill color in only one or two locations within your worksheet and to use only muted colors unless there is a compelling reason to do otherwise.

➦ Home→Font→Fill Color 🎨 ▾

Develop Your Skills EA2-D3

In this exercise, you will modify the income statement and the statement of owner's equity, and you'll create a balance sheet. Month-end asset and liability account balances for City Music World are as follows: Cash equals $104,000, Accounts Receivable equals $31,000, Equipment equals $83,000, and Accounts Payable equals $28,600.

1. Save your file as: **EA2-D3-FinancialStatements-[YourName]**

2. On the **Income Statement** tab, highlight the **range A1:D1** and choose **Home→ Alignment→Merge & Center**.

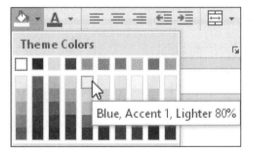

The top line within the three-line header has now been centered across columns A–D.

3. Merge and center the **range A2:D2** and the **range A3:D3**.

4. Select the **range A1:A3**.

Notice that, as a result of the previously applied Merge & Center commands, the range A1:D3 is highlighted when you select the range A1:A3.

5. Choose **Home→Font→Fill Color ▼→Blue, Accent 1, Lighter 80%**.

The header now has a more distinct appearance from the rest of the statement. Note that the name of each fill color (such as Blue, Accent 1, Lighter 80%) appears as a ScreenTip when you hover the mouse pointer over the colors.

6. On the **Statement of O.E.** tab, highlight the **range A1:C3** and choose **Home→Alignment→Merge & Center ▼→Merge Across**.

Each row within the three-line header (across columns A–C) has been merged.

7. Choose **Home→Alignment→Center**.

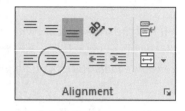

8. Select the **range A1:A3** and choose **Home→Font→Fill Color**.

   Note that the blue fill shade you chose earlier is applied to the range.

9. On the **Income Statement** tab, select **cells C11** and **D12** and then choose **Home→ Font→Borders ▼→Bottom Border**.

   The border below cell C11 indicates that all expense figures are being added to determine total expenses. The border below cell D12 indicates that the total expenses are being subtracted from the sales revenue to arrive at the net income.

10. Select **cell D13** and choose **Home→Font→Borders ▼→Bottom Double Border**.

    The double border below cell D13 indicates that the net income figure is the final figure in the income statement.

11. On the **Statement of O.E.** tab, select **cells C6** and **C8** and then choose **Home→Font→ Borders ▼→Bottom Border**.

12. Select **cell C9** and choose **Home→Font→Borders ▼→Bottom Double Border**.

Create the Balance Sheet and Begin Entering Data

13. If a third worksheet tab is visible to the right of the Statement of O.E. tab, select it; otherwise, click **New Sheet**.

14. Right-click the new worksheet tab, choose **Rename**, and then type **Balance Sheet** and tap ⌗Enter⌗.

15. On the **Statement of O.E.** tab, copy the **range A1:A3**.

16. Switch to the **Balance Sheet** tab, select **cell A1**, and press ⌗Ctrl⌗+⌗V⌗ to paste.

17. Type **Balance Sheet** in **cell A2** and **12/31/2016** in **cell A3**, and then tap ⌗Enter⌗ twice.

    This three-line header displays a single date on the third line, as the balance sheet is a snapshot *that conveys the position of a business on a single date but not information regarding the business' activity over a period of time.*

18. Enter this data:

Cell A5	Assets:
Cell A7	Cash
Cell C7	104,000
Cell A8	Accounts Receivable
Cell C8	31,000
Cell A9	Equipment
Cell C9	83,000
Cell A11	Total Assets
Cell C11	218,000

The balance sheet can be set up either with the assets positioned above or to the left of the liabilities and owner's equity. You displayed them above.

Cell C11 contains the figure $218,000, which represents the sum of the three asset figures.

Complete the Balance Sheet

19. Enter this data:

Cell A13	Liabilities:
Cell A15	Accounts Payable
Cell C15	28,600
Cell A17	Owner's Equity:
Cell A19	Harold Cameron, Capital
Cell C19	189,400
Cell A21	Total Liabilities & Owner's Equity
Cell C21	218,000

20. Highlight the **range C7:C21**, choose **Home→Number→Accounting Number Format**, and then click **Decrease Decimal** twice.

21. Select **cells A5**, **A13**, and **cell A17** and choose **Home→Font→Bold**.

22. Select **cells C9** and **C19** and choose **Home→Font→Borders ▾→Bottom Border**.

23. Select **cells C11** and **C21** and click the **Bottom Double Border** button.

24. Select **cell A8** and choose **Home→Alignment→Wrap Text**.

    You must increase the column width in order for Accounts Receivable to display properly. This will be done after the next few steps are completed.

25. Select **cell A15** and then click within the Formula Bar to the left of the *P* in *Payable*.

26. Tap ⌧Backspace⌧ and then hold ⌧Alt⌧, tap ⌧Enter⌧, and tap ⌧Enter⌧ again to confirm the entry.

    Tapping ⌧Backspace⌧ eliminated the space between Accounts and Payable. Holding ⌧Alt⌧ and tapping ⌧Enter⌧ applied a line break between the words, moving Payable to a new line within the same cell. The appearance of this entry will be corrected within the next few steps.

27. Select **cell A21** and choose **Home→Alignment→Wrap Text**.

28. Wrap the text in **cell A19**, choose **Home→Cells→Format→Column Width**, and then type **22** and click **OK**.

    Although text wrapping has been applied to cells A8 and A19, the entries within these cells now appear on one row, as the column is wide enough to allow this. However, the entry in cell A15, to which a line break was applied, has remained on two lines within the same cell.

29. Change the width of **cell A19** to **15**.

    Now that the column width has been reduced, all three cells display the respective entries on multiple lines.

30. Double-click the border between the **column C–D** headers.

    By double-clicking the right border of the column C header, you automatically decreased the width of the highlighted column to fit its entries.

31. Select **cell B5** and change the column width to **2**.

    Because the highlight is in column B, the width of this column has changed.

32. On all three tabs, set the **range A1:A3** in bold formatting.

33. On the **Balance Sheet** tab, highlight the **range A7:A9** and choose **Home→Alignment→ Increase Indent**.

34. Select the headers for **rows 6**, **10**, **14**, **16**, **18**, and **20**.

35. Choose **Home→Cells→Format→Row Height**, type **5**, and tap [Enter].

36. Set the height of **rows 19** and **21** to **32**.

37. Save and close your file.

REAL-WORLD Accounting

What Are the Benefits of Using Excel to Create Financial Statements?

Similar to journal entries, financial statements can be automatically generated using computerized accounting systems. Although many companies use such systems, it's not uncommon for small businesses to opt against them—often due to a desire to minimize costs and a lack of willingness to learn the computerized process. For these small businesses, Excel can increase efficiency and allow for effective comparisons to be made across accounting periods.

Creating templates in Excel for each of the four financial statements means you can copy and update the templates for each subsequent period, thus streamlining work. Through the use of multiple worksheet tabs, the financial statements can be maintained within the same file, allowing easy comparison between different periods.

Although increased efficiency and the ability to compare data are significant benefits, the knowledge gained from manually creating financial statements can be far more impactful. When using financial statements generated through accounting software, the user has not participated in their creation, whereas a careful review of every line item is inevitable when manually creating financial statements. As such, many owners find that they are better equipped to run their businesses when they use Excel to generate their monthly statements.

Self-Assessment

Check your knowledge of this chapter's key concepts and skills using the Self-Assessment here or in your eLab course.

1. When you delete cells, you must indicate how surrounding cells should shift.   *True   False*

2. A hidden row will appear when the worksheet is printed.   *True   False*

3. Neither row A nor column 1 can be hidden.   *True   False*

4. The deletion of a worksheet cannot be reversed with Undo.   *True   False*

5. All vertical alignment options are accessed directly on the Ribbon.   *True   False*

6. When a rotation option is applied, row height automatically adjusts to fit the rotated cell entry.

7. By default, text entries are right-aligned and number entries are left-aligned.   *True   False*

8. A cell entry can only be indented if it is left-aligned.   *True   False*

9. The Merge & Center command can be used to merge individual rows of data simultaneously.   *True   False*

10. The most recently selected border option is displayed on the Border button on the Ribbon.   *True   False*

11. When right-clicking to insert cells, which option does NOT appear?
    Entire Column
    Shift Cells Up
    Shift Cells Right
    Entire Row

12. Which element of a worksheet tab CANNOT be changed?
    Name
    Height
    Location
    Color

13. Which of these is NOT a horizontal alignment option?
    Middle
    Left
    Right
    Center

14. What does a single bottom border within a financial statement indicate?
    The above figure is the final figure within the statement.
    The above figure should be examined closely by management.
    A calculation is being performed on the figures above the border.
    The below figure is the final figure within the statement.

15. How is a line break applied?

Ctrl + Enter

Ctrl + Shift

Alt + Enter

Alt + Shift

16. Which of these options is NOT available on the Merge & Center menu on the Ribbon?
Merge & Center
Center
Merge Across
Unmerge Cells

17. The Increase Indent button is displayed within which group on the Home tab?
Clipboard
Font
Alignment
Number

18. Which of these options does NOT appear on the Fill Color menu?
Theme Colors
Gradient Colors
Standard Colors
More Colors

19. When a merge command is applied, the new merged cell takes on the name of which former cell?
The cell formerly located in the top left of the merged area
The cell formerly located in the top right of the merged area
The cell formerly located in the bottom left of the merged area
The cell formerly located in the bottom right of the merged area

20. When the Increase Indent command is applied, the cell entry:
is always indented from the right edge of the cell.
is indented from the right or left edge of the cell, depending on the type of entry.
is always indented from the left edge of the cell.
None of these; the user chooses how to indent.

Reinforce Your Skills

EA2-R1 Create Financial Statements for Pro Painting Inc.

In this exercise, you will create a monthly income statement, statement of owner's equity, and balance sheet in Excel for Pro Painting Inc. With the exception of the Giovanni Keith, Capital account (the balance for which is from 1/1/2016), the company had the following account balances as of 1/31/2016.

Accounts Receivable	$600	Maintenance Expense	$800
Auto Expense	$950	Notes Payable	$450
Cash	$3,100	Rent Revenue	$800
Delivery Expense	$350	Service Revenue	$3,600
Giovanni Keith, Capital – 1/1/2016	$5,050	Supplies	$700
Giovanni Keith, Drawing	$500	Tools	$1,100
Insurance Expense	$1,800		

1. Open a **Blank Workbook** and save the file in your **Chapter 02** folder as: **EA2-R1-FinancialStatements-[YourName]**

2. If necessary, use the **New Sheet** button to add worksheet tabs for a total of three.

3. Follow these steps to rename the tabs:
   - Double-click the first worksheet tab and type: **Income Statement**
   - Right-click the second worksheet tab, choose **Rename**, and type: **Statement of O.E.**
   - Select the third worksheet, choose **Home→Cells→Format→Rename Sheet**, and type: **Balance Sheet**

4. On the **Income Statement** tab, type the company name in **cell A1**, the statement name in **cell A2**, and the date in an appropriate format in **cell A3**.

5. Highlight the **range A1:D3**, choose **Home→Alignment→Merge & Center ▼→ Merge Across**, and then center the text.

6. On the **Statement of O.E.** tab, type the company name in **cell A1**, the statement name in **cell A2**, and the date in an appropriate format in **cell A3**.

7. Merge and center the contents in the **ranges A1:C1**, **A2:C2**, and **A3:C3**.

8. Repeat steps 6–7 on the **Balance Sheet** tab, taking care to use the correct statement name (cell A2) and date format (cell A3).

Enter Data for the Income Statement

9. On the **Income Statement** tab, type a revenue header in **cell A5**.

10. Enter the data as described:

In this cell or range:	Enter the data for:
Range B6:B7	Revenue account names (largest to smallest)
Range C6:C7	Revenue account balances
Cell A8	Total revenue description
Cell D8	Total revenue amount
Cell A10	Expenses header
Range B11:B14	Expense account names (largest to smallest)
Range C11:C14	Expense account balances
Cell A15	Total expenses description
Cell D15	Total expenses
Cell A16	Net income or loss entry
Cell D16	Net income or loss amount

11. Select **cells C7**, **C14**, and **D15** and then choose **Home→Font→Border ▼→ Bottom Border**.

12. Apply a bottom double border to **cell D16**.

13. In **cell A18**, type **Review maintenance expense for potential savings** and then choose **Home→Alignment→Orientation→Format Cell Alignment** and change the number in the Degrees box to **12**.

14. Right-click the **row 18** header and choose **Hide**.

15. Highlight the **range C6:D16**, choose **Home→Number→Accounting**, and then click **Decrease Decimal** twice.

16. Right-click the **column A** header and change the column width to **6**.

17. Highlight the headers for **columns B–D** and double-click the border between the **columns B–C** headers.

18. Highlight the **range A1:A3**, apply bold formatting, and then choose **Home→Font Fill Color ▼** and select **Blue-Gray**, **Text 2, Lighter 80%**.

Enter Data for the Statement of Owner's Equity

19. On the **Statement of O.E.** tab, enter the data as described:

In this cell:	Enter the data for the:
Cell A5	Beginning equity account name
Cell C5	Beginning equity amount
Cell A6	Name of the item to be added
Cell C6	Amount to be added
Cell C7	Subtotal of cells C5 and C6
Cell A8	Name of the item to be deducted
Cell C8	Amount to be deducted
Cell A9	Ending equity account name
Cell C9	Ending equity amount

20. Apply a bottom border to **cells C6** and **C8** and apply a bottom double border to **cell C9**.

21. Select **cells A5** and **A9** and choose **Home→Alignment→Wrap Text**.

22. Set the **range C5:C9** in the **Accounting** number format with no decimal places.

23. Using the right-click method, set the width of **column A** to **23** and the width of **column B** to **2**.

24. Double-click the border between the **columns C–D** headers.

25. Select the headers for **rows 5** and **9**, choose **Home→Cells→Format→Row Height**, and set the height to **30**.

26. Highlight the **range A1:A3**, apply bold formatting, and then choose **Home→Font→ Fill Color ▼→Blue-Gray**, **Text 2**, **Lighter 80%**.

Enter Data for the Balance Sheet

27. On the **Balance Sheet** tab, enter the data as described:

In this cell or range:	Enter the data for the:
Cell A5	Asset header
Range A6:A9	Asset account names (in the order Cash, Accounts Receivable, Supplies, Tools)
Cell A10	Total asset description
Cell A12	Liability header
Cell A13	Liability account name
Cell A15	Owner's equity header
Cell A16	Equity account name
Cell A18	Total liability and owner's equity description

28. Type the appropriate asset amount in **cell C6**. Continue by entering appropriate amounts in the **range C7:C10** as well as in **cells C13**, **C16**, and **C18**.

29. Highlight the **range A6:A9** and choose **Home→Alignment→Increase Indent** twice.

30. Apply a bottom border to **cells C9** and **C16** and apply a bottom double border to **cells C10** and **C18**.

31. Select **cell A7** and then click in the **Formula Bar** to the left of the *R* in *Receivable*, tap ⎡Backspace⎤, hold ⎡Alt⎤, tap ⎡Enter⎤, release ⎡Alt⎤, and tap ⎡Enter⎤.

32. Select **cell A18** and choose **Home→Alignment→Wrap Text**.

33. Set the **range C6:C18** in the **Accounting** number format with no decimal places.

34. Using the right-click method, set the width of **column A** to **21** and the width of **column B** to **2**.

35. Double-click the border between the **columns C–D** headers.

36. Select the headers for **rows 7** and **18**, choose **Home→Cells→Format→Row Height**, and set the height to **30**.

37. Set the row height of **cells A14** and **A17** to **5**.

38. Highlight the **range A1:A3**, apply bold formatting, and then choose **Home→Font→ Fill Color ▾→Blue-Gray, Text 2, Lighter 80%**.

39. Save and close your file.

EA2-R2 Create Financial Statements for Deep Freeze Co.

In this exercise, you will create a monthly income statement, statement of owner's equity, and balance sheet in Excel for Deep Freeze Co. With the exception of the Alistair Rowe, Capital account (the balance for which is from 6/1/2016), the company had the following account balances as of 6/30/2016.

Accounts Payable	$1,100	Rent Revenue	$2,000
Alistair Rowe, Capital – 6/1/2016	$21,700	Sales Revenue	$8,100
Alistair Rowe, Drawing	$1,600	Shipping Expense	$1,000
Building	$9,500	Supplies	$600
Cash	$14,000	Telephone Expense	$1,800
Insurance Expense	$2,100	Utilities Expense	$2,300

1. Open a **Blank Workbook** and save the file in your **Chapter 02** folder as: **EA2-R2-FinancialStatements-[YourName]**

2. If necessary, use the **New Sheet** button to add worksheet tabs for a total of three.

3. Follow these steps to rename the tabs:
    - Double-click the first worksheet tab and type: **Income Statement**
    - Right-click the second worksheet tab, choose **Rename**, and type: **Statement of O.E.**
    - Select the third worksheet, choose **Home→Cells→Format→Rename Sheet**, and type: **Balance Sheet**

4. On the **Income Statement** tab, type the company name in **cell A1**, the statement name in **cell A2**, and the date in an appropriate format in **cell A3**.

5. Highlight the **range A1:D3**, choose **Home→Alignment→Merge & Center ▾→ Merge Across**, and then center the text.

6. On the **Statement of O.E.** tab, type the company name in **cell A1**, the statement name in **cell A2**, and the date in an appropriate format in **cell A3**.

7. Merge and center the contents in the ranges **A1:C1**, **A2:C2**, and **A3:C3**.

8. Copy the **range A1:C3**, click the **Balance Sheet** tab, select **cell A1**, and press Ctrl + V.

9. Change the entry in **cell A2** to the correct statement name and change the entry in **cell A3** to an appropriate date format.

Enter Data for the Income Statement

10. On the **Income Statement** tab, type a revenue header in **cell A5**.

11. Enter the data as described:

In this cell or range:	Enter the data for:
Range B6:B7	Revenue account names (largest to smallest)
Range C6:C7	Revenue account balances
Cell A8	Total revenue description
Cell D8	Total revenue amount
Cell A10	Expenses header
Range B11:B14	Expense account names (largest to smallest)
Range C11:C14	Expense account balances
Cell A15	Total expenses description
Cell D15	Total expenses
Cell A16	Net income or loss entry
Cell D16	Net income or loss amount

12. Select **cells C7**, **C14**, and **D15** and then choose **Home→Font→Borders ▾→ Bottom Border**.

13. Apply a bottom double border to **cell D16**.

14. In **cell A18**, type **Review rent revenue to maximize profit** and then choose **Home→Alignment→Orientation→Format Cell Alignment** and change the number in the Degrees box to **8**.

15. Highlight the **range C6:D16**, choose **Home→Number→Accounting Number Format**, and then click **Decrease Decimal** twice.

16. Right-click the **column A** header and change the column width to **6**.

17. Highlight the headers for **columns B–D** and double-click the border between the **columns B–C** headers.

18. Select the **range A1:A3** and choose **Home→Font→Bold**.

Enter Data for the Statement of Owner's Equity

19. On the **Statement of Owner's Equity** tab, enter the data as described:

In this cell:	Enter the data for the:
Cell A5	Beginning equity account name
Cell C5	Beginning equity amount
Cell A6	Name of the item to be added
Cell C6	Amount to be added
Cell C7	Subtotal of cells C5 and C6
Cell A8	Name of the item to be deducted
Cell C8	Amount to be deducted
Cell A9	Ending equity account name
Cell C9	Ending equity amount

20. Apply a bottom border to cells **C6** and **C8** and apply a bottom double border to **cell C9**.

21. Select **cells A5** and **A9** and choose **Home→Alignment→Wrap Text**.

22. Set the range **C5:C9** in the **Accounting** number format and with no decimal places.

23. Using the right-click method, set the width of **column A** to **22** and the width of **column B** to **2**.

24. Double-click the border between the **columns C–D** headers.

25. Select the headers for **rows 5** and **9**, choose **Home→Cells→Format→Row Height**, and set the height to **30**.

26. Set the **range A1:A3** in bold formatting.

Enter Data for the Balance Sheet

27. On the **Balance Sheet** tab, enter the data as described:

In this cell or range:	Enter the data for the:
Cell A5	Asset header
Range A6:A8	Asset account names (in the order Cash, Supplies, Building)
Cell A9	Total asset description
Cell A11	Liability header
Cell A12	Liability account name
Cell A14	Owner's equity header
Cell A15	Equity account name
Cell A17	Total liability and owner's equity description

28. Type the appropriate asset amount in **cell C6**. Continue by entering appropriate amounts in the **range C7:C9** as well as in **cells C12**, **C15**, and **C17**.

29. Highlight the **range A6:A8** and choose **Home→Alignment→Increase Indent** twice.

30. Apply a bottom border to **cells C8** and **C15** and apply a bottom double border to **cells C9** and **C17**.

31. Select **cell A17** and choose **Home→Alignment→Wrap Text**.

32. Set the **range C6:C17** in the **Accounting** number format with no decimal places.

33. Using the right-click method, set the width of **column A** to **20** and the width of **column B** to **2**.

34. Double-click the border between the **columns C–D** headers.

35. Select the headers for **row 17**, choose **Home→Cells→Format→Row Height**, and set the row height to **30**.

36. Set the row height of **cells A13** and **A16** to **5**.

37. Set the **range A1:A3** in bold formatting.

38. Save and close your file.

Apply Your Skills

EA2-A1 Create Financial Statements for Titan Industries

In this exercise, you will create a monthly income statement, statement of owner's equity, and balance sheet in Excel for Titan Industries. With the exception of the William Buffalo, Capital account (the balance for which is from 11/1/2016), the company had the following account balances as of 11/30/2016.

Accounts Payable	$3,500	Repair Expense	$2,500
Accounts Receivable	$7,000	Service Revenue	$13,000
Building	$13,000	Supplies	$1,000
Cash	$19,000	Supplies Expense	$700
Equipment	$10,000	Utilities Expense	$1,800
Office Expense	$6,200	William Buffalo, Capital – 11/1/2016	$40,200
Notes Payable	$5,000	William Buffalo, Drawing	$500

1. Open a **Blank Workbook** and save the file in your **Chapter 02** folder as:
   EA2-A1-FinancialStatements-[YourName]

2. Set the workbook to contain a total of three tabs, one for each financial statement and arranged in the order they will be completed.

3. In the **range A1:A3** on each tab:

   - Enter the appropriate three-line header for each, with bold formatting and the **Orange, Accent 2, Lighter 80%** fill color.
   - Merge and center the header rows across **columns A–D** (Income Statement) or **columns A–C** (Statement of O.E. and Balance Sheet).

Enter Data for the Income Statement

4. On the **Income Statement** tab, enter the data as described:

In this cell or range:	Enter the data for the:
Cell A5	Revenue account name
Cell D5	Revenue account amount
Cell A7	Expenses header
Range B8:B11	Expense account names (largest to smallest)
Range C8:C11	Expense account amounts
Cell A12	Total expenses description
Cell D12	Total expenses
Cell A13	Net income or loss entry
Cell D13	Net income or loss amount

5. Apply the appropriate border to **cells C11**, **D12**, and **D13**.

6. In **cell A15**, type a comment that indicates the largest expense and apply a **10% Orientation** to the cell; hide **row 15** so your comment is not visible.

7. Apply the **Accounting** number format with zero decimal places to all amounts in the statement and set appropriate column widths to **columns A–D**.

Enter Data for the Statement of Owner's Equity

8. On the **Statement of O.E.** tab, enter the data as described:

In this cell:	Enter the data for the:
Cell A5	Beginning equity account name
Cell C5	Beginning equity amount
Cell A6	Net income or loss title
Cell C6	Net income or loss amount
Cell C7	Subtotal of cells C5 and C6
Cell A8	Name of the appropriate account
Cell C8	Amount associated with cell A8
Cell A9	Ending equity account name
Cell C9	Ending equity amount

9. Apply the appropriate border to **cells C6**, **C8**, and **C9** and wrap the text in **cells A5** and **A9** to display the account names.

10. Apply the **Accounting** number format with zero decimal places to all amounts in the statement, set appropriate column widths to **columns A–C**, and set appropriate row heights to any rows requiring adjustment.

Enter Data for the Balance Sheet

11. On the **Balance Sheet** tab, enter the data as described:

In this cell or range:	Enter the data for the:
Cell A5	Asset header
Range A6:A10	Asset account names in order of liquidity (Cash, Accounts Receivable, Supplies, Equipment, Building)
Range C6:C10	Asset account amounts
Cell A11	Total assets name
Cell C11	Total assets amount

12. Apply the appropriate border to **cells C10** and **C11**.

13. Insert a line break in the appropriate location in the account name in **cell A7**.

14. Enter the data as described:

In this cell or range:	Enter the data for the:
Cell A13	Liabilities header
Range A14:A15	Liability account names (from short- to long-term)
Range C14:C15	Liability account amounts
Cell A16	Total liability name
Cell C16	Total liability amount
Cell A18	Owner's equity header
Cell A19	Equity account name
Cell C19	Equity account amount
Cell A21	Total liabilities and owner's equity name
Cell C21	Total liabilities and owner's equity amount

Hint: In this instance, the order of liabilities from short- to long-term is also the order from smallest to largest.

15. Wrap the text in **cells A19** and **A21** to display the account name.

16. Apply the appropriate border to cells **C15**, **C19**, and **C21**.

17. Apply the **Accounting** number format with zero decimal places to all amounts.

18. Apply appropriate column widths to **columns A–C**, indent the account names in the **range A6:A10** and the **range A14:A15**, and apply appropriate row heights as needed.

19. Save and close your file.

EA2-A2 Create Financial Statements for Metropolitan Corp.

In this exercise, you will create a monthly income statement, statement of owner's equity, and balance sheet in Excel for Metropolitan Corp. With the exception of the Terry Mattingly, Capital account (the balance for which is from 5/1/2016), the company had the following account balances as of 5/31/2016.

Accounts Payable	$27,000	Sales Revenue	$23,000
Accounts Receivable	$24,000	Service Revenue	$4,000
Cash	$57,000	Supplies Expense	$6,000
Land	$41,000	Tax Expense	$13,000
Maintenance Expense	$17,000	Telephone Expense	$10,000
Notes Payable	$9,000	Terry Mattingly, Capital – 5/1/2016	$118,000
Printing Expense	$11,000	Terry Mattingly, Drawing	$2,000

1. Open a **Blank Workbook** and save the file in your **Chapter 02** folder as: **EA2-A2-FinancialStatements-[YourName]**

2. Set the workbook to contain a total of three tabs, one for each financial statement and arranged in the order they will be completed.

3. In the **range A1:A3** on each tab:

   - Enter the appropriate three-line header with bold formatting and the **Green, Accent 6, Lighter 60%** fill color.
   - Merge and center the header rows across **columns A–D** (Income Statement) or **columns A–C** (Statement of O.E. and Balance Sheet).

Enter Data Within the Income Statement

4. On the Income Statement tab, enter the data as described:

In this cell or range:	Enter the data for the:
Cell A5	Header for revenues
Range B6:B7	Revenue account names (largest to smallest)
Range C6:C7	Revenue account amounts
Cell A8	Total revenue entry
Cell D8	Total revenue amount
Cell A10	Header for expenses
Range B11:B15	Expense account names (largest to smallest)
Range C11:C15	Expense account amounts
Cell A16	Total expenses entry
Cell A17	Net income or loss entry
Range D16:D17	Amounts associated with cells A16 and A17

5. Apply the appropriate border to **cells C7**, **C15**, **D16**, and **D17**.

6. In **cell A19**, type a comment that indicates the largest revenue item and apply a **15% Orientation** to the cell.

7. Apply the **Accounting** number format with zero decimal places to all amounts within the statement and apply appropriate column widths to **columns A–D**.

Enter Data for the Statement of Owner's Equity

8. On the Statement of O.E. tab, enter the data as described:

In this cell:	Enter the data for the:
Cell A5	Beginning equity account name
Cell C5	Beginning equity amount
Cell A6	Net income or loss title
Cell C6	Net income or loss amount
Cell A7	Appropriate account name
Cell C7	Amount associated with cell A7
Cell A8	Ending equity account name
Cell C8	Ending equity amount

9. Apply the appropriate border to **cells C7** and **C8** and use line breaks to display the account names in **cells A5** and **A8**.

10. Apply the **Accounting** number format with zero decimal places to all amounts.

11. Apply appropriate column widths to **columns A–C** and appropriate row heights to **rows 5** and **8**.

Enter Data Within the Balance Sheet

12. On the Balance Sheet tab, enter the data as described:

In this cell or range:	Enter the data for the:
Cell A5	Asset header
Range A6:A8	Asset account names in order of liquidity (Cash, Accounts Receivable, Land)
Range C6:C8	Asset account amounts
Cell A9	Total assets name
Cell C9	Total assets amount

13. Apply the appropriate border to **cells C8** and **C9**.

14. Wrap the text in **cell A7**.

15. Enter the data as described:

In this cell or range:	Enter the data for the:
Cell A11	Liabilities header
Range A12:A13	Liability account names (from short- to long-term)
Range C12:C13	Liability account amounts
Cell A14	Total liability name
Cell C14	Total liability amount
Cell A16	Owner's equity header
Cell A17	Equity account name
Cell C17	Equity account amount
Cell A19	Total liabilities and owner's equity name
Cell C19	Total liabilities and owner's equity amount

Hint: In this instance, the order of liabilities from short- to long-term is also the order from smallest to largest.

16. Indent the account names twice in the **ranges A6:A8** and **A22:A13**.

17. Apply the appropriate border to **cells C13**, **C17**, and **C19** and add a line break to the entry in **cell A19**.

18. Apply the **Accounting** number format with zero decimal places to all amounts.

19. Apply appropriate column widths to **columns A–C** and appropriate row heights as needed.

20. Save and close your file.

Extend Your Skills

EA2-E1 Create Financial Statements for Frozen Fractals Corp.

In this exercise, you will create an income statement, statement of owner's equity, and balance sheet in Excel for Frozen Fractals Corp. With the exception of the Jacqueline Elise, Capital account (the balance for which is from 12/1/2016), the company had the following account balances as of 12/31/2016.

Accounts Payable	$6,000	Land	$27,000
Accounts Receivable	$4,100	Office Expense	$4,000
Auto Expense	$9,400	Rent Revenue	$8,500
Cash	$61,000	Sales Revenue	$41,000
Furniture	$8,000	Supplies Expense	$2,500
Jacqueline Elise, Capital – 12/1/2016	$73,200	Telephone Expense	$6,100
Jacqueline Elise, Drawing	$3,000	Utilities Expense	$3,600

When creating the financial statements, be certain to use the techniques from this chapter to present each in good form.

EA2-E2 Create Financial Statements for BeBo Industries

In this exercise, you will create an income statement, statement of owner's equity, and balance sheet in Excel for BeBo Industries. With the exception of the Lily Ruth, Capital account (the balance for which is from 8/1/2016), the company had the following account balances as of 8/31/2016.

Accounts Payable	$3,700	Security Expense	$1,200
Accounts Receivable	$3,400	Service Revenue	$14,100
Cash	$27,000	Supplies Expense	$900
Equipment	$9,100	Telephone Expense	$1,500
Lily Ruth, Capital - 8/1/2016	$34,000	Utilities Expense	$2,100
Lily Ruth, Drawing	$1,400	Wages Expense	$3,300
Maintenance Expense	$1,900		

When creating the financial statements, be certain to use the techniques from this chapter to present each in good form.

EA2-E3 Create Financial Statements for Weather Watchers Co.

In this exercise, you will create an income statement, statement of owner's equity, and balance sheet in Excel for Weather Watchers Co. With the exception of the Jacob Wright, Capital account (the balance for which is from 3/1/2016), the company had the following account balances as of 3/31/2016.

Accounts Payable	$29,000	Salaries Expense	$51,000
Accounts Receivable	$9,000	Sales Revenue	$82,000
Building	$41,000	Service Revenue	$11,000
Cash	$17,000	Truck Expense	$8,000
Insurance Expense	$14,000	Utilities Expense	$13,000
Jacob Wright, Capital - 3/1/2016	$58,000	Wages Expense	$22,000
Jacob Wright, Drawing	$5,000		

When creating the financial statements, be certain to use the techniques from this chapter to present each in good form.

Critical Thinking

EA2-C1 Discuss Using Hide/Unhide

Many individuals are likely to review a company's financial statements. Among these stakeholders are executive managers, potential investors, loan officers, and prospective employees. When disseminating financial statements, it is not uncommon to include commentary or discussion points related to the figures. These comments are often intended for a limited audience. The Hide and Unhide commands can be used to ensure that comments are displayed within a worksheet only when desired.

Write a paragraph of at least five sentences in which you identify four stakeholders who are likely to review financial statements (use those referenced or others of your choosing) and why. Write a second paragraph of at least five sentences to discuss the type of commentary that would be appropriate to include for each stakeholder.

EA2-C2 Discuss Managing Workbooks in an Accounting Environment

Multiple worksheet tabs can be used to organize a company's financial statements for an accounting period. This technique can be used in a variety of other ways as well. Giving thought to these other uses can yield significant benefits down the road in terms of enhancing efficiency and ensuring quality analyses.

Write a paragraph of at least six sentences in which you identify four accounting-related tasks (other than completing financial statements) for which the use of multiple worksheets would be appropriate. Discuss how multiple worksheets within a workbook can be used for each task.

Statement of Cash Flows

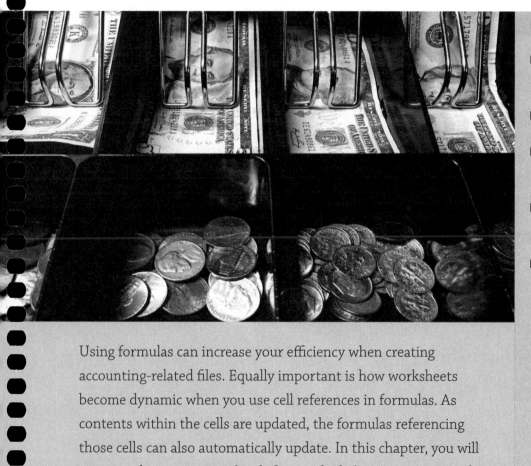

LEARNING OBJECTIVES

- Create a statement of cash flows

- Create formulas in Excel

- Use cell references in formulas

- Modify, copy, and correct formulas

- Find and replace cell contents and formats

Using formulas can increase your efficiency when creating accounting-related files. Equally important is how worksheets become dynamic when you use cell references in formulas. As contents within the cells are updated, the formulas referencing those cells can also automatically update. In this chapter, you will examine the statement of cash flows, which focuses on uses and sources of cash. Because a business must maintain sufficient cash flow for operations, understanding its cash position is vital. As this statement contains multiple sections, each of which can involve various calculations, the use of formulas is critical. While creating this financial statement, you will review how Excel formulas can be created, modified, copied, and corrected. You will also review how cell contents and formats can be located and modified, a skill that will prove useful when you must alter similar file elements in multiple locations.

PROJECT City Music World

City Music World is a retail store that sells musical equipment and offers lessons for beginning and experienced musicians. Although the company has not previously created a statement of cash flows, it would like to begin doing so to keep a closer eye on the movement of cash into and out of the business. You have been asked to create the current period's statement of cash flows using Excel formulas that can be easily modified when necessary.

In this chapter, you will learn how formulas can increase your efficiency when creating a worksheet and make your final file more user-friendly. You will use formulas to create a statement of cash flows that can be used from one accounting period to the next, and you will examine the simplest methods for updating the file.

City Music World
Statement of Cash Flows
For the Month Ended December 31, 2016

Operating Activities:				
Net Income	$	19,400		
Depreciation Expense	$	3,100		
Increase in A/R	$	(600)		
Increase in A/P	$	2,100		
Cash Flows From Operating Activities:			$	24,000
Investing Activities:				
Sale of Equipment	$	71,000		
Purchase of Equipment	$	(83,000)		
Cash Flows Used in Investing Activities:			$	(12,000)
Financing Activities:				
Harold Cameron, Drawing	$	(14,000)		
Decrease in N/P	$	(5,000)		
Cash Flows Used in Financing Activities:			$	(19,000)
Net Decrease in Cash			$	(7,000)
Cash (Beginning Balance)			$	111,000
Cash (Ending Balance)			$	104,000

Accounting Refresher — Statement of Cash Flows

Cash is the most important asset on any company's books, so keeping an eye on the factors that led to the current cash balance is vital. The statement of cash flows is devoted to displaying all activity related to the cash account.

The statement of cash flows includes three sections:

1. The *Operating Activities* section is listed first, showing cash-related activity associated with the company's standard revenue-generating operations. Basically, any receipt (inflow) or use (outflow) of cash associated with the daily running of the business is included.

2. The *Investing Activities* section is next. It displays any cash spent on long-term (fixed) assets or cash received for the sale of long-term assets.

3. The *Financing Activities* section is last. It shows cash-related activity associated with long-term liabilities (amounts owed for longer than one year), stocks, bonds, or withdrawals. Any cash received from these activities (such as from the issuance of stocks or bonds) or paid out for these activities (such as for payment of a long-term debt or the owner's cash withdrawal) is included.

WARNING! The statement of cash flows includes only activities in which cash has changed hands. So, a transaction for furniture purchased on account would not be displayed because it did not involve the Cash account.

When completing the Operating Activities section, a company can use one of two methods:

- The *indirect method* begins with the net income and makes any necessary adjustments. These adjustments include the impact of cash-related transactions that are not captured within net income and exclude the impact of non-cash-related transactions that are captured within net income.

- In the *direct method* all sources of cash (which belong within the Operating Activities section) are listed individually. The uses of cash are also listed on a line-by-line basis.

The final figure within the Operating Activities section is the same, regardless of the method used. The Investing Activities and Financing Activities sections are not impacted by the method selected.

Working with Formulas

Formulas begin with an equals sign, and Excel will automatically insert the equals sign if you first type a plus (+) or minus (–) sign. Formulas may be entered using numbers or, preferably, using cell references.

| =50+100 | =B2+C2 |

This formula uses numbers.   This formula uses cell references.

Cell and Range References

Formulas derive their power from the use of cell and range references. Using references in formulas ensures that formulas can be copied to other cells and that results are automatically recalculated when the data is changed in the referenced cell(s).

TIP!   Do not type the results of calculations directly into cells. Always use formulas to calculate those results instead.

The reason it's generally more efficient to complete accounting tasks in Excel versus on paper is due to time saved through the use of cell references. Getting accustomed to this approach will yield significant benefits over time.

The Language of Excel Formulas

Formulas can include any or all of the standard arithmetic operators shown in the following table. Keep in mind that each formula is entered into the same cell that displays the resulting calculation.

Arithmetic Operators in Formulas

Operator	Example	Comments
+ (addition)	= C7+C11	Adds the values in C7 and C11
- (subtraction)	= C7–C11	Subtracts the value in C11 from the value in C7
* (multiplication)	= C7*C11	Multiplies the values in C7 and C11
/ (division)	= C7/C11	Divides the value in C7 by the value in C11
^ (exponentiation)	=C7^3	Raises the value in C7 to the third power (C7*C7*C7)
% (percent)	=C7*12%	Multiplies the value in C7 by 12% (0.12)
( ) (grouping)	=C7/(D4-D2)	Subtracts the value in D2 from the value in D4 and then divides C7 by the subtraction result

TIP!   When typing a cell reference in a formula, you can type the column letter in lowercase and Excel will capitalize it for you.

Develop Your Skills EA3-D1

In this exercise, you will begin a statement of cash flows in Excel for City Music World for the month ended December 31, 2016. You will use the indirect method to complete the Operating Activities section. Monthly figures used in the Operating Activities section are shown here.

Net Income	$19,400	Accounts Receivable (ending balance)	$31,000
Depreciation Expense	$3,100	Accounts Payable (beginning balance)	$26,500
Accounts Receivable (beginning balance)	$30,400	Accounts Payable (ending balance)	$28,600

1. Start Excel. Open **EA3-D1-StatementofCF** from your **Chapter 03** folder and save it as: **EA3-D1-StatementofCF-[YourName]**

2. Type **Operating Activities:** in **cell A5**.

3. Type **Net Income** in **cell A6** and **19400** in **cell C6**.

   You entered Net Income because the indirect method of the statement of cash flows begins with this in the Operating Activities section. The amount is shown with a dollar sign because column C has been formatted to display Accounting number format.

4. Type **Depreciation Expense** in **cell A7** and **3100** in **cell C7**.

   In the Operating Activities section, the depreciation expense is always added back to the net income for the period. This is why the $3,100 is displayed as a positive amount here. The same process is used with an amortization expense (essentially the same as depreciation expense, but referring to an intangible asset) for the period.

5. Type **Increase in A/R** and **-600** in **row 8** and **Increase in A/P** and **2100** in **row 9**.

   Increases in current assets, such as accounts receivable (denoted by A/R), are subtracted from net income. This is why the $600 increase is displayed as a negative amount. Increases in current liabilities, such as accounts payable (denoted by A/P), are added back to net income, which is why the $2,100 increase is displayed as a positive amount.

TIP! If the current asset account balance had decreased during the year, that decrease would be added back to net income. If the current liability account balance had decreased during the year, that decrease would be subtracted from net income.

6. Type **Cash Flows From Operating Activities:** in **cell A10** and **=C6+C7+C8+C9** in **cell D10**.

   The formula result ($24,000) is displayed in cell D10. Because this result is a positive amount, the description in cell A10 includes the word From. Had the result been a negative amount, From would have been replaced with Used In.

7. Select **cell C9** and choose **Home→Font→Borders ▼→Bottom Border**.

8. Save your file.

   Unless otherwise directed, always keep your file open at the end of each exercise.

Using Cell References in Formulas

A cell reference identifies which cell or range of cells contains the values to use in a formula. By default, a cell reference is displayed as a *relative* reference.

Relative Cell References

When a cell reference is entered in a formula, Excel examines the cell reference to determine the distance between it and the cell in which the formula is written. For example, when you enter the formula =A3*B3 in cell C3, Excel notes that cell A3 is two cells to the left of the formula and cell B3 is one cell to the left of the formula. These are referred to as relative cell references because Excel is noting where the references are relative to the current position of the formula.

SUM	▼	⋮	✕	✓	*fx*	=A3*B3

◢	A	B	C	D
1	Units Sold	Sales Price	Revenue	
2	8	$ 5.65	$ 45.20	
3	12	$ 5.75	=A3*B3	

This feature is particularly important when copying the same formula to multiple locations throughout a worksheet.

What-If Analysis

The use of cell references allows you to easily perform a what-if analysis (also called sensitivity analysis) on worksheet elements. For example, if a formula containing cell references is used to estimate total accounts receivable for a business' first month of operations (before customers have made payments), it can be easily updated to determine the impact of different sales amounts. This type of simple change within a worksheet provides a wealth of information that can be used to plan business operations based on potential future outcomes.

1

C3	▼	⋮	✕	✓	*fx*	=C1*C2

◢	A	B	C	D
1	Total Sales:		$ 250,000	
2	% from Credit Sales		80%	
3	Accounts Receivable		$ 200,000	

C3	▼	⋮	✕	✓	*fx*	=C1*C2

◢	A	B	C	D
1	Total Sales:		$ 300,000	
2	% from Credit Sales		80%	
3	Accounts Receivable		$ 240,000	

2

1. The formula in cell C3 includes cell references for cells C1 and C2.

2. When the value in cell C1 is changed to $300,000, the result in cell C3 automatically updates.

Develop Your Skills EA3-D2

In this exercise, you will perform a what-if analysis in the statement of cash flows for City Music World for the month ended December 31, 2016.

1. Save your file as: **EA3-D2-StatementofCF-[YourName]**

2. Enter **27100** in **cell C6**.

   The Cash Flows from Operating Activities have increased to $31,700. A what-if scenario, such as this one in which a different net income figure is utilized, can be easily examined when using formulas in Excel.

3. Now enter **15800** in **cell C6**.

   Had the net income been $15,800 for the period, then (as seen in cell D10) the Cash Flows from Operating Activities would have been $20,400.

4. Click **Undo** twice to revert the amount in cell C6 to $19,400.

5. Save your file.

Modifying and Copying Formulas

You can modify (or edit) a formula in the Formula Bar or by double-clicking the formula cell. If you select a cell and enter a new formula, it replaces the previous contents. When you select a formula to edit it, you will see colored lines surrounding all of the cells that are referenced by the formula. This can help you to track the elements of the formula within the worksheet.

The C1 cell reference in the formula takes on the same blue color as the border surrounding cell C1. Cell C2 takes on a shade of red.

Circular References

A circular reference occurs when the formula refers to its own cell or to another formula that refers to that cell. For example, the formula in cell C3 is =C1*C3. Excel cannot complete the calculation because cell C3 is the formula cell, not a reference to a value that can be used in a calculation.

WARNING! You must correct the formula manually after you close Help or the Circular Reference Warning message.

C3	▼ :	× ✓ f_x	=C1*C3					
◢	A	B C	D	E	F	G	H	I
1	Total Sales:	$ 300,000						
2	% from Credit Sales	80%						
3	Accounts Receivable	=C1*C3						

Microsoft Excel ✕

⚠ There are one or more circular references where a formula refers to its own cell either directly or indirectly. This might cause them to calculate incorrectly.

Try removing or changing these references, or moving the formulas to different cells.

[OK]   [Help]

Copying Formulas

You can use Copy and Paste commands or AutoFill to copy formulas to new cells. To use AutoFill, you must first select the cell to copy and then drag the fill handle across the cells to which the formula will be pasted. In worksheets that display the same formula many times (especially when those formulas are adjacent to one another), copying the formula can save considerable time.

C2	▼ :	× ✓ f_x	=A2*B2		
◢	A	B	C	D E	F
1	Units Sold	Sales Price	Revenue		
2	8	$ 5.65	$ 45.20		
3	12	$ 5.75	$ 69.00		
4	14	$ 5.80	$ 81.20		
5	6	$ 5.80	$ 34.80		
6	3	$ 5.90	$ 17.70		
7	11	$ 5.95	$ 65.45		
8			⊞₊ ▼		
9				⦿ Copy Cells	
10				○ Fill Formatting Only	
11				○ Fill Without Formatting	
12				○ Flash Fill	
13					

You can change what is copied by clicking the AutoFill Options button.

When formulas are copied, the cell references within the formulas are updated. For example, if the formula =A2*B2 is entered in cell C2 and then copied to cell C3, the cell references will shift down by one row just as the formula itself has moved down one row (from row 2 to row 3). The resulting formula in cell C3 will read =A3*B3.

The formula in cell C2, which reads =A2*B2, was copied here to cell C3.

Develop Your Skills EA3-D3

In this exercise, you will continue with the statement of cash flows for City Music World for the month ended December 31, 2016. To complete the Investing Activities section, you will use these monthly figures: Equipment Sale #1 equals $71,000, Equipment Purchase #1 equals $61,000, and Equipment Purchase #2 equals $22,000.

1. Save your file as: **EA3-D3-StatementofCF-[YourName]**

2. Enter this data:

Cell A12	Investing Activities
Cell A13	Sale of Equipment
Cell C13	71000
Cell A14	Purchase of Equipment
Cell C14	-83000

The equipment sale resulted in cash flowing into the business, so that amount is displayed as a positive number. The equipment purchase resulted in cash flowing out of the business, so that amount is displayed as a negative number.

3. Select **cell C14** and then choose **Home→Font→Borders ▾→Bottom Border**.

4. Type **Cash Flows Used in Investing Activities:** in **cell A15**.

5. Select **cell D10** and choose **Home→Clipboard→Copy**. Then select **cell D15** and press Ctrl + V .

Just as the formula in cell D10 adds the contents of four cells in the adjacent column, the new formula pasted in cell D15 also sums four cells. Only two amounts need to be added here, so you must modify the formula.

6. Click in the Formula Bar to the left of *C13*, tap Backspace eight times to delete the first two cell references, and then type **D15+** and tap Enter.

   You removed cell references C11 and C12 from the formula, but, by then including cell D15, you created a circular reference.

7. Click **OK**. Then, select **cell D15**, click in the Formula Bar to the left of *C13*, tap Backspace four times, and tap Enter.

8. Save your file.

Using Excel's Find and Replace Commands

Excel's Find command can perform searches for a particular word, number, cell reference, formula, or format within a worksheet or an entire workbook. The Replace feature helps you to find an item and replace it with a specified item. When using these features, keep in mind that Excel searches for text without regard for upper- or lowercase but replaces text with the exact case you type.

↗ Home→Editing→Find & Select→Find | Ctrl+F

↗ Home→Editing→Find & Select→Replace | Ctrl+H

Replacing Cell Contents

Cell contents can be replaced individually with the Replace button or throughout an entire worksheet simultaneously with Replace All. The Replace command can be particularly useful when updating templates for financial statements and other similar reports. Company-specific information, such as company name and accounts names, can be easily changed in a template in this manner.

Replacing Cell Formats

Sometimes it's beneficial to replace cell formats throughout a worksheet while leaving the cell contents unchanged. For example, figures within a statement of cash flows can easily be changed from displaying as standard numbers to the accounting format using Replace.

1. You can limit the Find and Replace command to specific areas of a workbook.

2. You can find and replace items with specific cell formats.

Develop Your Skills EA3-D4

In this exercise, you will complete the statement of cash flows for City Music World for the month ended December 31, 2016. For the Financing Activities section, use these figures: Cash (beginning balance) equals $111,000, Harold Cameron, Drawing equals $14,000, Notes Payable (beginning balance) equals $5,000, and Notes Payable (ending balance) equals $0.

1. Save your file as: **EA3-D4-StatementofCF-[YourName]**

2. Enter this data:

cell A17	Financing Activities:
cell A18	Harold Cameron, Drawing
cell C18	-14000
cell A19	Decrease in Notes Payable
cell C19	-5000
cell A20	Cash Flows Used in Financing Activities:
cell D20	=C18+C19

3. Select **cells C19** and **D20** and then choose **Home→Font→Borders ▼→ Bottom Border**.

4. Type **Net Decrease in Cash** in cell **A22**, tap ⌷Tab⌷ three times, and type: **=D10+D15+D20**

   By adding the final figures in each section, you have arrived at the total change in cash for the period. As this is a negative amount, you have used Decrease in the description.

5. Type **Cash (Beginning Balance)** in cell **A23**, tap ⌷Tab⌷ three times, and type: **111000**

6. Type **Cash (Ending Balance)** in cell **A24**, tap ⌷Tab⌷ three times, and type: **=D22+D23**

7. Select **cell D24** and choose **Home→Font→Borders ▼→Top and Double Bottom Border**.

8. Choose **Home→Editing→Find & Select→Replace**.

9. Follow these steps to find and replace text:

A. Make sure the **Replace** tab is displaying.

B. Type **Notes Payable** in the **Find What** box.

C. Type **N/P** in the **Replace With** Box.

D. Click **Replace All**.

E. Click **OK** in the window that appears.

You replaced the phrase Notes Payable in cell A19 with the abbreviation N/P. Next you will find and replace formatting.

10. Highlight the contents of the **Find What** box and tap ⌷Delete⌷. Repeat for the **Replace With** box.

11. Click the **Options** button to expand the dialog box.

12. On the **Find What** row, choose **Format** ▼→**Choose Format from Cell**, and then click **cell C6**.

13. On the **Replace With** row, choose **Format** ▼→**Format**, click the **Number** tab and choose **Accounting**, enter **0** in the **Decimal Places** box, and click **OK**.

14. Click **Replace All** and then **OK**.

   Nine instances of the Accounting number format now show no decimal places. Because the format you highlighted in the Find What row did not include a border, cells with a border were not updated. You will now update these cells.

15. On the **Find What** row, click **Format** ▼→**Clear Find Format**.

16. Choose **Format** ▼→**Choose Format From Cell**, click **cell C9**, and click **Replace All**.

   Four more instances of the Accounting number format (those for which a bottom border is displayed) are now updated.

17. Click **OK** and then close the **Find and Replace** window.

18. Select **cell D24** and choose **Home→Number→Decrease Decimal** twice.

   As there was only one instance in which a cell contained a top and double bottom border, there was no benefit to using Find & Replace to update cell D24.

19. Save and close your file.

REAL-WORLD Accounting

What Are the Benefits of Using Excel to Create the Statement of Cash Flows?

Creating a statement of cash flows in Excel allows for the same efficiency and ease of comparisons across different time periods seen when creating other financial statements in Excel. Another benefit is the automatic generation of the statement of cash flows, once the proper formulas have been created.

Every element of the statement of cash flows can be located in another financial statement (net income, ending cash balance), calculated from figures in other financial statements (increase/decrease in Accounts Receivable or Notes Payable), or calculated from postings within the general ledger (Purchase of Equipment, Sale of Machinery). If these elements are included in Excel, then formulas can be written to calculate the amount in the statement of cash flows. And once a template is created, the statement can be automatically generated every month. In fact, other elements such as the general ledger don't need to be created in Excel as long as the figures in them can be exported to Excel in a consistent manner every period.

While the initial work is time consuming, the overall time savings each period will be significant. And because the elements of the statement of cash flows would be automatically populated, the statement could provide an up-to-date view of the cash-related operations of a business at any stage, assuming the other items in Excel are being updated in real time.

Self-Assessment

Check your knowledge of this chapter's key concepts and skills using the Self-Assessment here or in your eLab course.

1. You must use capital letters when typing cell references in formulas. *True* *False*

2. A relative cell reference in a formula will not change when the formula is copied to another cell. *True* *False*

3. By default, when a cell reference is first included in a formula (so that only the column and row references are included), it is displayed as a relative cell reference. *True* *False*

4. When an amount is changed within a cell that is referenced in a formula, the result of the formula updates accordingly. *True* *False*

5. A formula can be edited in the Formula Bar or by double-clicking the formula cell. *True* *False*

6. A circular reference will not prevent Excel from displaying the result of the formula in which it appears. *True* *False*

7. When a circular reference is included within a formula, a warning message is displayed. *True* *False*

8. AutoFill copies a formula from one cell to another. *True* *False*

9. With Find and Replace, each instance of the item entered in the Find box must be replaced individually. *True* *False*

10. Find and Replace can be used to replace both cell contents and cell formats. *True* *False*

11. Which of these is a correctly written cell reference?
    2C
    34
    AG
    D7

12. Which of these is NOT an operator that can be used within a formula?
    *
    @
)
    /

13. The formula =H3+J4 in cell A1 is copied to cell A2. How will the formula appear in cell A2?
    =H4+J5
    =I3+K4
    =H4+J4
    =I3+J5

14. When a formula is selected for editing, what happens to the cell references in the formula so they can be tracked to their respective locations within the worksheet?
    Their size is altered.
    They appear in bold.
    They are color-coded.
    They are italicized.

15. When a new formula is entered into a cell that already contains a formula, what happens to the original formula?
    It is retained, while the new formula is disregarded.
    It is deleted.
    It is added to the beginning of the new formula.
    It is added to the end of the new formula.

16. A circular reference occurs when a formula refers:
    to its own cell.
    to another formula that refers to the cell in which the original formula is written.
    to both its own cell and to another formula that refers to the cell in which the original formula
        is written.
    None of these options

17. Which of these is NOT an option associated with the AutoFill button?
    Paste Cells
    Copy Cells
    Fill Formatting Only
    Fill Without Formatting

18. Which statement best describes the impact on relative cell references in a formula being copied and pasted?
    The cell references appear identical to those within the copied formula.
    Only the column portion of the cell references (letter) may change in the copied formula.
    The cell references will update based on the distance between the location of the original formula and
        the new formula.
    Only the row portion of the cell references (number) may change in the copied formula.

19. When would you NOT use the Options button on the Replace tab in the Find and Replace window?
    When locating cell contents within a specific area of a worksheet
    When replacing specific cell formats
    When locating cell contents with a specific case
    When replacing specific cell contents

20. When using Find and Replace to locate a cell format, which of these CANNOT be used to populate the format within the Find row?
    Copying an existing cell format within the worksheet
    Manually selecting the number type from a variety of options
    Manually selecting the font size and type from a variety of options
    Copying a previously changed cell format that was originally part of the worksheet

Reinforce Your Skills

EA3-R1 Create the Statement of Cash Flows for Waterfall Management Inc.

In this exercise, you will use the indirect method to create a statement of cash flows in Excel for Waterfall Management Inc. The following amounts relate to April of 2016.

Net Income	$57,000	Purchase of Equipment	$31,000
Amortization Expense	$1,500	Purchase of Machinery	$18,500
Accounts Receivable (beginning)	$17,500	Notes Payable (beginning)	$20,000
Accounts Receivable (ending)	$4,500	Notes Payable (ending)	$9,000
Accounts Payable (beginning)	$1,200	Michael Elba, Drawing	$4,000
Accounts Payable (ending)	$9,200	Cash (beginning balance)	$147,000

1. Open **EA3-R1-StatementofCF** from your **Chapter 03** folder and save it as: **EA3-R1-StatementofCF-[YourName]**

2. In **cell A5**, type a header for the first section of the statement and do not include a colon at the end.

3. Enter the first item for this section in **cell A6** and its associated amount in **cell C6**.

4. Enter the name of the only expense item for this section in **cell A7** and its associated amount in **cell C7**.

5. Enter the remaining two items for this section on **rows 8–9** in the order they appear in the balance sheet.

6. In **cell A10**, begin typing **Cash Flows** and complete the entry based on the information in this section of the statement (do not include a colon).

7. Enter **=C6+C7+C8+C9** in **cell D10**.

8. Change **cell C6** to **27100** and then to **15800**, taking note of how cell D10 automatically updates each time, and then revert the cell to its original figure.

   Hint: Use the Undo command twice.

Complete the Second Section of the Statement of Cash Flows

9. In **cell A12**, type a header for the second section of the statement and do not include a colon at the end.

10. Enter the first item for this section (enter items alphabetically) in **cell A13** and its associated amount in **cell C13**.

    Hint: Enter any amounts that result in cash flowing out of the business as negative figures in this section.

11. Enter the second item in **cell A14** and its associated amount in **cell C14**.

12. In **cell A15**, begin typing **Cash Flows** and complete the entry based on the information in this section of the statement (do not include a colon).

13. Select **cell D10** and choose **Home→Clipboard→Copy**, click **cell D15**, press Ctrl+V, and tap Enter.

    The formula in cell D15 needs to be corrected.

14. Click in the **Formula Bar** to the left of *C13* and tap Backspace enough times to delete the first two cell references.

Complete the Third Section of the Statement of Cash Flows

15. In **cell A17**, enter a header for the third section of the statement with no colon at the end.

16. Type the account name for the owner's withdrawals in **cell A18** and the associated amount in **cell C18**.

17. Type the final item for the section in **cell A19** and its associated amount in **cell C19**.

18. In **cell A20**, begin typing **Cash Flows** and complete the entry based on the information in this section of the statement (do not include a colon).

19. Enter **=C18+C19** in **cell D20**.

20. Enter the appropriate description depending on whether total cash increased or decreased during the period in **cell A22**, tap Tab three times, and enter: **=D10+D15+D20**

21. Type the names of the appropriate Cash balances in **cells A23** and **A24** and their associated amounts in **cells D23** and **D24**.

22. Choose **Home→Editing→Find & Select→Replace**.

23. Fill in the fields on the **Replace** tab to find all instances of **Activities** and replace them all with **Activities:** (colon).

24. Clear the contents of the **Find What** and **Replace With** boxes using Delete and then click the **Options** button.

25. Complete the fields as indicated and then click **Replace All**:

    - Find What row: Choose **Format ▼→Choose Format from Cell** and click **cell C6**.
    - Replace With row: Choose **Format ▼→Format**, click the **Number** tab and choose **Accounting**, and set the decimal places to **0**.

26. Apply a bottom border to **cells C9**, **C14**, **C19**, and **D20** and then apply a top and double bottom border to **cell D24**.

27. Save and close your file.

EA3-R2 Create the Statement of Cash Flows for Hailstorm Co.

In this exercise, you will use the indirect method to create a statement of cash flows in Excel for Hailstorm Co. The following amounts relate to January of 2016.

Net Income	$3,100	Sale of Machinery	$1,900
Depreciation Expense	$400	Purchase of Equipment	$2,100
Accounts Receivable (beginning)	$1,900	Investment by Owner	$1,000
Accounts Receivable (ending)	$1,100	Lucas Schmidt, Drawing	$300
Accounts Payable (beginning)	$2,900	Cash (beginning balance)	$7,800
Accounts Payable (ending)	$1,700		

1. Open **EA3-R2-StatementofCF** from your **Chapter 03** folder and save it as:
   EA3-R2-StatementofCF-[YourName]

2. In **cell A5**, enter a header for the first section of the statement (without a colon at the end).

3. Enter the first item for this section in **cell A6** and its associated amount in **cell C6**.

4. Enter the name of the only expense item for this section in **cell A7** and its associated amount in **cell C7**.

5. Enter the remaining two items for this section on **rows 8–9** in the order they appear in the balance sheet.

   Hint: Any amounts that result in cash flowing out of the business should be entered as negative figures within this section.

6. In **cell A10**, type the appropriate cash flows description based on the information in this section of the statement (do not include a colon).

7. Enter **=C6+C7+C8+C9** in **cell D10**.

Complete the Second Section of the Statement of Cash Flows

8. In **cell A12**, enter a header for the second section of the statement (without a colon at the end).

9. Enter the first item for this section (enter items from largest to smallest in this section) in **cell A13** and its associated amount in **cell C13**.

10. Enter the second item for this section in **cell A14** and its associated amount in **cell C14**.

11. In **cell A15**, type the appropriate cash flows entry based on the information in this section of the statement (do not include a colon).

12. Click **cell D10** and press Ctrl+C, click **cell D15**, and choose **Home→Clipboard→Paste**.

    The formula in cell D15 needs to be corrected.

13. Click in the **Formula Bar** to the left of *C13* and tap Backspace enough times to delete the first two cell references.

Complete the Third Section of the Statement of Cash Flows

14. In **cell A17**, enter a header for the third section of the statement (without a colon at the end).

15. Enter the account name for the owner's investment in **cell A18** and its associated amount in **cell C18**.

16. Enter the final item for this section in **cell A19** and its associated amount in **cell C19**.

17. In **cell A20**, type the appropriate cash flows entry based on the information in this section of the statement (do not include a colon).

18. Enter **=C18+C19** in **cell D20**.

19. Enter the appropriate description depending on whether total cash increased or decreased during the period in **cell A22**, tap Tab three times, and enter: **=D10+D15+D20**

20. Type the names of the appropriate Cash balances in **cells A23** and **A24** and their associated amounts in **cells D23** and **D24**.

21. Choose **Home→Editing→Find & Select→Replace**.

22. Fill in the fields on the **Replace** tab to find all instances of *Activities* and replace them all with *Activities:* (colon).

23. Clear the contents of the **Find What** and **Replace With** boxes using Delete and then click the **Options** button.

24. Complete the fields as indicated, and then click **Replace All**:

    - Find What row: Choose **Format ▼→Format**, click the **Number** tab, choose **Accounting**.
    - Replace With row: Choose **Format ▼→Format**, click the **Number** tab, choose **Accounting**, and set the decimal places to **0**.

25. Apply a bottom border to **cells C9**, **C14**, **C19**, and **D20** and apply a top and double bottom border to **cell D24**.

26. Save and close your file.

·Apply Your Skills

EA3-A1 Create the Statement of Cash Flows for Tight Flying Co.

In this exercise, you will use the indirect method to create the statement of cash flows in Excel for Tight Flying Co. The following amounts relate to June of 2016.

Net Income	$28,000	Sale of Equipment	$1,700
Depreciation Expense	$2,000	Sale of Furniture	$9,300
Accounts Receivable (beginning)	$9,600	Notes Payable (beginning)	$15,800
Accounts Receivable (ending)	$13,200	Notes Payable (ending)	$4,800
Accounts Payable (beginning)	$4,600	Stacey Feinberg, Drawing	$20,000
Accounts Payable (ending)	$9,300	Cash (beginning balance)	$80,100

1. Open **EA3-A1-StatementofCF** from your **Chapter 03** folder and save it as:
   EA3-A1-StatementofCF-[YourName]

2. Enter the data as described into the correct cells for the first section of the statement:

In this row:	Enter the data for the:
Cell A5	Header (no colon at end)
Cells A6 and C6	First item in this section and its associated amount
Cells A7 and C7	Only expense item and its associated amount
Cells A8 and C8	First of the remaining two items and its associated amount
Cells A9 and C9	Final item and its associated amount
Cells A10 and D10	Final description for (no colon) and a formula to summarize the items in the first section

Hint: Enter the items in rows 8–9 in the order they would appear in the balance sheet.

Complete the Second Section of the Statement of Cash Flows

3. Enter the data as described into the correct cells for the second section of the statement:

In this row:	Enter the data for the:
Cell A12	Header (no colon at end)
Cells A13 and C13	First item in this section and its associated amount
Cells A14 and C14	Second item in this section and its associated amount
Cells A15 and D15	Final description for (no colon) and a formula to summarize the items in the second section

Hint: Enter items alphabetically in this section.

Complete the Third Section of the Statement of Cash Flows

4. Enter the data as described into the correct cells for the third section of the statement:

In this row:	Enter the data for the:
Cell A17	Header (no colon at end)
Cells A18 and C18	Account name for the owner's withdrawals and the associated amount
Cells A19 and C19	Final item in this section and its associated amount
Cells A20 and D20	Final description for (no colon) and a formula to summarize the items in the first section of the statement
Cells A22 and D22	Appropriate description for the change in Cash and the associated amount
Cells A23 and D23	Name of the appropriate Cash balance and its appropriate amount
Cells A24 and D24	Name of the appropriate Cash balance and its appropriate amount

5. Use Find and Replace to:

   - Replace *Activities* with *Activities:* (with a colon).
   - Replace all instances of the Accounting number format with the Accounting number format with zero decimal places.

6. Apply a bottom border to the cells for which it is appropriate and a top and double bottom border to the one cell that needs it.

7. Save and close your file.

EA3-A2 Create the Statement of Cash Flows for Fitness Pros Co.

In this exercise, you will use the indirect method to create a statement of cash flows in Excel for Fitness Pros Co. The following amounts relate to October of 2016.

Net Income	$9,000	Purchase of Furniture	$4,900
Depreciation Expense	$1,250	Purchase of Machinery	$8,800
Accounts Receivable (beginning)	$3,950	Notes Payable (beginning)	$0
Accounts Receivable (ending)	$10,750	Notes Payable (ending)	$4,500
Accounts Payable (beginning)	$8,300	Eva Bryant, Drawing	$6,000
Accounts Payable (ending)	$200	Cash (beginning balance)	$35,600

1. Open **EA3-A2-StatementofCF** from your **Chapter 03** folder and save it as:
   EA3-A2-StatementofCF-[YourName]

2. Enter the data as described into the correct cells for the first section of the statement:

In this row:	Enter the data for the:
Cell A5	Header (include a colon)
Cells A6 and C6	First item in this section and its associated amount
Cells A7 and C7	Only expense item and its associated amount
Cells A8 and C8	First of the remaining two items and its associated amount
Cells A9 and C9	Final item and its associated amount
Cells A10 and D10	Final description for (with colon) and a formula to summarize the items in the first section

Hint: Enter the items in rows 8–9 in the order they would appear in the balance sheet. Use an abbreviation when typing the description of the asset account.

Complete the Second Section of the Statement of Cash Flows

3. Enter the data as described into the correct cells for the second section of the statement:

In this row:	Enter the data for the:
Cell A12	Header (include a colon)
Cells A13 and C13	First item in this section and its associated amount
Cells A14 and C14	Second item in this section and its associated amount
Cells A15 and D15	Final description for (with colon) and a formula to summarize the items in the second section

Hint: Enter items alphabetically in this section.

Complete the Third Section of the Statement of Cash Flows

4. Enter the data as described into the correct cells for the third section of the statement:

In this row:	Enter the data for the:
Cell A17	Header (include a colon)
Cells A18 and C18	Description for the liability account that should be entered and the associated amount
Cells A19 and C19	Final item in this section and its associated amount
Cells A20 and D20	Final description for (with colon) and a formula to summarize the items in the first section of the statement
Cells A22 and D22	Appropriate description for the change in Cash and the associated amount
Cells A23 and D23	Name of the appropriate Cash balance and its appropriate amount
Cells A24 and D24	Name of the appropriate Cash balance and its appropriate amount

5. Use Find and Replace to:

   - Replace *A/R* with *Accounts Receivable*.
   - Replace all instances of the Accounting number format with the Accounting number format with zero decimal places.

6. Apply a bottom border to the cells for which it is appropriate and a top and double bottom border to the one cell that needs it.

7. Save and close your file.

Extend Your Skills

EA3-E1 Create the Statement of Cash Flows for Survive & Thrive Co.

In this exercise, you will use the indirect method to create a statement of cash flows in Excel for Survive & Thrive Co. These amounts relate to July of 2016.

Net Income	$4,500	Sale of Machinery	$21,000
Depreciation Expense	$900	Purchase of Equipment	$18,000
Accounts Receivable (beginning)	$6,200	Notes Payable (beginning)	$5,600
Accounts Receivable (ending)	$5,100	Notes Payable (ending)	$6,600
Accounts Payable (beginning)	$3,000	Travis Jackman, Drawing	$3,000
Accounts Payable (ending)	$4,800	Cash (beginning balance)	$37,400

Use the techniques from this chapter to present the statement in good form.

EA3-E2 Create the Statement of Cash Flows for Big League Bullseye Corp.

In this exercise, you will use the indirect method to create a statement of cash flows in Excel for Big League Bullseye Corp. These amounts relate to September of 2016.

Net Income	$300	Purchase of Equipment	$3,100
Depreciation Expense	$2,500	Purchase of Furniture	$2,400
Accounts Receivable (beginning)	$9,400	Investment by Owner	$1,800
Accounts Receivable (ending)	$12,500	Nicholas Winfield, Drawing	$1,500
Accounts Payable (beginning)	$7,300	Cash (beginning balance)	$11,300
Accounts Payable (ending)	$6,900		

Use the techniques from this chapter to present the statement in good form.

EA3-E3 Create the Statement of Cash Flows for Future Back Industries

In this exercise, you will use the indirect method to create a statement of cash flows in Excel for Future Back Industries. These amounts relate to February of 2016.

Net Loss	$1,200	Sale of Furniture	$750
Depreciation Expense	$800	Purchase of Machinery	$3,000
Accounts Receivable (beginning)	$3,100	Investment by Owner	$900
Accounts Receivable (ending)	$1,100	Richard Morse, Drawing	$1,200
Accounts Payable (beginning)	$900	Cash (beginning balance)	$44,200
Accounts Payable (ending)	$200		

Use the techniques from this chapter to present each in good form.

Critical Thinking

EA3-C1 Discuss Benefits of Using Relative Cell References

Many accounting-related worksheets require the same formula to be used in multiple locations. While certain worksheets, such as those containing a financial statement, are relatively small, others can extend for thousands of rows. As you learned, the Copy and Paste commands and the AutoFill option can be used to efficiently copy a formula from one location to another.

Identify four types of accounting-related worksheets (aside from the financial statements) for which the use of relative cell references within formulas would yield a significant benefit. Write a paragraph of at least six sentences to discuss the structure of the worksheets and why the use of relative cell references would be beneficial.

EA3-C2 Discuss What-If Analysis in Accounting Worksheets

What-if analyses can be easily performed in Excel by changing as few as one figure. As a business examines the possibilities surrounding its future performance, this type of analysis provides crucial information relative to best- and worst-case scenarios. As future planning becomes more complex, these what-if analyses can increase in complexity and usefulness.

Identify five what-if analyses that a business can perform when considering its performance for the upcoming year. Write a paragraph of at least four sentences in which you discuss the elements of your what-if analyses. Write a second paragraph with at least four sentences to discuss how the information obtained from the what-if analyses could be used to improve business planning.

Inventory Costing and Analysis

LEARNING OBJECTIVES

- Use functions in formulas to perform calculations and manipulate text

- Calculate inventory cost under the LIFO, FIFO, and weighted average methods

- Apply data bars to worksheets

- Create PivotTables

Working with Excel's built-in functions will allow you to fully realize the benefits of using formulas in worksheets. These built-in functions can automatically perform many numerical calculations and varying forms of text manipulation. Once the worksheet data has been properly entered, analysis tools (such a data bars and PivotTables) can prove to be invaluable. In this chapter, you will examine an inventory listing and calculate inventory cost. You'll use various methods to calculate the ending inventory balance. You will then ensure that specific information within the inventory listing is easily identified through the use of data bars. Last, you will see how PivotTables can be used to examine worksheet data.

City Music World

City Music World is a retail store that sells musical equipment and offers lessons for beginning and experienced musicians. The company carries an extensive array of products and would like to calculate the cost of this inventory and analyze the historical inventory levels more efficiently. You are tasked with completing the company's inventory listing and highlighting important elements of the worksheet.

In this chapter. you will complete the inventory listing using Excel's built-in functions. You will then use text-related functions while determining an inventory balance using the LIFO, FIFO, and weighted average methods. Last, you will use data bars and a PivotTable to highlight key information and analyze the inventory listing in multiple ways.

Product Manager	(Multiple Items)					
Sum of Ending Inventory Balance - Year 2	Column Labels					
Row Labels	Bass Software	Earbuds/In Ear	Guitar Accessories	Guitar Software	On-Ear Headphones	Ukuleles
Finland						3100
Germany			2600	1000		
Holland						
Italy					4800	
Sweden		0				
U.S.A.				900		
Grand Total	0	2600	1000	900	4800	3100

A PivotTable, combined here with slicers and a PivotChart, can be used to analyze data.

Inventory Costing Methods

Accounting Refresher ↻

As a merchandising business purchases inventory, which it intends to resell at a higher price, it typically finds that inventory cost increases over time. This is referred to as inflation. One implication of inflation is that different units of inventory within a business' warehouse will cost different amounts. While one unit may have been purchased two months earlier for $50, another unit may have been purchased more recently for $52.

How, then, does the business determine the cost of the inventory units remaining in the warehouse at the end of the period (the ending inventory balance for the period)? Typically it's too difficult to track the cost of each unit of inventory, so if the business has twelve units remaining in inventory at the end of the period, does it use the $50 or the $52 amount for each remaining unit? Or, does it average these figures to determine the ending inventory balance?

To answer this question, a business must choose one of three inventory costing methods: LIFO (last in, first out), FIFO (first in, first out), or weighted average.

LIFO (Last In, First Out)

Under the LIFO method, the business assumes that the most recent (or last) goods added to inventory are sold to customers before other goods in inventory (thus, they are the *first* goods *out* of the warehouse). When determining ending inventory balance, you use the cost of the earliest-obtained goods in the calculations—because the last goods obtained are assumed sold.

NOTE! As is consistent with the approach taken by the majority of small businesses, the periodic inventory system (under which the chosen inventory method is applied once at the end of the period) is assumed here and throughout this chapter.

FIFO (First In, First Out)

The FIFO method is essentially the opposite of the LIFO method. Under this method, the business assumes that the earliest (or first) goods added to inventory are sold to customers before other goods in inventory (thus, they are the *first* goods *out* of the warehouse). When determining ending inventory balance, you use the cost of the most recently obtained goods in the calculations—because the first goods obtained are assumed sold.

Weighted Average

The weighted average method typically results in an ending inventory balance that falls between the balances that would be calculated under the LIFO and FIFO methods. Under the weighted average method, the business divides the total cost of all goods that were in the warehouse during the period by the total number of units that were in the warehouse during the period. The result is a weighted average cost per unit. This weighted average cost is then multiplied by the number of units remaining in the warehouse at the end of the period in order to determine the ending inventory balance.

Working with Functions

A function is a prewritten formula that helps simplify complex procedures, both for numbers and text. For instance, a function can be used to sum a group of numbers, determine the payment amount on a loan, or convert a number to text. Many functions are invaluable when performing necessary accounting calculations. Some of the most basic functions are introduced here.

Using AutoSum to Create a SUM Formula

AutoSum automatically sums a column or row of numbers. When you click AutoSum, Excel starts the formula for you by entering =SUM() with a proposed range of adjacent cells in the parentheses. Excel first looks upward for a range to sum. If a range is not found there, it looks left. You can accept the proposed range, which can be viewed in the Formula Bar, or select a different range.

	C	D	E	F	G
SUM			fx	=SUM(F5:F83)	
78	Brown	Germany	Professional	$ -	$
79	Brown	U.S.A.	Professional	$ 790	$
80	Brown	France	Professional	$ 1,300	$
81	Brown	U.S.A.	Professional	$ 6,300	$
82	Brown	Germany	Beginner	$ 6,300	$
83	Brown	Spain	Casual User	$ 3,450	$
84				=SUM(F5:F83)	
85				SUM(number1, [number2], ...)	

1. The Formula Bar displays the formula.

2. A flashing marquee surrounds the proposed range (F5:F83) above the formula cell (F84).

In addition to summing a group of numbers, AutoSum can perform a number of other calculations.

Calculations Available Within AutoSum Menu

Function Name	Description
SUM	Adds the values in the cells
AVERAGE	Averages the values in the cells
COUNT NUMBERS	Counts the number of values in the cells; cells containing text and blank cells are ignored
COUNTA (under More Functions)	Counts the number of values and text entries in the cells; blank cells are ignored
MAX	Returns the highest value in the cells
MIN	Returns the lowest value in the cells

↗ Home→Editing→AutoSum   Alt + =

Status Bar Functions

You can customize the **status bar**, which is displayed at the bottom of the Excel window, to display all of the functions noted so far. To customize the status bar, right-click anywhere on it and choose the features to add or remove. You can customize other features of the status bar as well, such as zoom, permissions, macro recording, and more.

Intermediate	$	-	$	✓ Average	$4,338	$
Professional	$	-	$	✓ Count	4	$
Professional	$	790	$	Numerical Count		$
Professional	$	1,300	$	Minimum		$
Professional	$	6,300	$	Maximum		$
Beginner	$	6,300	$	✓ Sum	$17,350	$
Casual User	$	3,450	$	✓ Upload Status		$
	$	275,760		✓ View Shortcuts		
				✓ Zoom Slider		
⊕				✓ Zoom	100%	▶

Average: $4,338   Count: Sum: $17,350   — ——|—— + 100%

By default, the status bar displays the functions to calculate averages, count of values, and sum of the selected range.

Formula AutoComplete

Formula AutoComplete assists you in creating and editing formulas. Once you type an equals (=) sign and any letters, Excel will display a list of functions beginning with the typed letters below the active cell.

Function Syntax

A function is a predefined formula that performs calculations or returns a desired result. Most functions are constructed using similar basic rules, or syntax. This syntax also applies to the MIN, MAX, AVERAGE, COUNT, and COUNTA functions.

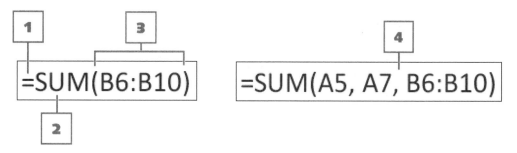

1. Formulas containing functions begin with an equals sign.

2. The function name follows the equals sign.

3. Parentheses surround the argument, which is usually a range of cells.

4. In this formula, cells A5 and A7 are added to the range B6:B10.

Insert Function

The Insert Function option displays the Insert Function dialog box. Within this dialog box you can locate a function by typing a description or searching categories. When you locate the desired function and click OK, the Function Arguments box appears, providing a straightforward method for entering each component (or argument) of a function.

TIP!   As you use more of Excel's advanced functions, you will find these dialog boxes increasingly beneficial.

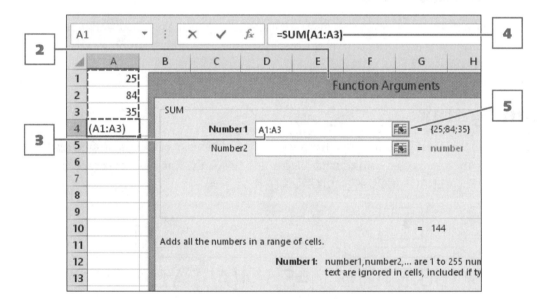

1. You can search for a function by typing a description or choosing a category.

2. The Function Arguments box appears when you choose a function.

3. The argument (typically a range) can be typed here or selected from the worksheet.

4. The function appears in the Formula Bar.

5. The Collapse button hides the Function Arguments box while you select the desired range.

You can move the Function Arguments dialog box around the screen to better view the worksheet by dragging its title bar.

↗ Formulas→Function Library→Insert Function | Shift + F3

Develop Your Skills EA4-D1

In this exercise, you will use functions to summarize data within an inventory listing. You will also review and modify information provided in the status bar.

1. Start Excel. Open **EA4-D1-Inventory** from your **Chapter 04** folder and save it as: **EA4-D1-Inventory-[YourName]**

2. On the Inventory Listing tab, type the following in **cell B2**: **=COUNTA(**

3. Highlight the **range A5:A83**, type **)** (a closed parenthesis), and tap Enter.

   The total number of inventory categories is now prominently displayed at the top of the worksheet.

4. Type **=COU** in **cell J5**, double-click the **Count** function in the list, highlight the **range E5:I5**, type **)** (a closed parenthesis), and tap Enter.

   Because there is no entry within cell I5 at this point, the result of this formula is 4.

5. Select **cell K5** and choose **Formulas→Function Library→Insert Function**.

6. Type **Average** in the **Search for a Function** box, click **Go**, click **Average** from the **Select a Function** box, and click **OK**.

7. Highlight the **range E5:I5** and click **OK** in the **Function Arguments** dialog box.

   You may need to move the Function Arguments dialog box by dragging its title bar in order to highlight the specified range.

8. Click **cell L5** and choose **Formulas→Function Library→Insert Function**.

9. Choose **Statistical** from the **Or Select a Category** drop-down menu, scroll through the list in the **Select a Function** box and click **Max**, and click **OK**.

10. Highlight the **range E5:I5** and click **OK** in the **Function Arguments** dialog box.

11. Click **cell M5** and **Home→Editing→AutoSum ▼→Min**, highlight the **range E5:I5**, and tap Enter.

12. Highlight the **range J5:M5**, click the fill handle, and drag down to **row 83**.

    The fill handle is the small square at the bottom right of the selected range.

13. Highlight the **range E84:I84** and choose **Home→Editing→AutoSum**.

14. Save your file.

    Unless otherwise directed, always keep your file open at the end of each exercise.

Using Functions to Format Text

When worksheet data is imported from sources other than Excel, the data may not be formatted as you wish. For example, employee last name, first name, and middle name may all be contained in one column when it would be beneficial if the names were separated into separate columns. Similarly, text within a worksheet may require manipulation so it conforms to a desired format. Excel's text functions allow the user to easily alter text in this manner.

LEFT, MID, and RIGHT to Extract Text

Data copied into an Excel worksheet from another application may contain characters you don't want. Alternatively, data may need to be modified to appear in a specific format, such as an identifying code for inventory that contains the first three letters of the item's name connected to the two-digit month and two-digit day on which it was obtained. You can use the LEFT, MID, and RIGHT functions to extract a certain number of characters, depending on their location in the text string.

The RIGHT function can be used to extract a specified number of characters from the right side of a text string, while the LEFT function accomplishes the same from the left side. The MID function counts the characters from the left until it arrives at the starting character number specified and then extracts the desired number of characters. The extracted characters display in the formula result cell and the original text is not affected.

LEFT, MID, and RIGHT Function Syntax

Function	Syntax
LEFT	LEFT(text,[number of characters])
MID	MID(text, character start number, number of characters)
RIGHT	RIGHT(text,[number of characters])

WARNING! While the number of characters is optional for the LEFT and RIGHT functions, it is mandatory for the MID function.

LEFT, MID, and RIGHT Function Arguments

Argument	Description
Text	The text characters to be counted or extracted.
Character start number	The starting character to be extracted. Used with the MID function to determine which character, counted from left to right, should be displayed first. If this argument is omitted, then the first character in the text string is the starting point.
Number of characters	The total characters to be extracted. If this argument is omitted, then only the first character is displayed. Optional for LEFT and RIGHT.

The LEFT function

The MID function

The RIGHT function

Flash Fill and the CONCATENATE Function

Flash Fill allows you to quickly create modified versions of text entries with similar characteristics. CONCATENATE is a function that can be used to combine multiple text entries within a single cell.

Flash Fill

You may find it useful to modify text so portions of it are copied to a new column. For example, when email addresses are listed in a column, Flash Fill can be used to insert the account name (the portion before the @ symbol) in an adjacent column. To do so, you simply type the account name for the first row (when using the Flash Fill button on the Ribbon) or first two rows (when using Excel's automatic suggestions for filled data), after which Excel completes all remaining cells.

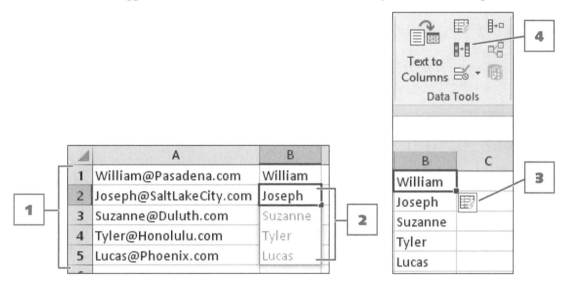

1. Original data

2. Flash Fill's suggestions based on data in the two cells above

3. Flash Fill Options button

4. Flash Fill Ribbon button

Flash Fill can also be used to combine text from multiple columns (such as combining first, middle, and last names from multiple columns into one) and to modify text (such as adding dashes to phone numbers to modify them from ########## to ###-###-####).

Data→Data Tools→Flash Fill 📇 │ Ctrl + E

CONCATENATE Function

The CONCATENATE function can also be used to combine existing text into a single cell. While it's appropriate to use Flash Fill when combining multiple columns of data, the CONCATENATE function is a better option when text entries from multiple locations within a worksheet are being combined. The syntax of the CONCATENATE function is *CONCATENATE(text1, [text2], ...).*

C1	▼	:	×	✓	*fx*	=CONCATENATE(A1, " ", B1)

◢	A	B	C	D	E	F
1	New	York	New York			

Text and blank spaces are displayed within quotation marks in a formula. Therefore, the " " results in a space displayed between *New* and *York*.

Nested Functions

A nested function is one that is included within a formula in which another function already appears. Essentially, the nested function serves as one of the arguments within the formula created using the original function.

fx	=CONCATENATE(LEFT(D1, 1), MID(D1, 5, 1))

	D	E	F	G
	New York	NY		

This CONCATENATE function includes a nested LEFT function and a nested MID function.

Develop Your Skills EA4-D2

In this exercise, you will calculate the ending inventory balance for one inventory category of City Music World using three inventory costing methods.

1. Save your file as: **EA4-D2-Inventory-[YourName]**

2. On the **Acoustic Guitars** tab, click **cell A17**.

   Here you will enter a description for the first inventory costing method, beside which you will calculate the ending inventory amount under this method.

   Do not complete the cell entries until instructed to do so in step 6.

3. Type this text: **=CONCATENATE(LEFT(A5, 1),**

   You are using the CONCATENATE function to create the description LIFO Inventory Balance: *and are partially basing this title on the entry in cell A5. The LEFT function here returns the first* L *from the entry in cell A5.*

4. Type this text: **MID(A5, 6, 1),**

   The MID function here returns the letter I, *which is the sixth character in cell A5.*

5. Type this text: **MID(A5, 10, 1), MID(A5, 16, 1),**

   The MID function here returns the tenth character (F) and the sixteenth character (O).

6. Type " **Inventory Balance:**") and tap Tab.

   This final portion of the description is enclosed in quotation marks. Be sure to include the space before Inventory, *as it's necessary to ensure a space displays between* LIFO *and* Inventory.

7. In **cell B17**, type **=D10+(F4-B10)*C11** and tap Enter.

   Under the LIFO method, the most recently obtained goods are assumed to have been sold and ending inventory is assumed to be of the earliest-obtained items. So, the twenty-one units from beginning inventory are assumed to be part of the twenty-three units in ending inventory. The other two units are assumed to have been a part of the next inventory layer (Purchase #1).

8. In **cell A18**, type: **=CONCATENATE(LEFT(A6, 1), MID(A6, 7, 1), MID(A6, 11, 1), MID(A6, 17, 1), " Inventory Balance:")**

9. In **cell B18**, type: **=D14+(F4-B14)*C13**

   With the FIFO method, it is assumed that ending inventory comprises the most recently obtained items. So, ending inventory includes the twenty units from Purchase #4 and three units from Purchase #3.

10. In **cell A19**, type: **=CONCATENATE(LEFT(A7, 1), MID(A7, 10, 1), " Inventory Balance:")**

11. In **cell B19**, type: **=(D15/B15)*F4**

    Under the weighted average method, an average cost per unit is determined (total cost in cell D15 divided by total units in cell B15) and then multiplied by the number of units in ending inventory (cell F4) to find the ending inventory balance.

12. Switch to the **Inventory Listing** tab and select **cell I5**.

    You have decided that, consistent with the approach used for other items in the inventory listing, you will use the LIFO method to determine the ending inventory balance for acoustic guitars. You will now modify the inventory listing to reflect this decision.

13. Type **=**, switch to the **Acoustic Guitars** tab, click **cell B17**, and tap Enter.

    The total count in cell J5 has been updated from 4 to 5, which is the result of an inventory cost being entered in cell I5.

14. Save your file.

Applying Conditional Formatting

The Conditional Formatting command applies formatting to cells that meet criteria that you set. Conditional formats are activated only when the criteria are met. For example, you may assign a yellow fill to a cell when its value is greater than twelve. You may apply conditional formatting to cells containing values, text, dates, blanks, or errors. This can be particularly useful when highlighting important information in a financial statement, inventory listing, etc.

You can choose to conditionally format cells with data bars, a color scale, or an icon set. Each of these can be used to quickly show how amounts within a worksheet relate. You can also easily remove conditional formatting.

Ending Inventory Balance - Year 1	Ending Inventory Balance - Year 2	Ending Inventory Balance - Year 3
$ 1,600	$ 3,100	⬤ $ -
$ 700	$ 900	⬤ $ 600
$ 1,100	$ 1,000	⬤ $ 1,000

Conditional formatting with data bars, a color scale, and icons helps you highlight data.

WARNING! Use consistent formatting and limit the use of data bars, color scales, and icon sets on one worksheet. Using multiple styles could confuse the reader.

Develop Your Skills EA4-D3

In this exercise, you will apply data bars that will allow you to easily review the relative differences between ending inventory levels for each inventory category.

1. Save your file as: **EA4-D3-Inventory-[YourName]**

2. Switch to the **Inventory Listing** tab, if necessary.

3. Highlight the **range K5:K83** and choose **Home→Styles→Conditional Formatting→ Color Scales→Blue – White – Red Color Scale**.

4. With the **range K5:K83** highlighted, choose **Home→Styles→Conditional Formatting→Icon Sets→3 Arrows (Colored)**.

   Multiple conditional formatting options can be applied simultaneously. You decide that you'd like to replace the conditional formatting shown.

5. With the **range K5:K83** highlighted, choose **Home→Styles→Conditional Formatting→ Clear Rules→Clear Rules from Selected Cells**.

6. With the **range K5:K83** highlighted, choose **Home→Styles→Conditional Formatting→ Data Bars→Gradient Fill→Purple Data Bar**.

   Review the average inventory costs in column K and note the ease with which you can compare amounts with the data bars displayed.

7. Save your file.

Creating PivotTables

PivotTables are powerful data analysis tools. They let you summarize data in various ways and instantly change the view you use. A PivotTable not only subtotals groups of related data, but it also compares one group to another. This has a variety of accounting-related applications, particularly when examining large data sets, such as an inventory listing.

Arranging the Source Data

A PivotTable is created from data in an Excel worksheet. The data should contain no blank rows or columns. The following examples illustrate two PivotTables based on the worksheet list shown here.

Inventory Category	Product Manager	Country of Manufacture	Primary End User	Ending Inventory Balance - Year 1	Ending Inventory Balance - Year 2	Ending Inventory Balance - Year 3	Ending Inventory Balance - Year 4
Acoustic Guitars	Williams	Mexico	Casual User	$ 2,000	$ 2,500	$ 2,200	$ 2,100
Electric Guitars	Williams	U.S.A.	Professional	$ 4,200	$ 4,500	$ 4,700	$ 4,400
Folk Instruments	Williams	Portugal	Intermediate	$ -	$ -	$ -	$ 2,000
Ukuleles	Williams	Finland	Beginner	$ 1,600	$ 3,100	$ -	$ 1,700
Guitar Software	Williams	U.S.A.	Beginner	$ 700	$ 900	$ 600	$ 200
Guitar Accessories	Williams	Germany	Beginner	$ 1,100	$ 1,000	$ 1,000	$ 1,000
Guitar Strings	Williams	Spain	Casual User	$ -	$ -	$ -	$ -
Guitar Amplifiers	Williams	U.S.A.	Professional	$ 200	$ 400	$ 350	$ -
Bass Amps	Jacobs	Mexico	Intermediate	$ 6,200	$ 5,700	$ 4,900	$ 5,300
Keyboard Amps	Jacobs	Spain	Professional	$ 7,100	$ 7,400	$ 7,500	$ 7,100
Guitar & Bass Effects	Jacobs	Italy	Beginner	$ 5,000	$ 5,000	$ 5,500	$ 5,300
Wireless Guitar Systems	Jacobs	France	Casual User	$ 3,600	$ 3,750	$ 3,900	$ 3,650
Wireless Bass Systems	Jacobs	Mexico	Intermediate	$ 2,800	$ 2,700	$ 2,500	$ 2,600
Bass Guitars	Clancy	Portugal	Intermediate	$ -	$ 4,700	$ 1,300	$ -
Bass Guitar Strings	Clancy	France	Professional	$ 350	$ 380	$ 900	$ 950
Bass Accessories	Clancy	France	Casual User	$ 1,120	$ 850	$ 1,100	$ 1,060
Bass Software	Clancy	Sweden	Beginner	$ -	$ -	$ -	$ 300
Over-Ear Headphones	Pouncey	Sweden	Professional	$ 6,200	$ 5,300	$ 3,000	$ 500
On-Ear Headphones	Pouncey	Italy	Beginner	$ 4,600	$ 4,800	$ 4,900	$ 4,600

PivotTable Example 1

You can sort the preceding table by country of manufacture or primary end user, but you cannot easily compare totals for the various countries in each end user category. A PivotTable can summarize some or all data in any number of ways and can create grand totals. Each column in a PivotTable is a field. Examine the PivotTable and notice that the Primary End User field from the table is used for the row labels, the Country of Manufacture field for the column labels, and the Ending Inventory Balance - Year 2 field for the data area and grand totals. Each row displays the total inventory balance by the country of manufacture for each primary end user group.

Sum of Ending Inventory Balance - Year 2	Column Labels ▼											
Row Labels ▼	Finland	France	Germany	Greece	Holland	Iceland	Italy	Mexico	Norway	Portugal	Spain	Sweden
Beginner	4900		12400	4500	4200	0	18000	4200		0	3900	2800
Casual User	1950	4600	450	0	0	2600	10380	2500	4250	880	6000	
Intermediate	5300	15300	14100		4050	7600	4650	8400		4700	960	
Professional		2380	14100	3500	2300			1850	3900		26200	5300
Grand Total	12150	22280	41050	8000	10550	10200	33030	16950	8150	5580	37060	8100

This PivotTable summarizes inventory balances by country of manufacture.

PivotTable Example 2

In this example, data is summarized first by primary end user and then by country of manufacture. To create this type of view, the PivotTable layout shown in the following illustration contains the Primary End User and then Country of Manufacture fields for row labels, no column labels, and the Ending Inventory Balance - Year 2 field for the data area and totals.

Row Labels ▼	Sum of Ending Inventory Balance – Year 2
⊟ Beginner	62900
Finland	4900
Germany	12400
Greece	4500
Holland	4200
Iceland	0
Italy	18000
Mexico	4200
Portugal	0
Spain	3900
Sweden	2800
U.S.A.	8000
⊟ Casual User	42630
Finland	1950
France	4600
Germany	450
Greece	0
Holland	0
Iceland	2600
Italy	10380
Mexico	2500
Norway	4250
Portugal	880
Spain	6000
U.S.A.	9020

This PivotTable layout summarizes contributions first by primary end user and then by country of manufacture.

How PivotTables Work

Each area of the PivotTable plays a role in data organization. The PivotTable Fields task pane displays after you define the worksheet range to be used. The areas of the task pane are explained in the following illustration, which displays the settings for PivotTable Example 1.

NOTE! You must select a cell in the PivotTable to display the PivotTable Fields task pane.

1. Here you choose columns that will appear in the PivotTable.

2. You can filter fields you have chosen by dragging them here.

3. Row labels are displayed here.

4. Column labels are displayed here.

5. The Values area displays the field on which a calculation is performed.

Where you place fields in the PivotTable Fields task pane determines how the PivotTable summarizes the data. By choosing different fields or moving (dragging and dropping) a field, you can quickly compare data in various ways. You can choose from several functions—such as SUM, COUNT, and AVERAGE—to calculate fields containing values.

Filtering a PivotTable with AutoFilter

You may set the PivotTable to filter, or include, specific items in the data summaries. The totals and subtotals are recalculated for the selected items. The Row Label and Column Label headings have an AutoFilter button that displays the same sorting and filtering options available on the columns of worksheet lists and tables. This feature is particularly useful when you are making a decision based on a specific portion of the data within a worksheet.

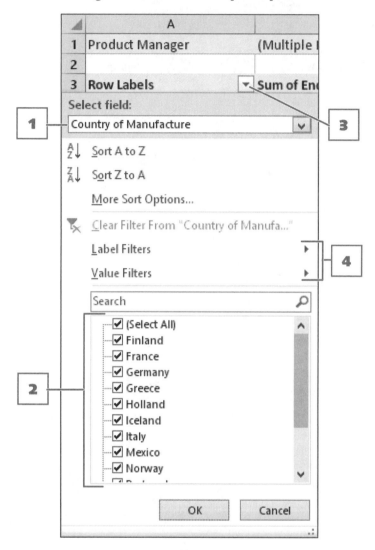

1. The field to be filtered is set here.

2. Select specific countries here.

3. This is the AutoFilter button.

4. Additional filtering commands, such as Begins With and Greater Than, are available here.

Filtering PivotTables with Slicers

Slicers are menu frames displayed on a worksheet that contain all filtering choices in one field. Selected items are highlighted in slicers, making it easy to identify applied criteria. Slicer frames can be resized, moved, and formatted with styles for a consistent appearance. Slicers can be shared in other worksheets in the same workbook for use with multiple PivotTables based on the same data set.

NOTE! Changing the filtering selections in a shared slicer causes all connected PivotTables to update automatically.

1. Highlighted items are included in the current filter

2. Multi-Select button

3. Clear Filter button

Develop Your Skills EA4-D4

In this exercise, you will create a PivotTable based on the inventory listing for City Music World. You will then modify the PivotTable to examine the inventory data.

1. Save your file as: **EA4-D4-Inventory-[YourName]**

2. Click **cell A5** and choose **Insert→Tables→PivotTable**.

3. Modify the contents of **Table/Range** box so *$M$84* is replaced with **$I$83** and then click **OK**.

   This modification excludes certain columns and the total row from the PivotTable.

4. Right-click the tab for the new sheet that has appeared and choose **Rename**, type **Inventory PivotTable**, and tap Enter.

5. In the PivotTable Fields task pane, click in the checkboxes, in order, for **Inventory Category**, **Country of Manufacture**, and **Ending Inventory Balance – Year 2**.

   The PivotTable displays each inventory category and then lists the country in which they are manufactured. A grand total is displayed at the bottom of the PivotTable.

6. In the **Rows** area in the **PivotTable Fields** task pane, drag the **Country of Manufacture** field above **Inventory Category**.

   The PivotTable now displays each country of manufacture and the inventory categories for goods produced in these countries. Note that the Ending Inventory – Year 2 Balance column displays a subtotal beside each country (which adds the total inventory balance for all inventory categories manufactured in that country).

7. Drag the **Inventory Category** field from the Rows area to the **Columns** area.

   You have now pivoted the table to display a column for each inventory category. Totals for the inventory balance within each country are displayed in the final column in the table.

8. Return the **Inventory Category** field to the **Rows** area.

9. Click the **Product Manager** checkbox near the top of the task pane and then drag that field from the **Rows** area to the **Filters** area.

   Although the Product Manager field is included within the filter area, the PivotTable currently displays the inventory balances for all product managers. Next you will exclude some of the managers from the displayed data.

10. Click the drop-down arrow in **cell B1** and then click the **Select Multiple Items** checkbox.

11. Click to remove the checkboxes beside **Clancy**, **Jacobs**, **Pouncey**, and **Williams** and then click **OK**.

Search	🔎
☑ (All)	
☑ Abbott	
☑ Brown	
☐ Clancy	
☑ Howard	
☐ Jacobs	
☑ Noone	
☐ Pouncey	
☐ Williams	

    ☑ Select Multiple Items

    OK   Cancel

    You have now filtered the PivotTable to display only the inventory balances associated with the four product managers whose checkboxes were not unchecked.

12. Close the **PivotTable Fields** task pane and then select **cell A4**.

    By selecting cell A4, the PivotTable Tools tabs become visible. Next you will filter the data using slicers, which are accessed through these tabs.

Use Slicers to Filter Data

13. Choose **PivotTable Tools→Analyze→Filter→Insert Slicer**, click in the checkboxes for **Primary End User** and **Product Manager**, and click **OK**.

    To view both slicer windows at the same time, you may need to drag one window beside the other. Notice that the Product Manager slicer highlights only the four product managers whose inventory figures are currently reflected within the PivotTable.

14. In the **Product Manager** slicer, choose **Clancy**.

    Choosing one product manager automatically deselects the others.

15. Still in the **Product Manager** slicer, click the **Multi-Select** button and then choose **Pouncey** and **Williams**.

16. In the **Primary End User** slicer, choose **Intermediate** and click the **Clear Filter** button.

    The Clear Filter button removed the Intermediate filter and restored data for all end users in the PivotTable.

17. In the **Primary End User** slicer, choose **Beginner**.

18. Click the **AutoFilter** button in **cell A3** and then click the drop-down arrow box under **Select Field**.

    You can filter either field included in the PivotTable rows.

19. Close the AutoFilter menu by clicking outside of it.

20. Save your file.

Creating PivotCharts

A PivotChart presents data from a PivotTable. There are two ways to create a PivotChart:

1. Chart an existing PivotTable by choosing a chart type from the Insert tab, as is done for a normal Excel chart.

2. Use the PivotChart command to create a PivotTable and PivotChart from the source data simultaneously. The chart builds as you choose fields in the PivotTable Fields task pane.

The fields in the values area of the PivotTable are displayed as data series in the chart. Row labels in the PivotTable are used as axis labels in the chart, while column labels are the data series in the chart legend.

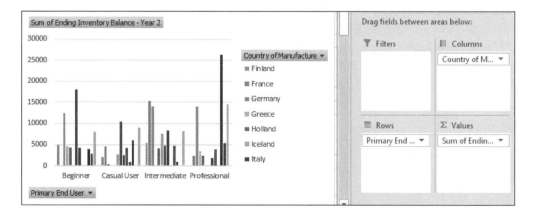

NOTE! PivotCharts are an excellent way to share accounting-related data without having to convey the detailed figures.

Filtering PivotCharts

A PivotChart can be filtered using the AutoFilter buttons on the chart, the AutoFilter buttons on the PivotTable, or slicers. Any filtering included in the PivotChart is applied to the related PivotTable as well.

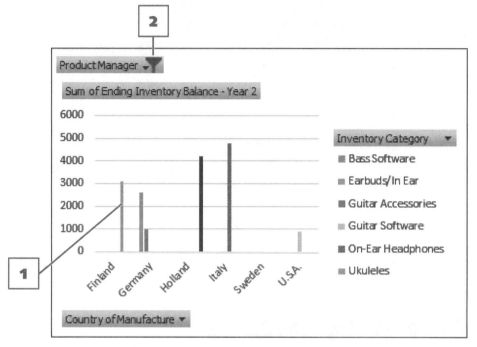

1. The chart columns depict the PivotTable column values.

2. The data may be filtered using the AutoFilter buttons.

TIP!   To retain an original PivotTable, copy it before creating a PivotChart, as any changes to the chart will update the PivotTable copy.

Develop Your Skills EA4-D5   Develop Your Skills EA4-D5

In this exercise, you will create a PivotChart based on your PivotTable. You will then modify the PivotChart to display the exact inventory data that you would like to review.

1. Save your file as: **EA4-D5-Inventory-[YourName]**

2. Click **cell A4** and choose **PivotTable Tools→Analyze→Tools→PivotChart**.

3. Choose **Column** and **Clustered Column**; click **OK**.

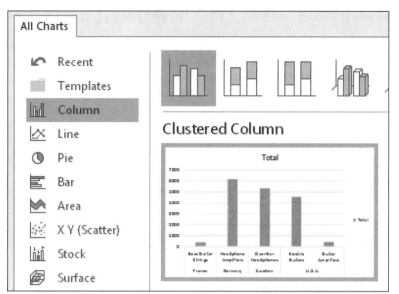

4. Click a blank area of the **PivotChart** and drag it below the **PivotTable**.

5. Choose **PivotChart Tools→Analyze→Show/ Hide→Field List** to display the PivotChart Fields task pane.

6. Drag the **Inventory Category** field from the Axis area to the **Legend** area.

    Notice that both the PivotTable and the PivotChart are updated based on this change.

7. Close the task pane and then drag each slicer below the PivotTable.

8. Save and close the file.

REAL-WORLD Accounting

What Are the Benefits of Using Excel to Examine and Analyze an Inventory Listing?

One of the primary benefits of using Excel when managing an inventory listing (or any large amount of data) is that data can be added and updated quickly. Data can similarly be summarized, through functions, and highlighted, through conditional formatting, more readily in Excel than it could be otherwise.

However, Excel's data analysis tools are what make the ideal environment to examine large batches of data. It's not uncommon for higher-level executives to request analyses on data accumulated over many years. As you have seen, PivotTables allow for data to be summarized based on any category in the data set. For example, if City Music World was considering ceasing its relationship with its German suppliers, the PivotTable completed in this chapter would provide valuable information as to the financial impact of such a decision.

These analyses are not limited to inventory data. A PivotTable would be equally effective in analyzing, for example, sales data across sixty stores for forty categories of clothing. This data could be analyzed based on the day of the week it was sold, whether it was sold at full price or for a reduced amount, etc. Such an analysis could provide key data leading to a decision to close a given store, lean more heavily toward non-discounted inventory, etc. It's the flexibility afforded to the end user that makes tools such as the PivotTable such powerful elements.

Self-Assessment

Check your knowledge of this chapter's key concepts and skills using the Self-Assessment here or in your eLab course.

1. A function is a prewritten formula built into Excel. *True   False*

2. The AutoSum button can be used only to create formulas with SUM. *True   False*

3. CONCATENATE is used to divide a single cell entry across multiple cells. *True   False*

4. Flash fill provides suggestions for cell entries based on previously entered data. *True   False*

5. The weighted average inventory method results in inventory costs that fall between those arrived at through the use of LIFO and FIFO. *True   False*

6. Conditional formatting should be used carefully, as it cannot be removed once applied. *True   False*

7. A PivotTable is a summary of worksheet data that can be arranged in a variety of ways. *True   False*

8. Data used to create a PivotTable must be contained within a table. *True   False*

9. The only way to filter PivotTable data is via a slicer. *True   False*

10. When a PivotChart is updated, the associated PivotTable is also automatically updated. *True   False*

11. Although each of these functions can be accessed via the AutoSum menu (under More Functions), which one is NOT listed on the AutoSum menu itself?
    Average
    Left
    Max
    Min

12. Which of these is NOT displayed for a range by default within the status bar?
    Average
    Count (of values)
    Sum
    Maximum

13. Under which tab is the Insert Function button located?
    Home
    Insert
    Formulas
    Data

14. For which of these functions must the Character Start Number be identified?
    LEFT
    MID
    RIGHT
    CONCATENATE

15. Which of these formulas contains a nested function?
    =MAX(A1:C7)
    =CONCATENATE(LEFT(A6, 2), " item")
    =MIN(D8:R13)+SUM(A3, A7)
    =AVERAGE(45, C2:E2)*20

16. The acronym LIFO stands for:
    Last in, first out
    Last in, function off
    Least in, first out
    Least in, function off

17. Which of these is NOT a conditional formatting option?
    Data bars
    Color scales
    Slicers
    Icon sets

18. Which of these is NOT an area displayed in the PivotTable Fields task pane?
    Filters
    Rows
    Values
    Axis

19. Which of these does NOT appear in a slicer?
    Label filters
    Field name
    Multi-Select button
    Clear Filter button

20. Which of these is NOT a location where a PivotChart may be filtered?
    AutoFilter buttons on the chart
    AutoFilter buttons on the associated PivotTable
    Formulas tab
    Associated slicers

Reinforce Your Skills

EA4-R1 Edit an Inventory Listing and Create a PivotTable for XL Sports Emporium

In this exercise, you will compile summary data based on an inventory listing for XL Sports Emporium. Then you will determine the inventory balance for a product using three methods. Last, you will create a PivotTable and a PivotChart.

1. Open **EA4-R1-Inventory** from your **Chapter 04** folder and save it as: **EA4-R1-Inventory-[YourName]**

   To begin, you will work with the Inventory Listing tab.

2. Click in **cell B2**, type **=COUNTA(** and highlight the **range A5:A70**, and then type **)** and tap ⎣Enter⎦.

3. In **cell J5**, type **=COU** and then double-click the **Count** function, highlight the **range E5:I5**, and then type **)** and tap ⎣Enter⎦.

4. Click **cell K5** and choose **Formulas→Function Library→Insert Function**.

5. Type **Average** in the search box and click **Go**, choose **Average** and click **OK**, highlight the **range E5:I5**, and then click **OK**.

   You may need to move the Function Arguments dialog box by dragging its title bar in order to highlight the specified range.

6. Click **cell L5**, choose **Formulas→Function Library→Insert Function**, click the arrow for **Or Select a Category**, choose **Statistical** and then **Max**, and click **OK**.

7. Highlight the **range E5:I5** and click **OK**.

8. Select **cell M5** and choose **Home→Editing→AutoSum ▾→Min**, highlight the **range E5:I5**, and tap ⎣Enter⎦.

9. Highlight the **range J5:M5**, click the fill handle, and drag down to **row 70**.

10. Highlight the **range E71:I71** and select **Home→Editing→AutoSum**.

Use Inventory Costing Methods

11. Switch to the **Treadmills** tab.

12. Enter the data as indicated:

Cell A17	=CONCATENATE(LEFT(A5, 1), MID(A5, 6, 1), MID(A5, 10, 1), MID(A5, 16, 1), " Inventory Balance:")
Cell B17	=D10+(F4-B10)*C11
Cell A18	=CONCATENATE(LEFT(A6, 1), MID(A6, 7, 1), MID(A6, 11, 1), MID(A6, 17, 1), " Inventory Balance:")
Cell B18	=D14+(F4-B14)*C13
Cell A19	=CONCATENATE(LEFT(A7, 1), MID(A7, 10, 1), " Inventory Balance:")
Cell B19	=(D15/B15)*F4

13. Switch to the **Inventory Listing** tab and select **cell I5**.

14. Type **=** and then click **cell B17** on the **Treadmills** tab and tap ⌷Enter⌷.

15. Highlight the **range K5:K70** and choose **Home→Styles→Conditional Formatting→ Data Bars→Solid Fill→Green Data Bar**.

    *Feel free to experiment with the conditional formatting options, including those for color scales and icon sets. Clear those rules **before** completing step 15.*

Insert a PivotTable

16. Select **cell A5** and choose **Insert→Tables→PivotTable**.

17. In the **Table/Range** box, replace *$M$71* with **$I$70** and click **OK**.

18. Right-click the new worksheet tab and rename it: **Inventory PivotTable**

19. In the **PivotTable Fields** task pane, click in order the checkboxes for **Warehouse Location**, **Manufacturer**, and **Ending Inventory Balance – Year 3**.

20. In the **Rows** area, drag the **Manufacturer** field above the **Warehouse Location** field.

21. Click the checkbox for **Department** and then drag that field to the **Filters** area.

22. Click the drop-down arrow in **cell B1**, click the checkbox beside **Select Multiple Items**, uncheck the boxes for **Cardio Equip.** and **Recovery**, and click **OK**.

23. Close the task pane and then select **cell A4**.

24. Choose **PivotTable Tools→Analyze→Filter→Insert Slicer**, click the checkboxes for **Warehouse Location** and **Department**, and click **OK**.

25. In the **Department** slicer, choose **Strength Train.** and then use the **Multi-Select** button to add **Bikes/Skates** and **Camping/Hiking**.

26. In the **Warehouse Location** slicer, choose **Oakland**.

Create a PivotChart

27. Click **cell A4** and choose **PivotTable Tools→Analyze→Tools→PivotChart**.

28. In the **Column** category, choose **Clustered Column** and click **OK**.

29. Click on a blank area of the PivotChart and drag it below the PivotTable.

30. Choose **PivotChart Tools→Analyze→Show/Hide→Field List** to display the **PivotChart Fields** task pane.

31. Drag the **Department** field to the **Legend** area, position the PivotChart below the PivotTable, and then close the task pane.

32. Position the slicers beside the PivotTable.

33. Save and close the file.

EA4-R2 Edit an Inventory Listing and Create a PivotTable for Housewares Kingdom

In this exercise, you will compile summary data based on an inventory listing for Housewares Kingdom. Then you will determine the inventory balance for a product category using three methods. Last, you will create a PivotTable and a PivotChart.

1. Open **EA4-R2-Inventory** from your **Chapter 04** folder and save it as: **EA4-R2-Inventory-[YourName]**

   To begin, you will work with the Inventory Listing tab.

2. Click in **cell B2**, type **=COU** and then double-click the **Counta** function, highlight the **range A5:A75**, and then type **)** and tap Enter.

3. In **cell J5**, type **=COUNT(** and then highlight the **range E5:I5**, and then type **)** and tap Enter.

4. Click **cell K5** and choose **Formulas→Function Library→Insert Function**.

5. Click the drop-down arrow for **Or Select a Category**, choose **Statistical** and then **Average**, and click **OK**.

6. Highlight the **range E5:I5** and click **OK**.

7. Select **cell L5**, choose **Formulas→Function Library→Insert Function**, type **Max** in the search box and click **Go**, choose **Max** and click **OK**, highlight the **range E5:I5**, and then click **OK**.

8. Select **cell M5** and choose **Home→Editing→AutoSum ▼→Min**, highlight the **range E5:I5**, and tap Enter.

9. Highlight the **range J5:M5**, click the fill handle, and drag down to **row 75**.

10. Highlight the **range E76:I76** and select **Home→Editing→AutoSum**.

Use Inventory Costing Methods

11. Choose the **Wall Art** tab.

12. Enter the data as indicated:

Cell A17	=CONCATENATE(LEFT(A5, 1), MID(A5, 6, 1), MID(A5, 10, 1), MID(A5, 16, 1), " Inventory Balance:")
Cell B17	=D10+(F4-B10)*C11
Cell A18	=CONCATENATE(LEFT(A6, 1), MID(A6, 7, 1), MID(A6, 11, 1), MID(A6, 17, 1), " Inventory Balance:")
Cell B18	=D14+(F4-B14)*C13
Cell A19	=CONCATENATE(LEFT(A7, 1), MID(A7, 10, 1), " Inventory Balance:")
Cell B19	=(D15/B15)*F4

13. Switch to the **Inventory Listing** tab and select **cell I5**.

14. Type **=** and then click **cell B17** on the **Wall Art** tab and tap ⌷Enter⌷.

15. Highlight the **range K5:K75** and choose **Home→Styles→Conditional Formatting→ Data Bars→Gradient Fill→Orange Data Bar**.

    *Feel free to experiment with the conditional formatting options, including those for color scales and icon sets. Clear those rules **before** completing step 15.*

Insert a PivotTable

16. Select **cell A5** and choose **Insert→Tables→PivotTable**.

17. In the **Table/Range** box, replace *$M$76* with **$I$75** and click **OK**.

18. Double-click the new worksheet tab and rename it **Inventory PivotTable**.

19. In the **PivotTable Fields** task pane, click in order the checkboxes for **Product Turnover**, **Classification**, and **Ending Inventory Balance – Year 1**.

20. In the **Rows** area, drag the **Classification** field above the **Product Turnover** field.

21. Click the checkbox for **Level 1 Department** and then drag that field to the **Filters** area.

22. Click the drop-down arrow in **cell B1**, click the checkbox beside **Select Multiple Items**, uncheck the boxes for **Lighting** and **Dining**, and click **OK**.

23. Close the task pane and then select **cell A4**.

24. Choose **PivotTable Tools→Analyze→Filter→Insert Slicer**, click the checkboxes for **Product Turnover** and **Level 1 Department**, and click **OK**.

25. In the **Level 1 Department** slicer, choose **Décor** and then use the **Multi-Select** button to add **Furniture** and **Bedroom**.

26. In the **Product Turnover** slicer, choose **High**.

Create a PivotChart

27. Click **cell A4** and choose **PivotTable Tools→Analyze→Tools→PivotChart**.

28. In the **Bar** category, choose **3-D Clustered Bar** and click **OK**.

29. Click on a blank area of the PivotChart and drag it below the PivotTable.

30. Choose **PivotChart Tools→Analyze→Show/Hide→Field List** to display the **PivotChart Fields** task pane.

31. Drag the **Level 1 Department** field to the **Legend** area, position the PivotChart below the PivotTable, and then close the task pane.

32. Position the slicers beside the PivotTable.

33. Save and close the file.

Apply Your Skills

EA4-A1 Edit an Inventory Listing and Create a PivotTable for Educational Endeavors

In this exercise, you will compile summary data based on an inventory listing for Educational Endeavors. Then you will determine the inventory balance for a product category using three methods. Last, you will create a PivotTable and a PivotChart.

1. Open **EA4-A1-Inventory** from your **Chapter 04** folder and save it as:
   EA4-A1-Inventory-[YourName]
2. Use a function to display the total number of product categories in **cell B2**.
3. Populate the cells as described for the **Construction Paper** product category:

In this cell:	Use a function to display the:
Cell J5	Number of years for which an inventory balance is displayed
Cell K5	Average inventory balance for the five years shown
Cell L5	Maximum inventory balance for the five years shown
Cell M5	Minimum inventory balance for the five years shown

   Hint: Make sure the formula in cell J5 will update properly if any currently blank cells are later filled in.

4. Copy the formulas in the **range J5:M5** and paste them such that the calculations will be performed for all product categories.
5. Enter formulas in the **range E63:I63** to add the inventory balances for each year.

Use Inventory Costing Methods

6. Switch to the **Construction Paper** tab.
7. Use the CONCATENATE function to enter *LIFO Inventory Balance* in **cell A17**.
8. Enter a formula in **cell B17** to calculate the ending inventory balance for construction paper under the LIFO method.
9. In **cell A18**, use the CONCATENATE function to enter *FIFO Inventory Balance*.
10. Enter a formula in **cell B18** to calculate the ending inventory balance for construction paper under the FIFO method.
11. In **cell A19**, use the CONCATENATE function to enter *WA Inventory Balance*.
12. Enter a formula in **cell B19** to calculate the ending inventory balance for construction paper under the weighted average method.
13. Enter a formula in the appropriate location on the **Inventory Listing** tab to display the fifth-year LIFO inventory balance for construction paper.
14. Apply the **3 Symbols (Uncircled)** icon set and **Red – White – Green** color scale to the **range K5:K62**.

Insert a PivotTable and a PivotChart

15. Create a PivotTable on the **Inventory Listing** tab based on the inventory balances displayed for all five years.

16. Rename the new worksheet tab containing the PivotTable.

17. Display the **Year 5 Inventory Balances** within the PivotTable with:

    - **Country of Manufacture** in the Rows area
    - **Product Category** in the Columns area
    - A filter that excludes the **Active** product department

18. Add a slicer that limits the data to product categories that earned at least a **3 of 5** online rating.

19. Create a **3-D Clustered Column** PivotChart and display the **Online Rating** category in the legend.

20. Position the PivotChart and slicer in a logical manner.

21. Save and close the file.

EA4-A2 Edit an Inventory Listing and Create a PivotTable for Electronic World

In this exercise, you will compile summary data based on an inventory listing for Electronic World. Then you will determine the inventory balance for a product category using three methods. Last, you will create a PivotTable and a PivotChart.

1. Open **EA4-A2-Inventory** from your **Chapter 04** folder and save it as: **EA4-A2-Inventory-[YourName]**

2. Use a function to display the total number of product categories in **cell B2**.

3. Populate the cells as described for the **4K Ultra HD TVs** product category:

In this cell:	Use a function to display the:
Cell J5	Number of years for which an inventory balance is displayed
Cell K5	Average inventory balance for the five years shown
Cell L5	Maximum inventory balance for the five years shown
Cell M5	Minimum inventory balance for the five years shown

Hint: Make sure the formula in cell J5 will update properly if any currently blank cells are later filled in.

4. Copy the formulas in the **range J5:M5** and paste them such that the calculations will be performed for all product categories.

5. Enter formulas in the **range E76:I76** to add all inventory balances for each year.

Use Inventory Costing Methods

6. Switch to the **4K Ultra HD TVs** tab.

7. Use the CONCATENATE function to enter *LIFO Inventory Balance* in **cell A17**.

8. Enter a formula in **cell B17** to calculate the ending inventory balance for 4K ultra HD TVs under the LIFO method.

9. In **cell A18**, use the CONCATENATE function to enter *FIFO Inventory Balance*.

10. Enter a formula in **cell B18** to calculate the ending inventory balance for 4K ultra HD TVs under the FIFO method.

11. In **cell A19**, use the CONCATENATE function to enter *WA Inventory Balance*.

12. Enter a formula in **cell B19** to calculate the ending inventory balance for 4K ultra HD TVs under the weighted average method.

13. Enter a formula in the appropriate location on the **Inventory Listing** tab to display the fifth-year LIFO inventory balance for 4K ultra HD TVs.

14. Apply the **Red Gradient Fill** data bars and **Green – White** color scale to the **range K5:K75**.

Insert a PivotTable and a PivotChart

15. Create a PivotTable on the **Inventory Listing** tab based on the inventory balances displayed for all five years.

16. Rename the new worksheet tab containing the PivotTable.

17. Display the **Year 5 Inventory Balances** within the PivotTable with:

    - **Department** in the Rows area
    - **Product Category** in the Columns area
    - A filter that excludes the **Northeast** shipping region

18. Add a slicer that limits the data to product categories with an internal classification of at least **Level 6**.

19. Create a **Clustered Bar** PivotChart and display the **Internal Classification** category in the legend.

20. Position the PivotChart and slicer in a logical manner.

21. Save and close your file.

Extend Your Skills

EA4-E1 Edit an Inventory Listing and Create a PivotTable for Gameroom Suppliers

In this exercise, you will compile summary data based on an inventory listing for Gameroom Suppliers. You will determine the inventory balance for a product category using three methods, and you will create a PivotTable based on the inventory listing.

Open **EA4-E1-Inventory**. Use one of Excel's built-in functions to enter the total number of product categories in an appropriate location. For each product category, use functions to enter the total number of years for which an inventory balance is displayed (include zero balances) and the average, maximum, and minimum inventory balances in appropriate locations. Then, use a function to enter the total inventory for each of the five years in the appropriate locations.

Determine the fifth-year inventory balance for air hockey tables using the LIFO, FIFO, and weighted average methods. Use formulas to determine the inventory balance under each. Ensure that the calculations are entered in appropriate locations on the Air Hockey Tables tab; label each calculation. Enter the LIFO inventory balance on the Inventory Listing tab as appropriate.

Last, create a PivotTable that displays the Year 3 inventory balances for products located in the Huntington or Smithtown warehouses and receiving at least a three-star rating. Label the new worksheet tab appropriately and use slicers to create the PivotTable. Create a PivotChart displaying the results of the PivotTable, using appropriate labeling and formatting throughout. Position the PivotChart and slicers in a logical manner.

EA4-E2 Edit an Inventory Listing and Create a PivotTable for Brown's Toy Store

In this exercise, you will compile summary data based on an inventory listing for Brown's Toy Store. You will determine the inventory balance for a product category using three methods, and you will create a PivotTable based on this inventory listing.

Open **EA4-E2-Inventory**. Use one of Excel's built-in functions to enter the total number of product categories in an appropriate location. For each product category, use functions to enter the total number of years for which an inventory balance is displayed (include zero balances) and the average, maximum, and minimum inventory balances in appropriate locations. Then, use a function to enter the total inventory for each of the five years in the appropriate locations.

Determine the fifth-year inventory balance for balance bikes using the LIFO, FIFO, and weighted average methods. Use formulas to determine the inventory balance under each. Ensure that the calculations are entered in appropriate locations on the Balance Bikes tab; label each calculation. Enter the LIFO inventory balance on the Inventory Listing tab as appropriate.

Last, create a PivotTable that displays the Year 4 inventory balances for products sold in-store or at trade shows and manufactured by Bouncing Balls or Toy Makerz. Label the new worksheet tab appropriately and use slicers to create the PivotTable. Create a PivotChart displaying the results of the PivotTable, using appropriate labeling and formatting throughout. Position the PivotChart and slicers in a logical manner.

EA4-E3 Edit an Inventory Listing and Create a PivotTable for Zeke's Hardware

In this exercise, you will compile summary data based on an inventory listing for Zeke's Hardware. Then you will determine the inventory balance for a product category using three methods, and you will create a PivotTable based on this inventory listing.

Open **EA4-E3-Inventory**. Use one of Excel's built-in functions to enter the total number of product categories in an appropriate location. For each product category, use functions to enter the total number of years for which an inventory balance is displayed (include zero balances) and the average, maximum, and minimum inventory balances in appropriate locations. Then, use a function to enter the total inventory for each of the five years in the appropriate locations.

Determine the fifth-year inventory balance for sanding accessories using the LIFO, FIFO, and weighted average methods. Use formulas to determine the inventory balance under each. Ensure that the calculations are entered in appropriate locations on the Sanding Accessories tab; label the calculations. Enter the LIFO inventory balance on the Inventory Listing tab as appropriate.

Last, create a PivotTable that displays the Year 1 inventory balances for products in departments 1A, 2B, or 3C and with internal classifications of Yellow or Blue. Label the new worksheet tab appropriately and use slicers to create the PivotTable. Create a PivotChart displaying the results of the PivotTable, using appropriate labeling and formatting throughout. Position the PivotChart and slicers in a logical manner.

Critical Thinking

EA4-C1 Discuss Conditional Formatting and Worksheet Readability

Worksheets are often created to summarize and share data with a colleague. Whether the colleague is a subordinate, peer, or high-level member of the management team, the goal of the worksheet is to ensure that key information can be effectively identified and understood. In this chapter, you saw how conditional formatting can be used to highlight key information in an inventory listing.

Identify four types of accounting-related worksheets (aside from inventory listings) for which the use of conditional formatting would improve the readability and effectiveness of a worksheet. Write a paragraph of at least six sentences to discuss the specific data for which conditional formatting would be applied and why doing so would provide a benefit to the end user.

EA4-C2 Discuss PivotTables and PivotCharts in an Accounting Environment

PivotTables and PivotCharts allow for efficient and flexible analysis of a data set. Although you focused on inventory listings in this chapter, these powerful analysis tools can be applied to many other accounting-related items as well. Businesses that become more adept at using these tools can benefit greatly. Decision-making is enhanced when the proper data is analyzed effectively, and PivotTables and PivotCharts allow for this type of analysis.

Write a paragraph of at least four sentences in which you identify four data sets (aside from an inventory listing) for which a business might use a PivotTable and PivotChart to complete an analysis. Write a second paragraph of at least six sentences to discuss how a PivotTable and a PivotChart would enhance the analysis of these data sets.

Bank Reconciliation

LEARNING OBJECTIVES

- Create a bank reconciliation

- Create headers and footers in a worksheet

- Use Format Painter

- Apply Quick Styles and conditional formatting

- Import data from multiple sources

As you have seen, formatting a worksheet is key to ensuring that the end user can efficiently interpret the worksheet's data. Visual alterations, such as those that can be applied using Quick Styles and conditional formatting, improve the appearance of and effectively convey the information in a worksheet. Conditional formatting calls attention to data that meets specific criteria. Other elements, such as headers and footers, are especially useful in lengthy worksheets, while Format Painter allows for quick formatting. In this chapter, you will create a bank reconciliation as you focus on methods that can improve the appearance of such a worksheet. You will also see how easily data can be imported, from QuickBooks and other sources, to add to the data in an existing worksheet.

PROJECT # City Music World

City Music World is a retail store that sells musical equipment and offers lessons for beginning and experienced musicians. As with most companies, City Music World keeps a close eye on its cash balance throughout the year. Part of this process is the creation of a monthly bank reconciliation. You are completing the reconciliation for the current month.

In this chapter, you will use a variety of data, some of which is imported from other programs, to create the bank reconciliation. You will apply preset styles to certain elements of the reconciliation and conditional formatting where appropriate. Last, you will create and add headers and footers to the worksheet.

City Music World
Bank Reconciliation
December 31, 2016

Beginning Bank Balance:		$35,550	**Beginning Book Balance:**		$33,344
Add:			**Add:**		
Deposits in Transit	$ 800		Notes Receivable		$ 1,400
	$1,250				
	$1,000	$ 3,050			
		$38,600			$34,744
Deduct:			**Deduct:**		
Outstanding Checks	$3,200		NSF Check	$528	
	$ 24		Bank Charges	$150	
	$1,610	$ 4,834	Check Error	$300	$ 978
Adjusted Bank Balance		$33,766	Adjusted Book Balance		$33,766

This bank reconciliation provides information about the current cash balance in an easily understandable format.

Accounting Refresher

Bank Reconciliations

There are certain business activities that occur during a month that are apparent to a company but not to its bank. Conversely, there are some activities that the bank knows about but the company doesn't. As a result, the balance displayed on a bank statement often differs from the cash balance in the general ledger. A bank reconciliation allows a business to examine these differences and ensure that all cash-related activity has been properly recorded.

A bank reconciliation is divided into two sides: the bank side on the left and the book (or company) side on the right. When considering where a reconciling item should be placed, a two-step process should be used. First, determine which party (bank or company) was unaware of the reconciling item. This is the side on which the reconciling item is placed. Second, determine whether the reconciling item increased or decreased the cash balance. This allows you to determine whether the item is added to or subtracted from its designated side.

There are a number of common reconciling items that appear on most bank reconciliations, including deposits in transit, outstanding checks, notes receivable collected by the bank, NSF checks, bank charges, and errors.

Deposits in Transit

A **deposit in transit** is a deposit made on one of the last days of the month. The bank was unable to process these deposits prior to the end of the month and, therefore, has not included them in the bank statement. However, since the company was aware of the deposit prior to the end of the month, it has included it in the cash balance. As the bank was unaware of this reconciling item, it is placed on the bank side. And as this deposit increases the cash balance, it is added to the bank side.

Outstanding Checks

An **outstanding check** is a check that has been written by the company but has not yet been cashed by the payee. Because the check has not been cashed, the bank is unaware of it. As these checks reduce the cash balance, they are subtracted from the bank side.

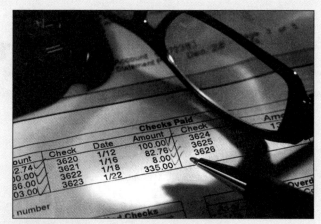

Notes Receivable Collected by the Bank

In some instances, a **note receivable** (an amount owed to the company by an outside party) can be paid by customers directly into a company's bank account. In this case the company is unaware that cash has been deposited. Since the deposit increases the cash balance, it is added to the book side.

(continued)

NSF Checks

An **NSF check** (often referred to as an insufficient or non-sufficient funds check) is received and deposited by the company into its bank account. However, because the payer doesn't have enough money in its account to cover the check, it is subsequently rejected (bounces). When this happens, the bank reduces the balance of the company's account, but the company is unaware of this. As this reversal of the deposited check decreases the cash balance, it is subtracted from the book side.

Bank Charges

These are levied by the bank for reasons such as low balances or the receipt of NSF checks. The company is not initially informed that these charges are being levied; it doesn't learn of this until the bank statement arrives. As these charges reduce the cash balance, they are subtracted from the book side.

TIP! The reconciling items discussed above always appear in the same location in every bank reconciliation. This differs from the next reconciling item, which can appear anywhere within the bank reconciliation.

Errors

Errors are the only reconciling items that can be found in different locations in the bank reconciliation. For example, assume the bank erroneously records a deposit of $2,000 as only $200. Since this error results in too little cash being added to the bank account, the $1,800 ($2,000 – $200) error must be added to the bank side. Alternatively, assume a check written by the company for $500 is recorded as only $50. Since this error results in too little of a reduction of the cash balance, the $450 ($500 – $50) error is subtracted from the book side.

WARNING! Always place a reconciling error on the side (bank or book) where the mistake was made.

Importing External Data

Brining data from other application programs into Excel is *importing*. Excel can import a variety of data into your workbooks. Converters are installed in Excel to import data from many popular applications, such as from a PDF file created using Adobe Acrobat.

If Excel can't import a specific type of data, check in the source application to see if you can save the data in a file format that is compatible with Excel. Do note that some loss of formatting may occur with this.

When completing a bank reconciliation, you use information from a number of sources. Being able to import data in a variety of ways is an important skill. There are three methods you can use to import data into Excel:

- Copy and paste
- Drag and drop
- Import a text file

Importing Data from QuickBooks with Copy and Paste

You can copy and paste text, numbers, images, and charts between another application and Excel. For example, to copy and paste a table or text from a Word document into an Excel worksheet, you simply select and copy (or cut) the data in Word and paste it into the desired cell in Excel. You can also use Paste Special to paste data, such as images, into Excel in a specific format.

An excellent example of a program from which data can be imported into Excel is QuickBooks. When reports are generated in QuickBooks, the data can then be displayed in an Excel worksheet.

Importing Data with Drag and Drop

You can drag and drop data between another application window and an Excel workbook. You select the data to be imported and then drag and drop it onto the desired worksheet. With this technique, data is cut from the source file, but if you close the source file without saving, the original data will be retained. This method can also be used to import data from a QuickBooks report.

Before using drag and drop, you must display the two application windows side by side. When dragging from a program other than Excel, the Restore Down button (which typically displays at the top right of a program window) can be used to display the program window within only a portion of the screen. The borders of both program windows can then be arranged side by side.

Alternatively, when dragging from one Excel worksheet to another, the Arrange All option can be used to display the two windows side by side. After selecting Arrange All, you can choose to orient the open windows vertically (left and right of the screen), horizontally (top and bottom of the screen), tiled (within rectangular windows), or cascading (each nearly full screen, and layered on top of one another).

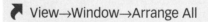 View→Window→Arrange All

Importing Data from a Text File

The Get External Data commands are used to import entire text files, Access tables, web page tables, or data sources such as a network server. The Get Data from Text command imports an entire text file into an Excel worksheet as data. The source file format may be tab delimited (.txt) or comma delimited (.csv). When another program is not compatible with Excel, you may need to save its data in one of those two formats. When you import a text file, Excel attempts to lay out the data neatly into rows and columns.

A tab-delimited (*.txt*) file

↗ Data→Get External Data→Get Data from Text

Develop Your Skills EA5-D1

In this exercise, you will create a bank reconciliation for City Music World for the month ended December 31, 2016. The reconciliation will be partly based on these figures: Bank Statement Balance (12/31/2016) equals $35,550; Notes Receivable equals $1,400; NSF Check equals $528; Bank Charges equals $150. During the previous month, the company erroneously recorded a check written by City Music World for $650 instead of the actual $950.

1. Start Excel. Open a **Blank Workbook** and save the file in your **Chapter 05** folder as:
   EA5-D1-BankRec-[YourName]

2. Enter this data and apply bold formatting to all three cells:

Cell A1	City Music World
Cell A2	Bank Reconciliation
Cell A3	`December 31, 2016

3. Highlight the **range A1:G3**, choose **Home→Alignment→Merge and Center ▾→ Merge Across**, and center-align the content.

4. Enter this data:

Cell A5	Beginning Bank Balance:
Cell E5	Beginning Book Balance:
Cells A6 and E6	Add:
Cells A9 and E9	Deduct:

   By first entering these elements, you have established a structure for the reconciliation. As you reconcile items, you can enter each within its proper section.

5. Set the width of **columns A and E** to **24**.

   Hint: The Ribbon path is Home→Cells→Format→Column Width.

6. Set the width of **column D** to **1**.

7. Type the bank statement balance of **35550** in **cell C5**.

8. Open **EA5-D1-QBReport** from your **Chapter 05** folder.

    The beginning book balance is derived from the company's records as of December 31, 2016. This file, which represents a report generated by QuickBooks, displays the activity and ending cash balance for the month of December.

9. In the QuickBooks report window, choose **View→Window→Arrange All**.

10. Click **Vertical** and then click **OK**.

11. In the bank reconciliation window, type `Outstanding Checks` in **cell A10**.

12. In the QuickBooks report window, click **cell N6** and then click the cell border and drag its contents to **cell B10** in the bank reconciliation window.

    This $3,200 figure represents the first of three outstanding checks in the QuickBooks report. Column K displays a checkmark for those checks that have cleared the bank, so to identify the outstanding checks you must look for those that do not have a checkmark in column K.

13. Continue to drag and drop contents from the QuickBooks report to the bank reconciliation as noted:

QuickBooks report location:	Bank reconciliation location:
Cell N8	Cell B11
Cell N10	Cell B12
Cell O14	Cell G5

    Cell O14 in the QuickBooks report shows the company's book balance at month end. This is the starting point for the company side of the reconciliation and so is dropped in cell G5. Note that cell G5 now contains the formula used to determine this balance in the QuickBooks report. You will now remove the formula.

14. In the bank reconciliation, click **cell G5** and choose **Home→Clipboard→Copy**, choose **Home→Clipboard→Paste ▼→Paste Values→Values**, and tap Esc.

    The formula that resulted in $33,344 appearing in cell G5 has been replaced with the value itself.

15. Close the QuickBooks report, choosing **Don't Save** when prompted.

    The drag-and-drop actions removed the cell contents from the QuickBooks report. By not saving the file when closing, you are retaining all content.

16. In the bank reconciliation, select the **row 7** header, scroll to the **row 8** header, and release the mouse button. Right-click either of the highlighted row headers and choose **Insert**.

    Three deposits in transit must be imported to the bank reconciliation. As there was only one row available for the inclusion of this data, two additional rows are added to accommodate the necessary information.

17. Click **cell B7**, choose **Data→Get External Data→From Text**, navigate to **EA5-D1-Deposits** in your **Chapter 05** folder, and click **Import**.

    The necessary deposit-in-transit information, which is also included in the QuickBooks report, has been consolidated in this text document.

    If you are unable to complete the Ribbon path shown in this step, your copy of Excel has been updated by Microsoft. To complete this and other exercises that involve importing data, add the legacy data tools in Excel by choosing File→Options→Data and then clicking in the checkbox for From Text. The Ribbon path to use when importing data is now Data→Get & Transform Data→Get Data→Legacy Wizard→From Text (Legacy).

18. Set the **Start Import at Row** option to **2** and click **Next** twice.

    The first row in the text document contains headers that are unnecessary for the bank reconciliation. They are excluded from the import by making this selection.

19. Make sure the first column in the preview at the bottom of the window is highlighted and then click in the circle for **Do Not Import Column (Skip)**.

20. Highlight the second column in the preview, click in the circle for **Do Not Import Column (Skip)**, and click **Finish**.

    The first column of the text document contains dates and the second column is blank. As neither of these columns contained data necessary for the reconciliation, you have excluded them from the import.

21. In the **Import Data** dialog box, click **OK** to import the data to the active cell in the worksheet.

    Note that the width of column B has been reduced. You will correct this as you progress through the bank reconciliation.

22. Type `Deposits in Transit` in cell **A7**.

23. Save your file.

    Unless otherwise directed, always keep your file open at the end of each exercise.

Using the Format Painter and Quick Styles

The Format Painter applies formatting from existing worksheet cells, while the Quick Styles option applies predefined formats to cells. Both of these tools can greatly simplify the formatting of a worksheet.

Format Painter

The Format Painter lets you copy text and number formats from one cell to another. This tool can be extremely helpful if you have a cell to which many formatting options have been applied and you do not wish to go through the process of applying each option individually to another cell or range of cells. Given the importance of a consistent appearance in accounting-related worksheets such as bank reconciliations, this is a tool you are likely to use often.

TIP!   You can double-click Format Painter to apply formatting to multiple locations.

 Home→Clipboard→Format Painter

Applying Quick Styles to Cells

You can apply Excel's built-in cell styles, also called Quick Styles, or create your own styles for a uniform worksheet design. A cell style's formatting may include the font, number format, borders, and fill.

New cell styles appear in the Custom section of the styles list. They are based on the workbook theme, so the colors change automatically to match any new theme that is applied. Among the built-in styles, only the Themed Cell Styles change colors. Any styles that you create or edit apply only to the currently open workbook. The Merge Styles command in the styles list allows you to import styles created in a different workbook into the current workbook.

Custom	
Custom Style...	
Good, Bad and Neutral	
Normal	Bad
Data and Model	
Calculation	Check Cell
Output	Warning Text
Titles and Headings	
Heading 1	Heading 2
Themed Cell Styles	
20% - Accent1	20% - Accent2
40% - Accent1	40% - Accent2
60% - Accent1	60% - Accent2
Accent1	Accent2
Number Format	
Comma	Comma [0]

The Cell Styles button allows for the application of both custom and built-in cell styles.

↗ Home→Styles→Cell Styles

Develop Your Skills EA5-D2

In this exercise, you will complete the bank reconciliation for City Music World using Format Painter and Quick Styles to easily modify its appearance.

Before You Begin: *Refer to the instructions in Develop Your Skills EA5-D1 for the figures associated with the reconciliation.*

1. Save your file as: **EA5-D2-BankRec-[YourName]**
2. Enter this data:

Cell E7	Notes Receivable
Cell G7	1400
Cell E12	NSF Check
Cell E13	Bank Charges
Cell E14	Check Error
Cell F12	528
Cell F13	150
Cell F14	300

You have now entered the remaining necessary data for the bank reconciliation. Next you will summarize the totals on each side of the reconciliation.

3. Type **=Sum(B7:B9)** in **cell C9**.
4. Copy **cell C9** and paste to **cells C14** and **G14**.
5. Type **=Sum(C5:C9)** in **cell C10** and then copy that cell and paste to **cell G10**.
6. Click **cell C15**, type **=C10-** and click **cell C14**, and tap Enter .
7. Copy **cell C15** and paste to **cell G15**.
8. Enter **Adjusted Bank Balance** in **cell A15** and **Adjusted Book Balance** in **cell E15**.

You have now completed data entry for the reconciliation, but the worksheet needs formatting so the contents can be clearly understood by the end user.

Format the Bank Reconciliation

9. Click **cell C5**, choose **Home→Number→Accounting Number Format**, and then click **Decrease Decimal** twice.

   This number format should be used throughout the reconciliation, so you will use Format Painter to apply the format to the remaining numbers in the worksheet.

10. Go to **Home→Clipboard** and double-click **Format Painter**.
11. Click once on every cell and range in which numbers are displayed and then choose **Home→Clipboard→Format Painter** to turn off the painter.

12. Select the headers for **columns B–C** and **columns F–G** and then double-click between the **columns B** and **C** headers.

13. Apply a bottom border to **cells C9**, **C14**, **G7**, and **G14**.

14. Apply a bottom double border to **cell C15** and then use Format Painter to copy that formatting to **cell G15**.

    Now that the formatting in the bank reconciliation has been improved, you will use Quick Styles to ensure that important headers stand out.

15. Select **cells A5**, **A15**, **E5**, and **E15** and then choose **Home→Styles→Cell Styles→ Heading 4**.

16. Save your file.

Using Preset and Customized Conditional Formatting

Conditional formatting allows for cells to be formatted based on whether they meet certain criteria. While Excel has a number of built-in conditional formatting options, you can also create formatting rules based on the elements in a worksheet.

 Home→Styles→Conditional Formatting

Presets and Multiple Conditions

You can choose from conditional formatting presets on the Conditional Formatting menu for frequently used criteria, such as Greater Than, Equal To, Above Average, and Top 10 Items. You can set any number of conditional formats and create multiple rules to check for more than one condition in a cell. Conditional formatting rules are applied in the priority order you set. The Stop If True option, when selected in any rule, prevents further formatting by the remaining rules after a criterion is evaluated as True.

For a report such as a bank reconciliation, which is typically completed on a monthly basis, the use of conditional formatting within the original template allows for easy identification of items that meet the desired criteria. This can save time, as the formatting rule must be applied only to the original template and will display for all reports based off the original file.

Home→Styles→Conditional Formatting→New Rule

Conditional Formatting Rules

If no preset item on the Conditional Formatting menu meets your desired criteria or formatting, you can create a new rule. The following illustration defines the parts of the New Formatting Rule dialog box. The options vary in the lower half of the dialog box, depending on the rule type you select.

1. The selected rule determines which options display below.

2. A preview of the formatted cell contents appears here.

3. The comparison operator and the value, text, date, or cell reference are shown in these boxes.

4. You can access the Format Cells dialog box with additional options via the Format button.

The Conditional Formatting Rules Manager

Conditional formatting rules can be created, edited, rearranged, and deleted within the Conditional Formatting Rules Manager dialog box, which allows you to work with all rules applied to a selected range or the entire worksheet. The following illustration displays the rules set within an entire worksheet.

1. You can choose to display the rules for the current selection or the entire worksheet.

2. These buttons are used to create a new rule and edit, delete, or rearrange the selected rule.

3. Here are the existing rules and their definitions.

Develop Your Skills EA5-D3

In this exercise, you will apply conditional formatting to figures in your bank reconciliation for City Music World so you can easily identify figures that require further examination.

1. Save your file as: **EA5-D3-BankRec-[YourName]**

2. Select **cell C5**.

   You want to be alerted if the bank balance drops below $40,000 at the end of any month so additional steps can be taken. To set up the alert, you will apply conditional formatting.

3. Choose **Home→Styles→Conditional Formatting→Highlight Cell Rules→Less Than** and then type **40000** and click **OK**.

   Cell C5 is now displayed with red text and a red background. As future reconciliations are completed, this conditional formatting rule will remain in cell C5. Therefore, if the bank balance is below $40,000 in future months, this formatting would appear again.

4. Choose **Home→Styles→Conditional Formatting→Manage Rules** to open the Conditional Formatting Rules Manager dialog box.

5. Click the **Edit Rule** button, highlight *=40000* in the **Edit the Rule Description** section, and then type **=30000** and click **OK** twice.

The cell is no longer highlighted, as the modified conditional formatting rule is not met. Upon reviewing this formatting, you decide that you would prefer a different approach. You will now replace this conditional formatting with a new conditional formatting rule.

6. Choose **Home→Styles→Conditional Formatting→Clear Rules→Clear Rules from Selected Cells**.

Now that you have removed the previously applied conditional formatting rule, you can create the new rule.

7. Choose **Home→Styles→Conditional Formatting→Manage Rules** and click the **New Rule** button in the dialog box that appears.

8. Follow these steps to complete the rule:

A. Choose **Use a Formula to Determine Which Cells to Format**.

B. Type **=$C$5<40000** here.

C. Click **Format** to open the Format Cells dialog box.

D. Click the **Fill** tab.

E. Choose the green color at the top-right corner of the palette.

9. Click **OK** three times.

10. Save your file.

Creating and Formatting Headers and Footers

Headers print at the top of every page, while footers print at the bottom of every page. Excel provides a variety of predesigned headers and footers. You can also create customized headers and footers. You can even create a different header and footer on odd and even pages for double-sided printing.

Completed by: William Stevens	Page 1 of 1				12/31/2016
City Music World					
Bank Reconciliation					

NOTE! Use Page Layout view or the Print Preview in Backstage view to see headers and footers. They do not display in Normal view.

Headers and footers are created most conveniently in Page Layout view. Excel divides headers and footers into left, center, and right sections of the page. You need not fill in all three sections. Click in a section to activate it and display the Design tab, which contains various options. When you choose an option from the Header & Footer Elements command group, Excel displays a code to represent the item. After you click outside the header section, Excel converts the code to properly display the selected option.

The Current Time code is shown on the left. On the right you can see how this code would look when printed.

TIP! You can format the font type, size, and color in headers and footers.

Develop Your Skills EA5-D4

In this exercise, you will create a header and a footer for City Music World's bank reconciliation.

1. Save your file as: **EA5-D4-BankRec-[YourName]**
2. Choose **Insert→Text→Header & Footer**.
3. Click in the right header section and choose **Header & Footer Tools→Design→ Header & Footer Elements→Current Date**.

   The Current Date code is displayed in the header. The actual current date will display after you click outside of the active header section.
4. Choose **Header & Footer Tools→Design→Navigation→Go to Footer**.
5. Click in the left footer section and choose **Header & Footer Tools→Design→ Header & Footer Elements→File Name**.
6. Choose **Header & Footer Tools→Design→Navigation→Go to Header**.
7. Save and close the file.

REAL-WORLD Accounting

What Are the Benefits of Using Excel to Create a Bank Reconciliation?

Because bank reconciliations are typically completed every month, you can create a template in Excel to use as your base file again and again. Quick Styles and conditional formatting can enhance such worksheets, and, while these are significant benefits, an even more significant reason to create a bank reconciliation in Excel is the ability to import data.

Bank reconciliations, perhaps more so than most accounting-related reports, require data from many different locations. For example, deposits in transit are identified through a comparison of deposits in the general ledger and bank statements. Outstanding checks are also identified through this comparison, while NSF checks and bank charges are identified solely within the bank statement. Errors may be identified by examining the bank statement but may also require

a review of accounts in the general ledger and/or entries in the general journal. For small businesses with relatively little activity, such comparisons are not complicated. But for larger companies with extensive activity, importing data (either into a bank reconciliation or a separate worksheet used for analysis) may be the most efficient way to complete this comparison.

Importing data from external sources is straightforward. In particular, Excel's ability to import data from a tab- (*.txt*) or comma- (*.csv*) delimited file means you can import data from many different programs. Whether an organization uses a program that can create Excel reports (such as QuickBooks) or not, the data from these programs can typically be imported and used to generate a bank reconciliation. Similarly, the format of the electronic bank statement will typically allow for the data contained therein to be imported. The importance of Excel's ability to import data from multiple sources cannot be overestimated.

Self-Assessment

Check your knowledge of this chapter's key concepts and skills using the Self-Assessment here or in your eLab course.

1. Drag and drop cannot be used to import data to a worksheet. *True False*

2. A *.csv* file is referred to as a comma-delimited file. *True False*

3. The Arrange All option can be used to display two windows side by side. *True False*

4. A bank reconciliation contains both an "add" and a "deduct" section within each of its three sides. *True False*

5. You must double-click Format Painter in order to apply formatting to a cell. *True False*

6. If you don't see your desired Quick Style in the cell styles menu, you can create a custom style. *True False*

7. Conditional formatting is not retained when a copy of a worksheet is created. *True False*

8. You can create multiple rules with the Conditional Formatting Rules Manager. *True False*

9. Both the header and footer areas of a worksheet are separated into three sections. *True False*

10. When entering the date or time in a header, the appropriate code cannot be entered via a selection on the Ribbon; it must be typed out. *True False*

11. Which items appear on the bank side of a bank reconciliation?
    Note receivable collected by bank
    Outstanding checks
    NSF checks
    Bank charges

12. Which items can appear on either side (bank and book) of a bank reconciliation?
    NSF checks
    Deposits in transit
    Outstanding checks
    Errors

13. Which of these CANNOT be used to insert external data in a worksheet?
    Format Painter
    Copy and Paste
    Drag and drop
    Importing a file

14. When using Arrange All, windows can be oriented in each way EXCEPT:
    Vertically
    Tiled
    Diagonally
    Cascade

15. What can Format Painter copy?
    Values
    Formulas
    Text
    Formatting

16. The cell styles option appears on the _____ tab of the Ribbon.
    Home
    Insert
    Data
    View

17. The Conditional Formatting Rules Manager allows for all of the following to be done to conditional formatting rules EXCEPT:
    Creating
    Editing
    Combining
    Deleting

18. Which of these is NOT a conditional formatting rule type in the New Formatting Rule dialog box?
    Format only cells that contain
    Format only top- or bottom-ranked values
    Format only unique or duplicate values
    Format only text entries

19. Which tab appears when a section of the header is activated?
    Formulas
    Design
    Data
    References

20. Which of these is NOT a footer section?
    Top
    Left
    Right
    Center

Reinforce Your Skills

EA5-R1 Create a Bank Reconciliation for Auto Salvage Co.

In this exercise, you will create a bank reconciliation for Auto Salvage Co. for the month ended December 31, 2016. The reconciliation will be partly based on these figures: Bank Statement Balance (12/31/2016) equals $17,000; Notes Receivable equals $1,300; NSF Check equals $1,200; Bank Charges equals $610. During the month, the company erroneously recorded a check written by Auto Salvage Co. as $600 instead of the actual amount of $400.

1. Open a **Blank Workbook** and save the file in your **Chapter 05** folder as: **EA5-R1-BankRec-[YourName]**

2. Enter this data and apply bold formatting to all three cells:

Cell A1	Auto Salvage Co.
Cell A2	Bank Reconciliation
Cell A3	`December 31, 2016

3. Highlight the **range A1:G3**, choose **Home→Alignment→Merge and Center ▼→ Merge Across**, and center-align the content.

4. Enter this data:

Cell A5	Beginning Bank Balance:
Cell E5	Beginning Book Balance:
Cells A6 and E6	Add:
Cells A9 and E9	Deduct:

5. Use the Ribbon to set the width of **columns A and E** to **24** and the width of **column D** to **1**.

6. Enter the bank statement balance of **17000** in **cell C5**.

7. Open **EA5-R1-QBReport** from your **Chapter 05** folder.

   The beginning book balance is derived from the company's records as of December 31, 2016. This file, which represents a report generated by QuickBooks, displays the activity and ending cash balance for the month.

8. In the QuickBooks report window, choose **View→Window→Arrange All** and then choose the **Vertical** option.

9. In the bank reconciliation window, type **Outstanding Checks** in **cell A10**.

10. In the QuickBooks report window, select **cell N7** and then click the cell border and drag the contents to **cell B10** in the bank reconciliation window.

    This $600 figure represents the first of three outstanding checks in the QuickBooks report. Column K displays a checkmark next to checks that have cleared the bank, so to identify the outstanding checks you must find those that do not have a checkmark in column K.

11. Continue to drag and drop contents from the QuickBooks report to the bank reconciliation as noted:

QuickBooks report location:	Bank reconciliation location:
Cell N9	Cell B11
Cell N11	Cell B12
Cell O14	Cell G5

Cell O14 in the QuickBooks report holds the company's book balance at month's end, which is the starting point for the company side of the bank reconciliation (cell G5). Cell G5 currently contains the formula from the QuickBooks report and should be replaced with the actual value.

12. In the bank reconciliation, click **cell G5** and press Ctrl+C, choose **Home→Clipboard→ Paste ▼→Paste Values→Values**, and tap Esc.

13. Close the QuickBooks report file, choosing not to save the changes.

14. Maximize the bank reconciliation window and then right-click the **row 7** header and choose **Insert**.

15. Select **cell B7**, choose **Data→Get External Data→From Text**, navigate to **EA5-R1-Deposits** in your **Chapter 05** folder, and click **Import**.

    This text file holds the necessary deposit-in-transit information that is also included in the QuickBooks report.

    If you are unable to complete the Ribbon path shown in this step, see EA5-D1, step 17, on page 133 for instructions.

16. Set the **Start Import at Row** option to **2** and click **Next** twice.

17. With the first column in the preview highlighted, click in the circle for **Do Not Import Column (Skip)**; then choose to skip the second column and click **Finish**.

18. In the **Import Data** dialog box, click **OK** to import the data to the active cell in your worksheet.

    The width of column B needs adjustment, which you will take care of later in the exercise.

19. Type **Deposits in Transit** in **cell A7**.

Use Format Painter and Quick Styles

20. Enter this data:

Cell E7	Notes Receivable
Cell E8	Check Error
Cell E11	NSF Check
Cell E12	Bank Charges
Cell F7	1300
Cell F8	200
Cell F11	1200
Cell F12	610

21. Enter **=Sum(B7:B8)** in **cell C8** and then use the Ribbon to copy **cell C8** and paste to **cells G8**, **C13**, and **G12**.

22. Select **cell C13**, highlight *B12* in the Formula Bar, click **cell B11**, and tap Enter.

23. Enter **=Sum(C5:C8)** in **cell C9** and then use keyboard shortcuts to copy **cell C9** and paste to **cell G9**.

24. Select **cell C14**, type **=C9-** and click **cell C13**, and tap Enter. Copy **cell C14** and paste to **cell G14** using the method of your choice.

25. With **cell G14** selected, highlight *G13* in the Formula Bar, click **cell G12**, and tap Enter.

26. Enter **Adjusted Bank Balance** in **cell A14** and **Adjusted Book Balance** in **cell E14**.

27. In **cell C5**, choose **Home→Number→Accounting Number Format** and then click **Decrease Decimal** twice.

28. Go to **Home→Clipboard** and double-click **Format Painter**.

29. Click once on every cell and range in which numbers are displayed and then choose **Home→Clipboard→Format Painter** to turn off Format Painter.

30. Select the headers for **columns B–C** and **columns F–G** and then double-click between the **columns F and G** headers.

31. Apply a bottom border to **cells C8**, **C13**, **G8**, and **G12**; set a bottom double border to **cell C14** and paint the formatting to **cell G14**.

32. Select **cells A5**, **A14**, **E5**, and **E14** and then choose **Home→Styles→Cell Styles→ Heading 4**.

Apply Conditional Formatting

You want to be alerted if the bank balance drops below $20,000 at the end of any month so additional steps may be taken. You will now apply conditional formatting to set up the alert.

33. Select **cell C5**, choose **Home→Styles→Conditional Formatting→Manage Rules**, and click the **New Rule** button.

34. Set up the rule as indicated:
    - Rule type: **Use a Formula to Determine Which Cells to Format**
    - Rule description: **=$C$5<40000**

35. Click the **Format** button to open the Format Cells dialog box.

36. Click the **Fill** tab, select any red color from the palette, and click **OK** three times.

Insert a Header and a Footer

37. Choose **Insert→Text→Header & Footer**.

38. Click in the right section of the header and choose **Header & Footer Tools→Design→ Header & Footer Elements→Current Time**.

39. Choose **Header & Footer Tools→Design→Navigation→Go to Footer** and add the code for the filename to the right section of the footer.

40. Save and close your file.

EA5-R2 Create a Bank Reconciliation for Mine Supplier Inc.

In this exercise, you will create a bank reconciliation for Mine Supplier Inc. for the month ended December 31, 2016. The reconciliation will be partly based on these figures: Bank Statement Balance (12/31/2016) equals $22,400; Notes Receivable equals $6,200; NSF Check equals $100; Bank Charges equals $90. During the previous month, the company erroneously recorded a check written by Mine Supplier Inc. for $1,100 instead of the actual amount of $2,700.

1. Open a **Blank Workbook** and save the file in your **Chapter 05** folder as:
    EA5-R2-BankRec-[YourName]

2. Enter this data and apply bold formatting to all three cells:

Cell A1	**Mine Supplier Inc.**
Cell A2	**Bank Reconciliation**
Cell A3	**'December 31, 2016**

3. Highlight the **range A1:G3**, choose **Home→Alignment→Merge and Center ▼→ Merge Across**, and center-align the content.

4. Enter this data:

Cell A5	**Beginning Bank Balance:**
Cell E5	**Beginning Book Balance:**
Cells A6 and E6	**Add:**
Cells A9 and E9	**Deduct:**

5. Use the Ribbon to set the width of **columns A and E** to **24** and the width of **column D** to **1**.

6. Enter the bank statement balance of **22400** in **cell C5**.

7. Open **EA5-R2-QBReport** from your **Chapter 05** folder.

8. In the QuickBooks report window, choose **View→Window→Arrange All** and then choose the **Vertical** option.

9. In the bank reconciliation window, type **Outstanding Checks** in cell **A10**.

10. In the QuickBooks report window, select **cell N7** and then click the cell border and drag the contents to **cell B10** in the bank reconciliation window.

11. Drag and drop contents from the QuickBooks report to the bank reconciliation as noted:

QuickBooks report location:	Bank reconciliation location:
Cell N10	Cell B11
Cell O14	Cell G5

12. In the bank reconciliation, click **cell G5**, press Ctrl+C, choose **Home→Clipboard→ Paste menu ▼→Paste Values→Values**, and tap Esc.

13. Close the QuickBooks report file, choosing not to save the changes.

14. Maximize the bank reconciliation window, select the headers for **rows 7–8**, and choose **Home→Cells→Insert**.

15. Select **cell B7**, choose **Data→Get External Data→From Text**, navigate to **EA5-R2-Deposits** in your **Chapter 05** folder, and click **Import**.

    If you are unable to complete the Ribbon path shown in this step, see EA5-D1, step 17, on page 133 for instructions.

16. Set the **Start Import at Row** option to **2** and click **Next** twice.

17. With the first column in the preview highlighted, click in the circle for **Do Not Import Column (Skip)**, choose to skip the second column, and click **Finish**.

18. In the **Import Data** dialog box, click **OK** to import the data to the active cell in your worksheet.

19. Type **Deposits in Transit** in **cell A7**.

Use Format Painter and Quick Styles

20. Enter this data:

Cell E7	Notes Receivable
Cell E12	NSF Check
Cell E13	Bank Charges
Cell E14	Check Error
Cell G7	6200
Cell F12	100
Cell F13	90
Cell F14	1600

21. Enter **=Sum(B7:B9)** in **cell C9** and then use the Ribbon to copy **cell C9** and paste it to **cells C13** and **G14**.

22. Select **cell C13**, highlight *B11* in the Formula Bar, and then type **B12** and tap Enter.

23. Enter **=Sum(C5:C9)** in **cell C10** and then use the keyboard to copy **cell C10** and paste it to **cell G10**.

24. Enter **=C10-C13** in **cell C15** and then copy **cell C15** and paste to **cell G15** using the method of your choice.

25. Select **cell G15**, highlight *G13* in the Formula Bar, and then type **G14** and tap Enter.

26. Enter **Adjusted Bank Balance** in **cell A15** and **Adjusted Book Balance** in **cell E15**.

27. In **cell C5**, choose **Home→Number→Accounting Number Format** and then click **Decrease Decimal** twice.

28. Go to **Home→Clipboard** and double-click **Format Painter**.

29. Click once on every cell and range in which numbers are displayed and then choose **Home→Clipboard→Format Painter** to turn off Format Painter.

30. Select the headers for **columns B–C** and **columns F–G** and then double-click between the **columns F and G** headers.

31. Apply a bottom border to **cells C9**, **C13**, and **G7**, a bottom double border to **cell C15**, and a top and double bottom border to **cell G15**.

32. Select **cells A5**, **A15**, **E5**, and **E15** and choose **Home→Styles→Cell Styles→Heading 4**.

Apply Conditional Formatting

33. Select **cell G5**, choose **Home→Styles→Conditional Formatting→Manage Rules**, and click the **New Rule** button.

34. Set up the rule as indicated, clicking **Format** when finished:

    - Rule type: **Use a Formula to Determine Which Cells to Format**
    - Rule description: **=$G$5>18000**

35. Click the **Font** tab, select any blue color, and click **OK** three times.

Insert a Header and a Footer

36. Choose **Insert→Text→Header & Footer**.

37. Click in the left section of the header and choose **Header & Footer Tools→Design→Header & Footer Elements→Current Date**.

38. Click in the center section of the header and enter the code for the current time.

39. Choose **Header & Footer Tools→Design→Navigation→Go to Footer**, click in the left section of the footer, and enter the code for the file path.

40. Save and close your file.

Apply Your Skills

EA5-A1 Create a Bank Reconciliation for Charleston Company

In this exercise, you will create a bank reconciliation for Charleston Company for the month ended December 31, 2016. The reconciliation should be partly based on these figures: Bank Statement Balance (12/31/2016) equals $149,800; Notes Receivable equals $5,500; NSF Check equals $2,500; Bank Charges equals $100. During the month, the bank erroneously deposited a $200 check written to Charleston Company into the bank account of Charley Town Company.

1. Open a **Blank Workbook** and save the file in your **Chapter 05** folder as: **EA5-A1-BankRec-[YourName]**

2. Enter the bank reconciliation headers in the **range A1:A3**; apply bold formatting.

3. Apply the **Merge & Center** command (from columns A–G) to each row in this range.

4. Using examples from the chapter, enter descriptions for the initial bank and book balances in the appropriate locations. Type the **Add:** and **Deduct:** labels in the proper cells on **rows 6 and 9**.

5. Set the width of **columns A and E** to **24** and the width of **column D** to **1**.

6. Enter the bank statement balance in the appropriate location.

7. Open **EA5-A1-QBReport** from your **Chapter 05** folder and arrange the window next to the bank reconciliation window.

8. Type **Outstanding Checks** in an appropriate location in the bank reconciliation.

9. Drag and drop each outstanding check and the book balance from the QuickBooks report to the appropriate cells in **columns B and G** of the bank reconciliation.

10. Copy the book balance in the bank reconciliation and use **Paste Values** in the same cell to override the existing formula with the value itself.

11. Close the QuickBooks report without saving.

12. If necessary, insert row(s) in the **Add:** section of the bank reconciliation to account for all items that will appear there.

13. Import the deposits in transit from **EA5-A1-Deposits** in your **Chapter 05** folder to the proper location in the bank reconciliation. (Hint: Use the Data tab.)

14. Type a description for the imported amounts in the proper cell of **column A**.

Use Format Painter and Quick Styles

15. Type the descriptions and amounts for the Notes Receivable, NSF Check, Bank Charges, and Check Error in the appropriate locations.

16. In the appropriate location, enter a formula to sum the items in the **Add:** section of the bank side of the reconciliation.

17. Sum the items in the **Deduct:** section on the bank side of the reconciliation by copying the previous formula and pasting it to the appropriate cell. If necessary, modify the copied formula.

18. If necessary, sum the items in the **Deduct:** section on the book side of the reconciliation by inserting appropriate formulas.

19. In the appropriate row, type a description for the final figures on each side of the reconciliation.

    Hint: Create two entries.

20. In the appropriate locations, enter formulas to calculate all remaining necessary figures on the bank side and book side of the reconciliation.

21. Apply the **Accounting** number format with zero decimal places to the beginning balance on the bank side and then use **Format Painter** to apply the formatting to all other dollar amounts.

22. Adjust column widths so all information is appropriately displayed.

23. Apply a bottom border to cells below which a calculation is completed and apply a bottom double border to cells that represent the final calculation in a column.

24. Apply the **Heading 4** Quick Style to the descriptions for the beginning and adjusted balances on each side of the reconciliation.

    Hint: Apply the setting to four cells.

Finalize the Bank Reconciliation

25. Create a new conditional formatting rule to the beginning bank statement balance such that the cell will contain a green fill color and red text if it drops below $155,000.

26. Insert the **Current Date** code in the right section of the footer and the **File Path** code in the left section of the header.

27. Save and close your file.

EA5-A2 Create a Bank Reconciliation for Tasters Club Corp.

In this exercise, you will create a bank reconciliation for Tasters Club Corp. for the month ended December 31, 2016. The reconciliation should be partly based on these figures: Bank Statement Balance (12/31/2016) equals $16,200; Notes Receivable equals $395; NSF Check equals $4,000; Bank Charges equals $550. During the month, the bank erroneously deposited a $505 check written to Pepper Products into the bank account of Tasters Club Corp.

1. Open a **Blank Workbook** and save the file in your **Chapter 05** folder as:
   EA5-A2-BankRec-[YourName]

2. Enter the bank reconciliation headers in the **range A1:A3**; apply bold formatting.

3. Apply the **Merge & Center** command (from columns A–G) to each row in this range.

4. Using examples from the chapter, enter descriptions for the initial bank and book balances in appropriate locations. Type the **Add:** and **Deduct:** labels in the proper cells in **rows 6** and **9**.

5. Set the width of **columns A and E** to **24** and the width of **column D** to **1**.

6. Enter the bank statement balance in the appropriate location.

7. Open **EA5-A2-QBReport** from your **Chapter 05** folder and arrange the window next to the bank reconciliation window.

8. Type **Outstanding Checks** in an appropriate location in the bank reconciliation.

9. Drag and drop each outstanding check as well as the book balance from the QuickBooks report to the appropriate cells in **columns B and G** of the bank reconciliation.

10. Copy the book balance in the bank reconciliation and use **Paste Values** in the same cell to override the existing formula with the value itself.

11. Close the QuickBooks report without saving.

12. If necessary, insert row(s) in the **Add:** section of the bank reconciliation to account for all items that will appear there.

13. Import the deposits in transit from **EA5-A2-Deposits** in your **Chapter 05** folder to the proper location in the bank reconciliation. (Hint: Use the Data tab.)

14. Type a description for the imported amounts in the proper cell of **column A**.

Use Format Painter and Quick Styles

15. Type the descriptions and amounts for the Notes Receivable, NSF Check, Bank Charges, and Check Error in the appropriate locations.

16. In the appropriate location, enter a formula to sum the items in the **Add:** section of the bank side of the reconciliation.

17. Sum the items in the **Deduct:** section of the bank side of the reconciliation by copying the previous formula and pasting it to the appropriate cell. If necessary, modify the copied formula.

18. If necessary, sum the items in the **Deduct:** section on the book side of the reconciliation by inserting appropriate formulas.

19. In the appropriate row, type a description for the final figures on each side of the bank reconciliation.

    Hint: Create two entries.

20. In the appropriate locations, enter formulas to calculate all remaining necessary figures on the bank side and book side of the reconciliation.

21. Apply the **Currency** format with zero decimal places to the beginning balance on the bank side and then use **Format Painter** to apply the formatting to all other dollar amounts.

22. Adjust column widths so all information is appropriately displayed.

23. Apply a bottom border to cells below which a calculation is completed and apply a bottom double border to cells that represent the final calculation in a column.

24. Apply the **Heading 4** Quick Style to the descriptions for the beginning and adjusted balances on each side of the reconciliation.

    Hint: Apply the setting to four cells.

Finalize the Bank Reconciliation

25. Create a new conditional formatting rule to the beginning bank statement balance such that the cell will contain a yellow fill color and blue text if it drops below $20,000.

26. Insert the **Current Time** code in the right section of the header and the **Current Date** code in the left section.

27. Insert the **File Path** code in the left section of the footer.

28. Save and close your file.

Extend Your Skills

EA5-E1 Complete a Bank Reconciliation for Jukebox Repair, Inc.

In this exercise, you will complete a bank reconciliation as of 12/31/2016 for Jukebox Repair, Inc. One of your primary goals is to ensure that the file can be easily understood by the end user. Use this information to populate the reconciliation:

- Deposits in Transit: $400 and $700
- NSF Check: $600
- Notes Receivable: $1,500
- Outstanding Checks: $1,000 and $500
- Bank Charges: $300
- When recording check #854 for $1,600, the company erroneously reduced the cash balance by $2,500.
- The bank statement reflects a 12/31/16 balance of $6,200, while the company's general ledger reflects a 12/31/16 cash balance of $4,300.

Modify the appearance of the reconciliation using Format Painter and Quick Styles. Set a conditional formatting rule that will highlight the bank balance if it exceeds $5,000. Apply a header that displays the filename and a footer that displays the current date. Ensure that all column widths, row heights, and font sizes are appropriately adjusted.

EA5-E2 Complete a Bank Reconciliation for Plastics Manufacturers

In this exercise, you will complete a bank reconciliation as of 12/31/2016 for Plastics Manufacturers. One of your primary goals is to ensure that the file can be easily understood by the end user. Use this information to populate the reconciliation:

- Deposits in Transit: $3,600
- NSF Check: $8,400
- Notes Receivable: $20,000
- Outstanding Checks: $3,000 and $1,800
- Bank Charges: $500
- When recording check #223 for $8,100, the company erroneously reduced the cash balance by $7,000.
- The bank statement reflects a 12/31/16 balance of $41,000, while the company's general ledger reflects a 12/31/16 cash balance of $29,800.

Modify the appearance of the reconciliation using Format Painter and Quick Styles. Set a conditional formatting rule that will highlight the bank balance if it falls below $45,000. Apply a header that displays the file path and a footer that displays the current date and time. Ensure that all column widths, row heights, and font sizes are appropriately adjusted.

EA5-E3 Complete a Bank Reconciliation for Pond Maintenance Corp.

In this exercise, you will complete a bank reconciliation as of 12/31/2016 for Pond Maintenance Corp. One of your primary goals is to ensure that the file can be easily understood by the end user. Use this information to populate the reconciliation:

- Deposits in Transit: $10,100 and $1,000
- NSF Check: $7,150
- Notes Receivable: $7,000
- Outstanding Checks: $3,100 and $600
- Bank Charges: $1,100
- The bank erroneously deposited a $250 check written to TreeSky Industries into the bank account of Pond Maintenance Corp.
- The bank statement reflects a 12/31/16 balance of $94,200, while the company's general ledger reflects a 12/31/16 cash balance of $102,600.

Modify the appearance of the reconciliation using Format Painter and Quick Styles. Set a conditional formatting rule that will highlight the bank balance if it exceeds $90,000. Apply a header that displays the filename and file path and a footer that displays the current time. Ensure that all column widths, row heights, and font sizes are appropriately adjusted.

Critical Thinking

EA5-C1 Discuss Importing Data into Accounting Worksheets

Creating accounting-related worksheets can be a daunting task. As you have seen in this chapter, your level of efficiency when creating these files is enhanced when you import data from outside programs. While it is common for data to be imported from QuickBooks, there is a variety of alternative sources from which accounting data can also be derived.

Write a paragraph with at least five sentences to identify three sources of accounting data not discussed in this chapter and the type of information you would derive from each. Write a second paragraph of at least four sentences in which you consider the types of accounting-related worksheets that would benefit from the inclusion of this data.

EA5-C2 Discuss Applying Headers/Footers to Accounting Worksheets

Headers and footers are vital elements of a properly designed worksheet. They can be used to convey an array of information in a streamlined manner. While a number of header and footer elements (such as page number, current date, and filename) can be selected from the Ribbon, you are not limited to these choices.

Write a paragraph of at least five sentences in which you identify four pieces of information (aside from those accessed via the Ribbon) that would be logical to include in the header or footer of an accounting-related worksheet. Write a second paragraph of at least five sentences to discuss why you believe it is appropriate to include each of these elements in a header or footer.

Depreciation Schedule

LEARNING OBJECTIVES

- Create a depreciation schedule

- Create a table

- Convert a range to a table, and vice versa

- Use the SLN, SYD, and DDB functions

- Sort, filter, and analyze table data

When dealing with multiple sets of similarly structured data, consistently presenting each set in your worksheet is important. One way to ensure this consistency is to use an Excel table. Not only do tables provide consistent formatting across all elements, they also allow the user to easily sort and filter the data within them. And the Quick Analysis button can help you further analyze table data. In this chapter, you will create a depreciation schedule, presenting the data in table form. You will sort, filter, and modify the table. Lastly, you will use built-in functions—such as SLN, SYD, and DDB—to quickly calculate the depreciation expense for the fixed assets within your table.

PROJECT	City Music World

City Music World is a retail store that sells musical equipment and offers lessons for beginning and experienced musicians. Over the years, City Music World has acquired a number of fixed assets, which are depreciated annually. To keep track of both the book value and depreciation expense for each asset, the company maintains a depreciation schedule. You are considering how best to present the depreciation schedule and to complete one that can be used on an ongoing basis.

In this chapter, you will create a table that includes all data necessary to calculate the depreciation expense for each fixed asset. You will modify the table and use functions to calculate depreciation expenses for each. You will also sort, filter, and analyze the table data.

Fixed Asset	Date of Acquisition	Cost	Salvage Value	Useful Life (years)	Accumulated Depreciation	Depreciation Expense	Year-End Book Value
Piano	1/1/2008	$ 12,400	$ 2,400	10	$ 9,000	$ 1,000	$ 3,400
Office Furniture	1/1/2013	$ 4,300	$ 800	7	$ 2,000	$ 500	$ 2,300
Equipment	1/1/2015	$ 24,000	$ -	12	$ 4,000	$ 2,000	$ 20,000
Studio Furniture	1/1/2016	$ 3,000	$ 300	9	$ 300	$ 300	$ 2,700
Total		$ 43,700	$ 3,500	9.5	$ 15,300	$ 3,800	$ 28,400

This depreciation schedule uses an Excel table to present the data in a consistent manner.

Accounting Refresher: Depreciation Expense

Over time, most **fixed assets** lose value. A fixed asset (also called a *long-term asset* or *plant asset*) is expected to be held for more than twelve months and cannot easily be converted to cash. This is in contrast to a **short-term asset** (or *current asset*), such as supplies or inventory, which is expected to be held for less than twelve months and can more easily be used up or converted to cash if necessary.

All fixed assets, with the notable exception of Land, are subject to **depreciation** as a result of the loss in value they experience. Depreciation expense represents an estimate of the loss in value that an asset experiences over time. Think about an office table that is purchased for $250. Could a company resell this table for the same amount five years later, after it has been used consistently? No. *If* a buyer could be found, she would not be willing to pay full price for such an item. Since this depreciation process consistently occurs, businesses must account for it over time. While multiple methods exist for the calculation of depreciation expense, the three most common are the straight-line, sum of the years' digits, and double-declining balance methods.

Straight-Line Depreciation

Under the straight-line method of depreciation, a company records the same amount of depreciation for each year of the asset's **useful life**. The useful life (number of years the company expects to use the asset) is estimated based on past experience. For the straight-line method, the **salvage value** (or **residual value**) is also estimated. This represents the amount the company expects to receive for the asset at the time of disposal (when it is sold or discarded). To calculate annual depreciation under the straight-line method, you subtract salvage value from item cost and then divide by the useful life. The resulting depreciation expense is the same for every year of the asset's useful life.

NOTE!   The straight-line depreciation method is, by far, the most commonly used depreciation method.

Sum of the Years' Digits Depreciation

The sum of the years' digits method is referred to as an *accelerated depreciation method*, as it results in more depreciation during the early years of an asset's useful life than in the later years. Under this method, the digits of each year within the useful life are added and then used to calculate each year's depre-

ciation. For example, one of the necessary calculations for an asset with a three-year useful life would require adding the digits 3 + 2 + 1 to arrive at 6. Here we will examine how this result can be used to arrive at the correct depreciation.

(continued)

In the first year, you subtract salvage value from cost. Then, the useful life is divided by the sum of all digits. These two figures are then multiplied to determine the depreciation expense.

For an asset with a cost of $1,200, a salvage value of $200, and a four-year useful life, the sum of the years' digits would be 4 + 3 + 2 + 1 = 10. To determine the depreciation expense, you subtract $200 from $1,200 to arrive at $1,000. Then you divide four years by ten years to arrive at 40%. Lastly, you multiply $1,000 by 40% to arrive at a depreciation expense of $400. The same calculation is done for every year, except that the numerator of the fraction that yields the depreciation percentage is reduced by 1 for each subsequent year (so the second-year depreciation percentage calculation for an asset with a four-year useful life would be 3/10 = 30%).

Double-Declining Balance Depreciation

Similar to the sum of the years' digits method, the double-declining balance method is an accelerated depreciation method. Calculating depreciation using this method requires a three-step process:

1. Determine the straight-line rate of depreciation by dividing 1 (number of years for which you are calculating depreciation; this number never changes) by useful life. For example, if the useful life is five years, the straight-line rate would be 20% (one year divided by five years).

TIP!   An alternate calculation for this step would be to divide 100% by the useful life.

2. Multiply the straight-line rate of depreciation by two. This is why the method is called *double*-declining balance. For example, a straight-line rate of depreciation of 20% would be multiplied by two to arrive at 40%.

3. Multiply the cost of the asset by the rate determined in step 2. For example, if the cost of the asset is $1,000, then the double-declining balance depreciation would be $400 ($1,000 multiplied by 40%).

In subsequent years, the same calculation is used, except that the current book value (cost minus accumulated depreciation) replaces the cost in step 3. For example, if a fixed asset cost $1,000, experienced $400 of depreciation during the first year, and has a useful life of 5 years, then the second year's double-declining balance depreciation would be $240 ([$1,000 minus $400] multiplied by 40%).

Up to this point, the salvage value has not impacted the calculation. The double-declining balance method doesn't factor in the salvage value until near the end of the useful life. As you calculate each year's depreciation, you must ensure that the asset's book value has not dropped below the salvage value. If this occurs in a given year, then you disregard the calculation for that year and substitute an amount that brings the book value down to, but not below, the salvage value (determine this by subtracting salvage value from current book value).

NOTE! Other declining-balance methods may also be used, such as triple-declining balance and 1.5-declining balance.

Working with Tables

You will often work with ordinary worksheet lists, and sometimes you'll want to convert a list to a table. An Excel table manages related data. For example, a table can hold the cost, accumulated depreciation, annual depreciation expense, and other information for all fixed assets of a company. The table data may be sorted, filtered, and calculated in various ways. Features specific to tables include:

- **Automatic expansion**—As you type more data rows at the bottom or columns to the right, the table expands. Cell formatting and formulas are copied automatically. For a circumstance in which table data is constantly expanding, such as when a company is obtaining new fixed assets over time, this allows for easy inclusion of the new fixed assets.
- **Calculated columns**—Entering a formula in one cell automatically copies the formula to all cells in the table column.
- **Table styles**—Selecting any of the formatting presets in the Table Style library applies consistent formatting to the entire table.
- **Filtering**—Displaying only those rows that meet certain criteria is available immediately after you create a table, but you must turn on filtering in columns of a worksheet list.
- **Functions**—You can display a total row and create summary formulas by choosing from a list of frequently used functions, like Sum and Average.

Creating a Table

You start a table by entering data in the worksheet cells as usual. Do not use blank rows or columns to separate areas within the list because Excel does not automatically include areas after blanks in a table. Note that a worksheet may include more than one table.

Fixed Asset	Date of Acqusition	Cost	Salvage Value	Useful Life (years)
Piano	1/1/2008	$12,400	$ 2,400	10
Office Furniture	1/1/2013	$ 4,300	$ 800	7
Equipment	1/1/2015	$24,000	$ -	12
Studio Furniture	1/1/2016	$ 3,000	$ 300	9

Worksheet data prior to creation of a table

Converting a Range to a Table

You can convert a worksheet list to a table by selecting any cell in the list and applying the Format as Table command. Excel includes all adjacent cells in the table until a blank row and column are encountered. You can change the suggested table range if it is not correct. The table appears in place of the original cells. During the conversion process, you choose a table style,

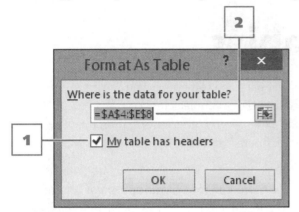

also known as a Quick Style. The Table Tools Design tab appears on the Ribbon after you create the table so you can apply additional formatting.

1. If checked, the first row will be used as the header row.

2. This is the table range.

Alternatively, you can start with blank cells in a table. After you select a range and choose the Format as Table command, the new table displays. Column headings and table data can then be entered.

TIP!   Use the customized Ribbon path to create a table using a specific table style.

↗ Insert→Tables→Table

↗ Home→Styles→Format as Table | Ctrl + T

Table Rows and Columns

In Excel, each row in a table holds a collection of facts about a certain person, event, or other item. For example, a fixed-assets table will have one row for each fixed asset. Each column in a table displays one characteristic of the individual row entries. For example, a fixed-assets table would have columns for items such as the asset name, asset cost, useful life, and salvage value.

Fixed Asset	Date of Acqusition	Cost	Salvage Value	Useful Life (years)
Piano	1/1/2008	$ 12,400	$ 2,400	10
Office Furniture	1/1/2013	$ 4,300	$ 800	7
Equipment	1/1/2015	$ 24,000	$ -	12
Studio Furniture	1/1/2016	$ 3,000	$ 300	9

1. Each table row contains data about one fixed asset.

2. Each column contains one type of data.

Populating and Formatting a Table

Excel names tables as Table1, Table2, and so on. Although you may use the generic names, renaming with descriptive titles that relate to the accounting worksheet is a good practice, as table names are often used in formulas. As with defined names for a cell or a range, table names may not include spaces but may include underscores.

 Table Tools→Design→Properties→Table Name

Header Row and Total Row

Always enter column headings in the first row of a table, which Excel treats as the header row. Excel uses the following rules for column headings:

- **One item per column**—Each column must contain one piece of information (such as asset name or accumulated depreciation) to enable full sorting and filtering.
- **Unique headings**—Each heading should be different.
- **Special characters**—You may use spaces, multiple capital letters, and special characters (such as a comma or dollar sign) in column headings. Avoid using the *at* symbol (@), pound sign (#), brackets ([ ]), and single quotes ('), as these have special meanings when used in formulas.

When a table cell is selected, the header row labels operate like frozen titles. They display in place of column headings (A, B, C, etc.) as you scroll down the table.

Fixed Asset	Date of Acq	Cost	Salvage V	Useful Life (
5 Piano	1/1/2008	$ 12,400	$ 2,400	10
6 Office Furniture	1/1/2013	$ 4,300	$ 800	7
7 Equipment	1/1/2015	$ 24,000	$ -	12
8 Studio Furniture	1/1/2016	$ 3,000	$ 300	9

You can display the total row below the last table row, or you can turn off the display. In a depreciation schedule, this would be particularly useful for columns containing figures such as total cost and accumulated depreciation. If the last table column contains numbers, a total is calculated automatically when the total row is displayed. If the last column contains text or dates, the populated cells in the column are counted instead of added together.

TIP! The total row can contain a variety of summary formulas, which can be accessed via a drop-down menu in each cell of the total row.

8	Studio Furniture	$ 3,000	$ 300
9	Total	$ 43,700	3,500
10		None	
11		Average	
12		Count	
		Count Numbers	
13		Max	
14		Min	
15		Sum	
		StdDev	
		Var	
16		More Functions...	

 Table Tools→Design→Table Style Options→Header Row

 Table Tools→Design→Table Style Options→Total Row

Formatting a Table

The Table Tools Design tab appears when any table cell is selected. From here you can change the table style and toggle on/off various options. Note that banded rows and columns, which are among the options that can be selected from this tab, contain light and dark fills that alternate for each row or column to facilitate reading of the table.

The table styles change to match the options set on the Design tab.

Develop Your Skills EA6-D1

In this exercise, you will begin a depreciation schedule for City Music World using an Excel table. These fixed assets, with associated data as of 12/31/2015, were acquired prior to the current year.

Fixed Asset	Date of Acquisition	Cost	Salvage Value	Useful Life (years)	Accumulated Depreciation
Office Furniture	1/1/2013	$4,300	$800	7	$1,500
Piano	1/1/2008	$12,400	$2,400	10	$8,000
Equipment	1/1/2015	$24,000	$0	12	$2,000

1. Open a **Blank Workbook** and save the file in your **Chapter 06** folder as:
   EA6-D1-Depreciation-[YourName]

2. Enter **City Music World** in **cell A1** and **Depreciation Schedule** in **cell A2**.

3. Type the fixed-asset data in the **range A4:F7**. Include the *Accumulated Depreciation* header but exclude its dollar amounts.

   You are not entering the accumulated depreciation amounts, as you will later calculate these as of 12/31/2016. Do not format the cells, as this will be done later as well.

4. Select **cell A4**, choose **Home→Styles→Format as Table→Gold, Table Style Medium 5**, and click **OK**.

5. Choose **Table Tools→Design→Properties**, click in the **Table Name** box, and then type `Depreciation _ Schedule` and tap Enter.

6. Choose **Table Tools→Design→Table Style Options→Total Row**.

   The count is displayed in the Accumulated Depreciation column, but the total row is blank in all other columns. Now you will populate the total row for certain of the displayed columns.

7. Select **cell C8**, click the drop-down arrow that appears, and choose **Sum**. Repeat for **cell D8**.

8. Select **cell E8**, click the drop-down arrow, and choose **Average**.

9. Choose **Table Tools→Design→Table Style Options→First Column**.

   The fixed-asset names are now displayed in bold (column A).

10. Save your file.

    Unless otherwise directed, always keep your file open at the end of each exercise.

Adding and Deleting Rows and Columns

As the depreciation schedule is used year after year, new fixed assets will be added when acquired. The simplest way to add rows is to include them at the end of the table, which can be done by tapping Tab while the right-most cell in the last data row is active. You use the Delete command to remove rows after selecting a cell in the desired row(s).

TIP! Click the Undo button if you accidentally tap Tab after the last cell in the row.

You can simply type in the blank column to the right of the last column to add it to the table. When new rows and/or columns are added to a table, calculations are updated and consistent formatting is applied. If you create a formula in one cell of a new column, Excel copies the formula to all other cells to create a calculated column. If you do not want a calculated column, type text or a number in at least one cell in the column before creating any formulas.

⤴ Home→Cells→Insert ▼→Insert Table Rows Above *or* Insert Table Rows Below

⤴ Home→Cells→Insert ▼→Insert Table Columns to the Left *or* Insert Table Columns to the Right

⤴ Home→Cells→Delete ▼→Delete Table Rows *or* Delete Table Columns

Selecting Table Rows and Columns

At times you may need to select all cells in a table row or column, such as when you would like to change their text color. Selecting a table row or column is different from selecting a work-sheet row or column in that you must click inside the first cell of the table's row or column, instead of the row or column header.

	A	B	C
		Date of	
4	**Fixed Asset** ▼	**Acqusition** ▼	**Cost** ▼
→ 5	**Piano**	1/1/2008 $	12,400
6	**Office Furniture**	1/1/2013 $	4,300

1

	A	B	C
		Date of	
4	**Fixed Asset** ▼	**Acqusition** ▼	**Cost** ▼
5	**Piano**	1/1/2008 $	12,400
6	**Office Furniture**	1/1/2013 $	4,300

2

	A	B	C
		Date of	
4	**Fixed Asset** ▼	**Acqusition** ▼	**Cost** ▼
5	**Piano**	1/1/2008 $	12,400
6	**Office Furniture**	1/1/2013 $	4,300

3

	A	B	C
		Date of	
4	**Fixed Asset** ▼	**Acqusition** ▼	**Cost** ▼
5	**Piano**	1/1/2008 $	12,400
6	**Office Furniture**	1/1/2013 $	4,300

4

1. Selects entire row through the end of the worksheet

2. Selects entire column through the end of the worksheet

3. Selects entire row within the table

4. Selects entire column within the table

TIP!   Select the header row just as you select a standard row.

Printing and Deleting a Table

The Print Selected Table option in the Print tab of Backstage view is used to print a table without including the other cells on the worksheet. The option is available only when you select a cell in the table before displaying the Print tab.

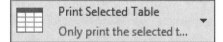

You can delete a table (as well as the data in it) by selecting all table cells, including the total row if visible, and tapping Delete or choosing the Delete Table Rows command on the Ribbon.

Develop Your Skills EA6-D2

In this exercise, you will add a fixed-asset row and multiple columns to the table. You will also preview how the table would look if printed. In addition to the assets previously included in the table, City Music World acquired studio furniture on 1/1/2016. The studio furniture has a cost of $3,000, an estimated salvage value of $300, and an estimated useful life of nine years.

1. Save your file as: **EA6-D2-Depreciation-[YourName]**

2. Select **cell F7** and tap Tab.

3. Enter the information for the new fixed asset in the **range A8:E8**.

   The figures in the total row have updated to include the new data.

4. Starting from **cell F8**, choose **Home→Cells→Insert ▼→Insert Table Columns to the Right** three times.

   You have added one more table column than is necessary, so you will now delete one.

5. Choose **Home→Cells→Delete ▼→Delete Table Columns**.

6. Type **Depreciation Expense** in **cell G4** and **Year-End Book Value** in **cell H4**.

7. Select the **row 4** header and choose **Home→Alignment→Wrap Text**.

8. Use the Ribbon to change the width of **columns B**, **E**, and **G:H** to **12**.

9. Use the right-click method to change the width of **column F** to **14** and the width of **column D** to **4**.

   Column D is now too narrow to display its data. You will fix this issue.

10. With **column D** highlighted, choose **Home→Cells→Format→AutoFit Column Width**.

11. Double-click between the **columns A** and **B** headers to autofit column A.

12. Double-click between the **rows 4** and **5** headers to autofit the height of row 4.

13. Select **cell A5** and choose **File→Print**.

14. In the Settings area, choose **Portrait Orientation→Landscape Orientation**.

15. Still in the Settings area, choose **Print Active Sheets→Print Selected Table**.

    The titles within rows 1 and 2 have now been excluded from the print area.

16. Click the **Back** button to exit Backstage view and then save your file.

Applying Depreciation Functions with Structured References

Depreciation methods can be used to determine annual depreciation for a fixed asset. As discussed, the most commonly used methods are the straight-line, sum of the years' digits, and double-declining balance methods. Excel functions can be used to calculated annual depreciation under each of these three methods.

In an Excel table, a calculated column is created when a formula is entered into any cell within the column. As a result, the formula is automatically copied to all other table cells in the column when it is first created. When a depreciation function is used to calculate depreciation expense for a fixed asset (in a single table row), the function will automatically do the same for all other fixed assets. This automatic calculation for the entire table can be toggled on/off using AutoCorrect Options.

TIP! If you don't want a formula to be copied throughout the column, choose Undo after confirming the formula to delete it from all but the cell in which it was entered.

🖈 File→Options→Proofing→AutoCorrect Options

As long as the cost, salvage value, and useful life of the asset are provided in the worksheet, these functions can be used to determine the applicable depreciation expense. Note that the period must also be entered when calculating depreciation expenses under the sum of the years' digits and double-declining balance methods. This allows Excel to determine the proper depreciation for each year of the asset's useful life.

NOTE! A factor can be entered to the double-declining balance formula to indicate a depreciation rate other than the default double rate. For example, triple-declining balance can be used by entering *3* as the optional factor in the formula.

	B	C
14	Cost	12400
15	Salvage Value	2400
16	Useful Life	10
17	Period	4
19	=SLN(C14,C15,C16)	Straight-Line Depreciation
20	=SYD(C14,C15,C16,C17)	Sum of the Years' Digits Depreciation
21	=DDB(C14,C15,C16,C17)	Double-Declining Balance Depreciation

The structure of each depreciation function within Excel can be seen here.

Structured References

Formulas in normal worksheet lists use cell references such as E7, but Excel uses structured references to refer to cells used in table formulas. Structured references allow formulas to adjust results automatically as rows and columns are added to or deleted from the table. They also adjust as you rename tables, edit column headings, and move or copy formulas. The generic syntax (language) of structured references allows you to create one formula in a calculated column so that the formula doesn't need to be copied to specific cells in the column as must be done in a normal worksheet range.

Formulas with Structured References

Review the following two formulas to understand how structured references differ from standard cell references.

	Cost	Salvage Value	Useful Life (years)	Accumulated Depreciation	Depreciation Expense	Year-End Book Value
	$ 12,400	$ 2,400	10	$ 9,000	$ 1,000	=C5-F5

1

2

	Cost	Salvage Value	Useful Life (years)	Accumulated Depreciation	Depreciation Expense	Year-End Book Value
	$ 12,400	$ 2,400	10	$ 9,000	$ 1,000	=[@Cost]-[@[Accumulated Depreciation]]

1. Worksheet formula with relative cell references

2. Table formula with structured references

The syntax of the table formula converts the relative reference of cell C5 to a structured reference containing brackets ([ ]) and the *at* symbol (@).

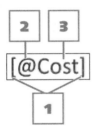

1. Brackets surround the reference.

2. The "at" symbol precedes the name.

3. This is the column heading.

Develop Your Skills EA6-D3

In this exercise, you will use Excel's depreciation functions to calculate the current year's depreciation expenses for each fixed asset. You will then use structured references to complete the remainder of the depreciation schedule. Recall the following accumulated depreciation figures as of 12/31/2015.

Fixed Asset	Accumulated Depreciation
Office Furniture	$1,500
Piano	$8,000
Equipment	$2,000
Studio Furniture	$0

1. Save your file as: **EA6-D3-Depreciation-[YourName]**

2. Navigate to the **Home** tab, if necessary, and then click **cell G5** and begin typing a formula with: **=SYD(**

3. Complete the formula: Select **cell C5** and type a comma, select **cell D5** and type a comma, and then select **cell E5** and type: **,4)**

   The formula is automatically copied to each row in the table and contains structured references. However, the period argument must be different for each fixed asset because they were acquired in different years, so you must edit rows 6–8.

4. With **cell G6** selected, replace the 4 in the Formula Bar with **9** and tap ⎣Enter⎦.

   As column G is a calculated column, every formula has been updated to reflect nine periods. Next you will reverse this so that the 9 is used only in the formula for cell G6.

5. Click **Undo** on the Quick Access toolbar.

   The formulas in cells G5, G7, and G8 show 4 again.

6. Select **cell G7**, and then replace the 4 in the Formula Bar with **2** and complete the entry.

   Because you used Undo to turn off the calculated column, the other formulas in the column do not update when a change is made to a single formula.

   Complete each of the next cell entries unless directed otherwise.

7. Select **cell G8** and replace the 4 in the Formula Bar with **1**.

   You have calculated the depreciation expense using the sum of the years' digits method. Now you want to see what the depreciation expense would be using the double-declining balance method.

8. Select **cell G5** and replace the *SYD* in the Formula Bar with **DDB**.

   The calculated depreciation expense has changed, as the double-declining balance method returns a different depreciation expense figure than the sum of the years' digits method.

9. Repeat step 8 for each cell in the **range G6:G8**.

   Now you will see how the numbers change when using the straight-line depreciation method.

10. Highlight the **range G5:G8** and tap ⎣Delete⎦.

11. To begin the new formula, select **cell G5** and type **=SLN(** but do not complete the entry.

12. Select **cell C5** and type a comma, select **cell D5** and type a comma, select **cell E5** and type a closed parenthesis, and tap ⎣Enter⎦.

    Notice that this has become a calculated column again, in which the straight-line depreciation is automatically calculated for all fixed assets in subsequent rows. Consistent with prior periods, you decide to use the straight-line depreciation method and will now complete the remainder of the table.

13. Select **cell F5**, type **=1500+** and select **cell G5**, and then tap ⎣Enter⎦.

14. Click **Undo** on the Quick Access toolbar.

    The formula includes structured references, instead of standard cell references. Clicking Undo turned off calculated columns, which was necessary as the accumulated depreciation prior to the current year is different for each fixed asset and, therefore, cannot be copied to the other rows.

15. Repeat step 13 for each cell in the **range F6:F8**.

    Hint: Use the correct accumulated depreciation amount at the beginning of each formula (see the exercise instructions).

16. Select **cell H5** and type an equals sign, select **cell C5** and type a minus sign, select **cell F5**, and tap ⏎Enter.

    As the year-end book value for each fixed asset is calculated by subtracting the accumulated depreciation from the cost, this calculated column can remain within the table.

17. Select **cell F9**, click the drop-down button, and choose **Sum**. Repeat for **cells G9** and **H9**.

18. Save your file.

Using Enhanced Sorting and Filtering

Excel's AutoFilter feature operates in the same manner for both lists and tables. While a table automatically displays an AutoFilter button in each column heading, these buttons can be turned on when using a normal worksheet list. AutoFilter allows you to sort and filter displayed data. You can either use the search box to add items to the filter or select them from the list.

> ⬈ Data→Sort & Filter→Filter (to toggle the display of column heading buttons)

Sorts

To sort on one column in a table, you can use the *A to Z* or *Z to A* commands via the column heading AutoFilter buttons. A column heading's AutoFilter button changes to indicate that the table or list is sorted based on that column. An up arrow indicates a sort from lowest to highest, and a down arrow indicates highest to lowest.

You can sort table data on multiple columns using the Sort dialog box, which can be accessed from the Custom Sort Option on the AutoFilter button menu. The Move Up and Move Down buttons within the Sort dialog box can be used to change the sort order.

	1		
Fixed Asset	**Date of Acquisition** ▼	**Cost** ▼	
Equipment	1/1/2015	$ 24,000	
Office Furniture	1/1/2013	$ 4,300	
Piano	1/1/2008	$ 12,400	
Studio Furniture	1/1/2016	$ 3,000	
Total		$ 43,700	

1. This up arrow indicates that the table is sorted by fixed asset from A to Z.

Filters

Filtering allows you to display only rows that meet certain criteria. For example, you may display just the records for which the fixed-asset cost is greater than $50,000 or only records for fixed assets with a useful life of at least five years. The records not meeting your criteria are hidden until you clear the filter. You can filter by text color, cell fill color, or cell contents including text, numbers, and dates. You can filter for a color or icon that has been applied through conditional formatting. The column heading AutoFilter button displays a filter icon to alert you that the table is filtered and does not currently display all rows. The current filter setting appears in a ScreenTip when you hover the mouse pointer over the button. You can filter on multiple columns using AutoFilter.

4	Fixed Asset	Date of Acqusition	Cost
5	Equipment	1/1/2015	$ 24,000
7	Piano	1/1/2008	$ 12,400
8	Studio Furniture	1/1/2016	$ 3,000
9	Total		$ 39,400

1. Row numbers change color to indicate that some are temporarily hidden.

2. The AutoFilter button indicates that a filter is in effect.

3. Formulas in the total row recalculate for the filtered records.

Filtering with Multiple Criteria and Searches

An AutoFilter list contains all unique items in the column. After removing the checkmark from Select All, you can choose one or more items to include in the filter. Alternatively, you can search for filters within the Search box.

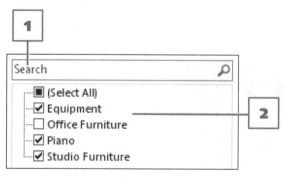

1. Search box

2. Listing of all items in the column

Custom Filters

The Custom Filter command, accessed via the column heading AutoFilter list, displays a dialog box that can be used to filter by two criteria in the same column. For example, you may filter for records with accumulated depreciation between $20,000 and $40,000, using the And option as shown. The Or option displays every record that meets either of the two criteria—not necessarily both. The dialog box also displays after you choose any text filter option or some of the number and date filter options. You can choose one or both specifications in the dialog box as needed.

Custom AutoFilter	?	×
Show rows where:		
Accumulated Depreciation		
is greater than ⌄	20000	⌄
● And ○ Or		
is less than ⌄	40000	⌄
Use ? to represent any single character		
Use * to represent any series of characters		
	OK	Cancel

Develop Your Skills EA6-D4

In this exercise, you will sort and filter the depreciation schedule.

1. Save your file as: **EA6-D4-Depreciation-[YourName]**

2. Select **cell B7** and choose **Data→Sort & Filter→Sort Oldest to Newest**.

   Note that the name of this button on the Ribbon changes to reflect the data in the column with the active cell. The button currently shows Sort Oldest to Newest because the active cell is in a column that displays dates.

3. Click the drop-down arrow in **cell E4** and then uncheck the box next to **12** and click **OK**.

   The Equipment row is no longer visible. Notice how the drop-down arrow look has changed to indicate that a filter is applied to this column.

4. Select any table cell and choose **Data→Sort & Filter→Filter**.

   The filter has been toggled off and the table now displays all fixed assets, including Equipment. Notice that the drop-down arrows have disappeared from the header cells.

5. Choose **Data→Sort & Filter→Filter**.

6. Click the drop-down arrow in **cell H4** and choose **Number Filters→Custom Filter**.

7. In the Custom AutoFilter dialog box, click in the *equals* box and choose **is greater than**, type **3000** in the box to the right, and click **OK**.

   The only two fixed assets now displayed are Piano and Equipment.

8. Save your file.

Using Quick Analysis

The Quick Analysis button allows you to more easily apply options also available on the Ribbon to data within both data tables and standard worksheet lists.

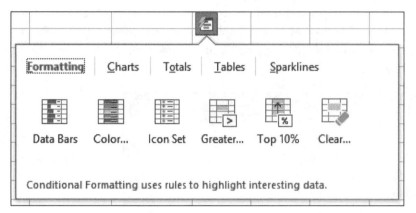

Available options include a variety of formatting, as well as the application of charts, column or row totals, and sparklines. In addition, the Quick Analysis button can be used to convert standard worksheet data into a table. You can also preview the impact of many of these options by holding the mouse pointer over the option. An analysis of fixed assets within a depreciation schedule can be simplified through the use of the Quick Analysis options.

Develop Your Skills EA6-D5

In this exercise, you will use Quick Analysis to create a pie chart based on the data in your depreciation schedule.

1. Save your file as: **EA6-D5-Depreciation-[YourName]**

2. Highlight the **range A4:H9** and click the **Quick Analysis** button at the bottom-right corner of the range.

3. Choose the **Charts** category and click **More**.

4. In the Insert Chart dialog box, click the **All Charts** tab, choose **Pie** from the menu on the left, and click **OK**.

   The pie chart is based on the first column of data adjacent to the row headers, which is Date of Acquisition. You don't want to graph the date of acquisition for the fixed assets, so you will change the data displayed in the chart.

5. Drag the chart below the table so its top-left corner is in **cell A11**.

   Hint: Click in the blank (white) portion of the chart area and drag the chart as needed.

6. Choose **Chart Tools→Design→Data→Select Data**, highlight the **range A4:A7**, hold [Ctrl], highlight the **range H4:H7**, and click **OK**.

   The pie chart now reflects the year-end book value for the two fixed assets currently displayed within the table.

7. Click the filter button in **cell H4** and choose **Clear Filter From "Year-End Book Value."**

   The pie chart updates to include Office Furniture, as this fixed asset is no longer hidden from view as a result of a filter. Because you previously selected source data for the pie chart that only extends through row 7, Studio Furniture (row 8) remains excluded from the pie chart.

8. Click in the chart and choose **Chart Tools→Design→Data→Select Data**.

   The Select Data Source dialog box appears.

9. In the **Chart Data Range** box, replace *$A$7* with **$A$8** and replace *$H$7* with **$H$8**; click **OK**.

   The source data for the pie chart has been extended through row 8, and the pie chart includes all four fixed assets.

10. Apply the **Accounting** number format with zero decimal places to the **ranges C5:D9** and **F5:H9**.

    These changes ensure that the data is displayed logically in the final version of the table.

11. Save and close your file.

REAL-WORLD Accounting

What Are the Benefits of Using Excel to Populate a Depreciation Schedule?

While maintaining schedules for a handful of fixed assets is not overly time-consuming, a business with dozens or hundreds of fixed assets must make every effort to efficiently maintain records. Tables allow for the simple inclusion of additional records (when fixed assets are acquired) and deletion of existing records (when fixed assets are disposed). Simple functions can be used to automatically calculate depreciation expenses and entries in a table can be modified when, for example, a salvage value or useful life estimate is revised.

Excel offers the most efficient method for maintaining a depreciation schedule, particularly for large organizations. While the organized structure of a table and functions save time, it is the worksheet flexibility that provides the greatest benefit. Modifying estimates and adding/deleting records can result in confusing reports when handwritten. And, although there are advanced accounting programs that can accomplish these goals, they almost universally require more training for the end user than is required with Excel.

Clearly, a depreciation schedule can be easily created and modified when structured as an Excel table. Aside from that benefit, the available Quick Analysis tools allow for faster and more extensive data analysis than is available through most other approaches. Remember that the goal of a schedule like this is to convey information efficiently. Quick Analysis tools are an excellent method through which key information can be highlighted and examined. Overall, the ease of use, flexibility, and analysis options associated with an Excel table make it an outstanding option for the completion of a depreciation schedule.

Self-Assessment

Check your knowledge of this chapter's key concepts and skills using the Self-Assessment here or in your eLab course.

1. A table can be created only if data has already been entered in a list within Excel.   *True   False*

2. Excel tables allow calculated columns and filtering.   *True   False*

3. A table can include both a header row and a total row.   *True   False*

4. Table column headings can include any special characters, such as the pound sign or brackets.   *True   False*

5. The factor variable in a double-declining balance function is optional.   *True   False*

6. A structured reference is one that uses standard cell references, such as A1.   *True   False*

7. A structured reference includes both brackets and the *at* symbol (@).   *True   False*

8. AutoFilter buttons allow you to sort and filter data in a table.   *True   False*

9. Records in a table that do not meet applied filtering criteria are hidden from view.   *True   False*

10. The Quick Analysis button provides access to features not included on the Ribbon.   *True   False*

11. Features specific to tables include each of these EXCEPT:
    Automatic expansion
    Calculated columns
    Depreciation functions
    Table Styles

12. Which special character can be used in a table header?
    Dollar sign ($)
    At symbol (@)
    Pound sign (#)
    Single quotes (')

13. Which of these is NOT an accelerated depreciation method?
    Straight-line depreciation
    Sum of the years' digits depreciation
    Double-declining balance depreciation
    Triple-declining balance depreciation

14. Which of these is NOT a table style option available on the Ribbon?
    Header Row
    Total Row
    Banded Columns
    Calculated Rows

15. When the right-most cell of the last data row in a table is active, tapping _____ creates a new row at the bottom of the table.

    <kbd>Ctrl</kbd>
    <kbd>Tab</kbd>
    <kbd>Alt</kbd>
    <kbd>Shift</kbd>

16. The table styles option appears under the _____ tab of the Ribbon.
    Page Layout
    Review
    View
    Design

17. Which of these is NOT required when using depreciation functions (SLN, SYD, or DDB)?
    Cost
    Salvage Value
    Useful Life
    Factor

18. Structured references allow formulas to adjust automatically when each of these actions EXCEPT _____ is taken.
    renaming tables
    editing column headings
    deleting tables
    deleting columns

19. What AutoFilter button image indicates that a list is sorted from lowest to highest?
    A filter icon
    A down arrow
    An up arrow
    A pyramid

20. Which of these is NOT available via the Quick Analysis button menu?
    Formatting
    Charts
    Alignment
    Sparklines

Reinforce Your Skills

EA6-R1 Complete a Depreciation Schedule for Linen Wholesalers

In this exercise, you will create a depreciation schedule for Linen Wholesalers using an Excel table. You will then sort, filter, and analyze the data. These fixed assets, with associated data as of 12/31/2015, were acquired prior to the current year.

Fixed Asset	Date of Acquisition	Cost	Salvage Value	Useful Life (years)	Accumulated Depreciation
Office Tables	1/1/2015	$1,400	$200	6	$0
Furniture	1/1/2010	$6,000	$0	12	$3,000
Warehouse Machinery	1/1/2012	$17,500	$1,500	16	$4,000

Linen Wholesalers also acquired office equipment on 1/1/2016. The office equipment had a cost of $4,200, an estimated salvage value of $700, and an estimated useful life of seven years.

1. Open a **Blank Workbook** and save the file in your **Chapter 06** folder as:
   EA6-R1-Depreciation-[YourName]

2. Type **Linen Wholesalers** in **cell A1** and **Depreciation Schedule** in **cell A2**.

3. Enter the fixed asset data in the **range A4:F7**. Include the *Accumulated Depreciation* header but exclude its amounts. Also exclude the newly acquired asset for now.

4. Select **cell A4**, choose **Home→Styles→Format as Table→Blue, Table Style Light 13**, and click **OK**.

5. Choose **Table Tools→Design→Properties**, enter **Depreciation _ Schedule** for the table name, and tap ⌷Enter⌷.

6. Choose **Table Tools→Design→Table Style Options→Total Row**.

7. One by one, select the cells listed and choose the indicated formula from the drop-down menu:

   - Cell C8: **Sum**
   - Cell D8: **Sum**
   - Cell E8: **Average**

8. Choose **Table Tools→Design→Table Style Options→First Column**.

Adjust Table Rows and Columns

9. Select **cell F7**, tap ⌷Tab⌷, and enter the information for the newly acquired fixed asset into the **range A8:E8**.

10. Click in **cell F8** and choose **Home→Cells→Insert ▼→Insert Table Columns to the Right** two times.

11. Type **Depreciation Expense** in **cell G4** and **Year-End Book Value** in **cell H4**.

12. Wrap the text in **row 4**.

13. Use the Ribbon to set the width of **columns G:H** to **12** and the right-click method to set the width of **column F** to **14**.

14. Use the ⌷Ctrl⌷ key to select the **columns B and E** headers then use the Ribbon to set the width of both to **12**.

15. Set the width of **column D** to **4** using any method and then choose **Home→Cells→Format→AutoFit Column Width**.

16. Double-click between the **columns A–B** headers to autofit column A.

17. Autofit the height of **row 4**.

18. Select **cell A5** and choose **File→Print**.

19. In the Settings area, choose **Portrait Orientation→Landscape Orientation** and then choose **Print Active Sheets→Print Selected Table**.

Use Depreciation Functions

20. Click the **Back** button to exit Backstage view and then navigate to the **Home** tab, if necessary.

21. Select **cell G5**, type **=DDB(** and select **cell C5**, type a comma, select **cell D5**, type a comma, select **cell E5**, and then type **,2)** and tap ⌷Enter⌷.

22. With **cell G6** selected, click in the Formula Bar, replace 2 with **7** and tap ⌷Enter⌷, and then click **Undo** on the Quick Access toolbar.

23. Edit the formulas in the Formula Bar for the cells as indicated:

    - In **cell G7**, change 2 to **5**.
    - In **cell G8**, change 2 to **1**.

24. For each cell in the **range G5:G8**, edit the formulas in the Formula Bar to replace *DDB* with **SYD**.

25. Delete the contents in the **range G5:G8**.

26. Select **cell G5**, type **=SLN(** and select **cell C5**, type a comma, select **cell D5**, type a comma, select **cell E5**, and then type a closed parenthesis and tap ⌷Enter⌷.

27. Select **cell F5**, type **=0+** and select **cell G5**, and then tap ⌷Enter⌷.

28. Press ⌷Ctrl⌷+⌷Z⌷.

29. Repeat step 26 for each cell in the **range F6:F8**. Ensure that the correct accumulated depreciation amount is entered at the beginning of each formula (based on the information provided in the instructions).

30. Select **cell H5** and type an equals sign, select **cell C5** and type a minus sign, select **cell F5**, and tap ⌷Enter⌷.

31. Select **cell F9**, click the drop-down button, and choose **Sum**. Repeat for **cells G9 and H9**.

Sort and Filter a Table

32. Select **cell C7** and choose **Data→Sort & Filter→Sort Smallest to Largest**.

33. Click the drop-down arrow in **cell E4** and then uncheck the box next to **12** and click **OK**.

34. Click the drop-down arrow in **cell H4** and choose **Number Filters→Custom Filter**.

35. In the dialog box, click in the **Equals** box and choose **is greater than**, type **1500** in the box to the right, and click **OK**.

Create a Chart Using Quick Analysis

36. Highlight the **range A4:H9** and click the **Quick Analysis** button in the bottom-right corner of the range.

37. Choose the **Charts** category and click **More**.

38. Click the **All Charts** tab, choose **Pie** from the menu, and click **OK**.

39. Drag the chart so its top-left corner is in **cell A11**.

40. Choose **Chart Tools→Design→Data→Select Data**, highlight the **ranges A4:A8** and **H4:H8**, and click **OK**.

41. Click the filter button in **cell H4** and choose **Clear Filter From "Year-End Book Value."**

42. Apply the **Accounting** number format and zero decimal places to the **ranges C5:D9** and **F5:H9**.

43. Save and close your file.

EA6-R2 Complete a Depreciation Schedule for High-Up Corp.

In this exercise, you will create a depreciation schedule for High-Up Corp. using an Excel table. You will then sort, filter, and analyze the data. These fixed assets, with associated data as of 12/31/2015, were acquired prior to the current year.

Fixed Asset	Date of Acquisition	Cost	Salvage Value	Useful Life (years)	Accumulated Depreciation
Office Furniture	1/1/2014	$2,900	$100	7	$800
Machinery	1/1/2011	$5,100	$600	9	$2,500
Retail Equipment	1/1/2008	$9,200	$200	20	$3,600

High-Up Corp. also acquired lobby furniture on 1/1/2016. The Lobby Furniture had a cost of $6,300, an estimated salvage value of $800, and an estimated useful life of eleven years.

1. Open a **Blank Workbook** and save the file in your **Chapter 06** folder as: **EA6-R2-Depreciation-[YourName]**

2. Type **High-Up Corp.** in **cell A1** and **Depreciation Schedule** in **cell A2**.

3. Enter the fixed-asset data in the **range A4:F7**. Include the *Accumulated Depreciation* header but exclude its amounts. Also exclude the newly acquired asset for now.

4. Select **cell A4**, choose **Home→Styles→Format as Table→Dark Blue, Table Style Dark 2**, and click **OK**.

5. Choose **Table Tools→Design→Properties**, enter **Depreciation _ Schedule** for the table name, and tap Enter.

6. Choose **Table Tools→Design→Table Style Options→Total Row**.

7. One by one, select the cells listed and choose the indicated formula from the drop-down menu:

   - Cell C8: **Sum**
   - Cell D8: **Sum**
   - Cell E8: **Average**

8. Choose **Table Tools→Design→Table Style Options→Banded Rows** to deselect banded rows and then choose **Table Tools→Design→Table Style Options→ Banded Columns**.

Adjust Table Rows and Columns

9. Select **cell F7**, tap Tab, and enter the information for the newly acquired fixed asset into the **range A8:E8**.

10. Click in **cell F8** and choose **Home→Cells→Insert ▼→Insert Table Columns to the Right** two times.

11. Type **Depreciation Expense** in **cell G4** and **Year-End Book Value** in **cell H4**.

12. Wrap the text in **row 4**.

13. Use the Ribbon to set the width of **columns G:H** to **12** and the right-click method to set the width of **column F** to **14**.

14. Use the Ctrl key to select the **columns B** and **E** headers and then use the Ribbon to set the width of both to **12**.

15. Set the width of **column D** to **4** using any method and then choose **Home→Cells→ Format→AutoFit Column Width**.

16. Double-click between the **column A–B** headers to autofit column A.

17. Autofit the height of **row 4**.

18. Select **cell A5** and choose **File→Print**.

19. In the Settings area, choose **Portrait Orientation→Landscape Orientation** and then **Print Active Sheets→Print Selected Table**.

Utilize Depreciation Functions

20. Click the **Back** button to exit Backstage view and then navigate to the **Home** tab, if necessary.

21. Select **cell G5**, type **=SYD(** and select **cell C5**, type a comma, select **cell D5**, type a comma, select **cell E5**, and then type **,3)** and tap Enter.

22. With **cell G6** selected, click in the Formula Bar, replace *3* with **6** and tap Enter, and then click **Undo** on the Quick Access toolbar.

23. Edit the formulas in the Formula Bar for the cells as indicated:

    - In **cell G7**, change the *3* to **9**.
    - In **cell G8**, change the *3* to **1**.

24. For each cell in the **range G5:G8**, edit the formulas in the Formula Bar to replace *SYD* with **DDB**.

25. Delete the contents of the **range G5:G8**.

26. Select **cell G5**, type **=SLN(** and select **cell C5**, type a comma, select **cell D5**, type a comma, select **cell E5**, type a closed parenthesis, and then tap $\boxed{\text{Enter}}$.

27. Select **cell F5**, type **=800+** and select **cell G5**, and then tap $\boxed{\text{Enter}}$.

28. Click **Undo** on the Quick Access toolbar.

29. Repeat step 26 for each cell in the **range F6:F8**. Ensure that the correct accumulated depreciation amount is entered at the beginning of each formula (based on the information provided in the instructions).

30. Select **cell H5** and type an equals sign, select **cell C5** and type a minus sign, select **cell F5**, and tap $\boxed{\text{Enter}}$.

31. Select **cell F9**, click the drop-down button, and choose **Sum**. Repeat for **cells G9 and H9**.

Sort and Filter a Table

32. Select **cell E7** and choose **Data→Sort & Filter→Sort Largest to Smallest**.

33. Click the drop-down arrow in **cell D4**, uncheck the box next to **$600**, and click **OK**.

34. Click the drop-down arrow in **cell H4** and choose **Number Filters→Custom Filter**.

35. In the dialog box, click in the **Equals** box and choose **is less than**, type **5500** in the box to the right, and click **OK**.

Create a Chart Using Quick Analysis

36. Highlight the **range A4:H9** and click the **Quick Analysis** button in the bottom-right corner of the range.

37. Choose the **Charts** category and click **More**.

38. Click the **All Charts** tab, choose **Bar** from the menu, and click **OK**.

39. Click the chart below so its top-left corner is in **cell A11**.

40. Choose **Chart Tools→Design→Data→Select Data**, highlight the **ranges A4:A8** and **G4:G8**, and click **OK**.

41. Click the filter button in **cell H4** and choose **Clear Filter From "Year-End Book Value"**.

42. Apply the **Accounting** number format and zero decimal places to the **ranges C5:D9** and **F5:H9**.

43. Save and close your file.

Apply Your Skills

EA6-A1 Complete a Depreciation Schedule for JCW Supplies

In this exercise, you will create a depreciation schedule for JCW Supplies as of 10/31/2017 using an Excel table. You will then sort, filter, and analyze the data in the table. These fixed assets, with associated data as of 10/31/2016, were acquired prior to the current year.

Fixed Asset	Date of Acquisition	Cost	Salvage Value	Useful Life (years)	Accumulated Depreciation
Furniture	11/1/2014	$3,400	$400	6	$1,000
Office Equipment	11/1/2012	$7,000	$700	9	$2,800
Machinery	11/1/2015	$6,500	$100	4	$1,600

JCW Supplies also acquired office furniture on 11/1/2016. The office furniture had a cost of $1,200, an estimated salvage value of $100, and an estimated useful life of eleven years.

1. Open a **Blank Workbook** and save the file in your **Chapter 06** folder as: **EA6-A1-Depreciation-[YourName]**

2. Enter appropriate bank reconciliation headers in the **range A1:A2**; apply bold formatting.

3. Enter the fixed-asset data in the **range A4:F7**; for the accumulated depreciation, enter the title but not the dollar amounts.

4. Format the **range A4:F7** as a table using **Light Orange, Table Style Light 17** and add the table name **Depreciation _ Schedule**.

5. Add a total row that shows sums in **columns C:D** and an average in **column E**.

6. Turn on the **First Column** table style option.

Adjust Table Rows and Columns

7. From within **cell F7**, extend the table to add one additional row and then enter all fixed-asset information for the newly acquired asset.

8. In order, add these two columns to the far right of the table: **Depreciation Expense** and **Year-End Book Value**

9. Wrap the text in the headers.

10. Apply appropriate column widths and, if necessary, autofit the header row height.

11. Change the worksheet orientation to **Landscape** and set the option so only the table will print.

Use Depreciation Functions

12. Use an Excel function to calculate depreciation expense for each fixed asset under the double-declining balance depreciation method.

    Hint: Turn off calculated columns when entering the formulas for each fixed asset.

13. Replace the formula with one that uses an Excel function to calculate depreciation expense for each fixed asset under the straight-line depreciation method. Use calculated columns so you can enter the formula in a single row and have it automatically extend to all other fixed assets.

14. Use structured references to calculate the accumulated depreciation for each fixed asset.

15. Use structured references with calculated columns to calculate the year-end book value for each fixed asset.

16. Use the **Sum** function on **columns F:H**.

Sort and Filter a Table

17. Sort the table data based on salvage value from largest to smallest.

18. Filter the table to hide fixed assets with a cost of $7,000.

19. Clear all filters; apply a new filter that displays only fixed assets with a cost greater than $2,000.

Create a Chart Using Quick Analysis

20. Use **Quick Analysis** to create a column chart displaying the accumulated depreciation for each fixed asset presently displayed in the table. Position the chart below the table.

21. Apply the **Accounting** number format with zero decimal places to all dollar amounts.

22. Save and close your file.

EA6-A2 Complete a Depreciation Schedule for Furniture Resellers

In this exercise, you will create a depreciation schedule for Furniture Resellers as of 12/31/2016 using an Excel table. You will then sort, filter, and analyze the data in the table. These fixed assets, with associated data as of 12/31/2015, were acquired prior to the current year.

Fixed Asset	Date of Acquisition	Cost	Salvage Value	Useful Life (years)	Accumulated Depreciation
Machinery	1/1/2007	$8,200	$700	10	$6,750
Garage Equipment	1/1/2009	$11,000	$200	9	$8,400
Computers	1/1/2013	$4,000	$0	5	$2,400

Furniture Resellers also acquired lobby furniture on 1/1/2016. The lobby furniture had a cost of $2,000, an estimated salvage value of $400, and an estimated useful life of eight years.

1. Open a **Blank Workbook** and save the file in your **Chapter 06** folder as: **EA6-A2-Depreciation-[YourName]**

2. Enter appropriate bank reconciliation headers in the **range A1:A2**; apply italic formatting.

3. Enter the fixed-asset data in the **range A4:F7**; for the accumulated depreciation, enter the title but not the dollar amounts.

4. Format the **range A4:F7** as a table using **Blue, Table Style Dark 6** and add `Depreciation _ Schedule` as the table name.

5. Add a total row to the table that shows sums in **columns C:D** and an average in **column E**.

6. Turn on the **First Column** and **Last Column** table style options.

Adjust Table Rows and Columns

7. From within **cell F7**, extend the table to add one additional row and enter all fixed-asset information for the newly acquired asset.

8. Add **two columns** to the far right of the table with the headers `Depreciation Expense` and `Year-End Book Value`, in that order.

9. Wrap the text in the headers.

10. Apply appropriate column widths and, if necessary, autofit the header row height.

11. Change the orientation of the worksheet to **Landscape**.

Use Depreciation Functions

12. Use an Excel function to calculate depreciation expense for each fixed asset under the sum of the years' digits method.

    Hint: Turn off calculated columns when entering the formulas for each fixed asset.

13. Replace the formula with one that uses an Excel function to calculate depreciation expense for each fixed asset under the straight-line depreciation method. Use calculated columns so you can enter the formula in a single row and have it automatically extend to all other fixed assets.

14. Use structured references to calculate the accumulated depreciation for each fixed asset.

15. Use structured references with calculated columns to calculate the year-end book value for each fixed asset.

16. Use the **Sum** function on **columns F:H**.

Sort and Filter a Table

17. Sort the data based on accumulated depreciation from smallest to largest.

18. Filter the table to not display fixed assets with a salvage value of $200.

19. Clear all filters; apply a new filter that displays only fixed assets with a useful life greater than six years.

Create a Chart Using Quick Analysis

20. Use **Quick Analysis** to create a bar chart displaying the year-end book value for each fixed asset presently displayed in the table. Position the chart below the table.

21. Apply the **Accounting** number format with zero decimal places to all dollar amounts.

22. Save and close your file.

Extend Your Skills

EA6-E1 Complete a Depreciation Schedule for Bill's Bakery

In this exercise, you will complete a depreciation schedule for Bill's Bakery. You will use the techniques from this chapter to enter fixed-asset data in an Excel table, calculate depreciation expense, and analyze the table data. A primary goal is to ensure that the depreciation schedule can be easily understood by the end user.

Use this information (provided as of 8/31/2015) to create the depreciation schedule as of 8/31/2016 for Bill's Bakery using appropriate headers and a table in which all pertinent information is displayed.

Fixed Asset	Date of Acquisition	Cost	Salvage Value	Useful Life (years)	Accumulated Depreciation
Office Furniture	9/1/2013	$3,700	$200	7	$1,000
Oven	3/1/2012	$12,400	$2,400	10	$3,500
Equipment	9/1/2014	$24,000	$0	12	$2,000

Bill's Bakery uses the straight-line method of depreciation. In addition to the fixed assets shown, Bill's Bakery acquired a new refrigerator on 3/1/2016. It cost $7,700, has an estimated seven-year useful life, and has an estimated salvage value of $700.

Create the table so there is a column for each item (note that some figures may appear different in your 8/31/2016 table than they do in the 8/31/2015 chart). Include columns for the annual depreciation expense and year-end book value. Use a function to calculate depreciation expense and structured references when calculating the year-end book value. Sort the table by depreciation expense in descending order. Filter the table to display only assets for which the estimated salvage value is greater than $0. Last, use Quick Analysis to apply data bars to the figures in the Accumulated Depreciation column.

EA6-E2 Complete a Depreciation Schedule for Main Street Theatre

In this exercise, you will complete a depreciation schedule for Main Street Theatre. You will use the techniques from this chapter to enter fixed-asset data in an Excel table, calculate depreciation expense, and analyze the table data. A primary goal is to ensure that the depreciation schedule can be easily understood by the end user.

Use this information (provided as of 12/31/2015) to create a depreciation schedule as of 12/31/2016 for Main Street Theatre using appropriate headers and a table in which all pertinent information is displayed.

Fixed Asset	Date of Acquisition	Cost	Salvage Value	Useful Life (years)	Accumulated Depreciation
Theatre Equipment	1/1/2009	$18,000	$2,000	10	$14,254.55
Lobby Furniture	1/1/2012	$5,000	$500	5	$4,200
Carousel	1/1/2002	$10,000	$1,000	18	$8,473.68
Office Furniture	1/1/2014	$3,000	$200	7	$1,300

Main Street Theatre uses the sum of the years' digits method of depreciation. In addition to fixed assets shown, Main Street Theatre acquired new ticketing equipment on 1/1/2016. The ticketing equipment cost $8,000, has an estimated ten-year useful life, and has an estimated salvage value of $2,000.

Create the table so there is a column for each item (note that some figures may appear different in your 12/31/2016 table than they do in the 12/31/2015 chart). Include columns for the annual depreciation expense and year-end book value. Use a function to calculate depreciation expense and structured references when calculating the year-end book value. Sort the table by cost in ascending order. Filter the table to display only assets for which the estimated useful life is less than twelve years. Last, use Quick Analysis to apply an icon set to the figures in the Annual Depreciation Expense column.

EA6-E3 Complete a Depreciation Schedule for Woodworkers Corp.

In this exercise, you will complete a depreciation schedule for Woodworkers Corp. You will use the techniques from this chapter to enter fixed-asset data in an Excel table, calculate depreciation expense, and analyze the table data. A primary goal is to ensure that the depreciation schedule can be easily understood by the end user.

Use this information (provided as of 4/30/2015) to create a depreciation schedule as of 4/30/2016 for Woodworkers Corp. using appropriate headers and a table in which all pertinent information is displayed.

Fixed Asset	Date of Acquisition	Cost	Salvage Value	Useful Life (years)	Accumulated Depreciation
Office Equipment	5/1/2010	$24,000	$1,500	10	$16,135.68
Manufacturing Equipment	5/1/2008	$44,000	$8,000	20	$22,954.94
Office Furniture	5/1/2013	$5,000	$500	6	$2,777.78

Woodworkers Corp. uses the double-declining balance method of depreciation. In addition to the fixed assets shown, Woodworkers Corp. acquired new lobby furniture on 5/1/2015. The lobby furniture cost $15,000, has an estimated fifteen-year useful life, and has an estimated salvage value of $1,000.

Create the table so there is a column for each item (note that some figures may appear different in your 4/30/2016 table than they do in the 4/30/2015 chart). Include columns for the annual depreciation expense and year-end book value. Use a function to calculate depreciation expense and structured references when calculating the year-end book value. Sort the table by accumulated depreciation in ascending order. Filter the table to display only assets for which the date of acquisition is after 1/1/2009. Last, use Quick Analysis to create a bar chart displaying the annual depreciation for each of the displayed fixed assets.

Critical Thinking

EA6-C1 Discuss Using Tables to Consolidate Accounting Data

As you have seen in this chapter, fixed assets can be efficiently summarized in an Excel table. Excel tables can also be used to organize and examine other accounting-related data as well. The effective use of Excel in an accounting environment entails the identification of all areas in which features, such as Excel tables, can provide a benefit to the end user.

Write a paragraph of at least five sentences to identify three types of accounting data (other than fixed assets/depreciation) that can be summarized in an Excel table. Write a second paragraph of at least five sentences to discuss how the use of an Excel table would facilitate analyses of each of your identified data types.

EA6-C2 Discuss Performing Quick Analyses on Table Data

While tables allow for the straightforward accumulation of data, this may not be the only goal when completing an accounting-related worksheet. As you have seen in this chapter, the Quick Analysis button provides an easy method through which the table data can be analyzed. The Quick Analysis options can also be used to highlight certain data points in a table such that the end user can easily identify pertinent information.

Identify one type of accounting data that can be displayed in a table (aside from the fixed-asset/depreciation data examined in this chapter). If you prefer, your selection can be one of the sets of data identified in Critical Thinking EA6-C1. Write a paragraph of at least four sentences in which you identify at least three types of analyses (accessible via the Quick Analysis button) that would be logical to perform on your identified data set. Write a second paragraph of at least five sentences to discuss why these analyses would provide a benefit to the end user.

Payroll Register

7

Payrolls

LEARNING OBJECTIVES

- Create a payroll register

- Use the ROUND and IF functions

- Distinguish between absolute cell references and mixed cell references

- Use VLOOKUP and HLOOKUP functions

- Improve worksheet layout readability

As your worksheets become more complex and the interrelation between financial figures increases, you can use advanced functions to automate calculations. For example, the ROUND function can eliminate unnecessary decimal places from figures, the IF function facilitates calculations that are dependent on the result of a logical test, and LOOKUP functions allow for the correct figure to be identified from an array of options. Absolute and mixed cell references can be used in conjunction with functions. In this chapter, you will use advanced functions to create a payroll register. You will calculate figures, such as total earnings, using the ROUND function, and you'll use the IF function to calculate total earnings and a nested IF function to calculate Social Security tax. Absolute and mixed cell references will be used in multiple locations, including within calculations for Medicare tax and voluntary withholdings. You will examine VLOOKUP and HLOOKUP functions as you modify overtime earnings. Last, you will enhance the layout of your worksheet.

PROJECT   City Music World

City Music World is a retail store that sells musical equipment and offers lessons for beginning and experienced musicians. The company has a number of employees and follows the common practice of summarizing payroll data in a payroll register, which maintains employee hours worked, earnings, deductions, and net pay. You have been asked to populate the payroll register and structure the required elements in an easy-to-read manner.

In this chapter, you will populate a payroll register using functions, including ROUND, IF, VLOOKUP, and HLOOKUP. You will also use absolute and mixed cell references in your formulas. Last, you will improve the appearance of the payroll register so the end user can quickly understand the data and identify the key elements.

Payroll Register

Pay Period   1/31/2016
Pay Date   2/3/2016

Employee Name	Regular Hours	Regular Rate	Regular Earnings	Overtime Hours	Overtime Rate	Overtime Earnings	Total Earnings	FWT	SWT	Social Security	Medicare	Hospital Donation	School Donation	Check Number	Net Pay
						Earnings				Deductions					
Lassiter, Z	40	$ 11.00	$ 440.00	5	$ 16.50	$ 82.50	$ 522.50	$ 16.00	$ 10.00	$ 32.40	$ 7.58	$ 10.45	$ 15.68	507	$ 430.39
Gomez, J	40	$ 11.00	$ 440.00	0	$ 16.50	N/A	$ 440.00	$ 17.00	$ 12.00	$ -	$ 6.38	$ 4.40	$ 8.80	508	$ 391.42
Applebaum, X	40	$ 11.00	$ 440.00	0	$ 16.50	N/A	$ 440.00	$ 11.00	$ 7.00	$ 15.50	$ 6.38	$ 4.40	$ 8.80	509	$ 386.92
Cerino, L	40	$ 11.00	$ 440.00	9	$ 16.50	$ 148.50	$ 588.50	$ 24.00	$ 16.00	$ 36.49	$ 8.53	$ 14.71	$ 20.60	510	$ 468.17
Miller, R	40	$ 11.00	$ 440.00	3	$ 16.50	$ 49.50	$ 489.50	$ 22.00	$ 15.00	$ 30.35	$ 7.10	$ 7.34	$ 12.24	511	$ 395.47
Totals:			$ 2,200.00			$ 280.50	$ 2,480.50	$ 90.00	$ 60.00	$ 114.74	$ 35.97	$ 41.30	$ 66.12		$ 2,072.37

Total Earnings	Hosp. Don.	Sch. Don.
$ 400	1.0%	2.0%
$ 450	1.5%	2.5%
$ 500	2.0%	3.0%
$ 550	2.5%	3.5%
$ 600	3.0%	4.0%

	SS%	Medicare %
	6.20%	1.45%
SS Wage Base		
$ 118,500		

Name	Prior Earnings
Lassiter, Z	$ 8,900
Gomez, J	$ 214,000
Applebaum, X	$ 118,250
Cerino, L	$ 96,500
Miller, R	$ 51,000

Accounting Refresher: Payroll Register

For many businesses, salaries and wages represent one of the largest expenses incurred each year. To maintain control over this important asset, and to ensure compliance with federal and state tax withholding requirements, a **payroll register** should be created for each pay period. The top of the payroll register contains the pay period ending date and the employees' pay date. The main body of the register displays earnings, deductions, and **net pay** information. Additional data, such as tax rates and incentive plan rates (often used in earnings and/or deduction formulas), can be inserted below the payroll register.

Pay Period Ending Date and Pay Date

You create an individual payroll register for each pay period. A pay period represents the period of time for which the employees are being compensated. The pay period ending date, which is displayed at the top of the payroll register, is the final date of the pay period. The pay date, which is the date employees receive their paychecks, can be on or after the pay period ending date. Each business determines the schedule on which paychecks are distributed—and then must consistently follow that schedule.

Earnings Section of the Payroll Register

In the payroll register, data for each employee is held in a single row. The earnings section is located adjacent to the employee name column on the far left of the worksheet. The earnings section contains all information needed to calculate total earnings for each employee, such as the number of regular and overtime hours worked and regular/overtime wage rates. Regular earnings are then determined by multiplying the regular hours worked by the regular wage rate. Similarly, overtime earnings are determined by multiplying the overtime hours worked by the overtime wage rate. Last, total earnings (also referred to as **gross pay**) represent the sum of regular earnings and overtime earnings.

Deductions Section of the Payroll Register

Employee taxes are paid as part of a pay-as-you-go system, meaning that taxes must be paid as the employee earns compensation. The employee is not permitted to, for example, wait until year end and pay all taxes owed at once. To facilitate this process, employers are required to withhold taxes from employees and to periodically remit these taxes to the appropriate governmental entity. Among these taxes are federal income tax, state income tax, Social Security tax, and Medicare tax.

- **Federal withholding tax** Also referred to as FWT or federal income tax, this tax is collected by the federal government to fund a range of governmental agencies. An employer can use either the **wage-bracket method** or the **percentage method** to determine the proper withholding amount. In either case, the employer uses tax tables, which are updated and published annually by the Internal Revenue Service (IRS), to determine the proper amount to withhold from taxable pay.

(continued)

- **State income tax** This tax is similar to federal income tax, but the tax is used to fund operations at the state level. Just as tax tables are used to determine the proper amount of federal income tax to withhold from gross pay, state-specific tax tables are used to determine this figure for state income tax.

TIP! While most states do collect state income tax, there are a handful that do not at all or that only collect taxes on dividend and interest income.

- **Social security tax** Also referred to as old age, survivors, and disability insurance, or OASDI, this tax funds the social security system, which pays benefits to retired or disabled workers and their dependents and survivors. This tax is subject to an income threshold. In 2016, for example, it was calculated as 6.2% of the first $118,500 earned during the year. The $118,500 threshold is referred to as the social security tax wage base.

- **Medicare tax** Also referred to as hospital insurance or HI, this tax funds the Medicare federal health insurance program that covers individuals 65 years of age or older and certain disabled individuals. This tax is calculated as 1.45% of all employee earnings.

In addition to these taxes, each of which is a **mandatory deduction**, employees can choose to be subject to any of a number of **voluntary deductions**. Among the amounts that employees can choose to have withheld from gross pay are those for union dues, retirement plan payments, medical plan payments, cafeteria plan payments, and charitable donations.

Net Pay

The final column in the payroll register displays net pay, which is the amount an employee receives in his/her paycheck. It's calculated by subtracting all mandatory and voluntary deductions from the total earnings (gross pay).

NOTE! The paycheck number is usually listed in the column to the left of that displaying net pay.

Additional Data

Depending on the calculations required by an employer, it may be necessary to include additional data adjacent to the payroll register. Typically, this information is located below the payroll register, and it's used to automate the earnings and tax calculations. For example, if employees are offered the opportunity to have a percentage of total earnings withheld as charitable contributions, the different percentages at which these contributions can be withheld are listed below the payroll register.

Creating Formulas with ROUND and IF Functions

The ROUND and IF functions are useful when calculating figures for a payroll register. As most figures in a payroll register are expressed in dollar amounts, the ROUND function can be used to ensure that cents in these figures are expressed properly (with two decimal places). The IF function is used when different calculations could be appropriate in a single cell. This can be useful when calculating various taxes, including Social Security tax, for which different calculations may be appropriate as employees approach the annual wage base.

ROUND Function

Excel's ROUND function rounds a number or calculation to the desired number of decimal places. This is distinct from the Increase Decimal and Decrease Decimal buttons in the Number group on the Home tab. The ROUND function *modifies* the entry in a cell to include only the specified number of decimal places, while the Increase Decimal and Decrease Decimal buttons only alter the number of decimal places displayed (they don't change the cell entry).

For example, consider a cell containing the number 6.348. If you apply the ROUND function to reduce the number of decimal places to two, the cell would show 6.35 and the entry within the cell would be changed to 6.35. Any formulas created with the cell would consider 6.35 in the calculations.

If you instead used the Decrease Decimal command, the cell would display 6.35 but the cell entry would remain at 6.348. Any formulas created with the cell would consider 6.348 in the calculations.

ROUND Function Syntax

The generic elements of the ROUND function look like this.

ROUND(number, num_digits)

The *number* argument is the figure that you would like to round. It can be expressed as a number, calculation or cell reference.

The *num_digits* argument is the number of decimal places to be displayed. If negative, the figure will be rounded to the left of the decimal point.

> ⚡ Formulas→Insert Function→Math & Trig→ROUND

IF Function

Excel's IF function displays a value or text based on a logical test you create. The IF function will display one of two results, depending on the outcome of your logical test. For example, when calculating Social Security tax for an employee, the IF function could be used to display either total earnings multiplied by 6.2% (if the employee has not exceeded the Social Security tax wage base) or $0 (if the employee has previously exceeded the Social Security tax wage base).

IF Function Syntax

The generic elements of the IF function look like this.

IF(logical_test, value_if_true, value_if_false)

The *Logical_Test* argument is the condition being checked using a comparison operator, such as =, >, <, >=, <=, or <> (not equal to).

The *Value_If_True* argument is the value, text in quotation (") marks, or calculation returned if the logical test result is found to be true.

The *Value_If_False* argument is the value, text in quotation (") marks, or calculation returned if the logical test result is found to be false.

NOTE!   If you type the IF formula directly in its cell, you must add quotation marks around text arguments. If you use the Insert Function command, Excel will add the quotation marks for you.

> ↗ Formulas→Insert Function→Logical→IF

How the IF Function Works

Consider the formula =IF(F2>=118500, 0, E2*6.2%). Excel performs the logical test to determine whether the value in cell F2 is greater than or equal to the Social Security Wage Base of $118,500. A value of 118,500 or more would evaluate as true. A value less than 118,500, a blank cell, or text entered in cell F2 would all evaluate as false. If the logical test proves true, the value 0 (zero) displays in the formula cell because the employee is not subject to Social Security tax if prior period earnings exceed $118,500. If the logical test proves false, the calculation E2*6.2% is performed and the result displays in the formula cell. Note that 6.2% represents the Social Security tax rate in this example.

G2	▾	⋮	✕	✓	*fx*	=IF(F2>=118500, 0, E2*6.2%)	

	E	F	G	H
1	Gross Pay	Prior Period Earnings	Social Security Tax	
2	$ 1,750	$ 112,300	$ 109	

1

G2	▾	⋮	✕	✓	*fx*	=IF(F2>=118500, 0, E2*6.2%)	

	E	F	G	H
1	Gross Pay	Prior Period Earnings	Social Security Tax	
2	$ 1,750	$ 122,800	$ -	

2

1. This formula results in tax being calculated in cell G2, as prior period earnings are below $118,500.

2. This formula results in no tax in cell G2, as prior period earnings exceed $118,500.

You can also use the IF function to display a text message or leave the cell blank. Two examples that display text are shown in the following table.

Formula	Action If True	Action If False
IF(F3>0, "Worked Overtime", "No Overtime")	The text *Worked Overtime* displays	The text *No Overtime* displays
IF(D6<=400, "", "High Withholding")	The cell displays blank	The text *High Withholding* displays

TIP! If you type "" (quotation marks with no space between) as the value_if_true or value_if_false argument, Excel will return a blank cell.

Develop Your Skills EA7-D1

In this exercise, you will continue to populate an existing payroll register by completing the Overtime Earnings, Total Earnings, FWT, and SWT columns. Your manager has requested that N/A be displayed in the Overtime Earnings column for any employee who did not work overtime hours.

Use this information to complete the FWT and SWT columns.

Employee Name	Federal Withholding Tax (FWT)	State Withholding Tax (SWT)
Lassiter, Z	$16	$10
Gomez, J	$17	$12
Applebaum, X	$11	$7
Cerino, L	$24	$16
Miller, R	$22	$15

1. Open **EA7-D1-Payroll** from your **Chapter 07** folder and save it as:
   EA7-D1-Payroll-[YourName]

2. Select **cell H9**, choose **Formulas→Function Library→Insert Function**, select the **Logical** category, choose the **IF** function, and click **OK**.

3. Follow these steps to set up the IF function:

A. Type **F9=0** in the **Logical_Test** box.

B. Click in the **Value_If_True** box and type: **"N/A"**

C. Click in the **Value_If_False** box and type: **F9*G9**

D. Click **OK**.

This formula ensures that for those employees who did not work overtime hours, N/A will be displayed. For employees who did work overtime hours, overtime earnings will be calculated.

4. Double-click the fill handle at the bottom-right corner of the active cell.

The formula is copied to rows below the active cell for which adjacent data exists.

5. In **cell I9**, type: **=Round(IF(H9="N/A", E9, E9+H9), 2)**

*You have combined the ROUND and IF functions in one formula, which is called **nesting**. You have indicated that Excel should round the result of the IF function in cell I9. The 2 at the end of the formula indicates that the result should be rounded to two decimal places. Note that, for this formula, the only time rounding may be necessary is when an employee works and is given credit for a partial hour at either the regular or overtime rate.*

6. Select **cell I9** and double-click the fill handle in the bottom-right corner.

7. Enter the federal and state withholding tax figures in the **range J9:K13**.

8. Save your file.

Unless otherwise directed, always keep your file open at the end of each exercise.

Using Nested IF Functions and Absolute/Mixed Cell References

A nested IF function expands on the flexibility of an IF function by allowing for more than two possible outcomes in a single formula. Each cell reference in these (and other) formulas must be one of three types: relative, absolute, or mixed. We have been looking at relative cell references thus far. Now you will see that when formulas are copied, it is vital that absolute and mixed cell references are used properly.

Nested IF Function

In a nested formula, one function is contained within another function. For example, the formula =SUM(25, AVERAGE(B2:H2)) nests the AVERAGE function within the SUM function. It results in 25 being added to the average of the cells in the range B2:H2.

A single IF function is used when there can be only one of two results. If additional results are possible, a nested IF function can be used. A nested IF function uses one IF function within another IF function.

The "How the IF Function Works" section used an example involving the Social Security Wage Base of $118,500. A result of $0 was displayed if cell F2 was greater than or equal to $118,500. If cell F2 was less than $118,500, cell E2 was multiplied by 6.2%. This formula did not account for one possible circumstance: What if the employee's current period earnings, when combined with prior period earnings, cross the $118,500 threshold during the pay period? In that instance, only the portion of current period earnings that fall below the cumulative $118,500 wage base is subject to Social Security tax. As there are three possible results that could be displayed in this instance, a nested IF function is appropriate.

| H2 | ▾ | ⋮ | ✕ | ✓ | *fx* | =IF(F2>=G2,0,IF(E2+F2<G2,E2*6.2%,(G2-F2)*6.2%)) |

◢	E	F	G	H	I
1	Gross Pay	Prior Period Earnings	SS Wage Base	Social Security Tax	
2	$ 1,750	$ 122,800	$ 118,500	$ -	

The second argument in the first IF function returns a value of $0 here.

| H2 | ▾ | ⋮ | ✕ | ✓ | *fx* | =IF(F2>=G2,0,IF(E2+F2<G2,E2*6.2%,(G2-F2)*6.2%)) |

◢	E	F	G	H	I
1	Gross Pay	Prior Period Earnings	SS Wage Base	Social Security Tax	
2	$ 1,750	$ 47,200	$ 118,500	$ 108.50	

The second argument in the second IF function returns a value of $108.50 here.

| H2 | ▼ | : | ✕ ✓ | *fx* | =IF(F2>=G2,0,IF(E2+F2<G2,E2*6.2%,(G2-F2)*6.2%)) |

◢	E	F	G	H	I
1	Gross Pay	Prior Period Earnings	SS Wage Base	Social Security Tax	
2	$ 1,750	$ 118,300	$ 118,500	$ 12.40	

The third argument in the second IF function returns a value of $12.40 here.

By nesting this second IF function in the Value_If_False argument of the first IF function, the three possible results are accounted for. If the logical test in the first IF function is true, then the Value_If_True in the first IF function is displayed. If the Logical_Test in the first IF function is false, then the result of the Value_If_False section of the first IF function is followed. The result of this Value_If_False section is based on the second nested IF function; therefore, two different answers could be displayed, depending on the result returned from the second IF function.

Absolute Cell References

By default, a cell reference in a formula is a relative cell reference, meaning that the location of the cell reference is *relative* to the cell that contains the formula. For example, if you enter =A3–B3 in cell C3, Excel notes that cell A3 is two cells to the

| C4 | ▼ | : | ✕ ✓ | *fx* | =A4-B4 |

◢	A	B	C
3	500	200	300
4	1200	400	800
5			

left of the formula and cell B3 is one cell to the left of the formula. When you copy the formula, the cell references update automatically. So, if you copy the formula to cell C4, the new formula would be =A4–B4.

You may not want references updated when a formula is moved or copied. In this instance, you can use an **absolute cell reference**, which always refers to the same cell, even when the formula is copied to another location. You create

| C4 | ▼ | : | ✕ ✓ | *fx* | =$A$3-$B$3 |

◢	A	B	C	D
3	500	200	300	
4	1200	400	300	
5				

absolute references by placing dollar signs in front of the column and row components of the reference. For example, if the formula =$A$3–$B$3 were entered in cell C3 and then copied to cell C4, the formula within cell C4 would still read =$A$3–$B$3.

Mixed Cell References

Mixed cell references have a combination of relative and absolute references. For example, the reference $C1 is a combination of an absolute reference to column C and a relative reference to row 1. This can be useful when copying a formula both across a row and down a column.

▲	A	B	C
1		400	600
2	0.05	=$A2*B$1	=$A2*C$1
3	0.1	=$A3*B$1	=$A3*C$1
4	0.15	=$A4*B$1	=$A4*C$1
5	0.2	=$A5*B$1	=$A5*C$1
6	0.25	=$A6*B$1	=$A6*C$1

Here the formula in cell B2 is copied to the range B2:C6. Note the difference in location of the dollar sign between the A2 and B1 cell references.

TIP! The F4 function key can be used to insert the dollar signs in a cell reference. The first press places dollar signs in front of the column and row components of the cell reference, a second tap places a dollar sign in front of only the row component, a third tap places a dollar sign in front of only the column component, and a fourth tap removes all dollar signs.

This table indicates what happens to different types of cell references when their formulas are copied to other locations.

Cell Reference	Type	Copy-and-Paste Action	Result When Pasted
B6	Relative	One column to the right	C6
B6	Relative	One row down	B7
$B$6	Absolute	One column to the right	$B$6
$B$6	Absolute	One row down	$B$6
$B6	Mixed	One column to the right	$B6
$B6	Mixed	One row down	$B7
B$6	Mixed	One column to the right	C$6
B$6	Mixed	One row down	B$6

Develop Your Skills EA7-D2

In this exercise, you will calculate social security tax for each employee using a nested IF function. You will also use both absolute and mixed formatting within formulas for social security tax and Medicare tax.

1. Save your file as: **EA7-D2-Payroll-[YourName]**

   Do not complete the cell entries unless directed.

2. In **cell L9**, type: **=ROUND(IF(I27>L24, 0,**

This first portion of this IF function instructs Excel to enter 0 in the active cell if the employee's prior earnings exceed $118,500. As $118,500 is the Social Security Wage Base, the employee does not owe Social Security taxes if he/she has already earned more than this amount during the current year. It's standard to begin tax calculations with the ROUND function.

3. Continue typing **IF(I27+I9<L24, I9*L22,** in the formula for **cell L9**.

You have nested a second IF function in the Value_If_False section of the first IF function. So, if the first IF function is not true (if prior earnings don't exceed the $118,500 wage base), then Excel will turn to the second IF function to determine what to enter in cell L9. The Logical_Test is whether prior earnings plus total earnings for the current period are less than $118,500. If so, all current period earnings are subject to Social Security tax and, therefore, the Value_If_True argument of the second IF Function dictates that cell L9 should display total earnings multiplied by the Social Security tax rate of 6.2%.

4. Type **(L24-I27)*L22)), 2)** and then tap Enter.

In this Value_If_False argument of the second IF function, the formula dictates what should be displayed if prior earnings do not exceed $118,500 and if prior earnings plus total earnings for the current period are not below $118,500. In this instance, the wage base is exceeded during the current period, so only the portion of earnings below the wage base is subject to Social Security tax. To determine the portion of earnings below the wage base, subtract prior period earnings (cell I27) from the wage base (cell L24). Then, multiply the result by the Social Security tax rate (cell L22) to arrive at the correct social security tax amount. The two closed parentheses at the end of the formula close the second and first IF function, respectively.

5. Select **cell L9** and double-click the fill handle at the bottom-right corner.

The Social Security tax does not populate properly for the remaining employees because both the Social Security tax rate (cell L22) and the Social Security Wage Base (cell L24) are relative cell references—so they change when the formula is copied down column L. You will now add absolute formatting for these cells to correct this issue.

6. Select **cell L9**; in the Formula Bar, type **$** in front of the column and row references for the first two instances of *L24*.

The first two instances of L24 should now appear as $L$24.

7. With **cell L9** still active, click anywhere in the first instance of *L22* in the Formula Bar and tap F4.

The relative cell reference L22 has been changed to the absolute cell reference $L$22.

8. Insert absolute formatting for the final instances of *L24* and *L22* in the formula.

9. Select **cell L9** and double-click the fill handle.

The social security tax is now properly calculated for each employee.

10. In **cell M9**, type **=ROUND(** and click **cell I9**, type ***** and click **cell M22**, and then tap F4.

11. Complete the formula with **, 2)** and then double-click the fill handle in **cell M9**.

12. Save your file.

Using VLOOKUP and HLOOKUP Functions

The VLOOKUP (Vertical Lookup) and HLOOKUP (Horizontal Lookup) functions retrieve a piece of data from a lookup table located in the same worksheet, a separate worksheet, or a different workbook.

Total Earnings	Hosp. Don.	Sch. Don.
$ 400	1.0%	2.0%
$ 450	1.5%	2.5%
$ 500	2.0%	3.0%
$ 550	2.5%	3.5%
$ 600	3.0%	4.0%

Total Earnings	$ 400	$ 450	$ 500	$ 550	$ 600
Hosp. Don.	1.0%	1.5%	2.0%	2.5%	3.0%
Sch. Don.	2.0%	2.5%	3.0%	3.5%	4.0%

The same data arranged in a vertical lookup table (left) and a horizontal lookup table (right)

Lookup Function Syntax

The structure of the HLOOKUP and VLOOKUP functions looks like this.

HLOOKUP(lookup value, table array, column index number, [range lookup])

VLOOKUP(lookup value, table array, column index number, [range lookup])

The *lookup value* is the value in the worksheet to be looked up in the first column of the table array.

The *table array* refers to the cell range containing the lookup table, which may be expressed as absolute cell references or a defined name. Excel searches for the data to be retrieved within this array.

The *column index number* refers to the column number in the table array that contains the corresponding data to be retrieved.

The *range lookup* is optional. It's a logical value that specifies a search for an exact or approximate value in the table array (TRUE, the default) or an exact match only (FALSE).

> ⤴ Formulas→Defined Names→Define Name

How the VLOOKUP Function Works

In the formula =VLOOKUP($I9,Donation_Percentages,2), cell I9 contains the lookup value, the defined name Donation_Percentages indicates the table array in which the search takes place, and the number 2 (column index number) indicates that the corresponding award rate will be retrieved from the second column of the lookup table. The search is conducted down the first column of the table array until the highest value not greater than the lookup value is located.

WARNING! Defined names are meant to describe the cell or range to which they are assigned. However, you cannot use spaces or cell references when creating a defined name.

5

| N9 | | ▼ | : | × | ✓ | f_x | =VLOOKUP($I9, Donation_Percentages, 2)*$I9 |

4

	I	J	K	L	M	N	O
6				**Deductions**			
7	Total	FWT	SWT	Social	Medicare	Hospital	School
8	Earnings			Security		Donation	Donation
9	$ 522.50	$ 16.00	$ 10.00	$ 32.40	$ 7.58	$ 10.45	$ 15.68
10	$ 440.00	$ 17.00	$ 12.00	$ -	$ 6.38	$ 4.40	$ 8.80
11	$ 440.00	$ 11.00	$ 7.00	$ 15.50	$ 6.38	$ 4.40	$ 8.80
12	$ 588.50	$ 24.00	$ 16.00	$ 36.49	$ 8.53	$ 14.71	$ 20.60
13	$ 489.50	$ 22.00	$ 15.00	$ 30.35	$ 7.10	$ 7.34	$ 12.24
14							
15							
16	$ 2,480.50	$ 90.00	$ 60.00	$ 114.74	$ 35.97	$ 41.30	$ 66.12

1

	Total Earnings	Hosp. Don.	Sch. Don.
19			
20	$ 400	1.0%	2.0%
21	$ 450	1.5%	2.5%
22	$ 500	2.0%	3.0%
23	$ 550	2.5%	3.5%
24	$ 600	3.0%	4.0%

2   **3**

1. Cell N9 contains the VLOOKUP formula.

2. Excel searches the first column of the lookup table and stops at row 22 because the lookup value is at least $500 but not $550.

3. The hospital donation percentage of 2% here is returned to cell N9.

4. The VLOOKUP result of 2% is multiplied by total earnings in cell I9.

5. The lookup value is the first argument in the VLOOKUP formula.

When a lookup formula will be copied to other cells, the cell range of the table array should be expressed in the formula as a defined name or absolute cell references. This can be done either through the Ribbon or the Name Box, where the defined name can be easily entered.

| Donation_Percentages ▼ | ⋮ | × | ✓ | *fx* | 400 |

◢	A	B	C	D	E
1					
2		Total Earnings	Hosp. Don.	Sch. Don.	
3		$ 400	1.0%	2.0%	
4		$ 450	1.5%	2.5%	
5		$ 500	2.0%	3.0%	
6		$ 550	2.5%	3.5%	
7		$ 600	3.0%	4.0%	
8					

The Name Box displays the defined name for the range B3:D7.

When the range lookup argument is TRUE (either by default or written out), the table array must be sorted on the first column from lowest to highest (A to Z). This sorting is unnecessary when the range lookup argument is FALSE. Note that when FALSE is specified as the range lookup argument and an exact match cannot be located within the table array, *#N/A* is displayed in the formula cell.

Develop Your Skills EA7-D3

In this exercise, you will use a VLOOKUP function to complete the donation columns in the payroll register. You will then populate the final two columns of the payroll register.

Use this information to complete the Check Number column of the register.

Employee Name	Check Number
Lassiter, Z	507
Gomez, J	508
Applebaum, X	509
Cerino, L	510
Miller, R	511

1. Save your file as: **EA7-D3-Payroll-[YourName]**
2. Highlight the **range B25:D29** and choose **Formulas→Defined Names→Define Name**.
3. In the **Name** box of the New Name window, type **Donation _ Percentages** and click **OK**.

   This defined name will be used in a LOOKUP function to populate the donation columns.

4. In **cell N9**, type **=ROUND(VLOOKUP(** but do not complete the entry.

   The donation amounts are based on a percentage of total earnings. These percentages are provided in the range C25:D29. Because they are listed in a table array, you will use the VLOOKUP function to populate these cells. The ROUND function begins the formula so that the ultimate result will be rounded to two decimal places.

5. Continue with the formula by typing **I9, do** and double-clicking **Donation_Percentages** from the list that appears; type **,2)*I9, 2)** and tap Enter.

   The lookup function searches for the highest figure not exceeding the value in cell I9 (total earnings) from the table array and returns the percentage in the second column of the array. This percentage is multiplied by total earnings in cell I9 and the result is rounded to two decimal places.

6. Select **cell N9**, click within the first instance of *I9* in the Formula Bar, and tap F4 three times. Click before the *I* in the second instance of *I9*, and then type **$** and tap Enter.

   You want to be able to copy this formula to all other cells in the two donation columns. For this, you need a mixed reference for cell I9. The dollar sign is placed in front of the I in each instance of I9 so total earnings in column I are always referenced in the formula. Each 9 does not require a dollar sign because the row number should change when the formula is copied.

7. Copy **cell N9** and paste to **cell O9**.

   Because the formula includes a mixed reference for cell I9, each instance of cell I9 is unchanged as the formula was copied one cell to the right. Therefore, the result of the formula is also unchanged. Next you will modify the formula in cell O9 to look up the percentage in the third row of the table array.

8. In the Formula Bar, replace the *2* in the third argument of the VLOOKUP function (the first instance of *2* in the formula) with **3**.

9. Highlight the **range N9:O9** and double-click the fill handle at the bottom-right corner of the active cell.

10. In the **range P9:P13**, type the appropriate check number for each employee.

11. In **cell Q9**, type: **=I9-sum(J9:O9)**

    This formula is one of the primary reasons why you have used the ROUND function in previous formulas. If you hadn't, then fractions of cents from the previous calculations could be summed in this formula, resulting in an incorrect total. Since all previous calculations were rounded, you are calculating a rounded net pay figure now.

12. Copy **cell Q9**, highlight the **range Q10:Q13**, and choose **Home→Clipboard→Paste**.

13. In **cell H16**, type **=SUM(** and highlight the **range H9:H13**, type a closed parenthesis, and then tap Enter.

14. Copy **cell H16** and paste to the **range I16:O16** and then to **cell Q16**.

15. Save your file.

Ensuring Effective Worksheet Layout

An Excel worksheet is designed to convey information to the end user. Whether creating financial statements, a payroll register, or any other accounting-related worksheet, the final product will be reviewed by a variety of interested parties. As such, a primary goal of any worksheet is to provide key data in an easily understandable manner.

A common mistake is to focus exclusively on the content of a worksheet without giving sufficient attention to how the information is presented. Of course, it's vital to ensure the accuracy of the worksheet data, but if the end user can't quickly comprehend this data, the worksheet will not achieve its desired goal. Spending time on worksheet layout and appearance is key to maximizing worksheet value.

Enhancing Worksheet Readability

When examining worksheet design, there are very few hard-and-fast rules. Some techniques work better in certain worksheets than in others. However, the following are a few general rules that should be followed in most circumstances:

- Align data such that tables, lists, and charts begin in the same column. If such an alignment is not possible, ensure that worksheet elements are displayed adjacent to one another.

- Distinguish between different data sets with borders.

- Separate different sets of data with blank rows and columns. The width of these columns and/or height of these rows can be reduced to keep blank space in the worksheet to a reasonable level.

1

	A	B	C	D
1				
2		Employee Name	Net Pay	
3		Williams, H.	$ 650	
4		Allens, B.	$ 820	
5		Strong, K.	$ 1,430	
6		Johnson, W.	$ 1,190	
7		Total	$ 4,090	
8			Donation Type	Donation Percentage
9			Hospital Donation	2.0%
10			School Donation	1.5%
11			Community Donation	2.5%
12				

	A	B	C
2		Employee Name	Net Pay
3		Williams, H.	$ 650
4		Allens, B.	$ 820
5		Strong, K.	$ 1,430
6		Johnson, W.	$ 1,190
7		Total	$ 4,090
9		Donation Type	Donation Percentage
10		Hospital Donation	2.0%
11		School Donation	1.5%
12		Community Donation	2.5%
13			

2

1. The data is illogically structured here.

2. Layout guidelines, Wrap Text, and other adjustments have been made here.

Highlighting Key Headers and Data

While the specific elements of a worksheet for which highlighting is appropriate will change from one Excel file to another, every worksheet contains a certain number of key components. Consideration must be given to which elements will allow the end user to arrive at a logical conclusion based on the worksheet data. As the goal is to draw the end user's attention to these elements, they should be highlighted. Additionally, headers and titles should be easily distinguishable from other content. Here are some guidelines to help ensure key data is highlighted and headers have a distinct appearance:

- Use bold/italic formatting; different font types, sizes, colors; and cell highlighting to set headers apart from other content. Use a maximum of two elements, though, as more will create a cluttered appearance.

- As is standard in accounting-related worksheets, use a bottom border below data for which a calculation is being performed and a bottom double border below data representing the final figure in a column.

- Use conditional formatting to highlight at most one set of key data.

	A	B	C
1			
2		Employee Name	Net Pay
3		Williams, H.	$ 650
4		Allens, B.	$ 820
5		Strong, K.	$ 1,430
6		Johnson, W.	$ 1,190
7		Total	$ 4,090
8			
9			
10		Donation Type	Donation Percentage
11		Hospital Donation	2.0%
12		School Donation	1.5%
13		Community Donation	2.5%
14			

This worksheet has been enhanced with distinct headers, the total with proper borders, and the largest net pay highlighted using conditional formatting.

Develop Your Skills EA7-D4

In this exercise, you will modify the appearance of the worksheet data so it is easy to understand at a glance. You will also highlight key elements.

1. Save your file as: **EA7-D4-Payroll-[YourName]**

2. Highlight the **range B24:D29**, choose **Home→Clipboard→Cut**, right-click **cell B19**, and choose **Paste**.

   The worksheet data should be positioned in an orderly manner that minimizes blank space between the various elements. Here you moved one element; you will continue to reposition the data over the next few steps.

3. Highlight the **range B26:G31** and choose **Home→Cells→Delete ▼→Delete Cells**.

4. In the Delete window, choose **Shift Cells Left** and click **OK**.

5. Highlight the **range L21:M24** and choose **Home→Font→Borders ▼→All Borders**.

6. Right-click the highlighted range and choose **Cut**; then select **cell L19** and paste the contents.

7. Use the Ribbon to set the height of **rows 18** and **25** to **7**.

   Empty space in a worksheet can be minimized by reducing the size of columns and rows that separate data. A good rule of thumb is to reduce by approximately half of the default size.

8. Apply bold formatting to the **range C6:O6** and italic formatting to the **range B7:Q8**.

   These headers within the payroll register now appear distinct from the below data.

9. Highlight the **range Q9:Q13** and choose **Home→Styles→Conditional Formatting→Top/Bottom Rules→Top 10 Items**.

10. In the Top 10 Items window, change *10* to **2** and choose **Green Fill with Dark Green Text**; click **OK**.

11. Save and close your file.

What Are the Benefits of Using Excel to Create a Payroll Register?

Excel formulas provide enormous benefits. When examining a payroll register, we see that the IF function is particularly useful, as there are multiple cells for which different results may be appropriate. The payroll register is unique in this regard. Another benefit of using Excel is the ability to create and use templates. Once again, this benefit is greater for the payroll register than most other accounting-related worksheets. A single payroll register is used for each pay period and most businesses use weekly or biweekly pay periods, which means twenty-six or fifty-two payroll registers per year. The ability to easily replicate the structure of a worksheet is another reason why Excel is a logical choice when completing a payroll register.

Microsoft Office is a popular piece of software. Most end users of the payroll register will have Excel loaded on their computers and at least some experience using it. This results in Excel being more versatile than any comparable program. For a report such as a payroll register, this ensures that all interested parties can review the worksheet and make modifications when necessary.

Self-Assessment

Check your knowledge of this chapter's key concepts and skills using the Self-Assessment here or in your eLab course.

1. The ROUND function requires the insertion of two arguments in a formula. *True False*

2. The Logical_Test must be entered as the first argument in an IF function. *True False*

3. The Value_If_False argument is optional in the IF function. *True False*

4. A nested IF function contains at least two standard IF functions. *True False*

5. When a formula is copied, any absolute cell reference in it will change based on the distance between the original and the copied formula. *True False*

6. A mixed cell reference contains a dollar sign in front of the column or row reference, but not both. *True False*

7. You can use F4 to toggle the dollar sign in front of one, both, or no column/row references in a cell reference. *True False*

8. The VLOOKUP and HLOOKUP functions must be used together to work properly. *True False*

9. The range lookup argument in the VLOOKUP function is optional. *True False*

10. The lookup table must be established before the HLOOKUP function can provide a result. *True False*

11. What CANNOT be entered in the num_digits argument of the ROUND function?
    The number zero
    A text entry
    A positive number
    A negative number

12. The IF function is found in the _____ category of the Insert Function dialog box.
    Logical
    Statistical
    Math & Trig
    Financial

13. Which of these does NOT appear in a standard payroll register?
    Net Pay
    Overtime Hours Worked
    Pay Date
    State Withholding Allowances

14. Which of these is NOT an argument within the IF function?
    Value_If_True
    Logical_Test
    Number
    Value_If_False

15. Which of these represents an absolute cell reference?
    $D$7
    D7
    $D7
    D$7

16. How will the mixed cell reference $H8 appear in the new cell if the formula containing the cell reference is dragged one cell to the right?
    $H9
    $G8
    $H8
    $G9

17. Which of these is NOT an argument in the VLOOKUP function?
    lookup value
    logical test
    table array
    column index number

18. What is entered in the range lookup argument of the VLOOKUP function to require an exact match in the lookup table?
    FALSE
    EXACT
    TRUE
    " " (a blank space)

19. Which statement is accurate for when the range lookup argument in the VLOOKUP function is TRUE?
    The second column of the table array must be sorted from lowest to highest.
    The second column of the table array must be sorted from highest to lowest.
    The first column of the table array must be sorted from lowest to highest.
    The first column of the table array must be sorted from highest to lowest.

20. What is the final column in the payroll register?
    Regular Hours
    Check Number
    Total Earnings
    Net Pay

Reinforce Your Skills

EA7-R1 Create a Payroll Register for Audio Warehouse

In this exercise, you will create a payroll register for Audio Warehouse using ROUND, IF, and VLOOKUP functions. You will also modify the worksheet's layout and highlight key elements.

Use this information to complete the payroll register.

Employee Name	FWT	SWT	Check Number
Ventura, G	$18	$12	881
Carrey, Y	$28	$19	882
Stewart, J	$32	$20	883
Armstrong, S	$16	$11	884
Roberts, F	$10	$6	885

1. Open **EA7-R1-Payroll** from your **Chapter 07** folder and save it as: **EA7-R1-Payroll-[YourName]**
2. Select **cell H9**, choose **Formulas→Function Library→Insert Function**, select the **Logical** category and then choose the **IF** function, and click **OK**.
3. Fill in the Function Arguments dialog box as indicated, clicking **OK** when finished:
   - Logical_Text box: **F9=0**
   - Value_If_True box: **"N/A"**
   - Value_If_False box: **F9*G9**
4. Copy **cell H9** to the **range H10:H13**.
5. Select **cell I9**, choose **Formulas→Function Library→Insert Function**, select the **Math & Trig** category and the **Round** function, and click **OK**.
6. In the **Number** box, type **IF(H9="N/A", E9, E9+H9)** and in the **Num_digits** box, type **2**; click **OK**.
7. Copy **cell I9** to the **range I10:I13**.
8. Enter the federal and state withholding tax figures in the **range J9:K13**.

Use Nested IF Functions, Absolute Formatting, and Mixed Formatting

9. In **cell L9**, type: **=ROUND(IF(I27>$L$24, 0, IF(I27+I9<$L$24, I9*$L$22, ($L$24-I27)*$L$22)), 2)**
10. Double-click the fill handle in **cell L9** to copy the formula to the **range L10:L13**.
11. In **cell M9**, type **=ROUND(** and click **cell I9**, type ***** and click **cell M22**, tap F4, and then type **, 2)** and tap Enter.
12. Double-click the fill handle in **cell M9**.

Add a Lookup Function

13. Highlight the **range B25:D29**, choose **Formulas→Defined Names→Define Name**, type **Donation _ Percentages** as the name, and click **OK**.

14. In **cell N9**, type **=ROUND(VLOOKUP(I9, do** and double-click **Donation_Percentages** in the list that appears; then type **,2)*I9, 2)** and tap Enter.

15. Select **cell N9**, click in the first instance of *I9* in the Formula Bar, and tap F4 three times. Then click before the *I* in the second instance of *I9*, type **$**, and tap Enter.

16. Copy **cell N9** to **cell O9**.

17. In the Formula Bar, replace the *2* in the third argument of the VLOOKUP function with **3**.

18. Highlight the **range N9:O9** and double-click the fill handle at the bottom-right corner of the active cell.

19. Enter the appropriate check numbers into the **range P9:P13**.

20. Type **=I9-sum(J9:O9)** in **cell Q9**.

21. Copy **cell Q9** to the **range Q10:Q13**.

22. In **cell H16**, type **=SUM(** and highlight the **range H9:H13** and then type a closed parenthesis.

23. Copy **cell H16** to the **range I16:O16** and **cell Q16**.

Finalize the Worksheet

24. Cut the **range B24:D29** and paste to **cell B19**.

25. Highlight the **range B26:G31**, choose **Home→Cells→Delete ▼→Delete Cells**, choose **Shift Cells Left**, and click **OK**.

26. Highlight the **range L21:M24** and choose **Home→Font→Borders ▼→All Borders**; then cut the highlighted range and paste to **cell L19**.

27. Set the height of **rows 18 and 25** to **7**.

28. Set the **range C6:O6** in bold and the **range B7:Q8** in italic.

29. Highlight the **range Q9:Q13** and choose **Home→Styles→Conditional Formatting→Top/Bottom Rules→Top 10 Items**.

30. In the dialog box, call for the top two cells to appear with a **Light Red Fill with Dark Red Text**; click **OK**.

31. Save and close your file.

EA7-R2 Create a Payroll Register for H.F. Landscaping

In this exercise, you will create a payroll register for H.F. Landscaping using ROUND, IF, and VLOOKUP functions. You will also modify the worksheet's layout and highlight key elements.

Use this information to complete the payroll register.

Employee Name	FWT	SWT	Check Number
Burnham, U	$16	$11	364
White, C	$24	$16	365
Henson, P	$13	$9	366
Jones, G	$19	$13	367
Lawless, A	$18	$13	368

1. Open **EA7-R2-Payroll** from your **Chapter 07** folder and save it as: **EA7-R2-Payroll-[YourName]**

2. Select **cell H9**, choose **Formulas→Function Library→Insert Function**, select the **Logical** category and the **IF** function, and click **OK**.

3. Fill in the Function Arguments dialog box as indicated and click **OK** when finished:
   - Logical_Test box: **F9=0**
   - Value_If_True box: **"N/A"**
   - Value_If_False box: **F9*G9**

4. Copy **cell H9** to the **range H10:H13**.

5. Type **=ROUND(IF(H9="N/A", E9, E9+H9), 2)** in **cell I9**.

6. Copy **cell I9** to the **range I10:I13**.

7. Enter the federal and state withholding tax figures in the **range J9:K13**.

Use Nested IF Functions, Absolute Formatting, and Mixed Formatting

8. Select **cell L9**, choose **Formulas→Function Library→Insert Function**, select the **Math & Trig** category and the **Round** function, and click **OK**.

9. In the **Number** box, type **IF(I27>$L$24, 0, IF(I27+I9<$L$24, I9*$L$22, ($L$24-I27)*$L$22))** and in the **Num_digits** box, type **2**; click **OK**.

10. Double-click the fill handle at the bottom-right corner of **cell L9**.

11. In **cell M9**, type **=ROUND(** and click **cell I9**, type ***** and click **cell M22**, tap F4, and then type **, 2)** and tap Enter.

12. Copy **cell M9** and paste to the **range M10:M13**.

Add a Lookup Function

13. Highlight the **range B25:D29**, type the defined name **Donation _ Percentages** in the **Name Box**, and tap Enter.

14. In **cell N9**, type **=ROUND(VLOOKUP($I9, do** and double-click **Donation_ Percentages** in the list that appears; then type **,2)*$I9, 2)** and tap Enter.

15. Copy **cell N9** to **cell O9**.

16. In the Formula Bar, replace the 2 in the third argument of the VLOOKUP function with **3**.

17. Highlight the **range N9:O9** and double-click the fill handle at the bottom-right corner of the active cell.

18. Enter the appropriate check numbers into the **range P9:P13**.

19. Type **=I9-sum(J9:O9)** in **cell Q9**.

20. Select **cell Q9** and drag the fill handle over the **range Q10:Q13**.

21. In **cell H16**, type **=SUM(** and highlight the **range H9:H13** and then type a closed parenthesis.

22. Copy **cell H16** to the **range I16:O16** and **cell Q16**.

Finalize the Worksheet

23. Highlight the **range B24:D29** and drag the outside border of the selection to the **range B19:D24**.

24. Highlight the **range B26:G31**, choose **Home→Cells→Delete ▼→Delete Cells**, choose **Shift Cells Left**, and click **OK**.

25. Right-click the **range L21:M24** and choose **Format Cells**.

26. Click the **Border** tab, choose the **Outline** option, and click **OK**.

27. Set the height of **rows 18 and 25** to **7**.

28. Set the **range C6:O6** in bold and the **range B7:Q8** in italic.

29. Highlight the **range Q9:Q13** and choose **Home→Styles→Conditional Formatting→Top/Bottom Rules→Top 10 Items**.

30. In the dialog box, call for the top two cells to appear with a **Light Red Fill**; click **OK**.

31. Save and close your file.

Apply Your Skills

EA7-A1 Create a Payroll Register for Athletics Supply House

In this exercise, you will create a payroll register for Athletics Supply House using ROUND, IF, and VLOOKUP functions. You will also modify the worksheet's layout and highlight key elements.

Use this information to complete the payroll register.

Employee Name	FWT	SWT	Check Number
Thomas, T	$15	$10	118
Kirkpatrick, I	$23	$16	119
Fitzgerald, R	$20	$14	120
Marshall, N	$9	$6	121
Abbott, P	$27	$9	122

1. Open **EA7-A1-Payroll** from your **Chapter 07** folder and save it as:
   EA7-A1-Payroll-[YourName]
2. In **cell H9**, create an **IF** function to display *N/A* for employees who do not work overtime and the overtime earnings for employees who do work overtime hours.
3. Copy the formula to the **range H10:H13**.
4. In **cell I9**, nest an **IF** function within the **ROUND** function such that regular earnings and overtime earnings are added.
5. Copy the formula to the **range I10:I13**.
6. Enter the federal and state withholding tax figures in the **range J9:K13**.

Use Nested IF Functions, Absolute Formatting, and Mixed Formatting

7. In **cell L9**, nest an **IF** function within the **ROUND** function to calculate Social Security tax using absolute and/or mixed references where necessary.
8. Copy the formula to the **range L10:L13**.
9. In **cell M9**, enter a **ROUND** function to calculate Medicare tax using absolute and/or mixed references as necessary.
10. Copy the formula to the **range M10:M13**.

Add a Lookup Function

11. Assign an appropriate defined name to the **range B25:D29**.
12. In **cell N9**, nest a **LOOKUP** function within the **ROUND** function to calculate the hospital donation amounts using absolute and/or mixed references as necessary.
13. Copy the formula to the **range N10:N13** and then to **cell O9**, modifying it to properly calculate the school donation amounts.
14. Enter the appropriate check numbers into the **range P9:P13**.

15. In **cell Q9**, enter a formula to calculate the net pay; copy it to the **range Q10:Q13**.

16. Enter a formula to calculate all appropriate totals in **row 16**.

Finalize the Worksheet

17. Move worksheet elements as necessary so they are appropriately aligned.

18. Apply borders and bold or italic formatting where necessary to distinguish sets of data and ensure that the headers stand out.

19. Apply conditional formatting to the **Net Pay** column such that the two largest checks are highlighted in **Yellow Fill with Dark Yellow Text**.

20. Save and close your file.

EA7-A2 Create a Payroll Register for Veterinary Supplies Corp.

In this exercise, you will create a payroll register for Veterinary Supplies Corp. using ROUND, IF, and VLOOKUP functions. You will also finalize the worksheet's layout and highlight key elements.

Use this information to complete the payroll register.

Employee Name	FWT	SWT	Check Number
Holt, W	$19	$12	934
Cooper, T	$17	$11	935
O'Reilly, J	$21	$14	936
Adams, M	$20	$14	937
Hamilton, B	$16	$10	938

1. Open **EA7-A2-Payroll** from your **Chapter 07** folder and save it as:
EA7-A2-Payroll-[YourName]

2. In **cell H9**, create an **IF** function to display *N/A* for employees who do not work overtime and the overtime earnings for employees who do work overtime hours.

3. Copy the formula to the **range H10:H13**.

4. In **cell I9**, nest an **IF** function within the **ROUND** function such that regular earnings and overtime earnings are added.

5. Copy the formula to the **range I10:I13**.

6. Enter the federal and state withholding tax figures in the **range J9:K13**.

Use Nested IF Functions, Absolute Formatting, and Mixed Formatting

7. In **cell L9**, nest an **IF** function within the **ROUND** function to calculate Social Security tax using absolute and/or mixed references where necessary.

8. Copy the formula to the **range L10:L13**.

9. In **cell M9**, enter a **ROUND** function to calculate Medicare tax using absolute and/or mixed references as necessary.

10. Copy the formula to the **range M10:M13**.

Add a Lookup Function

11. Assign an appropriate defined name to the **range B25:D29**.

12. In **cell N9**, nest a **LOOKUP** function within the **ROUND** function to calculate the hospital donation amounts using absolute and/or mixed references as necessary.

13. Copy the formula to the **range N10:N13** and then to **cell O9**, modifying it to properly calculate the school donation amounts.

14. Enter the appropriate check numbers into the **range P9:P13**.

15. In **cell Q9**, enter a formula to calculate the net pay; copy it to the **range Q10:Q13**.

16. Enter a formula to calculate all appropriate totals in **row 16**.

Finalize the Worksheet

17. Move worksheet elements as necessary so they are appropriately aligned.

18. Apply borders and bold or italic formatting where necessary to distinguish sets of data and ensure that the headers stand out.

19. Apply conditional formatting to the Net Pay column such that the two largest checks are highlighted in **Red Text**.

20. Save and close your file.

Extend Your Skills

EA7-E1 Complete a Payroll Register for Ashley's Auto Sales

In this exercise, you will complete a payroll register for Ashley's Auto Sales. You will use the techniques from this chapter to enter earnings, deduction, and net pay data. You will also modify the payroll register to ensure optimal layout and formatting.

Open **EA7-E1-Payroll**. Use an IF function to populate the Overtime Earnings and Total Earnings columns. Ensure that *N/A* is displayed in the Overtime Earnings column for employees who did not work overtime hours during the period. Populate the FWT and SWT columns using these figures.

Employee Name	FWT	SWT	Check Number
Stanley, J	$24	$16	682
Campbell, Y	$18	$12	683
Raimi, A	$12	$8	684
Williams, N	$33	$22	685
McCann, V	$16	$10	686

Create a nested IF function to calculate Social Security tax and a separate formula to calculate Medicare tax for each employee. Use absolute formatting as appropriate.

Use the appropriate LOOKUP function to calculate the charitable contributions and medical plan payment amounts for each employee. Note that the percentages in the range C25:D29 represent the percent of total earnings contributed to the respective voluntary withholdings. Use these in your LOOKUP function. Complete the payroll register by entering the check numbers and creating a formula to calculate each employee's net pay.

Adjust the worksheet layout by adding borders around distinct sets of data, adjusting column widths and/or row heights between sets of data, and minimizing blank space between data sets. Last, use appropriate formatting to distinguish the headers in rows 6–8 from the data below and conditional formatting to highlight the two largest Net Pay amounts.

EA7-E2 Complete a Payroll Register for Brochure Specialists

In this exercise, you will complete a payroll register for Brochure Specialists. You will use the techniques from this chapter to enter earnings, deduction, and net pay data. You will also modify the payroll register to ensure optimum layout and formatting.

Open **EA7-E2-Payroll**. Use an IF function to populate the Overtime Earnings and Total Earnings columns. Ensure that *N/A* is displayed in the Overtime Earnings column for employees who did not work overtime hours during the period. Populate the FWT and SWT columns using these figures.

Employee Name	FWT	SWT	Check Number
Addison, K	$17	$12	209
Sampson, W	$21	$14	210
Smith, Q	$20	$14	211
Vanegas, P	$13	$8	212
Spencer, O	$25	$16	213

Create a nested IF function to calculate Social Security tax and a separate formula to calculate Medicare tax for each employee. Use absolute formatting as appropriate.

Use the appropriate LOOKUP function to calculate the charitable contributions and medical plan payment amounts for each employee. Note that the percentages in the range C25:D29 represent the percent of total earnings contributed to the respective voluntary withholdings. Use these in your LOOKUP function. Complete the payroll register by entering the check numbers and creating a formula to calculate each employee's net pay.

Adjust the worksheet layout by adding borders around distinct sets of data, adjusting column widths and/or row heights between different sets of data, minimizing blank space between data sets. Last, use appropriate formatting to distinguish the headers in rows 6–8 from the data below and conditional formatting to highlight the two largest Net Pay amounts.

EA7-E3 Complete a Payroll Register for Upholstery Designers

In this exercise, you will complete a payroll register for Upholstery Designers. You will use the techniques from this chapter to enter earnings, deduction, and net pay data. You will also modify the payroll register to ensure optimum layout and formatting.

Open **EA7-E3-Payroll**. Use an IF function to populate the Overtime Earnings and Total Earnings columns. Ensure that *N/A* is displayed in the Overtime Earnings column for employees who did not work overtime hours during the period. Populate the FWT and SWT columns using these figures.

Employee Name	FWT	SWT	Check Number
Forbath, B	$11	$8	43
Carpenter, I	$28	$18	44
Quinn, L	$15	$10	45
Chang, H	$16	$10	46
Carter, M	$20	$14	47

Create a nested IF function to calculate Social Security tax and a separate formula to calculate Medicare tax for each employee. Use absolute formatting as appropriate.

Use the appropriate LOOKUP function to calculate the charitable contributions and medical plan payment amounts for each employee. Note that the percentages provided in the range C25:D29 represent the percent of total earnings contributed to the respective voluntary withholdings. Use these in your LOOKUP function. Complete the payroll register by entering the check numbers and creating a formula to calculate each employee's net pay.

Adjust the worksheet layout by adding borders used around distinct sets of data, adjusting column widths and/or row heights between sets of data, and minimizing blank space between data sets. Last, use appropriate formatting to distinguish the headers in rows 6–8 from the data below and conditional formatting to highlight the two largest Net Pay amounts.

Critical Thinking

EA7-C1 Discuss Using the IF Function

The IF function is one of the most versatile functions available in Excel. Even the simplest IF function can add great benefit to a worksheet. In this chapter, you saw how the IF function can be used in a payroll register to ensure that correct earnings and withholding amounts are entered for each employee. However, the payroll register is not the only accounting-related worksheet within which the IF function can be used.

Identify three types of accounting worksheets (other than the payroll register) that can benefit from the use of the IF function. Write a paragraph of at least five sentences in which you identify these worksheets. Write a second paragraph of at least five sentences to discuss how the IF function can be used within each worksheet and why it would be beneficial to do so.

EA7-C2 Discuss Maximizing Worksheet Readability

As you have seen, worksheet layout is a vital element of any Excel report. Layout is also the most commonly overlooked component of an effective worksheet, as the desire to produce relevant data often take center stage. While certain general rules for an effective layout have been provided in this chapter, they are by no means the only methods that can be used to improve worksheet appearance.

Write a paragraph of at least four sentences in which you identify four techniques (aside from those discussed in this chapter) they can improve a worksheet's appearance. Write a second paragraph of at least sentences to identify at least one accounting-related worksheet in which each technique could be used. Be certain to discuss why each technique is appropriate for your identified worksheets.

Bond Amortization

LEARNING OBJECTIVES

- Create a bond amortization schedule

- Use the PV, FV, and PMT functions

- Protect worksheet elements

- Automate processes with macros

Financial functions are among Excel's more complex elements. However, it's worth taking the time to master their use, as these functions can save substantial time. Commonly used financial functions are present value (PV), future value (FV), and payment (PMT). Because of the complexity of these functions, you may find it necessary to protect some or all of a worksheet that includes them. You may also find that automating processes involving these functions with macros allows for a greater efficiency. In this chapter, you will use financial functions while creating a bond amortization schedule. You will begin by calculating different features of a bond using PV, FV, and PMT functions. You will create a bond amortization schedule for this bond and protect various worksheet elements. Last, you will create a macro to automate the completion of a bond amortization table.

PROJECT	City Music World

City Music World is a retail store that sells musical equipment and offers lessons for beginning and experienced musicians. The company is considering issuing bonds to fund a potential expansion of its operations. Before doing so, the company wants to review the necessary payment schedule and purchase price of bonds with different characteristics. You are creating a bond amortization schedule that can be updated for different bonds. You will protect key worksheet elements and automate as much of the schedule completion as possible.

In this chapter, you will create a bond amortization schedule using PV, FV, and PMT functions. You will also apply different levels of worksheet protection for different users. Last, you will create macros to automate populating the bond amortization schedule once key bond data has been entered.

	A	B	C	D	E	F	G
2		**Bond Details**			**Populate Schedule**		
3		Date	1/1/2012				
4		Face Value	$ 100,000.00				
5		Contract Rate	10%				
6		Effective Rate	12%				
7		Life (years)	5				
8		Payments per Yea	2				
9							
10		**Bond Calculations**					
11		Present Value	$ 92,639.91				
12		Future Value	$ 100,000.00				
13		Payment	$ 5,000.00				
14							
15		Date	Interest Payment	Interest Expense	Amortization of Bond Discount	Bond Discount Balance	Carrying Value
16		1/1/2012				$ 7,360.09	$ 92,639.91
17		6/30/2012	$ 5,000.00	$ 5,558.39	$ 558.39	$ 6,801.69	$ 93,198.31
18		12/31/2012	$ 5,000.00	$ 5,591.90	$ 591.90	$ 6,209.79	$ 93,790.21
19		6/30/2013	$ 5,000.00	$ 5,627.41	$ 627.41	$ 5,582.38	$ 94,417.62
20		12/31/2013	$ 5,000.00	$ 5,665.06	$ 665.06	$ 4,917.32	$ 95,082.68
21		6/30/2014	$ 5,000.00	$ 5,704.96	$ 704.96	$ 4,212.36	$ 95,787.64
22		12/31/2014	$ 5,000.00	$ 5,747.26	$ 747.26	$ 3,465.11	$ 96,534.89
23		6/30/2015	$ 5,000.00	$ 5,792.09	$ 792.09	$ 2,673.01	$ 97,326.99
24		12/31/2015	$ 5,000.00	$ 5,839.62	$ 839.62	$ 1,833.39	$ 98,166.61
25		6/30/2016	$ 5,000.00	$ 5,890.00	$ 890.00	$ 943.40	$ 99,056.60
26		12/31/2016	$ 5,000.00	$ 5,943.40	$ 943.40	$ (0.00)	$ 100,000.00
27		Totals	$ 50,000.00	$ 57,360.09	$ 7,360.09		

This bond amortization schedule has been fully populated through the use of a macro that automates the creation of all formulas.

Bond Amortization Schedule

When a business seeks to raise cash to fund a large expenditure, such as for the building of a new facility or the development of a new product, it will typically raise capital by issuing additional shares of stock (**equity financing**) or borrowing money (**debt financing**). One financial instrument that can be used when pursuing debt financing is a bond.

When a business issues a bond, it receives a lump payment from the bondholder to be used by the business to pursue its intended expenditure. In exchange, the bondholder receives periodic payments over the life of the bond (interest payments) and a lump-sum payment equal to the **face value** of the bond at the end of the bond's life (principal payment). To determine figures such as the initial selling price of the bond and interest payments, you must understand the various bond characteristics. When using the most commonly applied effective interest method, these characteristics include the face value, life of the bond, **contract interest rate**, and **effective interest rate**.

NOTE!   The effective interest method is the amortization method examined here, as it requires the completion of a bond amortization schedule. The alternative, though far less widespread, is to use straight-line amortization.

Face Value

The face value of a bond is the amount paid to the bondholder on the **maturity date** (the end of the bond's life). If the **issue price** of the bond equals the face value, then the bond is being sold at its par value. However, oftentimes bonds are sold at more than their face value (sold at a premium) or less than their face value (sold at a discount).

Life of the Bond

The life of the bond represents the period of time over which the bond will be outstanding before it matures. A bond is often held by a single bondholder over the course of its life, but it's also common for bonds to be sold from one bondholder to another. Periodic interest payments are made to the current bondholder throughout the life of the bond, and the face value of the bond is paid to the bondholder upon bond maturity. Note that the bond will indicate the frequency with which interest payments are made (annually, semiannually, etc.), and this schedule is followed throughout the life of the bond.

Contract Interest Rate vs. Effective Interest Rate

The contract interest rate is attached to the bond and used to calculate interest payments periodically made to the bondholder. Conversely, the effective interest rate (also called the market interest rate) factors in the impact of compounding on the interest payments. When completing a bond amortization table, the contract interest

(continued)

rate is used to calculate actual interest payments, while the effective interest rate is used to calculate the present value of the bond.

These interest rates can be used to quickly identify whether a bond will be sold at a discount, face value, or a premium. When the contract interest rate and effective interest rate are the same, the bond sells at face value. If the contract rate is below the effective rate, then the bond can be considered less desirable than a similar bond that could be purchased elsewhere. This bond will sell at a discount from the face value. Conversely, if the contract rate is above the effective rate, then the bond is considered more attractive than a similar bond that could be purchased elsewhere and will sell at a premium above face value.

Amortizing Bond Discount or Premium

When a bond is issued at a discount or premium, the impact of this discount or premium within the financial records of the bond issuer is spread over the life of the bond. This **bond amortization** either increases the interest expense recorded when each bond payment is made (in the case of a discount) or reduces the interest expense (in the case of a premium). The total interest expense for each period is calculated as the interest payment plus amortized discount *or* minus amortized premium.

Carrying Value

The **carrying value** of a bond can be calculated as face value minus unamortized discount (or plus the unamortized premium). When the bond is issued, the unamortized discount or premium equals the total discount or premium for the bond. As the discount or premium is amortized, the unamortized portion of the discount or premium is gradually reduced (leading to a gradual increase in the carrying value when there is a discount or a gradual decrease when there is a premium). The result is that once the bond matures, the discount or premium will have been amortized to $0, and the bond's carrying value will equal its face value.

Working with Financial Functions

Excel includes a variety of financial functions that can simplify the creation of accounting-related worksheets. For example, there are basic financial functions for determining monthly payments on loans, total interest paid on loans, and the future value of investments. When examining the characteristics of a specific bond or other financial instrument, the PMT, PV, and FV functions are useful.

PMT Function

For the PMT function to calculate the required payment for a bond, you must specify the bond interest rate, number of payments to be made, present value, and future value of the payment at maturity.

The interest rate and number of payments must be carefully considered. The effective interest rate (not the contract interest rate) is the first argument. It's typically expressed in annual terms, so if a bond requires an alternative payment schedule (such as semiannual instead of annual payments), the interest rate entered in the formula must be adjusted. For example, if the effective interest rate is 14% and a bond requires semiannual interest payments, then there are two interest payments every year. You divide 14% by two payments per year to arrive at an interest rate of 7%, which is what is entered as the first argument in the function.

The number of payments will often differ from the number of years in the life of the bond. If a bond with semiannual interest payments has a five-year life, then it will have a total of ten payments (five years * two payments per year).

One additional element to review is how the PMT function expresses periodic payments. By default, the result of the PMT function is displayed as a negative

```
=-PMT(C6/C8, C7*C8, C11, -C4)
```

number. When writing the formula it is common to place a negative sign before the function. This reverses the result from a negative to a positive figure. Similar consideration is given to the individual arguments of the PMT function. Because the FV argument represents a lump payment at the end of the bond's life, it should also be expressed as a negative number when writing the formula.

↗ Formulas→Function Library→Insert Function→Financial→PMT Function

PV Function and FV Function

The PV function calculates the present value of a bond when you specify the bond interest rate, number of payments, interest payment amount, and future value of the payment at maturity. The FV function calculates the future value of a bond when you specify the bond interest rate, number of payments, interest payment amount, and present value.

```
=PV(C6/C8,C7*C8,-C4*C5/C8,-C4)
=-FV(C6/C8,C7*C8,-C4*C5/C8,C11)
```

The PV and FV functions typically require negative symbols in their formulas.

The same considerations must be made for these functions as are made for the PMT function. Both the effective interest rate argument and the number of payments argument are entered per the earlier discussion. Additionally, the interest payment amount and future value of the payment at maturity must be expressed in negative terms. For the FV function, then, a negative sign is added before the *FV* at the beginning of the formula. The present value is considered to be a positive amount in Excel (since it does not represent a payment), so a negative sign is not needed before the *PV* at the beginning of that formula.

↗ Formulas→Function Library→Insert Function→Financial→PV Function

↗ Formulas→Function Library→Insert Function→Financial→FV Function

Financial Function Syntax

You create financial functions using actual values or cell references. Remember that using cell references offers more flexibility and is preferable.

PMT, PV, and FV Function Syntax

Function	Syntax
PMT (Payment)	PMT (rate, periods, present value, [future value], [type])
PV (Present Value)	PV (rate, periods, payment, [future value], [type])
FV (Future Value)	FV (rate, periods, payment, [present value], [type])

These financial functions can be used when the payment amount remains constant, such as with most bonds, car loans, and fixed-rate mortgages.

The *rate* argument is the interest rate for each period of the bond or loan. Although these interest rates are quoted as annual rates, payments usually are made more frequently. For monthly payments, as an example, you divide the interest rate by twelve. You can enter the result or the calculation details (such as 7%/12) in the formula.

The *periods* argument is the number of payments for the bond or loan, or the number of deposits for an investment.

The *payment* argument for a bond or loan is the required periodic interest payment. For an investment, it's the amount invested in each period. In either case, the payment is always the same for each period.

The *future value* argument is optional. It is the balance that will be owed at the bond maturity date or the amount desired at the end of an investment. This must be entered when determining the present value of, or payments for, a bond but is not required if the balance of an investment will be zero.

The *present value* argument is the value, in today's dollars, of a bond or loan. It must be entered when determining the future value of a bond. Or, it can be the starting balance of an investment (not required if the starting balance is zero). This argument is optional for the FV function.

The *type* argument indicates when payments are due. You are not required to enter the default argument 0 (zero) if payments are made at the end of the period. Enter 1 if payments are due at the beginning of the period. This is an optional argument.

Develop Your Skills EA8-D1

In this exercise, you will use financial functions to calculate the present value, future value, and payments associated with a bond. You will then create a bond amortization schedule.

Base your spreadsheet on a bond with a $100,000 face value, a five-year life, semiannual interest payments, a coupon interest rate of 10%, and an effective interest rate of 12%. The bond is issued on 1/1/2012.

1. Open a **Blank Workbook** and save the file in your **Chapter 08** folder as:
    EA8-D1-Bond-[YourName]

    You will begin by preparing the worksheet for the data to be entered.

2. Set the width of **column A** to **0.75** and the height of **row 1** to **7.2**.

    This creates nice spacing that improves worksheet readability.

3. Merge and center the **range B2:C2**, add bold formatting, and enter **Bond Details**.

4. In order, type these headers in the **range B3:B8**: **Date**, **Face Value**, **Contract Rate**, **Effective Rate**, **Life (years)**, and **Payments per Year**

5. Enter **1/1/12** in **cell C3**.

6. Enter **100000** in **cell C4** and apply the **Accounting** number format.

7. Enter **.1** in **cell C5** and **.12** in **cell C6** and then select the **range C5:C6** and choose **Home→Number→Percent Style**.

8. Select **cell C7**, type **5** and tap Enter, and then type **2** and tap Enter.

9. Center-align the contents of the **range C3:C8**.

10. Highlight the **range B2:C8** and choose **Home→Font→Borders ▼→Outside Borders**; also apply an outside border around **cell B2**.

11. Autofit **column B** and set the width of **column C** to **12**.

12. Merge and center the **range B10:C10**, add outside borders and bold formatting, and enter **Bond Calculations**.

13. In order, type these headers in the **range B11:B13**: **Present Value**, **Future Value**, and **Payment**

Enter Financial Functions

14. In **cell C11**, type **=PV(C6/C8,** but do not complete the entry.

    The effective interest rate is used for the first argument. It is divided by two because the effective rate is expressed in annual terms, but the bond pays interest semiannually.

15. Enter the next part of the formula: **C7*C8,**

    The second argument (number of interest payments) is calculated by multiplying the total number of years of the bond's life by the payments per year.

16. Enter the next part of the formula: **−C4*C5/C8,**

    In the third argument, the contract rate of interest is multiplied by the face value of the bond to determine the periodic interest payments. Just as the effective interest rate was divided by the number of payments per year, the contract interest rate is divided by the number of payments to arrive at a prorated contract interest rate for each payment period. A negative sign is placed in front of C4 because the interest payments represent cash outflows.

17. To complete the formula, type **–C4)** and tap Enter.

   The fourth argument represents the face value of the bond at maturity. As this is an outflow of cash, a negative sign is placed in front of C4.

18. In **cell C12**, type **=-FV(C6/C8, C7*C8, -C4*C5/C8, C11)** and tap Enter.

   The arguments in the FV function are similar to those in the PV function. Note the negative sign at the beginning of the formula.

19. With **cell C13** selected, choose **Formulas→Function Library→Insert Function**, select the **Financial** category and the **PMT** function, and click **OK**.

20. Complete the Function Arguments box as shown and then click **OK**:

PMT		
Rate	C6/C8	= 0.06
Nper	C7*C8	= 10
Pv	C11	= 92639.91295
Fv	-C4	= -100000
Type		= number

21. With **cell C13** still active, click between the equals sign and *PMT* in the Formula Bar, type a minus sign, and tap Enter.

   Just as the interest payments were preceded by a negative sign in the PV and FV functions because they represent cash outflows, the PMT function includes a negative sign here as well.

22. Apply the **Accounting** number format to the **range C11:C13** and add an outside border to the **range B10:C13**.

23. Select the headers for **columns D–G** and use the right-click method to set the width to **15**.

Complete the Amortization Schedule

24. Starting with **cell B15**, highlight the **range B15:G15**, apply an outside border, add bold formatting, and set the Wrap Text option and Center alignment.

25. In **cell B15**, type **Date** and tap Tab; continue typing **Interest Payment**, **Interest Expense**, **Amortization of Bond Discount**, **Bond Discount Balance**, and **Carrying Value** in the remaining highlighted cells, tapping Tab between each entry.

   Cells E15 and F15 indicate that a bond discount is being amortized. This can be verified by noting that the present value of the bond is less than its future value. If the present value had been greater than the future value, the cells would show a bond premium being amortized.

26. Enter **1/1/2012** in **cell B16**, **6/30/2012** in **cell B17**, and **12/31/2012** in **cell B18**.

27. Highlight the **range B17:B18** and then drag the fill handle at the bottom-right corner of the range through **cell B26**.

   The bond depreciation schedule begins with the date on which the bond is issued and includes one row for every date on which an interest payment is made.

28. In **cell B27**, enter **Totals** and right-align the text.

29. Type **=C12-C11** in **cell F16**, tap Tab, and then type **=C11** and tap Enter.

   These figures, which are based on the financial figures previously calculated, create the foundation for the remainder of the bond amortization schedule.

30. In **cell C17**, type **=C13** and tap F4, and then tap Tab.

   The interest payment was previously calculated and is based on the contract interest rate. It remains constant for every period, so you are using absolute formatting.

31. Enter **=G16*$C$6/$C$8** in **cell D17**.

   The total interest expense for each period is calculated by multiplying the current carrying value of the bond (which, as seen in cell G16, equals face value minus current balance within the bond discount) by the effective interest rate. As we have seen, the interest rate is divided by the number of payments per year.

32. Enter **=D17-C17** in **cell E17**.

   The difference between the interest payment and the interest expense, as calculated here, represents the amortization of the discount for the current period.

33. Enter **=F16-E17** in **cell F17**.

   The bond discount balance is reduced by the amortization amount each period. The bond discount is gradually reduced until it reaches zero at the end of the life of the bond.

34. Enter **=G16+E17** in **cell G17**.

   Just as the bond discount balance decreases by the bond amortization amount each period, the carrying value of the bond (when it is issued at a discount) increases each period by the bond amortization amount.

35. Highlight the **range C17:G17** and use the fill handle to copy the formulas through **row 26.**

36. Highlight the **range C27:E27**, choose **Home→Editing→AutoSum**, and then choose **Home→Font→Borders ▼→Top and Double Bottom Border**.

37. Apply the **Accounting** number format to the **range C16:G27**.

38. Save your file.

   Unless otherwise directed, always keep your file open at the end of each exercise.

Protecting Workbooks and Worksheets

You protect a file to prevent accidental or intentional modification. Excel offers three levels of protection:

- *Workbook-level protection* protects the structure of the entire workbook, preventing changes to the way worksheets are displayed.
- *Worksheet-level protection* restricts changes to certain objects on worksheets.
- *Cell-level protection* limits access to certain cells on worksheets.

Protecting the Workbook Structure

Protecting a workbook prevents structural changes from being made. For example, you cannot delete, rename, copy, or move worksheets while the structure is protected.

The Protect Workbook command displays the Protect Structure and Windows dialog box. Using an optional password allows you to control who can switch this protection on and off.

1. The Structure option protects worksheets from being reordered, copied, or deleted.

2. The Windows option is disabled in Excel 2013 and 2016 and, therefore, cannot be used.

↗ Review→Changes→Protect Workbook

Protecting the Worksheet Elements

You can turn on protection for individual worksheets in a workbook. The Protect Sheet command even allows you to restrict activity to specific actions, such as selecting cells, formatting rows and columns, and inserting/deleting rows and columns.

Turning Protection On and Off

Although it might appear that you would turn worksheet protection on/off using the Protect Worksheet and Contents of Locked Cells checkbox, that is not the case. That option always should have a checkmark. Clicking OK actually turns on worksheet protection.

Allowing User Changes

By default, two user options are selected in the Protect Sheet dialog box, giving users permission only to click on cells. If you remove those checkmarks, users can scroll through the worksheet but cannot select any cells. You can specify that users are allowed to change certain other items in a protected worksheet.

In a bond depreciation schedule, the user should need to change only a few input cells (including those for effective interest rate, face value, and bond life). Once entered, these figures should allow for the automatic completion of the body of the schedule. As such, it's common for users to be given access to only those cells that require initial inputs.

Password Protection

For the highest level of protection, add a password. Users must enter the password to unprotect the worksheet and make further changes. For worksheets that are accessible by many employees but used only by a select few, including a password can help ensure that data is not improperly accessed.

WARNING! Keep track of your passwords! Workbook-protection passwords cannot be retrieved. If you forget your password, you must re-create the workbook.

↗ Review→Changes→Protect Sheet *or* Home→Cells→Format→Protect Sheet

Develop Your Skills EA8-D2

In this exercise, you will protect your bond amortization schedule so that users can alter only certain elements.

1. Save your file as: **EA8-D2-Bond-[YourName]**
2. Choose **Review→Changes→Protect Workbook**.
3. Follow these steps to protect the workbook:

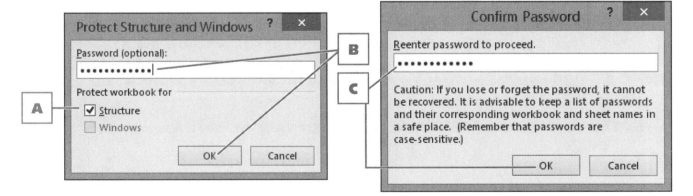

A. If necessary, click to place a checkmark in the **Structure** checkbox.

B. Type **Amortization** as the password and click **OK**.

C. In the **Confirm Password** dialog box, retype **Amortization** and click **OK**.

4. Double-click the **Sheet1** tab.

   An error message appears because protecting the workbook structure prevents the renaming of sheet tabs.

5. Click **OK**, choose **Review→Changes→Protect Workbook**, and then type the password **Amortization** and click **OK**.

   The workbook is no longer protected.

6. Choose **Home→Cells→Format→Protect Sheet** and confirm that the boxes for these items are checked (if not, click to add checkmarks):

   • Protect Worksheet and Contents of Locked Cells
   • Select Locked Cells
   • Select Unlocked Cells

7. Click the checkbox for **Format Cells**, type **Bond** as the password, and click **OK**.

8. Confirm the password when prompted.

9. Right-click the **column D** header.

   As a result of the protection you applied, some options in the pop-up menu are grayed out, or disabled.

10. Select **cell C17** and then click the **Insert** tab on the Ribbon.

    Notice that the majority of options on the Insert tab are also disabled.

11. Highlight the **range B27:E27** and choose **Home→Font→Bold**.

    You can apply the bold formatting even though the workbook protection is active because you allowed this in step 7.

12. Choose **Review→Changes→Unprotect Sheet** and then enter the password **Bond** and click **OK**.

13. Save your file.

Protecting Individual Cells

You can protect the contents and formatting of certain cells. You can also hide formulas so they don't display in the Formula Bar or when the Show Formulas command is used. All worksheet cells are locked by default until you unlock them. Why, then, have you been able to edit all locked cells? The cells' locked/unlocked condition has no effect until worksheet protection is turned on.

NOTE!   Remember that worksheet protection can be turned on through the Home or Review tab.

The Protection Tab of the Format Cells Dialog Box

You can open the Format Cells dialog box via the menu that appears when you right-click a highlighted area of a worksheet.

The Protection tab in the Format Cells dialog box allows you to change options for selected cells. There are two cell protection options you can set:

- *Locked:* Check or uncheck this option to lock/unlock the currently selected cells.
- *Hidden:* This option affects only the display of formulas. It does not hide labels, values, or formula results.

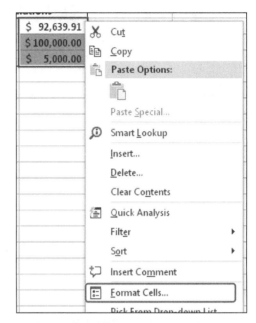

Unlocking Cells in a Protected Worksheet

When the Locked option is unchecked, selected cells are unlocked. Unlocked cells can be edited even though the overall worksheet is protected. This way, you can protect formulas and labels while still allowing data entry in other areas. The unlocked portion of the worksheet is referred to as the *changes area*. You must unlock the cells before protecting the worksheet.

TIP!   For rapid data entry into unlocked cells, tap ⌊Tab⌋ after entering data in each. When you reach the end of a row in the changes area and tap ⌊Tab⌋, the insertion point wraps to the next row.

↗ Home→Cells→Format→Lock Cell

To Lock or Not to Lock?

If your worksheet contains only a few cell ranges that users are allowed to change, unlock those cells. The rest of the worksheet will remain locked when you turn on worksheet protection. If most of the worksheet needs to be accessible for updating, you may want to use the Select All option and unlock all cells and then lock just the cells you want to protect.

TIP! Use the [Ctrl] key to select multiple cell ranges and then select Unlock, Lock, or Hidden to apply the option to multiple ranges at once.

Develop Your Skills EA8-D3

In this exercise, you will unlock cells that require modification to complete the bond amortization schedule. You will then protect the worksheet so only the unlocked cells can be modified.

1. Save your file as: **EA8-D3-Bond-[YourName]**
2. Highlight the **ranges C3:C8** and **B16:G27** and choose **Home→Cells→Format→ Lock Cell**.

    As these cells were locked by default, they are now unlocked.
3. Highlight the **range C11:C13**, right-click, and choose **Format Cells**.

    The Format Cells dialog box opens.
4. Switch to the **Protection** tab, check the box for **Hidden**, and click **OK**.
5. Choose **Review→Changes→Protect Sheet**, enter **Interest** as the password, and click **OK**; confirm the password in the next dialog box.
6. Select **cell C12**.

    Notice that the Formula Bar is empty. This cell is in the range for which the Hidden option was selected.
7. Type any letter in **cell E2**.

    You did not unlock this particular cell prior to protecting the worksheet, so a warning message displays to indicate that you cannot type in this cell.
8. Click **OK** to close the warning message.
9. Use the right-click method to change the name of the **Sheet1** tab to **Bond Schedule**.

    The worksheet is protected but the workbook remains unprotected; therefore, the workbook structure, including the worksheet tab names, can be modified.
10. Save your file.

Using Macros

A macro is a recorded set of mouse and keyboard actions that can be played back at any time. Macros are useful for automating routine tasks, especially lengthy tasks. Be aware that macros can contain viruses, so be cautious about opening workbooks containing macros you receive from others.

Security Levels

You change macro security in the Trust Center section of Excel Options. The setting there is in effect for all workbooks opened on your computer. The setting is not embedded in any workbooks that you save and share with others.

You can choose among four levels of security that control whether macros in an opened workbook are available or disabled:

- *Disable All Macros Without Notification:* Only macros in workbooks that you place in a trusted location of the Trust Center will run. All other digitally signed and unsigned macros are disabled.
- *Disable All Macros with Notification:* This is the default option. It displays a message allowing you to enable macros in the specified workbook if you wish or use the workbook without enabling macros.
- *Disable All Macros Except Digitally Signed Macros:* This option automatically disables unsigned macros and enables macros from publishers previously added as a trusted publisher in the Trust Center.
- *Enable All Macros:* You are not protected from potentially unsafe macros. This option is not recommended for general use.

If you have antivirus software installed, the file will be scanned for viruses before it is opened regardless of the security level set.

NOTE! Your network system administrator may set macro security and prevent users from changing it.

⏺ File→Options→Trust Center→Trust Center Settings→Macro Settings

Recording Macros

Excel's macro recording feature is similar to a video camera. You turn it on, record your actions, and then stop the recorder. You can play back the recorded keystrokes and mouse actions as many times as you want.

1. When a macro is recording, the Stop Recording button appears on the status bar.

2. After a first macro has been recorded, you can click this icon on the status bar to record subsequent macros.

⏺ View→Macros→View Macros ▾→Record Macro

Naming a Macro

You can add custom names for your macros or use Excel's default names (Macro1, Macro2, etc.). Macro names cannot contain spaces but can include capital letters and underscores.

Recording Macro Steps

Most actions—including mouse actions, choosing Ribbon commands, selecting options in dialog boxes, using arrow keys to navigate, and typing text—are recorded in a macro. Any mistakes and corrections you make during recording also are saved. If the final result is correct, you can include the mistakes and their corrections in the macro; otherwise, just rerecord the macro using the proper actions.

TIP!   Practice the procedure you wish to automate before recording the macro to reduce the risk of making mistakes during the recording process.

Storing Macros

Macros are available only in the workbook in which you create them unless you assign them to the Personal Macro Workbook, which is a hidden file used to make macros available to all open workbooks. Some macros are useful only in a particular workbook. For these macros, choose the *This Workbook* storage option. Other macros can benefit multiple workbooks, and these are the ones to assign to the Personal Macro Workbook.

Saving a Workbook Containing Macros

If you attempt to save a workbook containing macros using the normal Excel Workbook file format, Excel displays the message: "The following features cannot be saved in macro-free workbooks: VB Project." Clicking No in the message box displays the Save As dialog box, where you should choose the Excel Macro-Enabled Workbook file format. The file is saved with the extension .xlsm to indicate that it contains a macro.

Running Macros

You can run macros from the Macro dialog box, but they're much more accessible if you assign them to shortcut keys, custom buttons or graphics on a worksheet, or buttons on the Quick Access toolbar.

↗ View→Macros→View Macros │ Alt + F8

Develop Your Skills EA8-D4

In this exercise, you will record a macro that will complete the bond amortization schedule. You will then run the macro.

1. Save your file as: **EA8-D4-Bond-[YourName]**

2. Choose **File→Options→Trust Center→Trust Center Settings→Macro Settings**, ensure that **Disable All Macros with Notification** is selected, and click **OK** twice.

3. Highlight the **range C16:G27** and tap Delete.

    You will now re-create the bond amortization schedule while recording a macro, which can be saved and used later when completing subsequent schedules.

4. Choose **View→Macros→Macros ▼→Record Macro** to open the Record Macro dialog box.

5. Enter **Amortization _ Schedule** as the macro name and click **OK**.

6. Select **cell F16**, type **=C12-C11** and tap Tab, and then type **=C11** and tap Enter.

7. Select **cell C17**, type **=$C$13** and tap Tab, type **=G16*$C$6/$C$8** and tap Tab, type **=D17-C17** and tap Tab, type **=F16-E17** and tap Tab, and then type **=G16+E17** and tap Enter.

8. Highlight the **range C17:G17** and drag the fill handle through **row 26**.

9. In **cell C27**, enter: **=SUM(C17:C26)**

10. Copy **cell C27**, paste in the **range D27:E2**, and tap Esc.

11. Choose **View→Macros→Macros ▼→Stop Recording**.

12. Delete the contents of the **range C16:G27**.

    You will now run the macro to ensure that it was properly recorded. In doing so, you will repopulate the bond amortization schedule.

13. Choose **View→Macros→Macros** and click **Run**.

    The bond amortization schedule is once again complete.

14. Choose **Review→Changes→Unprotect Sheet** and then type **Interest** and tap Enter.

    You have temporarily unprotected the sheet so you can insert a text box.

15. Choose **Insert→Illustrations→Shapes** and click **Text Box** in the **Basic Shapes** section.

16. Click near the top-left corner of **cell E2** and drag to the bottom right of **cell E5** to create a text box over the **range E2:E5**.

17. Type **Populate Schedule** and format the text with bold and a 16-point font size.

18. Right-click the text box, choose **Assign Macro**, click the **Amortization_Schedule** macro from the list, and click **OK**.

19. Choose **Review→Changes→Protect Sheet**, enter **Schedule** as the password, and click **OK**; confirm the password when prompted.

20. Delete the contents of the **range C16:G27**.

    You will now run the macro from the object that you have entered within the spreadsheet.

21. Click the text box to initiate the macro.

    The bond amortization schedule is once again complete.

22. Save a copy of your file as a **Macro-Enabled Workbook** and then close it.

    Hint: Choose File→Save As and choose Macro-Enabled Workbook from the Save as Type box.

REAL-WORLD Accounting

What Are the Benefits of Using Excel to Create a Bond Amortization Schedule?

There are a few characteristics of a bond amortization schedule that make it ideal for completion in Excel. You have seen how financial functions can streamline bond-related calculations. More important, because the body of the schedule requires identical formulas in multiple rows, using macros is ideal. As a result, only a small number of items must be entered (effective interest rate, number of periods, etc.) before the automated portion can be completed, allowing for the use of protection throughout the majority of the worksheet.

As macros can be assigned to worksheet objects, Excel provides a simple forum for the automatic completion of a bond amortization schedule. This allows novice users to benefit from the full power of Excel without extensive knowledge of the program. Once the macro has been created, any user can easily employ it. This level of accessibility for all users is rare within accounting-related programs.

The use of workbook and/or worksheet protection also ensures that novice users do not accidentally introduce errors in a worksheet. Again, Excel is unique in its extensive ability to limit user access solely to the few elements that require modification. The result of using both macros and workbook/worksheet protection is that a relatively complex schedule, such as that for bond amortization, can be efficiently completed by users with relatively little experience in the program.

Self-Assessment

Check your knowledge of this chapter's key concepts and skills using the Self-Assessment here or in your eLab course.

1. The PMT, PV, and FV functions are displayed in the Financial section of the Insert Function dialog box. *True   False*

2. In the PMT, PV, and FV functions, the interest rate argument is always expressed in annual terms. *True   False*

3. The number 1 represents the default entry for the *type* argument in PMT, PV, and FV functions. *True   False*

4. Cell references CANNOT be used with PV and FV functions. *True   False*

5. In Excel 2016, the Windows protection option has been disabled. *True   False*

6. The Protect Sheet command can be accessed on the Review and Home tabs. *True   False*

7. When protecting a worksheet, you must create a password. *True   False*

8. The Tab key can be used to move through unlocked cells in a worksheet. *True   False*

9. All worksheet cells are unlocked by default. *True   False*

10. Macro names CANNOT include spaces. *True   False*

11. Interest rates, including the effective interest rate and contract interest rate, are typically expressed in _____ terms.
    weekly
    monthly
    semiannual
    annual

12. For a bond, which formula argument represents a payment and requires the inclusion of a negative sign before the argument to reverse its sign within financial formulas?
    Rate
    Future Value
    Present Value
    Periods

13. What is the optional argument for PMT, PV, and FV functions?
    Rate
    Periods
    Payment
    Type

14. What is the first argument in the PV function?
    Type
    Periods
    Rate
    Payment

15. Which of these is NOT an available level of protection in Excel?
    Excel-level protection
    Workbook-level protection
    Worksheet-level protection
    Cell-level protection

16. When the Hidden option on the Protection tab of the Format Cells dialog box is checked, what is NOT displayed in the worksheet?
    Formulas
    Labels
    Values
    Formula Results

17. Which of these is NOT an option in the Protect Sheet dialog box?
    Select unlocked cells
    Format rows
    Select locked sheets
    Insert hyperlinks

18. On what tab is the Record Macro option found?
    Insert
    Formulas
    Data
    View

19. Which of these is NOT an available level of security in Excel?
    Disable all macros
    Disable all macros except digitally signed macros
    Disable all macros with notification
    Disable all macros without notification

20. Which of these CANNOT be used to run a macro?
    Shortcut keys
    Custom buttons
    Quick Access toolbar
    Page Layout tab

Reinforce Your Skills

EA8-R1 Create a Bond Amortization Schedule for Electronics Warehouse

In this exercise, you will complete a bond amortization schedule for Electronics Warehouse. You will calculate the bond characteristics and generate a schedule with key components. You will also protect worksheet elements and create a macro.

The bond is issued on 1/1/11 and has a $200,000 face value, a twelve-year life, semiannual interest payments, a contract interest rate of 8%, and an effective interest rate of 7%.

1. Open a **Blank Workbook** and save the file in your **Chapter 08** folder as: **EA8-R1-Bond-[YourName]**

2. Prepare the worksheet as indicated:

   - Set the width of **column A** to **0.75** and the height of **row 1** to **7.2**.
   - Merge and center the **range B2:C2**, add bold formatting, and enter: **Bond Details**
   - In order, enter these headers in the **range B3:B8**: **Date, Face Value, Contract Rate, Effective Rate, Life (years), Payments per Year**
   - Apply center alignment to the **range C3:C8**.

   Now you are ready to begin populating the worksheet with the bond data.

3. Enter this data and apply any indicated formatting:

In this cell:	Type this:	And add this formatting:
Cell C3	1/1/11	
Cell C4	200000	Accounting number format
Cell C5	.08	Percent style
Cell C6	.07	Percent style
Cell C7	12	
Cell C8	2	

4. Highlight the **range B2:C8** and choose **Home→Font→Borders ▼→Outside Borders**; apply an outside border around **cell B2**.

5. Autofit **column B** and then highlight the **range C3:G3** and set the column width to **15**.

6. Merge and center the **range B10:C10**, add bold formatting and outside borders, and enter: **Bond Calculations**

7. Enter this data:

Cell B11	Present Value
Cell C11	=PV(C6/C8, C7*C8, -C4*C5/C8, -C4)
Cell B12	Future Value
Cell C12	=-FV(C6/C8, C7*C8, -C4*C5/C8, C11)
Cell B13	Payment

8. In **cell C13**, choose **Formulas→Function Library→Insert Function**, select the **Financial** category and the **PMT** function, and click **OK**.

9. Fill in the Function Arguments box as indicated, clicking **OK** when finished:
   - Rate box: **C6/C8**
   - Nper box: **C7*C8**
   - Pv box: **C11**
   - Fv box: **–C4**

10. With **cell C13** still active, click in the Formula Bar between the equals sign and *PMT* and type a minus sign.

11. Apply the **Accounting** number format to the **range C11:C13** and add an outside border around the **range B10:C13**.

Complete the Amortization Schedule

12. In the **range B15:G15**, set text wrapping and center alignment, apply an outside border, and add bold formatting.

13. In order, enter these headers in the **range B15:G15**: `Date`, `Interest Payment`, `Interest Expense`, `Amortization of Bond Premium`, `Bond Premium Balance`, `Carrying Value`

14. Type **1/1/2011** in **cell B16**, **6/30/2011** in **cell B17**, and **12/31/2011** in **cell B18**.

15. Highlight the **range B17:B18** and then drag the fill handle through **cell B40**.

16. In **cell B41**, type `Totals` and right-align the text.

17. Enter this data:

Cell F16	=C11-C12
Cell G16	=C11
Cell C17	=$C$13
Cell D17	=G16*$C$6/$C$8
Cell E17	=C17-D17
Cell F17	=F16-E17
Cell G17	=G16-E17

18. Copy the **range C17:G17** and paste to the **range C18:G40**.

19. Highlight the **range C41:E41** and choose **Home→Editing→AutoSum**; choose **Home→ Font→Borders ▼→Top and Double Bottom Border**.

20. Apply the **Accounting** number format to the **range C16:G41**.

Protect a Workbook and a Worksheet

21. Choose **Review→Changes→Protect Workbook** and, if necessary, add a checkmark in the **Structure** checkbox.

22. Enter **Protected** as the password and click **OK**; confirm the password when prompted.

23. Choose **Review→Changes→Protect Workbook**, enter the password, and click **OK**.

24. Choose **Home→Cells→Format→Protect Sheet** and, as necessary, add checkmarks next to the boxes for these options and click **OK** when finished:

    - Protect Worksheet and Contents of Locked Cells
    - Select Locked Cells
    - Select Unlocked Cells
    - Format Columns

25. Use a Ribbon command to set the width of **cell C17** to **12**.

26. Choose **Review→Changes→Unprotect Sheet**.

Protect Individual Cells

27. Highlight the **ranges C3:C8** and **B16:G41** and choose **Home→Cells→Format→ Lock Cell**.

28. Highlight the **range C11:C13**, right-click, and choose **Format Cells**.

29. Switch to the **Protection** tab, check the box for **Hidden**, and click **OK**.

30. Choose **Review→Changes→Protect Sheet** and add the password **Worksheet**, confirming the password when prompted.

31. In **cell G7**, type **k** and then click **OK** in the dialog box.

32. Rename the **Sheet1** tab to **Bond Schedule**.

Record and Run a Macro

33. Choose **File→Options→Trust Center→Trust Center Settings→Macro Settings**, ensure that **Disable All Macros with Notification** is selected, and click **OK** twice.

34. Delete the contents of the **range C16:G41**.

35. Choose **View→Macros→Macros ▼→Record Macro**, enter **Amortization_Schedule** as the macro name, and click **OK**.

36. Complete these actions in order for the new macro:

    - Select **cell F16**, type **=C11-C12** and tap Tab, and then type **=C11** and tap Enter.
    - Select **cell C17**, type **=$C$13** and tap Tab, type **=G16*$C$6/$C$8** and tap Tab, type **=C17-D17** and tap Tab, type **=F16-E17** and tap Tab, and then type **=G16-E17** and tap Enter.
    - Highlight the **range C17:G17** and drag the fill handle through **row 40**.
    - Enter **=SUM(C17:C40)** in **cell C41**.
    - Copy **cell C41** to the **range D41:E41** and tap Esc.

37. Click the **Stop Recording** button in the status bar.

38. Delete the contents of the **range C16:G41** then choose **View→Macros→Macros** and click **Run**.

39. Choose **Review→Changes→Unprotect Sheet**, enter the password **Worksheet**, and tap Enter.

40. Choose **Insert→Illustrations→Shapes**, click the **Text Box** shape, and draw a text box over the **range E2:E5**.

41. Type **Populate Schedule** in the text box, add italic formatting, and set the font size to **16**.

42. Right-click the text box, choose **Assign Macro**, click **Amortization_Schedule** in the list, and click **OK**.

43. Choose **Review→Changes→Protect Sheet** and enter **Finalized** as the password, confirming when prompted.

44. Delete the contents of the **range C16:G41** and then click the text box to run the macro.

45. Save your file as a **Macro-Enabled Workbook** and then close it.

EA8-R2 Create a Bond Amortization Schedule for Software Developers Co.

In this exercise, you will complete a bond amortization schedule for Software Developers Co. You will calculate the bond characteristics and generate a schedule with key components. You will also protect worksheet elements and create a macro.

The bond is issued on 1/1/13 and has a $180,000 face value, a four-year life, quarterly interest payments, a contract interest rate of 9%, and an effective interest rate of 10%.

1. Open a **Blank Workbook** and save the file in your **Chapter 08** folder as: **EA8-R2-Bond-[YourName]**

2. Prepare the worksheet as indicated:
   - Set the width of **column A** to **0.75** and the height of **row 1** to **7.2**.
   - Merge and center the **range B2:C2**, add bold formatting, and enter: **Bond Details**
   - In order, enter these headers in the **range B3:B8**: **Date**, **Face Value**, **Contract Rate**, **Effective Rate**, **Life (years)**, **Payments per Year**
   - Apply center alignment to the **range C3:C8**.

   Now you are ready to begin populating the worksheet with the bond data.

3. Enter this data and apply any indicated formatting:

In this cell:	Type this:	And add this formatting:
Cell C3	1/1/13	
Cell C4	180000	Accounting number format
Cell C5	.09	Percent Style
Cell C6	.1	Percent Style
Cell C7	4	
Cell C8	4	

4. Highlight the **range B2:C8** and choose **Home→Font→Borders ▼→Outside Borders**; apply an outside border around **cell B2**.

5. Highlight the **range B3:G3** and use the Ribbon to change the column width to **15**.

6. Merge and center the **range B10:C10**, add bold formatting and outside borders, and enter: **Bond Calculations**

7. Enter this data:

Cell B11	`Present Value`
Cell C11	`=PV(C6/C8, C7*C8, -C4*C5/C8, -C4)`
Cell B12	`Future Value`
Cell C12	`=-FV(C6/C8, C7*C8, -C4*C5/C8, C11)`
Cell B13	`Payment`

8. In **cell C13**, choose **Formulas→Function Library→Insert Function**, select the **Financial** category and the **PMT** function, and click **OK**.

9. Fill in the Function Arguments box as indicated, clicking **OK** when finished:

   - Rate box: **C6/C8**
   - Nper box: **C7*C8**
   - Pv box: **C11**
   - Fv box: **−C4**

10. With **cell C13** still active, click in the Formula Bar between the equals sign and *PMT* and type a minus sign.

11. Apply the **Accounting** number format to the **range C11:C13** and add outside borders to the **range B10:C13**.

Complete the Amortization Schedule

12. In the **range B15:G15**, set text wrapping and center alignment, apply an outside border, and add bold formatting.

13. In order, enter these headers in the range **B15:G15**: `Date`, `Interest Payment`, `Interest Expense`, `Amortization of Bond Discount`, `Bond Discount Balance`, `Carrying Value`

14. Type **1/1/2013** in **cell B16**, **3/31/2013** in **cell B17**, **6/30/2013** in **cell B18**, **9/30/2013** in **cell B19**, and **12/31/2013** in **cell B20**.

15. Highlight the **range B17:B20** and then drag the fill handle through **cell B32**.

16. In **cell B33**, type **Totals** and right-align the text.

17. Enter this data:

Cell F16	`=C12-C11`
Cell G16	`=C11`
Cell C17	`=$C$13`
Cell D17	`=G16*$C$6/$C$8`
Cell E17	`=D17-C17`
Cell F17	`=F16-E17`
Cell G17	`=G16+E17`

18. Copy the **range C17:G17** and paste to the **range C18:G32**.

19. Highlight the **range C33:E33**, choose **Home→Editing→AutoSum**, and choose **Home→Font→Borders ▼→Top and Double Bottom Border**.

20. Apply the **Accounting** number format to the **range C16:G33**.

Protect a Workbook and a Worksheet

21. Choose **Review→Changes→Protect Workbook** and, if necessary, add a checkmark in the **Structure** checkbox; click **OK**.

22. Turn off protection by choosing **Review→Changes→Protect Workbook**.

23. Choose **Home→Cells→Format→Protect Sheet** and, as necessary, add checkmarks in the boxes next to these options:

    - Protect Worksheet and Contents of Locked Cells
    - Select Locked Cells
    - Select Unlocked Cells
    - Format Columns

24. Enter **Accounting** as the password and click **OK**; confirm the password when prompted.

25. Use the right-click method to change the width of **column C** to **12** and then autofit **column B**.

26. Choose **Review→Changes→Unprotect Sheet**, enter the password, and click **OK**.

Protect Individual Cells

27. Highlight the **ranges C3:C8** and **B16:G33** and choose **Home→Cells→Format→ Lock Cell**.

28. Highlight the **range C11:C13**, right-click, and choose **Format Cells**.

29. Switch to the **Protection** tab, check the box for **Hidden**, and click **OK**.

30. Choose **Review→Changes→Protect Sheet** and add the password **Excel** (confirming when prompted).

31. In **cell G7**, type **w** and then click **OK** in the dialog box.

32. Rename the **Sheet1** tab to **Bond Schedule**.

Record and Run a Macro

33. Choose **File→Options→Trust Center→Trust Center Settings→Macro Settings**, ensure that **Disable All Macros with Notification** is selected, and click **OK** twice.

34. Delete the contents of the **range C16:G33**.

35. Choose **View→Macros→Macros ▼→Record Macro**, enter **Amortization_Schedule** as the macro name, and click **OK**.

36. Complete these actions in order for the macro:

    - Select **cell F16**, type **=C12-C11** and tap [Tab], and then type **=C11** and tap [Enter].
    - Select **cell C17**, type **=$C$13** and tap [Tab], type **=G16*$C$6/$C$8** and tap [Tab], type **=D17-C17** and tap [Tab], type **=F16-E17** and tap [Tab], and then type **=G16+E17** and tap [Enter].
    - Highlight the **range C17:G17** and drag the fill handle through **row 32**.
    - Enter **=SUM(C17:C32)** in **cell C33**.
    - Copy **cell C33** to the **range D33:E33** and tap [Esc].

37. Click the **Stop Recording** button in the status bar.

38. Delete the contents of the **range C16:G33** and then choose **View→Macros→Macros** and click **Run**.

39. Choose **Review→Changes→Unprotect Sheet** and then enter the password **Excel** and tap Enter.

40. Choose **Insert→Illustrations→Shapes**, click the **Text Box** shape, and draw a text box over the **range E2:E5**.

41. Type **Populate Schedule** in the text box, add bold formatting, and set the font size to **16**.

42. Right-click the text box, choose **Assign Macro**, click **Amortization_Schedule** in the list, and click **OK**.

43. Choose **Review→Changes→Protect Sheet** and enter **Macro** as the password, confirming when prompted.

44. Delete the contents of the **range C16:G33** and then click the text box to run the macro.

45. Save your file as a **Macro-Enabled Workbook** and then close it.

Apply Your Skills

EA8-A1 Create a Bond Amortization Schedule for Kim's Kitchen

In this exercise, you will complete a bond amortization schedule for Kim's Kitchen. You will calculate the bond characteristics and generate a schedule with key components. You will also protect worksheet elements and create a macro.

The bond is issued on 1/1/10 and has a $120,000 face value, a seven-year life, semiannual interest payments, a contract interest rate of 12%, and an effective interest rate of 10%.

1. Open a **Blank Workbook** and save the file in your **Chapter 08** folder as: **EA8-A1-Bond-[YourName]**

2. Change the width of **column A** to **0.75** and the height of **row 1** to **7.2**.

3. Merge and center the **range B2:C2**, type **Bond Details** in the merged cell, and bold the entry.

4. In the **range B3:B8**, enter the descriptions **Date**, **Face Value**, **Contract Rate**, **Effective Rate**, **Life (years)**, and **Payments per Year**.

5. Enter the bond details in the **range C3:C8**; center these entries.

6. Apply borders to the appropriate locations in the **range B2:C8**.

7. Adjust the column width of **columns B:G** to **15**.

8. Merge and center the **range B10:C10**, type **Bond Calculations** in the merged cell, and bold the entry.

9. In the **range B11:B13**, enter the descriptions **Present Value**, **Future Value**, and **Payment**.

10. In the **range C11:C13**, enter appropriate formulas that contain solely cell references and apply the **Accounting** number format.

11. Apply borders to the appropriate locations in the **range B10:C13**.

Complete the Amortization Schedule

12. In the **range B15:G15**, set text wrapping and center alignment, apply an outside border, and add bold formatting.

13. In the **range B15:G15**, enter the column descriptions for the bond amortization schedule.

14. In the **range B16:B18**, enter dates for the bond issuance and the first two interest payments.

15. Apply additional dates as appropriate in **column B**.

16. Type appropriate formulas in the necessary cells in **rows 16–17** of the bond amortization schedule.

17. Copy the formulas in **row 17** to the remaining rows in the bond amortization schedule.

18. In **column B** below the final populated row of the bond amortization schedule, enter **Totals** and right-align the text.

19. Use **AutoSum** in the Totals row to calculate the appropriate columns and apply the **Accounting** number format.

20. Add appropriate borders to the entire bond amortization schedule.

Protect a Workbook and a Worksheet

21. Use the **Protect Workbook** command and apply a password.

22. Turn off workbook protection.

23. Use the **Protect Worksheet** command, ensuring that all cells can be selected and all columns can be formatted while worksheet protection is on; apply a password.

24. Set the width of **column C** to **12** and autofit the width of **column B**.

25. Turn off worksheet protection.

Protect Individual Cells

26. Toggle off the **Lock Cell** command for all cells in the Bond Details and bond amortization schedule sections.

27. Hide the formulas in the Bond Calculations section.

28. Use the **Protect Sheet** command, ensuring that all cells can be selected while worksheet protection is on; apply a password.

29. Rename the worksheet to: **Bond Schedule**

Record and Run a Macro

30. Ensure that **Disable All Macros with Notification** is the active macro setting.

31. Delete all data in the bond amortization schedule except the dates and headers.

32. Record a macro that populates the bond amortization schedule, applying an appropriate name for the macro.

33. Delete all data in the bond amortization schedule except the dates and headers and then run your macro.

34. Unprotect the worksheet.

35. Insert a text box from which to run the macro in an appropriate location and add an appropriate name in bold; assign your macro to the text box.

36. Use the **Protect Sheet** command, ensuring that all cells can be selected while worksheet protection is on; apply a password.

37. Delete all data in the bond amortization schedule except the dates and headers and then use the text box to run your macro.

38. Save your file as a **Macro-Enabled Workbook** and then close it.

EA8-A2 Create a Bond Amortization Schedule for Cubby Manufacturing

In this exercise, you will complete a bond amortization schedule for Cubby Manufacturing. You will calculate the bond characteristics and generate a schedule with key components. You will also protect worksheet elements and create a macro.

The bond is issued on 1/1/12 and has a $60,000 face value, a five-year life, quarterly interest payments, a contract interest rate of 12%, and an effective interest rate of 14%.

1. Open a **Blank Workbook** and save the file in your **Chapter 08** folder as: **EA8-A2-Bond-[YourName]**

2. Change the width of **column A** to **0.75** and the height of **row 1** to **7.2**.

3. Merge and center the **range B2:C2**, type **Bond Details** in the merged cell, and bold the entry.

4. In the **range B3:B8**, enter the descriptions **Date, Face Value, Contract Rate, Effective Rate, Life (years)**, and **Payments per Year**.

5. Enter the bond details in the **range C3:C8**; center these entries.

6. Apply borders to the appropriate locations in the **range B2:C8**.

7. Adjust the column width of **columns B:G** to **15**.

8. Merge and center the **range B10:C10**, type **Bond Calculations** in the merged cell, and bold the entry.

9. In the **range B11:B13**, enter the descriptions **Present Value, Future Value**, and **Payment**.

10. In the **range C11:C13**, enter appropriate formulas that contain solely cell references and apply the **Accounting** number format.

11. Apply borders to the appropriate locations in the **range B10:C13**.

Complete the Amortization Schedule

12. In the **range B15:G15**, set text wrapping and center alignment, apply an outside border, and add bold formatting.

13. In the **range B15:G15**, enter the column descriptions for the bond amortization schedule.

14. In the **range B16:B20**, enter dates for the bond issuance and the first four interest payment dates.

15. Apply additional dates as appropriate in **column B**.

16. Type appropriate formulas in the necessary cells in **rows 16–17** of the bond amortization schedule.

17. Copy the formulas in **row 17** to the remaining rows in the bond amortization schedule.

18. In **column B** below the final populated row of the bond amortization schedule, enter **Totals** and right-align the text.

19. Use **AutoSum** in the Totals row to calculate the appropriate columns and apply the **Accounting** number format.

20. Add appropriate borders to the entire bond amortization schedule.

Protect a Workbook and a Worksheet

21. Use the **Protect Workbook** command and apply a password.

22. Turn off workbook protection.

23. Use the **Protect Worksheet** command, ensuring that all cells can be selected and all columns can be formatted while worksheet protection is on; apply a password.

24. Set the width of **column C** to **12** and autofit the width of **column B**.

25. Turn off worksheet protection.

Protect Individual Cells

26. Toggle off the **Lock Cell** command for all cells within the Bond Details and bond amortization schedule sections.

27. Hide the formulas in the Bond Calculations section.

28. Use the **Protect Sheet** command, ensuring that all cells can be selected while worksheet protection is on; apply a password.

29. Rename the worksheet to: `Bond Schedule`

Record and Run a Macro

30. Ensure that **Disable All Macros with Notification** is the active macro setting.

31. Delete all data in the bond amortization schedule except the dates and headers.

32. Record a macro that populates the bond amortization schedule, applying an appropriate name for the macro.

33. Delete all data in the bond amortization schedule except the dates and headers and then run your macro.

34. Unprotect the worksheet.

35. Insert a text box from which to run the macro in an appropriate location and add an appropriate name in italic; assign your macro to the text box.

36. Use the **Protect Sheet** command, ensuring that all cells can be selected while worksheet protection is on; and apply a password.

37. Delete all data in the bond amortization schedule except the dates and headers and then run your macro.

38. Save your file as a **Macro-Enabled Workbook** and then close it.

Extend Your Skills

EA8-E1 Complete a Bond Amortization Schedule for Townline Construction

In this exercise, you will complete a bond amortization schedule for Townline Construction. You will calculate the bond characteristics and generate a schedule with key components. You will protect worksheet elements and create a macro.

Start a new file. Reduce the width of column A to 0.75 and the height of row 1 to 7.20. Enter the bond details in the range B2:C8. Include a centered header and appropriate titles. Enter the details for a bond with a $260,000 face value, a four-year life, semiannual interest payments, a contract interest rate of 10%, and an effective interest rate of 11%. The bond is issued on 1/1/13. (Hint: Values must be entered here so they can be used in subsequent formulas.)

Enter bond calculations for the present and future values and the payments in the range B10:C13. The future value and payment calculations will generate results that match figures given above; you complete these calculations to check your work. Create a bond amortization schedule beginning in cell B15. Use headers that are consistent with those used in this chapter. Calculate totals for the appropriate columns. Assign an appropriate name to the worksheet tab.

Record a macro that generates every formula in the worksheet after the bond details (in the range B2:C8) and dates have been entered. Run the macro to ensure it operates properly. Insert a text box in an appropriate location, add an appropriate name in the text box, and assign the macro to this text box.

Protect the workbook structure and apply a password. Modify cell protection for all cells containing formulas in column G such that formulas are hidden. Then protect the worksheet by only allowing users to select locked and unlocked cells; insert hyperlinks and apply a password.

Save your file as a Macro-Enabled Workbook.

EA8-E2 Complete a Bond Amortization Schedule for Stationery Specialists

In this exercise, you will complete a bond amortization schedule for Stationery Specialists. You will calculate the bond characteristics and generate a schedule with key components. You will protect worksheet elements and create a macro.

Start a new file. Reduce the width of column A to 0.75 and the height of row 1 to 7.20. Enter the bond details in the range B2:C8. Include a centered header and appropriate titles. Enter the details for a bond with a $140,000 face value, a six-year life, quarterly interest payments, a contract interest rate of 8%, and an effective interest rate of 7%. The bond is issued on 1/1/11. (Hint: Values must be entered here so they can be used in subsequent formulas.)

Enter bond calculations for the present and future values and the payments in the range B10:C13. The future value and payment calculations will generate results that match figures given above; you complete these calculations to check your work. Create a bond amortization schedule beginning in cell B15. Use headers that are consistent with those used in this chapter. Calculate totals for the appropriate columns. Assign an appropriate name to the worksheet tab.

Record a macro that generates every formula in the worksheet after the bond details (in the range B2:C8) and dates have been entered. Run the macro to ensure it operates properly. Insert a text box in an appropriate location, add an appropriate name in the text box, and assign the macro to this text box.

Protect the workbook such that worksheets cannot be reordered, copied, or deleted. Modify cell protection for all cells containing formulas in column G such that the formulas are hidden. Protect the worksheet by allowing users to format only cells, columns, and rows; apply a password.

Save your file as a Macro-Enabled Workbook.

EA8-E3 Complete a Bond Amortization Schedule for Dan's Refinishing

In this exercise, you will complete a bond amortization schedule for Dan's Refinishing. You will calculate the bond characteristics and generate a schedule with key components. You will protect worksheet elements and create a macro.

Start a new file. Reduce the width of column A to 0.75 and the height of row 1 to 7.20. Enter the bond details in the range B2:C8. Include a centered header and appropriate titles. Enter the details for a bond with a $200,000 face value, an eight-year life, semiannual interest payments, a contract interest rate of 7%, and an effective interest rate of 9%. The bond is issued on 1/1/09. (Hint: Values must be entered here so they can be used in subsequent formulas.)

Enter bond calculations for the present and future values and the payments in the range B10:C13. The future value and payment calculations will generate results that confirm figures given above; you complete these calculations to check your work. Create a bond amortization schedule beginning in cell B15. Use headers that are consistent with those used in this chapter. Calculate totals only for the appropriate columns. Assign an appropriate name to the worksheet tab.

Record a macro that generates every formula in the worksheet after the bond details (in the range B2:C8) and dates have been entered. Run the macro to ensure it operates properly. Insert a text box in an appropriate location, add an appropriate name in the text box, and assign the macro to this text box.

Protect the workbook such that the worksheets cannot be copied, reordered, or deleted. Apply a password when protecting the workbook. Modify cell protection for all cells containing formulas in columns F:G such that the formulas are hidden. Then protect the worksheet by only allowing users to sort data.

Save your file as a Macro-Enabled Workbook.

Critical Thinking

EA8-C1 Discuss Worksheet Protection

Protection can be used at multiple levels to protect workbooks, worksheets, and individual cells. In the case of the bond amortization schedule, this protection ensures that users adjust only certain cells and cannot inadvertently alter elements that should remain static. However, a bond amortization schedule is not the only worksheet for which protection is appropriate. Depending on factors such as the frequency with which a worksheet is disseminated and the number of users with access to the file, various levels of protection can be beneficial for many of the accounting-related spreadsheets.

Write a paragraph of at least five sentences to identify four types of accounting worksheets (other than the bond amortization schedule) within which some level of protection would be appropriate. Write a second paragraph of at least eight sentences to discuss why that protection is appropriate and what level of protection you would implement for each.

EA8-C2 Discuss Macros and Worksheet Automation

Efficiency is a key goal when completing any Excel worksheet. As the size and scope of the schedule grow, taking an efficient approach to populating it becomes increasingly vital. In the case of the bond amortization schedule, you have seen how macros can be used to complete the entire body of the schedule. Macros can similarly be used in other accounting-related spreadsheets that contain repetitious and/or predictable elements.

Consider how macros can be used to increase efficiency. Write a paragraph of at least four sentences in which you identify three accounting-related spreadsheets (other than the bond amortization schedule) that can benefit from the use of macros. Write a second paragraph of at least five sentences to discuss how macros can be used in each worksheet to improve the manner in which they are populated.

Financial Statement Analysis

LEARNING OBJECTIVES

- Perform a vertical analysis
- Perform a horizontal analysis
- Calculate financial ratios
- Create charts
- Insert and reply to cell comments

Charts are among the most basic and powerful tools for quickly conveying financial information. While creating an Excel chart is straightforward, identifying the correct chart to use in a given circumstance can be more challenging. For conclusions that cannot be neatly drawn from a chart, you can add comments with text explanations. These comments are visible to others and allow you to add information without altering workbook structure. In this chapter, you will use charts and cell comments to highlight important data derived from financial statement analyses. You will perform vertical and horizontal analyses on financial statements and create charts to illustrate key relationships among the data. Finally, you will calculate financial ratios and insert cell comments.

PROJECT	City Music World

City Music World is a retail store that sells musical equipment and offers lessons for beginning and experienced musicians. The company is examining its financial statements to determine how well it performed during the previous year and how well-positioned it is to move forward with potential projects. As part of this examination, the company is performing financial statement analyses. You have been asked to create a worksheet that includes various types of financial statement analyses and highlights key insights gleaned from the analyses.

In this chapter, you will perform a vertical analysis and a horizontal analysis on the company's financial statements. You will then create charts based on these analyses to highlight key data. Last, you will calculate financial ratios and add cell comments to identify important takeaways from these calculations.

City Music World
Comparative Income Statement
For the Years Ended December 31, 2017 and December 31, 2018

	2018	2017	Dollar Change	Percent Change
Revenues:				
Sales Revenue	$ 48,750	$ 39,000	$ 9,750	25.00%
Interest Revenue	1,350	1,425	$ (75)	-5.26%
Total Revenue	50,100	40,425	$ 9,675	23.93%
Expenses:				
Rent Expense	14,250	14,250	$ -	0.00%
Cost of Goods Sold	8,750	7,200	$ 1,550	21.53%
Auto Expense	3,550	3,550	$ -	0.00%
Utilities Expense	1,875	1,220	$ 655	53.69%
Supplies Expense	1,530	1,620	$ (90)	-5.56%
Telephone Expense	1,300	740	$ 560	75.68%
Miscellaneous Expense	475	500	$ (25)	-5.00%
Total Expenses	31,730	29,080	$ 2,650	9.11%
Net Income	$ 18,370	$ 11,345	$ 7,025	61.92%

Expense Change

This horizontal analysis is accompanied by a chart that displays key elements of the analysis.

Accounting Refresher ⟳ Financial Statement Analysis

An important part of running any business is analyzing its performance to help identify potential improvements. This consists of making comparisons between the company's account balances for the most recent period and other useful **benchmarks**. Here are some common benchmarks:

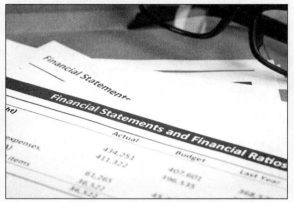

- *Prior performance:* Making comparisons to prior periods allows you to examine trends in accounts.

- *Competitor's balances:* Fluctuations in market conditions can result in specific financial results appearing more impressive at certain times. Comparisons to competitors who face the same market conditions can eliminate the need to consider these external impacts.

- *Industry standards:* A single financial figure can be viewed differently, depending on the business' industry. Comparing results to established industry standards can give you a clearer view of a company's performance.

Horizontal Analysis

One way a company's performance can be compared to any of the benchmarks is through a **horizontal analysis**. A horizontal analysis is typically performed on the income statement and balance sheet. When completing a horizontal analysis, account balances are compared across time to determine the dollar and percentage differences between them. When determining the dollar change, you subtract the base year account balance from the current year account balance. The percentage change can then be determined by dividing the dollar change by the base year account balance.

These account changes can provide a good deal of information regarding a company's performance. For example, a significant increase in a supplies expense could indicate that supplies are being inefficiently used. A thorough analysis can provide more information about this potential issue. After completing a horizontal analysis, the account changes can be viewed against comparable changes from competitors or industry averages to glean further information.

Vertical Analysis

Similar to a horizontal analysis, a **vertical analysis** is often performed on an income statement and balance sheet. Unlike a horizontal analysis, in which account balances for two periods are compared, a vertical analysis compares account balances in the same period. When used in conjunction with a horizontal analysis, a vertical analysis can provide a fuller picture of a business' performance.

(continued)

When performing a vertical analysis, you assign 100% to the base figure in the financial statement. This base figure is total assets (or total liabilities and owner's equity, which equals total assets) in the balance sheet. In the income statement, the base figure is total revenue. All other account balances in the financial statement are compared to the base figure to determine the percentage of the base figure represented by each account. For example, you determine the percentage for the Cash account by dividing the Cash account balance by the Total Assets balance. These percentages can be used to examine whether certain account balances are disproportionately large or small.

Ratio Analysis

Ratio analysis examines relationships between specific account balances. These relationships can provide further evidence as to a company's current level of success and its future prospects. Different ratios provide information about different elements of a company:

- **Liquidity ratios** indicate how quickly a company can convert assets to cash. They include the **current ratio** (current assets / current liabilities) and the **quick ratio** ((cash + short-term investments + accounts receivable) / current liabilities).

- **Solvency ratios** gauge a company's ability to meet long-term obligations. They include the **debt ratio** (total liabilities / total assets), **equity ratio** (total equity / total assets), and **debt-to-equity ratio** (total liabilities / total equity).

- **Profitability ratios** provide insight into a company's ability to effectively generate income. They include the **profit margin**(net income / revenue) and **return on assets** (net income / average total assets).

WARNING! No single piece of analysis can provide a full picture of how well a company has performed. A thorough analysis includes the examination of a variety of data.

Creating Charts in Excel

Many people are visual learners and find that numerical data is easier to interpret when presented in a chart. Charts are linked to the data from which they are created. They are automatically updated when worksheet data changes. You can apply options and enhancements to each chart element, such as the title, legend, plot area, value axis, category axis, and data series.

> [Insert] → [Charts]

You have the option of either embedding a new chart into the current worksheet where the data resides or placing it on a separate sheet (with the [F11] function key). This can be done when the chart is first created or at any time thereafter.

TIP! When you place a full-size chart on a separate worksheet, it will be based on the default chart type. You can change the chart type if desired.

Choosing the Proper Data Source and Chart Type

It's important to select the appropriate data and the proper row and column headings for certain types of charts (most notably column and bar charts) to ensure the chart displays properly. Typically, you will not include individual category data and totals because this will cause the individual data to appear distorted.

1
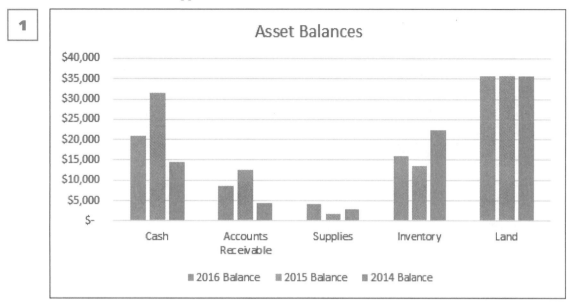

2
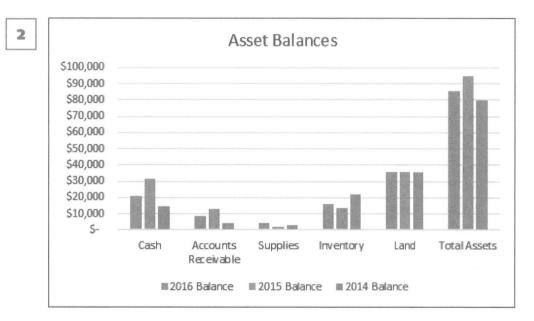

1. It's easy to see the relative differences between the account balances in this chart.

2. Here the relative differences between account balances are difficult to see because of the inclusion of Total Assets, which is significantly larger than the balance in the individual accounts.

Excel provides a variety of chart types and several subtypes for each. Each chart type displays data differently. You can also create customized charts (which can be used as templates) to meet your needs.

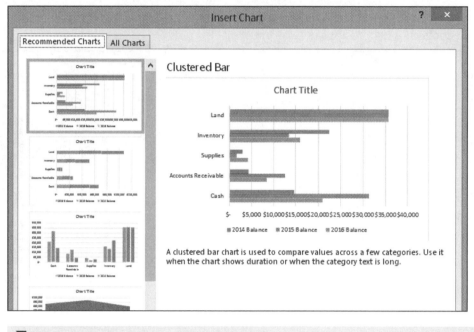

Insert→Charts→Recommended Charts

Chart and Axis Titles

You can create titles for your charts, as well as for the value and category axes. If you choose a range of information that includes what appears to Excel to be a title, Excel will include it in the new chart.

	A	B	C	D
1	Account Name	2016 Balance	2015 Balance	2014 Balance
2	Cash	$ 21,000	$ 31,400	$ 14,600
3	Accounts Receivable	$ 8,500	$ 12,600	$ 4,350
4	Supplies	$ 4,200	$ 1,640	$ 3,010
5	Inventory	$ 16,000	$ 13,500	$ 22,400
6	Land	$ 35,700	$ 35,700	$ 35,700
7	Total Assets	$ 85,400	$ 94,840	$ 80,060

The data shown here was used to create the following chart, which compares values using vertical bars. Each column within the chart represents a single account balance.

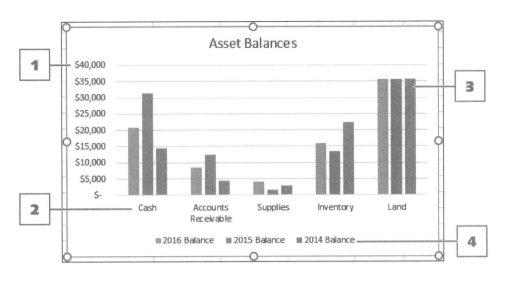

1. Vertical value axis

2. Horizontal category axis

3. Columns representing various balance sheet account values

4. Legend

Chart Formatting Control

To quickly preview and select chart elements, styles, and filters, you can use the formatting buttons that appear beside a selected chart. When you scroll over an option, a preview of that option appears in your chart.

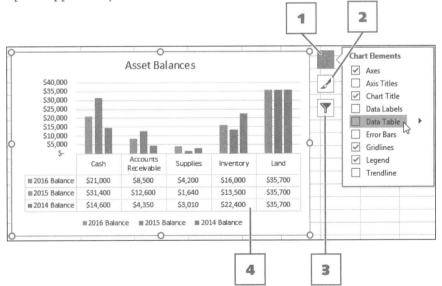

1. Chart Elements button

2. Chart Styles button

3. Chart Filters button

4. Preview of a data table's appearance

Moving, Sizing, and Deleting Charts

Charts that are embedded in a worksheet can be moved to a new location by clicking in the chart area and dragging.

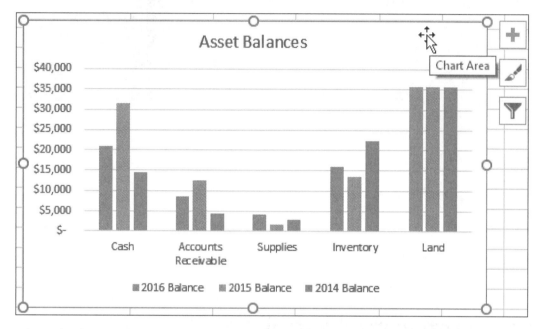

A four-pointed arrow (along with a ScreenTip) indicates that you can drag to move this selected chart.

To size a chart, it must first be selected. You can drag a sizing handle when the double-arrow mouse pointer is displayed. To change a chart size proportionately, hold Shift while dragging a corner handle. If you want to only change the height or width of a chart, do not hold Shift.

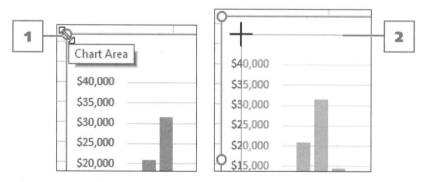

1. A double arrow appears when you point at a chart's sizing handle.

2. As you drag to size a chart, a black line displays the new size.

You can delete an embedded chart by selecting the chart area and tapping Delete. If the chart is contained on its own tab, you can delete the entire worksheet.

Changing the Chart Type and Source Data

It is easy to change the chart type using the Change Chart Type dialog box.

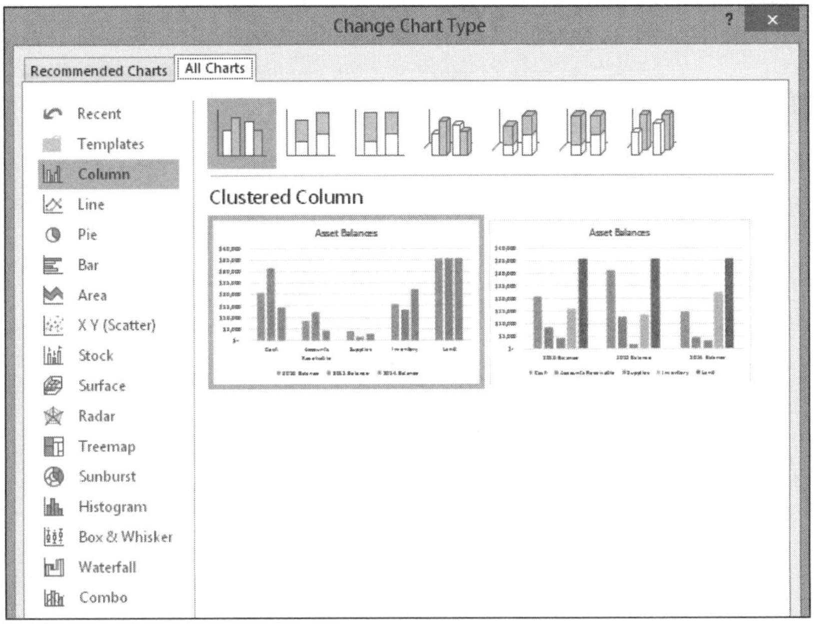

Chart Tools→Design→Type→Change Chart Type

You can also change the Source Data from within the Select Data Source dialog box. You may find it easier to edit the existing data range by using the collapse button. Aside from editing the data range, you can also alter individual data series and the horizontal axis. Note that the Switch Row/Column option swaps the data in the vertical and horizontal axes.

The Collapse button, often located to the right of a data range box in a dialog box, reduces the size of the dialog box, allowing you to more easily select cells and ranges in the worksheet.

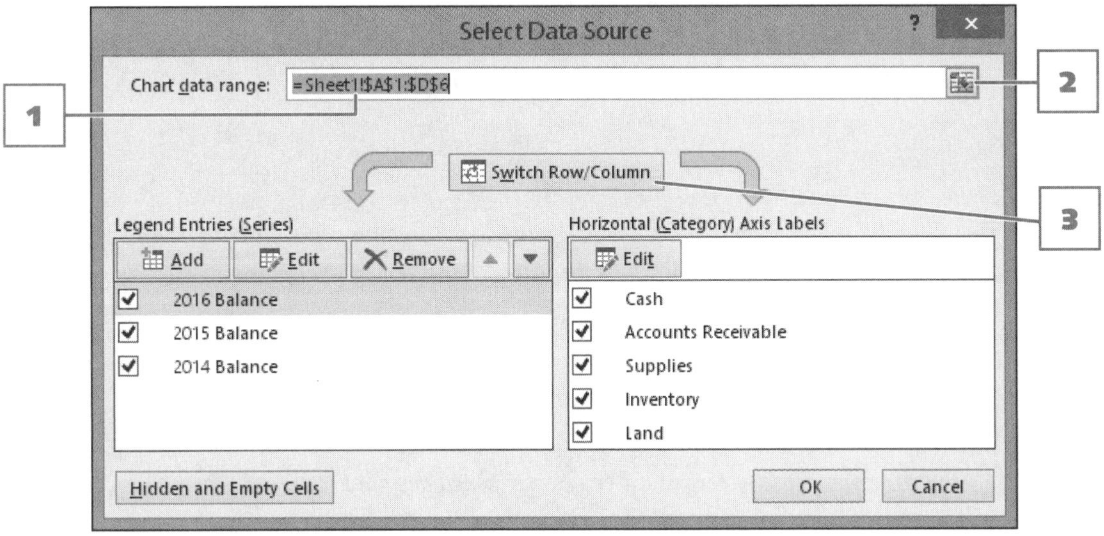

1. Worksheet name followed by an exclamation point

2. Collapse button

3. Switch Row/Column option

WARNING! Using the arrow keys while attempting to edit a data range in a text box results in unwanted characters. For best results, reselect a data range by highlighting in the worksheet.

↗ Chart Tools→Design→Data→Select Data

Modifying and Formatting Chart Elements

The legend, titles, and columns are all types of chart elements. Once selected, you can delete, move, size, and format different elements. You can move a selected element by dragging it with the mouse when you see the move pointer or change its size by dragging a sizing handle.

You can modify any chart element after the chart has been created by double-clicking the chart element to display a Format task pane with many options for that element. For example, options in the Format Chart Title dialog box allow you to adjust the vertical alignment, adjust the text direction, and apply a fill, border, or other visual effects.

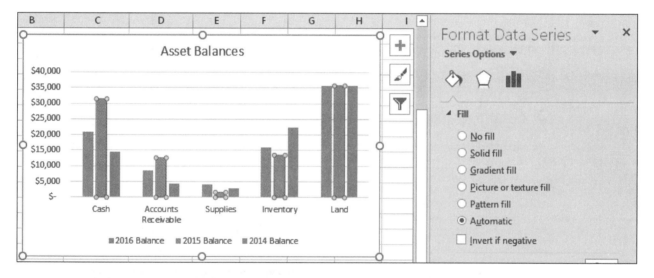

The Format task pane allows for the modification of the selected chart element.

In this exercise, you will complete a horizontal analysis on an income statement and a vertical analysis on a balance sheet. You will also chart the results of your analyses.

1. Open **EA9-D1-FSA** from your **Chapter 09** folder and save it as:
   EA9-D1-FSA-[YourName]

2. On the **Horizontal Analysis** tab, select **cell K8**, type **=** and select **cell G8**, type **–** and select **cell I8**, and then tap ⌷Enter⌷.

   This is a comparative income statement, as it includes data for more than one accounting period.

3. Select **cell M8**, type **=** and select **cell K8**, type **/** and select **cell I8**, and then tap ⌷Tab⌷.

   A horizontal analysis can be performed on any financial statement by dividing the increase or decrease in each account balance by the account balance from the base (earlier) year.

4. Copy the **range K8:M8**, highlight the **ranges K9:M10** and **K12:M20**, and choose **Home→Clipboard→Paste ▼→Formulas & Number Formatting**.

5. Highlight the **ranges C12:C19** and **K12:K19** and choose **Insert→Charts→ Insert Column or Bar Chart→Clustered Column**.

6. Drag the chart so the top-left corner is positioned at the top of **cell O2**.

   Hint: Click in the chart area and then drag.

7. Drag the bottom-right corner of the chart to the bottom-right of **cell V16**.

8. Choose **Chart Tools→Design→Data→Select Data**, highlight the **range C12:C18**, hold Ctrl, highlight the **range K12:K18**, and click **OK**.

   You removed the total expenses from the data range, thus improving readability of the chart.

9. With the chart selected, click the **Chart Elements** button (plus sign at the top-right corner) and add a checkmark next to **Chart Title**.

   A Chart Title text box appears in the chart.

10. Replace the default *Chart Title* with **Expense Change** and then click outside of the chart.

11. Switch to the **Vertical Analysis** tab and in **cell K8** enter **=G8/$G$13**.

    Cell G13 is used here, as Total Assets represents the base figure for the vertical analysis of each asset account.

12. In **cell L8**, enter **=I8/$I$13**.

13. Copy the **range K8:L8** and then select the **range K9:L13** and choose **Home→Clipboard→ Paste ▼→Formulas & Number Formatting**.

14. In **cell K15** enter **=G15/$G$18** and in **cell L15** enter **=I15/$I$18**.

    Here total liabilities and owner's equity are used as the base figures for the vertical analysis of each liability and equity account.

15. Copy the **range K15:L15** and then select the **range K17:L18**, right-click, and choose **Paste Special→Formulas & Number Formatting**.

16. Highlight the **range K8:K13** and tap F11.

    A column chart is created on a new tab. You will now modify this chart to suit your needs.

17. Rename the **Chart1** tab to: **Asset Chart – 2018**

18. Click in the chart area, choose **Chart Tools→Design→Data→Select Data**, select the **ranges C8:C13** and **K8:K13**, and tap Enter.

    Horizontal axis headers have been added to the chart because you modified the data range to include the account names.

19. Change the default name *Chart Title* to: **Asset Percentages – 2018**

20. Save your file.

    Unless otherwise directed, always keep your file open at the end of each exercise.

Working with Line and Pie Charts

Line charts show the progression of data over time, while pie charts are suitable when examining data that represent portions of a whole (just as pieces of an apple pie, when combined, represent the entire pie).

Line charts are most useful for comparing trends over a period of time. Like column charts, line charts have category and value axes. Line charts also use the same or similar objects as column charts.

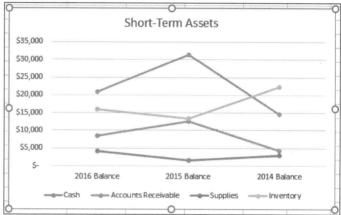

▲	A	B	C	D
1	Account Name	2016 Balance	2015 Balance	2014 Balance
2	Cash	$ 21,000	$ 31,400	$ 14,600
3	Accounts Receivable	$ 8,500	$ 12,600	$ 4,350
4	Supplies	$ 4,200	$ 1,640	$ 3,010
5	Inventory	$ 16,000	$ 13,500	$ 22,400
6	Land	$ 35,700	$ 35,700	$ 35,700
7	Total Assets	$ 85,400	$ 94,840	$ 80,060

The chart was created using the selected data.

Pie charts typically involve the selection of only two sets of data. These two sets are the values to be represented by the pie slices and the labels to identify the slices.

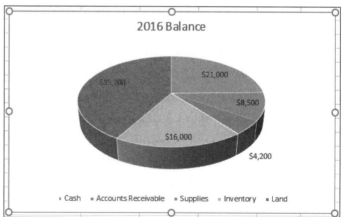

▲	A	B	C	D
1	Account Name	2016 Balance	2015 Balance	2014 Balance
2	Cash	$ 21,000	$ 31,400	$ 14,600
3	Accounts Receivable	$ 8,500	$ 12,600	$ 4,350
4	Supplies	$ 4,200	$ 1,640	$ 3,010
5	Inventory	$ 16,000	$ 13,500	$ 22,400
6	Land	$ 35,700	$ 35,700	$ 35,700
7	Total Assets	$ 85,400	$ 94,840	$ 80,060

This pie chart is based on the selected data.

Exploding, Rotating, and Elevating Pie Slices

You may want to draw attention to a particular slice of a pie chart. You can make one slice explode from the chart simply by dragging it away from the other slices.

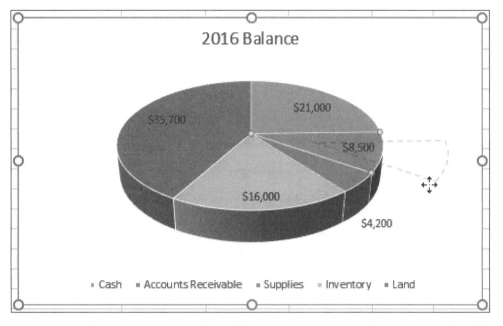

As you drag a slice out to give it an exploded effect, Excel shows a dashed line where the slice will land.

You can change the rotation and perspective (or elevation) of pie charts to display data in a different position or change the angle at which it is viewed.

NOTE!   While you can rotate other types of 3-D charts as well, you cannot rotate 2-D charts.

In this exercise, you will change your column charts to a line and a pie chart. You will then adjust the charts to ensure they effectively convey the data.

21. Save your file as: **EA9-D2-FSA-[YourName]**

22. On the **Asset Chart – 2018** tab, choose **Chart Tools→Design→Type→ Change Chart Type**.

23. Switch to the **All Charts** tab if necessary, choose the **Pie** category in the left pane, choose the **3-D Pie** type, and click **OK**.

    Notice that half of the pie chart is a single color. This half represents the total assets included in the data range. The inclusion of this total distorts the pie chart, so you will remove it.

24. Choose **Chart Tools→Design→Data→Select Data**, select the **ranges C8:C12** and **K8:K12**, and click **OK**.

    Although the pie chart is no longer distorted, you can't tell what each pie slice represents. Next you will add a legend.

25. Choose **Chart Tools→Design→Chart Layouts→Add Chart Element→Legend→ Bottom** and then click the **Chart Elements** button and choose **Data Labels→ Outside End**.

   In addition to adding a legend, you also added data labels.

26. Double-click the chart area to open the Format Chart Area task pane.

27. In the task pane under **Chart Options**, click the **Effects** button and choose **3-D Rotation→ Y Rotation**.

28. Change the existing entry to **30**.

   You have adjusted the rotation of the pie chart, which now efficiently conveys the data.

29. Double-click the chart title; in the task pane, choose **Fill & Line→Fill→Solid Fill** and choose **Green** from the color palette.

   Hint: The Green color is under Standard Colors.

30. Click the **Land – NY** pie slice twice and drag it away from the center of the chart.

   The first click selects the entire pie and the second click selects just the slice.

31. Switch to the **Horizontal Analysis** tab, click in the chart area, and choose **Chart Tools→ Design→Type→Change Chart Type**.

32. Choose the **Line** chart category and the **Line with Markers** chart type; click **OK**.

   This chart type uses markers to highlight the data points plotted in the chart; however, as a line chart is designed to show numerical progression over time, it's not a good option for this data.

33. Choose **Chart Tools→Design→Type→Change Chart Type**, select **Clustered Bar** from the **Bar** section, and click **OK**.

   A bar chart is similar to a column chart but the data is displayed horizontally (as opposed to vertically within a column chart).

34. Choose **Chart Tools→Design→Chart Layouts→Add Chart Element→Gridlines→ Primary Major Vertical**.

   The vertical gridlines interfered with the vertical axes data labels, so you removed them.

35. Save your file.

Applying Chart Layouts and Styles and Creating Sparklines

Chart layouts, also known as Quick Layouts, are designs that contain various preset chart elements. Choosing a chart layout saves time versus adding and formatting chart elements one at a time. Chart Styles are based on the workbook theme. There are many preset styles that you can apply to each chart type. The available chart layouts and styles change based on the chart type selected.

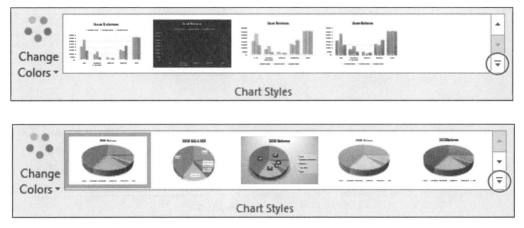

The More button displays additional options.

When you choose a chart style, the colors and effects (such as fill effects) will change to match the style selected. Data in worksheet cells is not affected by any styles you apply to charts. Excel does not allow you to create your own styles, but you can save the formatting from a selected chart as a template to use as the basis for future charts.

Sparklines

Sparklines appear as miniature charts in worksheet cells. They allow you to show data graphically without creating a larger chart. You can select a cell range and create sparklines for every row or column at once. Changes to data are reflected immediately in sparklines adjacent to the data. Each sparkline charts the data in one row or column.

	A	B	C	D	E
1	Account Name	2016 Balance	2015 Balance	2014 Balance	Sparklines
2	Cash	$ 21,000	$ 31,400	$ 14,600	
3	Accounts Receivable	$ 8,500	$ 12,600	$ 4,350	
4	Supplies	$ 4,200	$ 1,640	$ 3,010	
5	Inventory	$ 16,000	$ 13,500	$ 22,400	
6	Land	$ 35,700	$ 35,700	$ 35,700	
7	Total Assets	$ 85,400	$ 94,840	$ 80,060	

Sparklines display data trends within a single cell.

You may format a sparkline as a line, column, or win-loss. The win-loss format shows whether figures are positive or negative. You may format sparklines with different styles and choose to display data points in various ways. Note that the same formatting must be applied to sparklines that were created all at once.

↗ Insert→Sparklines→Line Sparkline *or* Column Sparkline *or* Win/Loss Sparkline

In this exercise, you will continue to improve the appearance of your charts and add sparklines.

36. Save your file as: **EA9-D3-FSA-[YourName]**

37. With the **Expense Change** chart selected, click the **Chart Styles** (paintbrush) button and choose **Style 12**.

38. Choose **Chart Tools**→**Design**→**Chart Layouts**→**Quick Layout**→**Layout 5**.

    This layout provides additional information in the chart, but you've decided that the change is unnecessary, so you will revert the chart to its previous appearance.

39. Click **Undo** on the Quick Access toolbar.

40. Switch to the **Asset Chart – 2018** tab and choose **Chart Tools**→**Design**→ **Chart Layouts**→**Quick Layout**→**Layout 1**.

    This layout provides most of the same information that you already had but does so in a different configuration.

41. Choose **Chart Tools**→**Design**→**Chart Styles**→**Style 3**.

42. Click the **Chart Filters** button in the chart, uncheck **Cash**, and click **Apply**.

    With the Cash account filtered out of the chart, note the manner in which the other pie slices expand to fill the pie chart. In this instance, it is beneficial to include the Cash account within the pie chart, so you will now add it back.

43. Check **Cash** and click **Apply**.

44. Switch to the **Vertical Analysis** tab, select the **range N8:N12**, and choose **Insert**→ **Sparklines**→**Line Sparkline**.

45. Select the **range K8:L12** and click **OK**.

    These sparklines will allow the user to see whether each account's vertical analysis percentage has increased or decreased. Alternatively, sparklines that cover more than two periods provide an excellent method by which financial trends can be displayed.

46. Click **cell N15**, choose **Insert**→**Sparklines**→**Line Sparkline**; the **Data Range** box active in the **Create Sparklines** dialog box, highlight the **range K15:L15** and click **OK**.

47. Click **cell N17**, choose **Insert**→**Sparklines**→**Line Sparkline**, select the **range K17:L17**, and click **OK**.

48. Select the **range N2:N19** and choose **Home**→**Font**→**Border** ▼→**No Border**; then select the **range B2:N19** and apply an outside border.

49. Type **Sparkline Trends** in **cell N6** and then apply bold formatting, center alignment, and text wrapping.

50. Save your file.

Inserting and Modifying Cell Comments

Excel's Comment feature is a great tool for online collaboration. A comment is a text note that you can embed inside a workbook cell without cluttering the normal view of the workbook. You can display all comments on a worksheet and even print them.

Comments are appropriate in a variety of circumstances, including:

- To document the formula or value in a cell
- To record a question about the worksheet data that can be resolved later
- To ask a question of an online collaborator without placing it into the normally printed page of the workbook

When someone inserts a comment, Excel places a small red triangle at the top-right corner of the cell. When you point at the cell containing the red triangle, Excel displays the comment author and text. You also can display/hide one or all comments using commands in the Comments group on the Review tab.

	A	B	C	D	E	F
1	Account Name	2016 Balance	2015 Balance	2014 Balance	Student Name:	
2	Cash	$ 21,000	$ 31,400	$ 14,600	Investigate this reduced	
3	Accounts Receivable	$ 8,500	$ 12,600	$ 4,350	balance.	
4	Supplies	$ 4,200	$ 1,640	$ 3,010		
5	Inventory	$ 16,000	$ 13,500	$ 22,400		
6	Land	$ 35,700	$ 35,700	$ 35,700		
7	Total Assets	$ 85,400	$ 94,840	$ 80,060		

Inserting and Deleting Comments

A comment is specific to a cell; therefore, you cannot assign a comment to a range of cells. You cannot insert more than one comment box in a cell, but you can add to an existing comment. After you give the command, a comment box appears in which you may type the text of the comment. Clicking outside the comment box hides it when *Show All Comments* is turned off. The Delete command on the Review tab will remove the selected comment from its cell.

You may jump from one comment to the next with the Next and Previous commands. This is especially useful in large worksheets. When you reach the last comment in the workbook, the Next command starts over with the first comment in the workbook.

Review→Comments→Insert a Comment │ Shift + F2

Adding to and Formatting Comments

You can add to comments from others by clicking in the comment box and typing. If the comment is not displayed, select the cell and choose Edit Comment. Typing your name in bold is recommended to identify your portion of the comment. You can also apply a different text color to your response to distinguish it from the original comment. You can change most text attributes for comments using commands on the Home tab, but the Font Color can be changed only by selecting the Format Comment command in the context menu.

NOTE!   The Insert a Comment command on the Ribbon changes to Edit Comment when the selected cell contains a comment.

⊿	A	B	C	D	E	F
1	Account Name	2016 Balance	2015 Balance	2014 Balance	**Student Name:** Investigate this reduced balance.	
2	Cash	$ 21,000	$ 31,400	$ 14,600		
3	Accounts Receivable	$ 8,500	$ 12,600	$ 4,350	**Manager Name:** Balance dropped temporarily due to timing of payments.	
4	Supplies	$ 4,200	$ 1,640	$ 3,010		
5	Inventory	$ 16,000	$ 13,500	$ 22,400		
6	Land	$ 35,700	$ 35,700	$ 35,700		
7	Total Assets	$ 85,400	$ 94,840	$ 80,060		

You can move a comment box by dragging its border or using the arrow keys on the keyboard. And to resize a comment box, you drag any of the handles that appear around its edges. A comment box does not expand automatically to display all the text of a lengthy comment, but you can scroll through text in a comment.

D	E	F	G
2014 Balance	**Student Name:** Investigate this reduced balance.		
$ 14,600			
$ 4,350			
$ 3,010	**Manager Name:** Balance dropped temporarily due to timing of payments.		
$ 22,400			
$ 35,700			
$ 80,060			

Although Excel's default is to suppress the printing of comments, you can change this in the Page Setup dialog box. When printing comments, choose a printing mode in the Page Setup dialog box. You can print each currently displayed comment where it appears on the worksheet or print all comments (whether displayed or not) on a separate sheet.

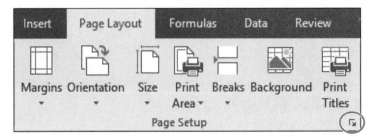

The dialog box launcher in the Page Setup group opens the Page Setup dialog box.

In this exercise, you will calculate ratios for City Music World. You will then insert comments that provide analyses of those ratios.

51. Save your file as: **EA9-D4-FSA-[YourName]**

52. Create a new worksheet tab named: **Ratio Analysis**

53. Enter **2018** in **cell B1** and **2017** in **cell C1**.

54. Highlight the **range B1:C1** and drag the fill handle through **cell F1**.

55. Apply center alignment, bold formatting, and a bottom border to the **range B1:F1**.

56. Enter the following in the **range A2:A4** in the order shown:

    - **Current Ratio**
    - **Debt Ratio**
    - **Profit Margin**

    A ratio analysis can consist of any combination of financial ratios. City Music World is examining these three.

57. Format the **range A2:A4** with bold formatting and set the column width to **12**.

58. In **cell B2**, type **=(** and switch to the **Vertical Analysis** tab, click **cell G8**, type **+** and click **cell G9**, type **+** and click **cell G10**, type **)/** and then click **cell G15**; tap Enter.

    The current ratio divides current assets by current liabilities. The only current assets in the balance sheet are Cash, Accounts Receivable, and Supplies, so these account balances comprise the numerator of the calculation.

59. In **cell C2** on the **Ratio Analysis** tab, repeat step 8 using the 2017 figures on the **Vertical Analysis** tab.

60. In **cell B3**, type **=** and click the **Vertical Analysis** tab, click **cell G15**, and then type **/** and click **cell G13**; tap Enter.

    Recall that the debt ratio is calculated as total liabilities divided by total assets.

61. In **cell C3** on the **Ratio Analysis** tab, repeat step 10 using the 2017 figures on the **Vertical Analysis** tab.

62. In **cell B4**, type **=** and click the **Horizontal Analysis** tab, click **cell G20**, and then type **/** and click **cell G10**; tap Enter.

    The profit margin is calculated as net income divided by total revenue.

63. In **cell C4** on the **Ratio Analysis** tab, repeat step 12 using the 2017 figures on the **Horizontal Analysis** tab.

64. Highlight the **range B2:F3** and choose **Home→Number→Comma Style**.

65. Highlight the **range B4:F4**, choose **Home→Number→Percent Style**, and then click **Increase Decimal**.

66. Type the following, in order, in the **range D2:F2**: **3.43**, **2.84**, and **2.67**

    These current ratios were previously determined for the years 2016, 2015, and 2014. You will now enter previously calculated debt ratios and profit margins.

67. Type the following, in order, in the **range D3:F3**: **.19**, **.27**, and **.26**

68. Type the following, in order, in the **range D4:F4**: **.18**, **.41**, and **.52**

69. Highlight the **range G2:G4**, choose **Insert→Sparklines→Column Sparkline**, highlight the **range B2:F4**, and click **OK**.

    These column sparklines illustrate the trends in the ratios over time.

70. Select **cell D2** and choose **Review→Comments→New Comment**.

    Note that your Microsoft Office username automatically appears in bold at the top of the comment.

71. Type **Investigate this increase** in the comment and then click anywhere outside the comment.

    Clicking outside the comment closes it. A red triangle appears at the top right of cell D2.

72. Right-click **cell G4** and choose **Insert Comment**; type **Is this trend sustainable?** and click **cell J1**.

73. Choose **Review→Comments→Next** to display the comment in **cell D2**. Click the **Next** button twice more to display the comment in **cell G4** and then display a dialog box.

    Clicking OK in this dialog box continues cycling through the worksheet comments; clicking Cancel leaves the current comment visible.

74. Click **OK**, choose **Review→Comments→Show/Hide Comment**, and select **cell K1**.

    The comment remains visible even after you have selected a different cell.

75. Choose **Review→Comments→Show All Comments**.

    All comments in the worksheet are visible.

76. Choose **Review→Comments→Show All Comments** to hide all comments.

77. Right-click **cell D2** and choose **Edit Comment**.

78. Tap ⌑Enter twice, choose **Home→Font→Bold**, type **Update:** and tap ⌑Enter, press ⌑Ctrl+⌑B, and type this text: **Year-end Cash balance was unusually high.**

79. Drag the bottom-right corner of the cell comment to the bottom-right corner of **cell G6**.

    You expanded the comment so it displays all text within it.

80. Select **cell A1** to hide the cell comment.

81. Save and close the file.

What Are the Benefits of Using Excel to Perform a Financial Statement Analysis?

As has been the case with many of the accounting-related worksheets you've examined, some of Excel's most useful features (including the ability to easily replicate worksheets and perform complex calculations) make it a logical choice for financial statement analyses. Excel's charts and cell comments also make the program an ideal option for this type of analysis.

Charts can be created in a variety of programs, but Excel's approach is unmatched in its simplicity. A few quick steps are all it takes to create a professional-looking chart to accompany worksheet data.

The flexibility that Excel offers in modifying charts is also unique. A financial statement analysis provides information to the end user so that decisions regarding the direction of a business can be made. These decisions are facilitated through the use of visual aids that efficiently convey key information. Excel charts are one such visual aid, and, because of the extensive manner in which they can be modified, you can adjust them to convey your desired message.

While charts convey key data from a financial statement analysis, we have seen that conclusions drawn from these analyses often require a different approach. Cell comments let you provide additional information without obscuring worksheet data. Financial statement analyses are meant to be examined and to then lead to actionable conclusions. Excel comments are particularly useful in this context.

Self-Assessment

Check your knowledge of this chapter's key concepts and skills using the Self-Assessment here or in your eLab course.

1. When you first create a chart, you can embed it in the current worksheet or place it on a separate worksheet. *True   False*

2. Chart and axis titles display in a new chart when included in the selected data range. *True   False*

3. Although you can move an embedded chart on its worksheet, you cannot change its size after it's been created. *True   False*

4. You can modify the range of data included in a chart after the chart is created via the Select Data Source dialog box. *True   False*

5. Pie charts are good for showing the progression of data over time. *True   False*

6. An exploded pie slice is not visible within a pie chart. *True   False*

7. A 2-D chart cannot be rotated. *True   False*

8. Sparklines can be thought of as miniature charts appearing in a single cell. *True   False*

9. Cell comments are always visible in a worksheet. *True   False*

10. The Insert Comment command changes to Edit Comment when the selected cell contains a comment. *True   False*

11. Which of these is NOT a category of ratios typically examined by businesses?
    Liquidity
    Solvency
    Qualitative
    Profitability

12. The Recommended Charts option is located on the _____ tab of the Ribbon.
    Home
    Insert
    Formulas
    Data

13. Which of these is NOT a chart formatting button?
    Chart Titles
    Chart Elements
    Chart Styles
    Chart Filters

14. Which of these is NOT a chart element of a column chart?
    Legend
    Titles
    Columns
    Data Range

15. How can you explode a pie slice?
Via the Ribbon
Right-click the pie slice
Drag the pie slice
Via a task pane

16. Which of these is NOT a type of sparkline?
Bar
Line
Column
Win/Loss

17. Where are sparklines located?
Within a chart
Within a single cell
Within a range of cells
Within a cell comment

18. Which of these is NOT a possible use of a cell comment?
To document a formula or value in a cell
To record a question
To change a formula and the result displayed within a cell
To communicate with an online collaborator

19. On what tab is the Insert a Comment option located?
Insert
Data
Review
View

20. How does Excel indicate that a cell contains a comment?
Green shading
An exclamation point
A yellow border
A small red triangle

Reinforce Your Skills

EA9-R3 Perform a Financial Statement Analysis for Ronald's Beverage Barn

In this exercise, you will perform a financial statement analysis for Ronald's Beverage Barn. You will perform horizontal/vertical analyses and create charts to highlight key information from these analyses. You will also calculate financial ratios and insert cell comments.

1. Open **EA9-R1-FSA** from your **Chapter 09** folder and save it as:
   EA9-R1-FSA-[YourName]

2. On the **Horizontal Analysis** tab, select **cell K8**, type **=** and select **cell G8**, and then type
   – and select **cell I8**; tap Enter.

3. Select **cell M8**, type **=** and select **cell K8**, and then type **/** and select **cell I8**; tap Tab.

4. Copy the **range K8:M8**, highlight the **range K10:M16**, and choose **Home→**
   Clipboard→Paste ▼→Formulas & Number Formatting.

5. Highlight the **ranges C10:C14** and **K10:K14** and choose **Insert→Charts→**
   Insert Column or Bar Chart→Clustered Column.

6. Position and size the chart so it covers the **range O2:V16**.

   Hint: Click the chart to select it, move it, and then resize it.

7. Replace the chart title default text with **Expense Change** and then click outside the
   chart.

8. Switch to the **Vertical Analysis** tab and enter **=G8/$G$13** in **cell K8**.

9. Enter **=I8/$I$13** in **cell L8**.

10. Copy the **range K8:L8** and then select the **range K9:L13** and choose **Home→Clipboard→**
    Paste ▼→Formulas & Number Formatting.

11. Enter **=G15/$G$18** in **cell K15** and **=I15/$I$18** in **cell L15**.

12. Copy the **range K15:L15**, then select the **range K17:L18**, right-click, and choose
    Paste Special→Formulas & Number Formatting.

13. Highlight the **range K8:K13** and tap F11.

14. Rename the **Chart1** tab to: **Asset Chart – 2018**

15. Click in the chart area and choose **Chart Tools→Design→Data→Select Data**, select the
    ranges C8:C13 and **K8:K13**, and click **OK**.

16. Click in the chart area; choose **Chart Tools→Design→Chart Layouts→**
    Add Chart Element→Chart Title→Centered Overlay and replace the default
    title with: **Asset Percentages – 2018**

Create Different Chart Types

17. Choose **Chart Tools→Design→Type→Change Chart Type**.

18. Switch to the **All Charts** tab if necessary, choose the **Pie** category and the **3-D Pie** type,
    and click **OK**.

19. Choose **Chart Tools→Design→Data→Select Data**, select the **ranges C8:C12** and **K8:K12**, and click **OK**.

20. Choose **Chart Tools→Design→Chart Layouts→Add Chart Element→Legend→ Bottom** and then click the **Add Chart Element** button and choose **Data Labels→ Outside End**.

21. Double-click the chart area; in the task pane, click **Effects** and choose **3-D Rotation→ Y Rotation** and change the existing entry to **30**.

22. Double-click the chart title; in the task pane, choose **Fill & Line→Fill→Solid Fill** and choose **Yellow** from the color palette.

23. Click the **Cash** pie slice twice and drag it away from the center of the pie chart.

24. Switch to the **Horizontal Analysis** tab, click in the chart area, choose **Chart Tools→ Design→Type→Change Chart Type**, choose **Clustered Bar** from the **Bar** category, and click **OK**.

25. Choose **Chart Tools→Design→Chart Layouts→Add Chart Element→Gridlines→ Primary Major Vertical**.

Apply Chart Layouts, Chart Styles, and Sparklines

26. Click the **Chart Styles** button and choose **Style 2**.

27. Switch to the **Asset Chart – 2018** tab and choose **Chart Tools→Design→ Chart Layouts→Quick Layout→Layout 6**.

28. Choose **Chart Tools→Design→Chart Styles→Style 6**.

29. Double-click a data label; in the task pane, navigate to **Label Options→ Label Options→Number** and choose **Percentage** (in the **Category** section).

30. Switch to the **Vertical Analysis** tab, select the **range N8:N12**, and choose **Insert→ Sparklines→Line Sparkline**.

31. Select the **range K8:L12** and click **OK**.

32. Click **cell N15**, choose **Insert→Sparklines→Line Sparkline**, highlight the **range K15:L15**, and click **OK**.

33. Select **cell N17**, choose **Insert→Sparklines→Line Sparkline**, highlight the **range K17:L17**, and click **OK**.

34. Highlight the **range N2:N19**, choose **Home→Font→Border ▼→No Border**, and then apply an outside border to the **range B2:N19**.

35. Type `Sparkline Trends` in **cell N6** and then apply bold formatting, center align-ment, and text wrapping.

Calculate Ratios and Insert Cell Comments

36. Create a new worksheet tab named: `Ratio Analysis`

37. Enter **2018** in **cell B1** and **2017** in **cell C1**.

38. Highlight the **range B1:C1** and drag the fill handle through **cell F1**.

39. Apply center alignment, bold formatting, and a bottom border to the **range B1:F1**.

40. Enter the following into the **range A2:A4** in the order shown:
    - `Current Ratio`
    - `Equity Ratio`
    - `Profit Margin`

41. Format the range with bold formatting and set the column width to **12**.

42. In **cell B2**, type **=(** and switch to the **Vertical Analysis** tab, click **cell G8**, type **+** and click **cell G9**, type **+** and click **cell G10**, type **+** and click **cell G11**, and then type **)/** and click **cell G15**; tap [Enter].

43. Repeat step 42 in **cell C2** using the 2017 figures.

44. In **cell B3**, type **=** and switch to the **Vertical Analysis** tab, click **cell G17**, and type **/** and click **cell G13**; tap [Enter].

45. Repeat step 44 in **cell C3** using the 2017 figures.

46. In **cell B4**, type **=** and switch to the **Horizontal Analysis** tab, click **cell G16**, and then type **/** and click **cell G8**; tap [Enter].

47. Repeat step 46 in **cell C4** using the 2017 figures.

48. Highlight the **range B2:F3** and choose **Home→Number→Comma Style**; then apply the **Percent Style** to the **range B4:F4** and choose **Home→Number→Increase Decimal**.

49. Enter this data:

Cell D2	0.28
Cell E2	0.30
Cell F2	0.57
Cell D3	0.32
Cell E3	0.21
Cell F3	0.26
Cell D4	.086
Cell E4	.234
Cell F4	.119

50. Select the **range G2:G4**, choose **Insert→Sparklines→Column Sparkline**, select the **range B2:F4**, and click **OK**.

51. Select **cell E3**, choose **Review→Comments→New Comment**, and enter this comment: **Investigate this decrease.**

52. Right-click **cell C4** and choose **Insert Comment**; then type **Why did profit decline?** and click **cell J1**.

53. Right-click **cell C4**, choose **Edit Comment**, tap [Enter] twice, type **Update:** in bold, and then turn off bold and type **Temporary economic slowdown.**

54. Drag the bottom-right corner of the comment to the bottom-right corner of **cell G8**.

55. Select **cell A1** to hide the cell comment.

56. Save and close the file.

EA9-R4 Perform a Financial Statement Analysis for Office Supply Superstore

In this exercise, you will perform a financial statement analysis for Office Supply Superstore. You will perform horizontal/vertical analyses and create charts to highlight key information from these analyses. You will also calculate financial ratios and insert cell comments.

1. Open **EA9-R2-FSA** from your **Chapter 09** folder and save it as:
   EA9-R2-FSA-[YourName]

2. On the **Horizontal Analysis** tab, select **cell K8**, type **=** and select **cell G8**, and then type **–** and select **cell I8**; tap Enter.

3. Enter **=K8/I8** in **cell M8**.

4. Copy the **range K8:M8**, highlight the **ranges K9:M13, K15:M16,** and **K18:M19,** and choose **Home→Clipboard→Paste ▼→Formulas & Number Formatting**.

5. Select the **ranges C8:C13** and **M8:M13** and choose **Insert→Charts→ Insert Column or Bar Chart→Clustered Column**.

6. Position the chart so it covers the **range O2:W17**.

7. Choose **Chart Tools→Design→Data→Select Data**, highlight the **ranges C8:C12** and **M8:M12**, and click **OK**.

8. With the chart selected, click the **Chart Elements** button and add a checkmark next to **Chart Title** and replace the default text with: **Asset Change**

9. Switch to the **Vertical Analysis** tab and enter **=G8/$G$8** in **cell K8**.

10. Enter **=I8/$I$8** in **cell L8**.

11. Copy the **range K8:L8** and then select the **range K10:L15** and choose **Home→Clipboard→ Paste ▼→Formulas & Number Formatting**.

12. Highlight the **range K10:K14** and tap F11.

13. Rename the **Chart1** tab as: **Expense Chart - 2018**

14. Click in the chart area, choose **Chart Tools→Design→Data→Select Data**, select the **ranges C10:C15** and **K10:K15**, and click **OK**.

15. Click the **Chart Filters** button, uncheck **Total Expenses**, and click **Apply**.

16. Click in the chart area, choose **Chart Tools→Design→Chart Layouts→ Add Chart Element→Chart Title→Centered Overlay**, and add the title: **Expense Percentages - 2018**

Create Different Chart Types

17. Choose **Chart Tools→Design→Type→Change Chart Type**.

18. Switch to the **All Charts** tab, if necessary, and then choose the **Pie** category and **Pie** type, and click **OK**.

19. Choose **Chart Tools→Design→Chart Layouts→Add Chart Element→Legend→ Bottom** and then click the **Add Chart Element** button and choose **Data Labels→ Best Fit**.

20. Double-click the title; in task pane, navigate to **Title Options→Fill & Line→Fill→ Solid Fill**, and choose **Red** from the palette.

21. Switch to the **Horizontal Analysis** tab, click in the chart area, choose **Chart Tools→Design→Type→Change Chart Type**, choose **Line with Markers** from the **Line** category, and click **OK**.

22. Choose **Chart Tools→Design→Type→Change Chart Type**, select the **All Charts** tab, select **Clustered Bar** from the **Bar** category, and click **OK**.

23. Choose **Chart Tools→Design→Chart Layouts→Add Chart Element→Gridlines→Primary Major Vertical**.

Apply Chart Layouts, Chart Styles, and Sparklines

24. Click the **Chart Styles** button and choose **Style 9**.

25. Switch to the **Expense Chart – 2018** tab and choose **Chart Tools→Design→Chart Layouts→Quick Layout→Layout 6**.

26. Choose **Chart Tools→Design→Chart Styles→Style 10**.

27. Double-click a data label; in the task pane, navigate to **Label Options→Label Options→Number** and choose **Percentage** (in the **Category** section).

28. Switch to the **Vertical Analysis** tab, highlight the **range N10:N13**, and choose **Insert→Sparklines→Line Sparkline**.

29. Select the **range K10:L13** and click **OK**.

30. Highlight the **range N2:N16**, choose **Home→Font→Border ▼→No Border**, and then apply an outside border to the **range B2:N16**.

31. Type `Sparkline Trends` in **cell N6** and then apply bold formatting, center alignment, and text wrapping.

Calculate Ratios and Insert Cell Comments

32. Create a new worksheet tab named: `Ratio Analysis`

33. Enter **2018** in **cell B1** and **2017** in **cell C1**.

34. Highlight the **range B1:C1** and drag the fill handle through **cell F1**.

35. Apply center alignment, bold formatting, and a bottom border to the **range B1:F1**.

36. Enter the following into the **range A2:A4** in the order shown:

    - `Current Ratio`
    - `Debt Ratio`
    - `Return on Assets`

37. Format the range with bold formatting and set the column width to **16**.

38. In **cell B2**, type **=(** and then switch to the **Horizontal Analysis** tab, click **cell G8**, type **+** and click **cell G9**, type **+** and click **cell G10**, type **+** and click **cell G11**, type **)/(** and click **cell G15**, type **+** and click **cell G16**, and then type **)** and tap Enter.

39. Repeat step 38 in **cell C2** using the 2017 figures.

40. In **cell B3**, type **=(** and switch to the **Horizontal Analysis** tab, click **cell G15**, type **+** and click **cell G16**, and then type **)/** and click **cell G13**; tap [Enter].

41. Repeat step 40 in **cell C3** using the 2017 figures.

42. In **cell B4**, type **=** and switch to the **Vertical Analysis** tab, click **cell G15**, type **/((** and switch to the **Horizontal Analysis** tab, select **cell G13**, type **+** and click **cell I13**, and then type **)/2)** and tap [Enter].

43. In **cell C4**, type **=** and switch to the **Vertical Analysis** tab, click **cell I15**, type **/** and switch to the **Horizontal Analysis** tab, and then select **cell I13**; tap [Enter].

    When calculating the return on assets you assume that ending total assets for 2017 equal ending total assets for 2016.

44. Highlight the **range B2:F3**, choose **Home→Number→Comma Style** and then apply the **Percent Style** to the **range B4:F4** and choose **Home→Number→Increase Decimal**.

45. Enter this data:

Cell D2	2.31
Cell E2	3.87
Cell F2	2.05
Cell D3	0.42
Cell E3	0.34
Cell F3	0.51
Cell D4	.234
Cell E4	.303
Cell F4	.397

46. Select the **range G2:G4**, choose **Insert→Sparklines→Column Sparkline**, select the **range B2:F4**, and click **OK**.

47. Select **cell C2**, choose **Review→Comments→New Comment**, and enter this comment: **Investigate this decrease**

48. Right-click **cell D4** and choose **Insert Comment** and then type **Examine this inefficiency** and click **cell J1**.

49. Right-click **cell D4**, choose **Edit Comment**, tap [Enter] twice, type **Update:** in bold, and then turn off bold and type: **Product mix issues, which led to this decrease, have been resolved.**

50. Drag the bottom-right corner of cell comment to the bottom-right corner of **cell G9**.

51. Select **cell A1** to hide the cell comment.

52. Save and close the file.

Apply Your Skills

EA9-A1 Perform a Financial Statement Analysis for Legal Services Co.

In this exercise, you will perform a financial statement analysis for Legal Services Co. You will perform horizontal/vertical analyses and create charts to highlight key information from these analyses. You will also calculate financial ratios and insert cell comments.

Use this information to complete the ratio analysis.

Ratio	2016	2015	2014
Quick Ratio	3.72	4.51	3.90
Debt Ratio	0.072	0.061	0.052
Profit Margin	.342	.294	.206

1. Open **EA9-A1-FSA** from your **Chapter 09** folder and save it as:
   EA9-A1-FSA-[YourName]

2. On the **Horizontal Analysis** tab, create formulas to calculate the dollar change in **column K** for all lines in the balance sheet.

3. In **column M**, create formulas to calculate the percent change for all lines.

4. Create an embedded **Clustered Column** chart based on the percent changes in each asset account.

5. Position the chart to the right of and top-aligned with the balance sheet.

6. Add an appropriate chart title and, if necessary, resize the chart so all elements are logically displayed.

7. Switch to the **Vertical Analysis** tab and create formulas to complete a vertical analysis on the income statement for 2018 and 2017.

8. Create a **Column Chart** on its own tab that is based on the 2018 expense account percentages. Include the Total Expenses and the Net Income rows in the chart.

9. Ensure that an appropriate chart title is centered and positioned on the column chart itself.

10. Rename the new worksheet tab to: **Expense Chart – 2018**

Create Different Chart Types

11. Change the chart type to **3-D Pie**.

12. Filter the chart to not display **Total Expenses**.

13. Display the legend at the bottom of the chart, display **Best Fit** data labels, and rotate the Y-axis of the chart to **40** degrees.

14. Add the **Yellow** fill to the background of the chart title.

15. Explode the largest pie slice.

16. Change the chart type associated with the balance sheet to **Clustered Bar** and remove gridlines.

Apply Chart Layouts, Chart Styles, and Sparklines

17. Apply **Layout 2** and **Style 3** to the **3-D Pie** chart.

18. Adjust the data labels to display as **Percentages** with **2** decimal places.

19. Display **Column Sparklines** to the right of each revenue and expense account in the income statement.

20. Adjust the borders around the income statement to include the sparklines.

21. Insert a **Sparkline Trends** header in the appropriate location, making sure its formatting is consistent with that of the adjacent cell entries.

Calculate Ratios and Insert Cell Comments

22. Create a new worksheet named **Financial Ratios**.

23. Enter headers for the five-year period from 2014–2018 in the **range B1:F1**, starting with the most recent year.

24. Enter the **Quick Ratio**, **Debt Ratio**, and **Profit Margin** headers in the **range A2:A4**, in that order.

25. Format all headers with bold formatting, add a bottom border and center alignment to all year headers, and expand the width of **column A** to **14**.

26. Create **formulas** to calculate the **ratios** for 2018 and 2017.

27. Enter the **ratios** for 2016, 2015, and 2014 based on the table in the instructions.

28. Apply **Comma Style** to all quick and debt ratios, add one decimal place to the debt ratios, and apply **Percent Style** with one decimal place to all profit margins.

29. Insert **Line Sparklines** to the right of each set of ratios, displaying all five years of ratio data.

30. Insert comments in the cells for the largest debt ratio and the smallest profit margin to indicate that they require further investigation.

31. Display all comments in the worksheet.

32. Enter a response in the comment for the smallest profit margin, indicating client attrition led to the reduced earnings for the year. Make sure the response is distinct from the original comment.

33. If necessary, resize the profit margin cell comment so it is entirely visible.

34. Embed a **Line** chart below the ratio data that displays the profit margin trend over the five-year period.

35. Modify the chart to include a chart title.

36. Save and close the file.

EA9-A2 Perform a Financial Statement Analysis for Water Feature Designers Inc.

In this exercise, you will perform a financial statement analysis for Water Feature Designers Inc. You will perform horizontal/vertical analyses and create charts to highlight key information from these analyses. You will also calculate financial ratios and insert cell comments.

Use this information to complete the ratio analysis.

Ratio	2016	2015	2014
Current Ratio	7.62	3.45	8.21
Debt-to-Equity Ratio	0.17	0.28	0.18
Profit Margin	.186	.292	.255

1. Open **EA9-A2-FSA** from your **Chapter 09** folder and save it as: **EA9-A2-FSA-[YourName]**

2. On the **Horizontal Analysis** tab, create formulas to calculate the dollar change in **column K** for all lines in the income statement.

3. In **column M**, create formulas to calculate the percent change for all lines.

4. Create an embedded **Clustered Column** chart based on the percent changes in each expense account.

5. Position the chart to the right of and top-aligned with the income statement.

6. Add an appropriate chart title and, if necessary, resize the chart so all elements are logically displayed.

7. Switch to the **Vertical Analysis** tab and create formulas to complete a vertical analysis on the balance sheet for 2018 and 2017.

8. Create a **Column Chart** on its own tab that is based on the 2018 asset account percentages. Include the Total Assets row in the chart.

9. Ensure that an appropriate chart title is displayed above the column chart and that it's positioned on the column chart itself.

10. Rename the new worksheet tab to: **Asset Chart - 2018**

Create Different Chart Types

11. Change the chart type to **3-D Pie**.

12. Filter the chart to not display **Total Assets.**

13. Display the legend at the bottom of the chart, display **Outside End** data labels, and rotate the Y-axis of the chart to **30** degrees.

14. Add the **Blue** fill to the background of the chart title.

15. Explode the smallest pie slice.

16. Change the chart type associated with the income statement to **Clustered Bar** and remove gridlines.

Apply Chart Layouts, Chart Styles, and Sparklines

17. Apply **Layout 6** and **Style 7** to the **3-D Pie** chart.

18. Use filters to remove **Land** from the 3-D Pie chart.

19. Adjust the data labels to display as **Percentages** with **2** decimal places.

20. Display **Column Sparklines** to the right of each asset, liability, and owner's equity account in the balance sheet.

21. Adjust the borders and the balance sheet to include the sparklines.

22. Insert a `Sparkline Trends` header in the appropriate location, making sure its formatting is consistent with that of the adjacent cell entries.

Calculate Ratios and Insert Cell Comments

23. Create a new worksheet named: `Financial Ratios`

24. Enter headers for the five-year period from 2014–2018 in the **range B1:F1**, starting with the most recent year.

25. In order, enter these headings in the **range A2:A4**: `Current Ratio`, `Debt-to-Equity Ratio`, and `Profit Margin`

26. Format all headers with bold formatting, add a bottom border and center alignment to all year headers, and expand the width of **column A** to **20**.

27. Create **formulas** to calculate the **ratios** for 2018 and 2017.

28. Enter the **ratios** for 2016, 2015, and 2014 based on the table in the instructions.

29. Apply **Comma Style** to all current and debt-to-equity ratios and apply **Percent Style** with one decimal place to all profit margins.

30. Insert **Line Sparklines** to the right of each set of ratios, displaying all five years of ratio data.

31. Insert comments in the cells for the largest profit margin and smallest debt-to-equity ratio to indicate that these require further investigation.

32. Display all comments in the worksheet.

33. Enter a response in the comment for the largest profit margin, indicating that a single large client led to inflated earnings for the year. Make sure the response is distinct from the original comment.

34. If necessary, resize the profit margin cell comment so it is entirely visible.

35. Embed a **Line** chart below the ratio data that displays the trend in the current ratio over the five-year period.

36. Modify the chart to include a chart title.

37. Save and close the file.

Extend Your Skills

EA9-E1 Perform a Financial Statement Analysis for Experienced Metalworks

In this exercise, you will perform a financial statement analysis for Experienced Metalworks. You will perform horizontal/vertical analyses and create charts to highlight key information from these analyses. You will also calculate financial ratios, insert cell comments, and create a chart for one set of ratio data.

Open **EA9-E1-FSA**. Complete a horizontal analysis on the 2018 and 2017 income statements and a vertical analysis on the 2018 and 2017 balance sheets. Embed two pie charts beside the balance sheet—one to display the 2017 asset account percentages and another to display the 2018 asset account percentages. Ensure that each has a chart title, legend, and data labels that are logically displayed.

Place a column chart on its own worksheet that displays each 2018 expense account percent change. Include a chart title and worksheet tab title.

Create a new worksheet to calculate the quick ratio, debt ratio, and profit margin for 2018 and 2017, and assign an appropriate worksheet title. Expand the worksheet to include these ratio results:

Ratio	2016	2015	2014
Quick Ratio	1.62	1.84	1.26
Debt Ratio	0.32	0.31	0.24
Profit Margin	0.36	0.52	0.50

Ensure that the ratios are presented logically and that cells are formatted to properly present the data. Enter cell comments for the largest quick ratio and smallest profit margin to indicate that further investigation is needed for each. Then add a response to the quick ratio comment, appropriately distinguished from the original, indicating that Accounts Receivable experienced a temporary increase at year-end, and size the comment appropriately.

Create column sparklines beside the financial ratios to show the trends over the five-year period. Embed a line chart below the financial ratios to display the debt ratio for all five years. Include a chart title within the chart.

EA9-E2 Perform a Financial Statement Analysis for Carpet Emporium

In this exercise, you will perform a financial statement analysis for Carpet Emporium. You will perform horizontal/vertical analyses and create charts to highlight key information from these analyses. You will also calculate financial ratios, insert cell comments, and create a chart for one set of ratio data.

Open **EA9-E2-FSA**. Complete a horizontal analysis on the 2018 and 2017 balance sheets and a vertical analysis on the 2018 and 2017 income statements. Embed two pie charts beside the income statement—one to display the 2017 expense account percentages and another to display the 2018 expense account percentages. Ensure that each has a chart title, legend, and data labels that are logically displayed.

Place a column chart on its own worksheet that displays each 2018 asset account dollar change. Include a chart title and worksheet tab title.

Create a new worksheet to calculate the current ratio, debt-to-equity ratio, and profit margin for 2018 and 2017, and assign an appropriate worksheet title. Expand the worksheet to include these ratio results:

Ratio	2016	2015	2014
Current Ratio	10.65	17.23	67.39
Debt-to-Equity Ratio	0.11	0.10	0.01
Profit Margin	0.46	0.19	0.26

Ensure that the ratios are presented logically and that cells are formatted to properly present the data. Enter cell comments for the largest profit margin and smallest debt-to-equity ratio to indicate that further investigation is needed for each. Then add a response to the profit margin comment, appropriately distinguished from the original, indicating that a temporary rent expense reduction was provided by the landlord due to building maintenance issues, and size the comment appropriately.

Create line sparklines beside the financial ratios to show the trend in each over the five-year period. Embed a line chart below the financial ratios to display the current ratio for all five years. Include a chart title within the chart.

EA9-E3 Perform a Financial Statement Analysis for Best Side Videography

In this exercise, you will perform a financial statement analysis for Best Side Videography. You will perform horizontal/vertical analyses and create charts to highlight key information from these analyses. You will also calculate financial ratios, insert cell comments, and create a chart for one set of ratio data.

Open **EA9-E3-FSA**. Complete a horizontal analysis on the 2018 and 2017 income statements and a vertical analysis on the 2018 and 2017 balance sheets. Embed two pie charts beside the balance sheet—one to display the 2017 asset account percentages and another to display the 2018 asset account percentages. Ensure that each has a chart title, legend, and data labels that are logically displayed.

Place a bar chart on its own worksheet that displays each 2018 expense account dollar change. Include a chart title and worksheet tab title.

Create a new worksheet to calculate the current ratio, equity ratio, and return on assets for 2018 and 2017, and assign an appropriate worksheet title. Assume that total assets on 12/31/2016 were equal to total assets on 12/31/2017. Expand the worksheet to include these ratio results:

Ratio	2016	2015	2014
Current Ratio	0.83	0.69	0.48
Equity Ratio	0.51	0.56	0.53
Return on Assets	0.88	0.63	1.71

Ensure that the ratios are presented logically and that cells are formatted to properly present the data. Enter cell comments for the largest return on assets and smallest current ratio to indicate that further investigation is needed for each. Then add a response to the return on assets comment, appropriately distinguished from the original, indicating that an unusually high one-time fee was earned during this year, leading to the increased return on assets for the year, and size the comment appropriately.

Create column sparklines beside the financial ratios to show the trends in each over the five-year period. Embed a line chart below the financial ratios to display the return on assets for all five years. Include a chart title within the chart.

Critical Thinking

EA9-C1 Discuss Creating Charts in Accounting-Related Worksheets

Charts are flexible visual aids and an invaluable resource in Excel. While you used them to illustrate key data from a financial statement analysis in this chapter, they have many other accounting-related uses. It is not uncommon for charts to be associated with a variety of worksheets, particularly those that will be disseminated to many end users.

Write a paragraph of at least six sentences in which you identify four types of accounting worksheets (other than financial statement analyses). Write a second paragraph of at least six sentences to discuss how the use of charts in each worksheet would provide a benefit to the end user.

EA9-C2 Discuss Using Cell Comments in Accounting-Related Worksheets

Even with the most complex worksheets, a primary goal is to ensure that the end user can fully read and comprehend the data. In this chapter, you saw how cell comments can be used to provide additional details, conclusions, etc. This supplemental information, when added to financial statement analyses, can be vital to ensuring that the data is properly interpreted. Cell comments provide similar clarification in other accounting-related worksheets.

Write a paragraph of at least five sentences in which you discuss four accounting-related worksheets (other than financial statement analyses) that would benefit from the inclusion of cell comments. Write a second paragraph of at least eight sentences to discuss both the worksheet data for which cell comments would be helpful and why you believe further information related to this data would be needed.

Budgeting and Cost Analysis

LEARNING OBJECTIVES

- Create cost and purchases budgets

- Perform a cost-volume-profit (CVP) analysis

- Freeze rows and columns

- Split a worksheet window

- Use Goal Seek

- Use Solver

As worksheets become more complex, being able to view them in different ways will be key to effectively examining the data. Freezing rows so they remain visible as you scroll through, splitting worksheets so two distant elements of the same worksheet can be viewed simultaneously, and using multiple worksheets greatly facilitate complicated analyses. In addition, the use of Excel's what-if analysis tools, such as Goal Seek and Solver, allows you to examine how worksheet results change based on different inputs. In this chapter, you will create budgets and perform a cost-volume-profit (CVP) analysis. An essential element of proper planning for any business is the estimation of potential financial outcomes; these budgets and costs analyses will assist the company in determining how it should proceed with operations during future periods.

PROJECT	# City Music World

City Music World is a retail store that sells musical equipment and offers lessons for beginning and experienced musicians. As part of its annual planning process, it is reviewing financial results to determine how the business should proceed. The company has determined that a thorough examination of cash, purchases, and overall costs is needed. You are creating cash and purchases budgets for the upcoming four quarters. You are also performing a cost-volume-profit (CVP) analysis for the same period.

In this chapter, you will begin by completing the cash and purchases budgets on different worksheets in the same workbook. You will freeze worksheet elements and split the worksheet window as part of this process. You will then perform what-if analyses to determine the potential scenarios involving costs for the upcoming year.

▲	A	B	C	D	I	J
1		City Music World				
2		Cash Budget				
3		For Quarters Ending in 2017				
4						
5				Quarter #4		Quarter #1
6	Beginning Cash Balance			$ 3,950		$ 23,000
7						
8	Add:	Cash Receipts from In-Store Customer Sales		$ 107,200		$ 122,000
9		Cash Receipts from Online Customer Sales		$ 29,300		$ 34,000
10		Cash Receipts from Services Rendered		$ 7,700		$ 18,000
11		Reduction in Accounts Receivable		$ 32,600		$ 42,000
17						
18	Less:	Cash Disbursements for Merchandise Purchases		$ 94,800		$ 103,000
19		Cash Disbursements for Operating Expenses		$ 60,900		$ 84,600
20		Loan Payments (Principal)		$ 13,200		$ 13,200
21		Loan Payments (Interest)		$ 1,800		$ 1,800
22	Total Cash Disbursements:			$ 170,700		$ 202,600

This cash budget is displayed using a split window.

Budgeting and Cost Analysis

Accounting Refresher

Budgeting is a process that is undertaken as part of overall planning for future periods. Budgeting can take on many forms and can be used to make determinations such as the cash required for future operations, the total that can be spent on expenses, and the merchandise purchases required to achieve various sales levels. Although the budgets completed by a given company will largely depend on the type of business, two common budgets are the **cash budget** and **purchases budget**.

Cash Budget

A cash budget can take on a number of forms. One can be created to estimate cash receipts from sales, another can estimate cash payments for operating expenses, and a third can combine estimated cash inflows and outflows to determine whether sufficient funds are available to pursue a large project. The key to producing actionable budgets, regardless of the  form, is to use well-researched estimates that lead to reasonable financial figures. These budgets are most useful when they approximate the financial results that ultimately occur. Accurate estimates lead to accurate budgets, so take care when creating estimates.

To establish estimates, a business reviews prior periods as well as industry and competitor results. These benchmarks, along with general economic projections for the future periods in question, help to establish reasonable estimates of items such as unit sales, bad debt expenses, and interest rates.

Purchases Budget

A purchases budget estimates merchandise purchases given the current level of inventory and the expected demand over the coming period. The goal is to ensure that the company neither runs out of products to sell nor holds too much product in inventory (as this can lead to increased expenses). To determine the proper level of purchases, the company estimates the cost of goods sold (based on projected sales levels) and determines the desired ending inventory (to have sufficient product available for the beginning of the subsequent period). When these two items are added and beginning inventory is subtracted from the total on hand, the company arrives at total budgeted purchases for the period.

(continued)

Cost-Volume-Profit (CVP) Analysis

A **cost-volume-profit (cvp) analysis** gauges the different income levels that can be expected based on the possible combinations of variable costs, fixed costs, and unit sales for a period. Just as with cash and purchases budgets, the company uses estimates to complete a CVP analysis. In fact, a company will often begin a CVP analysis by determining the **breakeven point**, which is the level of sales necessary to generate total net income of $0, based on the estimated variable and fixed costs. From there the business often calculates net income based on expected sales (instead of attempting to determine required sales that will lead to net income of $0). When performing CVP analyses, contribution margin is a key component. **Contribution margin** is the unit selling price minus the unit variable cost. For each additional unit sold, net income increases by the contribution margin.

Using Flexible Worksheet Views

Excel allows you to view two areas of a large worksheet that normally could not display together. You can easily restore the worksheet to its original view. Two or more worksheets in the same workbook or different workbooks can also be viewed at once.

Freezing Rows and Columns

When you select the Freeze Panes command, Excel freezes all rows above and all columns to the left of the selected cell. This locks the frozen rows and columns in place so they remain visible on the screen when you scroll. This can be particularly useful with worksheets that have many rows.

TIP!   To freeze rows only, select a cell in column A before choosing Freeze Panes. Similarly, to freeze columns only, select a cell in row 1 first.

 View→Window→Freeze Panes

Splitting the Worksheet Window

You may want to split the window to scroll within two areas of a worksheet. For example, a manager may want to compare budgetary data in rows 3–15 with that in rows 203–215. The Split button on the Ribbon toggles the split screen on/off.

Splitting Compared to Freezing

Freezing is useful to keep headings visible, but this may not allow you to view two nonadjacent groups of data. Splitting the window allows you to view two or four nonadjacent groups. Each pane has its own set of scroll bars. You can drag the split bar to adjust the number of rows or columns displayed in each pane.

[1]

	A	B	C	D	I	J
5				Quarter #4		Quarter #1
6	Beginning Cash Balance			$ 3,950		$ 23,000
7						
8	Add:	Cash Receipts from In-Store Customer Sales		$ 107,200		$ 122,000
9		Cash Receipts from Online Customer Sales		$ 29,300		$ 34,000
10		Cash Receipts from Services Rendered		$ 7,700		$ 18,000
18	Less:	Cash Disbursements for Merchandise Purchases		$ 94,800		$ 103,000
19		Cash Disbursements for Operating Expenses		$ 60,900		$ 84,600

[3]

[2]

	A	B	C	D	I	J
1		City Music World				
2		Cash Budget				
3		For Quarters Ending in 2017				
4						
5				Quarter #4		Quarter #1
6	Beginning Cash Balance			$ 3,950		$ 23,000
7						
8	Add:	Cash Receipts from In-Store Customer Sales		$ 107,200		$ 122,000
9		Cash Receipts from Online Customer Sales		$ 29,300		$ 34,000

1. You can scroll in each pane of this split window to view nonadjacent areas of the worksheet.

2. In this frozen window, the headings will remain visible as you scroll.

3. The split bar allows you to adjust how many rows or columns are displayed.

TIP! Use either Split or Freeze Panes, but not both together. One does not operate correctly when the other is in effect.

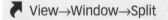 View→Window→Split

Viewing Worksheets in Multiple Windows

As an alternative to splitting the worksheet window, you can display two areas of a worksheet in separate windows. This method allows you to easily compare, copy, and move data. Each window is numbered, and only one window can be active at one time. You can even display two or more worksheets in this way. The worksheets can be from the same workbook or different workbooks.

Arranged windows can be scrolled independently with the scroll bars in each window. Or, you can use synchronous scrolling so the view in both windows moves simultaneously in the same direction as you scroll in the active window. This feature can keep the rows or columns aligned in the windows to help you compare data.

If more than two windows are open when the View Side by Side option is selected, a Compare Side by Side dialog box will appear. From this dialog box the user can select the second window (along with the one that is currently active) to display.

1. The active cell and brighter file name indicate that this window is active.

2. The windows are numbered.

3. Windows displayed side by side can be set to scroll in sync when you scroll in the active window.

➤ View→Window→New Window

➤ View→Window→View Side by Side

➤ View→Window→Synchronous Scrolling

Develop Your Skills EA10-D1

In this exercise, you will create a cash budget for City Music World. You will then freeze panes, split the window, and view worksheets side by side to review the results.

1. Open **EA10-D1-Budget** from your **Chapter 10** folder and save it as:
   EA10-D1-Budget-[YourName]

2. On the **Cash Budget** tab, enter **23000** in **cell J6**.

   This is the projected cash balance as of the beginning of the year and the starting point for the cash budget.

3. Enter the following, in order, in the **range J8:J13**: **122000**, **34000**, **18000**, **42000**, **1200**, and **0**

   These figures represent the projected itemized cash receipts for the first quarter. They are based on an analysis of previous periods and a review of expected economic conditions for the first quarter. All remaining projections have been determined in a similar manner.

4. Enter **=Sum(J8:J13)** in **cell J14** and **=J6+J14** in **cell J16**.

   The amount in cell J16 will be used to calculate the cash balance at the end of the quarter.

5. Enter the following, in order, in the **range J18:J21**: **103000**, **84600**, **13200**, and **1800**

6. Enter **=Sum(J18:J21)** in **cell J22** and **=J16-J22** in **cell J24**.

   Cell J24 indicates that the projected ending cash balance for the first quarter is $37,600. This amount, which is calculated as total cash available minus total cash disbursements, will be carried over as the projected beginning cash balance for the second quarter.

7. Enter **=J24** in **cell H6**.

8. Enter the following, in order, in the **range H8:H13**: **145000**, **37000**, **16000**, **39000**, **1240**, and **0**

9. Copy **cell J14** to **cells H14**, **F14**, and **D14**.

   Because the structure of the budget is the same for all four quarters, the formulas from the first quarter can be copied to the remaining three.

10. Copy **cell J16** to **cells H16**, **F16**, and **D16**.

11. Enter the following, in order, in the **range H18:H21**: **119000**, **103200**, **13200**, and **1800**

12. Copy the **range J22:J24** to the **ranges H22:H24**, **F22:F24**, and **D22:D24**.

    The ending cash balance for the second quarter is $38,640. The ending balance for the remaining two quarters will be populated once the cash receipt and cash disbursement projections are entered.

13. Copy **cell H6** to **cells F6** and **D6**.

    Just as with the beginning cash balance for the second quarter, the beginning cash balances for the remaining quarters are derived from the prior quarter's ending cash balance.

14. Enter these amounts:

	Quarter #4	Quarter #3
Cash Receipts from In-Store Customer Sales	$107,200	$184,500
Cash Receipts from Online Customer Sales	$29,300	$62,000
Cash Receipts from Services Rendered	$7,700	$21,800
Reduction in Accounts Receivable	$32,600	$28,000
Interest Received	$1,130	$1,110
Sale of Fixed Assets	$0	$3,400
Cash Disbursements for Merchandise Purchases	$94,800	$202,900
Cash Disbursements for Operating Expenses	$60,900	$117,600
Loan Payments (Principal)	$13,200	$13,200
Loan Payments (Interest)	$1,800	$1,800

The ending cash balance for the fourth quarter is $11,180.

Freeze Rows and Columns

15. Scroll so that **rows 1–5** and **columns A–B** are visible and then select **cell C6** and choose **View→Window→Freeze Panes→Freeze Panes**.

16. Scroll down so only cash disbursements and the ending cash balance show.

    Notice how much easier it is to review the displayed data with Freeze Panes.

17. Choose **View→Window→Freeze Panes→Unfreeze Panes**.

18. Choose **View→Window→Freeze Panes→Freeze Top Row**.

    This option freezes the highest visible row in the worksheet, regardless of which cell is active. As the budget worksheet contains more than one row of headers, this option is not beneficial here.

19. Choose **View→Window→Freeze Panes→Unfreeze Panes**.

Split the Worksheet

20. Click **cell C6** and choose **View→Window→Split**.

    The window is now split four ways. Because the data does not extend far enough to the right for a four-way split to be necessary, you will eliminate the vertical split bar.

21. Drag the vertical split bar to the left of **column A**.

    The worksheet is now only split horizontally.

22. In the top portion of the split window, scroll down so **row 8** is the first visible row.

23. Repeat the previous step for the bottom portion of the window, select **cell D8** in the top portion, and then type **108200** and tap ⌨Enter.

    The change you made in the top portion of the window is reflected in the bottom portion. The split is providing two different views of the same worksheet.

24. Undo the revised entry and then scroll down the bottom portion of the split window so **row 18** is the first visible row.

    Now the cash receipts and cash disbursements can be viewed together.

25. Choose **View→Window→Split** to return to one view of the worksheet.

View the Worksheet in Two Windows

26. Choose **View→Window→New Window** and then click the **View Side by Side** button.

    You are now viewing the worksheet in two separate windows.

WARNING! The zoom level for your original window may have changed. When the New Window command is applied, both windows display the zoom level of the window that was most recently displayed individually.

27. Scroll down in the top window.

    Synchronous scrolling was automatically activated when you chose the View Side by Side option.

28. In the top window, choose **View→Window→Synchronous Scrolling** and then scroll up so row 1 is displayed.

29. Scroll within the bottom window and enter **25000** in **cell J6**.

    Just as you saw with the split window, the change you made in the bottom window here is also made in the top window.

30. Undo the edit.

31. Choose **View→Window→View Side by Side** and close the window that shows :2 in the filename on the title bar.

32. Choose **View→Zoom→Zoom**, type **150** in the **Custom** box, and click **OK**.

33. Save your file.

    Unless otherwise directed, always keep your file open at the end of each exercise.

Printing Multipage Worksheets

Excel offers options that can improve the appearance of multipage worksheets when they are printed. When completing budgets, using these options can help ensure that printed versions are as user-friendly as the electronic versions.

Sizing Options

The Page Setup and Scale to Fit command groups on the Page Layout tab contain options to help fit large worksheets on printed pages.

TIP! You can use the orientation, margin, paper size, and scaling presets in the Print tab of Backstage view to correct the worksheet size just before printing.

Margins

Margins determine the space between the edge of the paper and the worksheet. You can choose from the three preset margin layouts—Normal, Wide, and Narrow—or use the Custom Margins option. Choose Narrow to fit more columns and rows on the printed page.

When you choose Custom Margins, the Page Setup dialog box opens with the Margins tab displayed. Here you can set specific margins and center the worksheet horizontally and/or vertically on the paper.

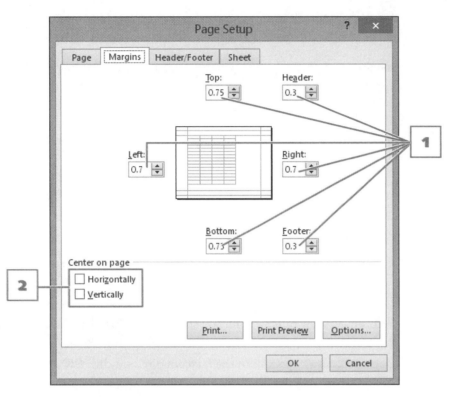

1. You can adjust the default margins (shown in inches) as you like.

2. Here you can choose to center the worksheet horizontally or vertically.

Orientation

Orientation refers to the direction of printing. Portrait is the default and prints across the narrow edge of the paper. Landscape orientation prints across the wide edge of the paper.

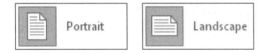

Size

The Size option refers to the paper size. The default paper size is Letter 8.5" x 11". A popular alternative to this is Legal 8.5" x 14".

Print Area

You can set any range of cells as the print area to print just that specific portion of the worksheet. The Set Print Area command makes the range permanent until you set a different range or choose Clear Print Area.

Scale to Fit

The Scale to Fit group on the Page Layout tab provides automated scaling options to adjust the worksheet size for printing.

Scaling Options

Setting	Notes
Width	Use to reduce the size of a worksheet containing many columns to fit its width on one, two, or more pages.
Height	Use to reduce the size of a worksheet containing many rows to fit its height on one, two, or more pages.
Scale	To adjust the width and height proportionally, you change the scale, which is set to 100 percent by default. When using the Scale option, the Width and Height options must be set to Automatic.

To reset the height and width to normal size, choose Automatic from each drop-down list. Make certain to change the Scale setting to 100 percent, as this doesn't happen automatically. The Undo command does not reverse Scale to Fit settings.

↗ Page Layout→Page Setup→Margins

↗ Page Layout→Page Setup→Page Orientation

↗ Page Layout→Page Setup→Page Size

↗ Page Layout→Page Setup→Print Area

↗ Page Layout→Scale to Fit→Scale

Develop Your Skills EA10-D2

In this exercise, you will modify the margins, page orientation, and print area of your cash budget. You will then use Scale to Fit options to further adjust how the worksheet will appear when printed.

1. Save your file as: **EA10-D2-Budget-[YourName]**
2. Choose **File→Print**.

   Review the Print Preview and note that the worksheet is currently set to print on two pages.

3. In the **Settings** section, choose **Normal Margins→Narrow**.

   The preview now displays the entire worksheet on one page. Notice that all data is positioned at the top of the page. Now you will change the orientation to better spread out the data across the page.

4. Click the **Back** button to return to the worksheet.
5. Choose **Page Layout→Page Setup→Orientation→Landscape** and then choose **File→Print**.

   Although the orientation has changed, the data is still displayed on a single page.

6. Return to the worksheet, choose **Page Layout→Page Setup→Size**, and review the menu options.

7. Choose **Page Layout→Page Setup→Margins→Normal** and change the orientation back to **Portrait**.

   You reverted the settings to their defaults so you can choose just a portion of the data to print.

8. Highlight the **range A1:J16** and choose **Page Layout→Page Setup→Print Area→Set Print Area**.

9. Choose **File→Print** to review the preview.

   You reduced the print area to only the cash receipt data. Notice that the worksheet is set to print on two pages, though. You will fix that next.

10. In the **Settings** section, choose **No Scaling→Fit All Columns on One Page**.

11. Still in the **Settings** section, choose **Portrait Orientation→Landscape Orientation** to change the orientation and then return to the worksheet.

12. Save your file.

Setting Additional Printing Options

In addition to adjusting the margins, page orientation, and page size to help improve the appearance of a printed worksheet, you can set additional Excel options, such as those for printing titles, gridlines, and headings.

Title Rows and Columns

You can specify one or more rows as title rows and one or more columns as title columns. Title rows and columns are printed on every page of a worksheet. This can be beneficial when complex data extends to multiple pages and requires headers for context.

TIP!   The Title Rows and Title Columns options are not available if you display the Page Setup dialog box from within the Print tab of Backstage view.

> ↗ Page Layout→Page Setup→Print Titles

Sheet Options

The Sheet Options group of the Page Layout tab contains commands that affect the worksheet view and all printed pages. You can choose some options separately for viewing a worksheet and others for printing.

Gridlines

By default, light gray gridlines surround every cell in the worksheet view—but these gridlines do not print by default. In large worksheets, you may find it useful to print gridlines to help track data across rows and down columns.

City Music World Cash Budget For Quarters Ending in 2017			City Music World Cash Budget For Quarters Ending in 2017		
		Quarter #4			Quarter #4
Beginning Cash Balance		$ 3,950	Beginning Cash Balance		$ 3,950
Add: Cash Receipts from In-Store Customer Sales		$ 107,200	Add: Cash Receipts from In-Store Customer Sales		$ 107,200
Cash Receipts from Online Customer Sales		$ 29,300	Cash Receipts from Online Customer Sales		$ 29,300
Cash Receipts from Services Rendered		$ 7,700	Cash Receipts from Services Rendered		$ 7,700
Reduction in Accounts Receivable		$ 32,600	Reduction in Accounts Receivable		$ 32,600
Interest Received		$ 1,130	Interest Received		$ 1,130
Sale of Fixed Assets		$ -	Sale of Fixed Assets		$ -
Total Cash Receipts:		$ 177,930	Total Cash Receipts:		$ 177,930

A worksheet without (left) and with (right) gridlines printed

Headings

By default, column headings (letters A, B, C, etc.) and row headings (numbers 1, 2, 3, etc.) do not print. Similar to gridlines, you can choose to have these headings appear on the printed worksheet.

> Page Layout→Sheet Options→View Gridlines *or* Print Gridlines

> Page Layout→Sheet Options→View Headings *or* Print Headings

Managing Multiple Worksheets

Excel prints the active worksheet when you choose the Quick Print command on the Quick Access toolbar. You can apply settings such as the margins, header and footers, and page orientation to multiple worksheets by first selecting the desired sheets (with Ctrl or Shift). You can print all sheets without selecting their tabs with the Print Entire Workbook command available in Backstage view. You can print just certain sheets by selecting the desired sheet tabs and choosing Print or Quick Print.

Develop Your Skills EA10-D3

In this exercise, you will complete a purchases budget for City Music World. You will then modify print settings in your cash and purchases budgets.

1. Save your file as: **EA10-D3-Budget-[YourName]**

2. Switch to the **Cash Budget** tab, select the **range A1:A3**, and choose **Home→Alignment→ Merge & Center**.

   You want to present the cash budget data on four printed pages, and you've temporarily removed the Merge & Center option so you can add the needed page breaks. Next you will remove the existing scaling so the page breaks will have the desired effect.

3. Choose **Page Layout→Scale to Fit→Width ▼→Automatic**.

4. Click **cell E1** and choose **Page Layout→Page Setup→Breaks→Insert Page Break**. Repeat in **cells G1 and I1**.

5. Replace the text in **cell A3** with: `For Quarters Ending in 2017`

6. Highlight the **range A1:D3**, choose **Home→Alignment→Merge & Center ▼→ Merge Across**, and center-align the content.

   The headers are now aligned over the columns that will appear on each printed page.

7. Choose **File→Print** and review all pages of the preview by clicking the **Next Page** button three times.

   The worksheet is displayed on four pages, but the row headers (in rows 1–3) and column headers (columns A–B) do not display on pages 2–4.

8. Switch back to the worksheet and choose **Page Layout→Page Setup→Print Titles**.

9. Click in the **Rows to Repeat at Top** box and then select **rows 1–3**.

   The three-row header will repeat at the top of every printed page.

10. Click in the **Columns to Repeat at Left** box, click anywhere in **column A**, and then replace the *D* with **B** and click **OK**.

Print titles	
Rows to repeat at top:	$1:$1
Columns to repeat at left:	$A:$B

   When you clicked column A, the range included columns A–D because Merge & Center is applied to the headers in the first three rows, which span those four columns.

11. Choose **File→Print** and review all pages in the preview.

   All four pages display the necessary headers.

   The merged data in the first three rows must be contained in the columns repeated at the left to appear on every page. If one of the headers had extended beyond column B, further adjustments (such as widening column B) would be needed to ensure that the complete header appeared on every page.

12. Switch to the **Purchases Budget** worksheet tab and enter **482400** in **cell C5** and **50000** in **cell C6**.

13. In **cell C7**, type **=SUM(** and highlight the **range C5:C6**, and then type **)** and tap Enter.

   The purchases budget will determine the merchandise purchases needed in order to satisfy expected product demand. The first step is to determine the total required merchandise inventory for the year, which is why you added projected cost of goods sold to the desired ending inventory.

14. Enter **12700** in **cell C8** and **=C7-C8** in **cell C9**.

   You subtract beginning inventory (as there is no need to purchase this merchandise) from the total inventory required to arrive at the required merchandise purchases for the year.

15. Choose **Page Layout→Sheet Options** and click in the **Print** box under **Headings**.

16. Choose **File→Print**.

   The preview displays the complete purchases budget with column and row headings visible. Notice that the headings display only for the columns and rows that contain data.

17. Switch back to the **Purchases Budget** tab, hold Ctrl, and select the **Cash Budget** tab.

    With both tabs selected, your next action will apply to both budgets simultaneously.

18. Choose **File→Print** and click the **Page Setup** link at the bottom of the **Settings** section.

    The Page Setup dialog box opens.

19. Switch to the **Sheet** tab in the dialog box, click in the **Gridlines** checkbox, and click **OK**. Then review all pages in the preview.

    Notice that both budgets now display gridlines, however the headers (which were previously visible for the Purchases Budget) have been removed, as that option was overridden by the selection you just made with both budget sheet tabs active.

20. Save your file.

Using Data Analysis Tools

Excel provides several tools to perform advanced what-if analyses, including Goal Seek and Solver. Each tool is best used in different scenarios. Goal Seek, for example, is useful when you have a worksheet result in mind but aren't sure how to adjust a specific value to achieve this solution.

Goal Seek

With Goal Seek, you set a goal for a specific formula result. For example, you can set the net income in a budget worksheet to equal $12,000. The goal cell must contain a formula, and you will instruct Goal Seek to adjust a variable to achieve the desired net income. Goal Seek adjusts only one variable at a time.

◢	A	B	C	D	E	F
1		City Music World				
2		CVP Income Statement				
3		For the Year Ending December 31, 2017				
4						
5		Goal Seek ? ×		Total		Per Unit
6	Sales Revenue	Set cell: D10 ⬆		$ 870,000		$ 100.00
7	Variable Costs	To value: 12000		$ 739,500		$ 85.00
8	Contribution Margin	By changing cell: $B$13 ⬆		$ 130,500		$ 15.00
9	Fixed Costs			$ 130,500		$ 15.00
10	Net Income	OK Cancel		$ 0		$ –
11						
12						
13	Units Sold:	8,700				

Here, Goal Seek will adjust units sold to arrive at a net income of $12,000.

➔ Data→Data Tools→What-If Analysis→Goal Seek

Solver

Excel's Solver tool can solve problems when more than one variable requires adjustment. You can specify a precise objective cell value, as with Goal Seek, or you can specify that Solver determine the maximum or minimum value. Solver also lets you specify one or more constraints, which gives you extra control by limiting a cell's possible range of values in the suggested solution.

TIP!   See Excel Help for more information on Solver's three solving methods: GRG Nonlinear, LP Simplex for linear problems, and Evolutionary for other problems.

1. Solver will change the values in these three cells to meet the objective and restraint.

2. A maximum value is set for the objective cell.

3. Constraint rules limit how the solution is calculated.

4. This option prevents unconstrained variables from being negative.

NOTE!   Solver is not part of the typical Office 2016 installation. It's an add-in program. Your network administrator may not grant permission to install add-ins.

↗ Data→Analyze→Solver

Develop Your Skills EA10-D4

In this exercise, you will create three CVP analyses. You will use Goal Seek to create a CVP analysis in which the company reaches the breakeven point. You'll also use Goal Seek to determine the unit sales necessary to generate net income of $12,000. Last, you will use Solver to determine the mix of sales price, variable costs, and fixed costs to maximize net income at a specific unit sales level.

1. Save your file as: **EA10-D4-Budget-[YourName]**

2. Switch to the **CVP Analysis #1** tab and enter this data:

Cell F6	100
Cell F7	85
Cell D9	130500

   These costs were previously determined.

3. Enter **=$B$13*F6** in **cell D6**, copy that cell, click **cell D7**, and choose **Home→Clipboard→Paste ▼→Formulas & Number Formatting**.

   Total sales revenue and total variable costs are calculated by multiplying units sold by their respective per-unit amounts. Cell D6 displays a zero, as one of the cells used in the formula (cell B13) has not yet been populated.

4. Enter **=D6-D7** in **cell D8**, copy that cell, click **cell F8**, and choose **Paste ▼→Formulas**.

5. Enter **=D9/B13** in **cell F9** and choose **Home→Number→Accounting** in **cell F9**.

6. Enter **=D8-D9** in **cell D10**, copy that cell, select **cell F10**, and choose **Paste ▼→Formulas**.

   Now that all of the formulas are properly entered, you can use Goal Seek to determine unit sales required to break even.

7. Click **cell D10** and choose **Data→Forecast→What-if Analysis→Goal Seek**.

   Notice that cell D10 appears by default in the Set Cell box.

8. Click in the **To Value** box and type **0**.

   Since you want to determine the unit sales necessary for City Music World to break even, you entered zero as the desired net income.

9. Click in the **By Changing Cell** box, select **cell B13**, and click **OK**.

   Goal Seek determines that 8,700 units must be sold for the company to break even.

10. Click **OK** to confirm the Goal Seek results.

    Now you will use Goal Seek to determine unit sales necessary to achieve a desired net income.

11. Right-click the **CVP Analysis #1** tab and choose **Move or Copy**, choose the **(move to end)** option, click the checkbox for **Create a Copy**, and click **OK**.

12. Rename the **CVP Analysis #1 (2)** tab to: **CVP Analysis #2**

13. Choose **Data→Forecast→What-if Analysis→Goal Seek** and complete the Goal Seek box as indicated:

    - Make sure the **Set Cell** box shows **D10** (change it if necessary).
    - Enter **12000** in the **To Value** box.
    - Enter **B13** in the **By Changing Cell** box.

    The Units Sold cell increased to 9,500 and the Fixed Costs Per Unit cell decreased to $13.74.

14. Click **OK** to close the Goal Seek Status dialog box.

    Now you want to consider how to maximize revenue by changing the sales price and costs. Past experience has indicated that the sales price cannot exceed $105, variable costs cannot be below $83 per unit, total fixed costs cannot be below $129,000, and the contribution margin must be at least 18% of the sales revenue. You will use Solver to determine the sales price and cost structure to maximize net income.

15. Choose **File→Options** and click **Add-Ins** in the left pane.

16. Make sure that **Excel Add-Ins** appears in the **Manage** box at the bottom of the window and click **Go**.

17. In the next window, click the checkbox for **Solver Add-In** and click **OK**.

    Solver has now been added to the far right of the Data tab on the Ribbon.

18. Right-click the **CVP Analysis #2** tab and choose **Move or Copy**, choose **(move to end)**, click the checkbox for **Create a Copy**, and click **OK**.

19. Rename the **CVP Analysis #2 (2)** tab to: **CVP Analysis #3**

20. Select **cell D10** and choose **Data→Analyze→Solver**.

21. Click in the **By Changing Variable Cells** box, click **cell F6**, type a comma and click **cell F7**, type a comma, and select **cell D9**.

    Note that the Set Objective box shows cell D10 and the Max option is selected. Solver will seek a solution that maximizes net income (cell D10). Solver can change values in cells F6, F7, and D9 to arrive at the solution.

22. Click the **Add** box and complete the Add Constraint dialog box as shown, clicking **OK** when finished.

This constraint ensures that Solver's solution will not reduce fixed costs below $129,000.

23. Repeat step 22 three times to constrain the solution such that **cell F6** is less than or equal to **105**, **cell F7** is greater than or equal to **83**, and **cell F8** is less than or equal to **cell F6** multiplied by **18%**.

    The final constraint includes a formula in which cell F6 is multiplied by 18%. Solver constraints can be entered as either numbers or formulas.

24. Click **Solve** and then click **OK** in the Solver Results dialog box.

The Solver Results display the maximum net income that can be earned if City Music World has sales of 9,500 units, maximizes the sales price per unit, and minimizes the total fixed costs. These estimated maximum and minimum achievable values were calculated via an examination of results from prior years. Notice that the variable cost per unit exceeds the minimum indicated in the Solver constraints, as the optimal solution does not call for the minimum variable cost level to be achieved.

TIP! If the parameters entered in Solver don't allow for a solution to be reached, an error message will display.

25. Save and close your file.

REAL-WORLD Accounting

What Are the Benefits of Using Excel to Complete Budgeting and Cost Analyses?

Excel's flexibility is exhibited in many ways. In this chapter, you saw how freezing rows and columns and splitting the worksheet window can allow for efficient data examination. This flexibility is a key reason why Excel is so frequently used for budgeting and cost analyses. However, when performing such analyses, where estimates and projections play a vital role, the availability of features such as Goal Seek and Solver are even more impactful.

While other programs offer what-if analysis tools, the ease with which options such as Goal Seek and Solver can be used in Excel makes the program the most logical choice. All budgetary and cost planning must, by definition, take estimates and projections into account. Because these variables can be changed so readily in Excel, different potential outcomes can be efficiently examined. CVP analyses, in particular, are most beneficial when different levels of variables (such as sales and variable costs) are reviewed. This efficiency saves time and ensures that alternatives can be considered and the most likely option is selected.

Ultimately, budgets and CVP analyses are useful only when they approximate the actual results that occur. Using Excel to create these scenarios increases the likelihood of data accuracy, thus increasing the usefulness of the worksheets.

Self-Assessment

Check your knowledge of this chapter's key concepts and skills using the Self-Assessment here or in your eLab course.

1. The Freeze Panes option can freeze columns and rows simultaneously. *True   False*

2. A worksheet window can be split only horizontally, not vertically. *True   False*

3. When viewing a worksheet in multiple windows, changes made in one window are not reflected in the other window. *True   False*

4. Synchronous scrolling works only when two windows for a single worksheet are viewed side by side. *True   False*

5. The Adjust Margins option is used to change the appearance of a printed worksheet. *True   False*

6. In Landscape orientation, the page width is longer than the page height. *True   False*

7. The Print Area option is located on View tab of the Ribbon. *True   False*

8. You can set the Print Titles option from the Print menu in Backstage view. *True   False*

9. Gridlines are set not to display by default. *True   False*

10. Solver can adjust multiple variables simultaneously. *True   False*

11. When using Freeze Panes to freeze only rows, the active cell must be located in:
    column A
    column B
    column C
    column D

12. What is the maximum number of groups that can be viewed simultaneously when splitting a window?
    1
    2
    3
    4

13. When using View Side by Side, how many windows can be active at one time?
    1
    2
    3
    4

14. Which of these CANNOT be set from the Print area in Backstage view?
    Orientation
    Print Titles
    Margin Presets
    Paper Size

15. Which of these is NOT a Margin option?
    Normal
    Tall
    Wide
    Narrow

16. Which of these is NOT a Scale to Fit option?
    Width
    Height
    Length
    Scale

17. Which of these is NOT a Sheet option?
    View Titles
    View Headings
    Print Headings
    Print Gridlines

18. Which what-if-analysis tool is best suited for arriving at a desired figure by adjusting a single variable?
    Goal Seek
    Solver
    Scenario Manager
    Data Tables

19. Solver can be set to determine a solution for each of these EXCEPT:
    The maximum value
    The minimum value
    The average value
    A specific value

20. On what Ribbon tab can Solver can be found?
    Insert
    Formulas
    Data
    Review

Reinforce Your Skills

EA10-R1 Complete Budgets and a CVP Analysis for Alphabet Industries

In this exercise, you will create budgets and perform CVP analyses for Alphabet Industries. You will first create a cash budget, adjusting settings to allow for efficient data examination. You will then create a purchases budget and adjust print settings. Lastly, you will perform CVP analyses using Goal Seek and Solver.

1. Open **EA10-R1-Budget** from your **Chapter 10** folder and save it as:
   EA10-R1-Budget-[YourName]

   To begin, you will populate the budget with data and formulas.

2. On the **Cash Budget** tab, enter **5700** in **cell J6**.

3. Enter the first quarter data:

Cell J8	37200	Cell J18	47200
Cell J9	41300	Cell J19	63400
Cell J10	58400	Cell J20	7200
Cell J11	4100	Cell J21	2100
Cell J12	300	Cell J22	=SUM(J18:J21)
Cell J13	17000	Cell J24	=J16-J22
Cell J14	=SUM(J8:J13)		
Cell J16	=J6+J14		

4. Enter the second quarter data:

Cell H6	=J24	Cell H13	0
Cell H8	21800	Cell H18	27300
Cell H9	20600	Cell H19	40000
Cell H10	41900	Cell H20	7200
Cell H11	400	Cell H21	2100
Cell H12	250		

   In steps 5–8, you will copy the formulas created for Quarter 1 to the appropriate locations in the columns for Quarters 2–4. Use **Ctrl** *to select the destination cells and paste the formulas to multiple cells at once.*

5. Copy **cell J14** to **cells H14**, **F14**, and **D14**.

6. Copy **cell J16** to **cells H16**, **F16**, and **D16**.

7. Copy the **range J22:J24** to the **ranges H22:H24**, **F22:F24**, and **D22:D24**.

8. Copy **cell H6** to **cells F6** and **D6**.

9. Enter the third and fourth quarter data:

	Quarter 4	Quarter 3
Cash Receipts from In-Store Customer Sales	31500	17300
Cash Receipts from Online Customer Sales	34800	23000
Cash Receipts from Consulting Services Rendered	17300	29800
Reduction in Notes Receivable	1600	850
Interest Received	320	270
Sale of Equipment	0	0
Cash Disbursements for Merchandise Purchases	41000	31000
Cash Disbursements for Operating Expenses	54600	51300
Loan Payments (Principal)	7200	7200
Loan Payments (Interest)	2100	2100

10. If necessary, scroll until **cell A1** is visible; then select **cell C6** and choose **View→Window→ Freeze Panes→Freeze Panes**.

11. Scroll to the right so only budgetary data for the first quarter is displayed and then scroll down so only cash disbursements and ending cash balance are displayed.

12. Choose **View→Window→Freeze Panes→Unfreeze Panes**.

Adjust Margins, Orientation, and Print Area

13. Choose **File→Print** and in the **Settings** section choose **Normal Margins→Narrow**.

14. Switch back to the **Cash Budget** tab, choose **Page Layout→Page Setup→ Orientation→Landscape**, and then review the print preview in Backstage view.

15. Switch back to the **Cash Budget** tab, change the margins to **Normal**, and set the orientation to **Portrait**.

16. Highlight the **range A1:J16** and choose **Page Layout→Page Setup→Print Area→ Set Print Area**.

17. Choose **File→Print** and in the **Settings** section choose **No Scaling→Fit All Columns on One Page** and then choose **Portrait Orientation→Landscape Orientation**.

Apply Print Titles, Headings, and Gridlines

18. Switch back to the **Cash Budget** tab and choose **Page Layout→Scale to Fit→ Width ▼→Automatic**.

19. Highlight the **range A1:A3** and choose **Home→Alignment→Merge & Center**.

20. Select **cell E1** and choose **Page Layout→Page Setup→Breaks→Insert Page Break**. Repeat for **cells G1** and **I1**.

21. Replace the contents of **cell A3** with: **For Quarters Ending in 2017**

22. Highlight the **range A1:D3**, choose **Home→Alignment→Merge & Center ▼→ Merge Across**, and then center-align the content.

23. Choose **File→Print** and use the **Next Page** button to review all pages in the preview.

24. Switch back to the **Cash Budget** tab and choose **Page Layout→Page Setup→ Print Titles**.

25. Click in the **Rows to Repeat at Top:** box and select **rows 1–3**. Click in the **Columns to Repeat at Left** box, click anywhere in **column A**, and then change the *D* to **B** and click **OK**.

26. Choose **File**→**Print** and use the **Next Page** button to review all pages in the preview.

27. Switch to the **Purchases Budget** tab; enter **159100** in **cell C5** and **18000** in **cell C6**.

28. In **cell C7**, type **=SUM(** and highlight the **range C5:C6**, and then type **)** and tap Enter.

29. Enter **30600** in **cell C8** and **=C7-C8** in **cell C9**.

30. Select the **Purchases Budget** and **Cash Budget** tabs and then choose **File**→**Print**.

31. Click the **Page Setup** link, switch to the **Sheet** tab, click the box for **Gridlines**, and click **OK**; review all pages in the preview.

Use Goal Seek and Solver

32. Switch to the **CVP Analysis #1** tab.

33. Enter **100** in **cell F6**, **81** in **cell F7**, and **74290** in **cell D9**.

34. Enter **=$B$13*F6** in **cell D6**; copy that cell, click **cell D7**, and choose **Home**→**Clipboard**→ **Paste ▼**→**Formulas & Number Formatting**.

35. Enter **=D6-D7** in **cell D8** and then use **Paste ▼**→**Formulas** to copy that formula to **cell D8**.

36. Enter **=D9/B13** in **cell F9** and choose **Home**→**Number**→**Accounting** in **cell F9**.

37. Enter **=D8-D9** in **cell D10** and then use **Paste ▼**→**Formulas** to copy that formula to **cell F10**.

38. Select **cell D10** and choose **Data**→**Forecast**→**What-if Analysis**→**Goal Seek**.

39. Change the **To Value** to **0**, click in the **By Changing Cell** box, select **cell B13**, and click **OK** twice.

40. Right-click the **CVP Analysis #1** tab and choose **Move or Copy**, choose **(move to end)**, check the box for **Create a Copy**, and click **OK**.

41. Rename the **CVP Analysis #1 (2)** tab to: **CVP Analysis #2**

42. Choose **Data**→**Forecast**→**What-if Analysis**→**Goal Seek**, ensure that the **Set Cell** entry is *D10*, set the **To Value** to **21200** and then set the **By Changing Cell** box to **B13**; click **OK** twice.

43. Make a copy of the **CVP Analysis #2** tab that will appear to the far right of the existing tab; name it: **CVP Analysis #3**

    Hint: See steps 40–41.

44. Select **cell D10** and then choose **Data**→**Analyze**→**Solver**; then click in the **By Changing Variable Cells** box, select **cell F6**, type a comma, select **cell F7**, type a comma, and select **cell D9**. Click the **Add** button.

45. Set up four constraints, one at a time, as indicated:

    Hint: Click Add to begin a new constraint and click OK after entering the details for each constraint.

Cell Reference		Constraint
Cell D9	>=	73000
Cell F6	<=	102
Cell F7	>=	79
Cell F8	<=	F6*22%

46. Click **Solve** and then click **OK** in the Solver Results dialog box.

47. Save and close your file.

EA10-R2 Complete Budgets and a CVP Analysis for Cara's Party Emporium

In this exercise, you will create budgets and perform CVP analyses for Cara's Party Emporium. You will first create a cash budget, adjusting settings to allow for efficient data examination. You will then create a purchases budget and adjust print settings. Lastly, you will perform CVP analyses using Goal Seek and Solver.

1. Open **EA10-R2-Budget** from your **Chapter 10** folder and save it as: **EA10-R2-Budget-[YourName]**

   To begin, you will populate the budget with data and formulas.

2. On the **Cash Budget** tab, enter **8500** in **cell J6**.

3. Enter the first quarter data:

Cell J8	151000	Cell J17	116000
Cell J9	15000	Cell J18	5600
Cell J10	600	Cell J19	3000
Cell J11	900	Cell J20	700
Cell J12	0	Cell J21	=SUM(J17:J20)
Cell J13	=SUM(J8:J12)	Cell J23	=J15-J21
Cell J15	=J6+J13		

4. Enter the second quarter data:

Cell H6	=J23	Cell H17	100500
Cell H8	141000	Cell H18	42000
Cell H9	11000	Cell H19	3000
Cell H10	820	Cell H20	700
Cell H11	750		
Cell H12	0		

   In steps 5–8, you will copy the formulas created for Quarter 1 to the appropriate locations in the columns for Quarters 2–4. Use Ctrl *to select the destination cells and paste the formulas to multiple cells at once.*

5. Copy **cell J13** to **cells H13**, **F13**, and **D13**.

6. Copy **cell J15** to **cells H15**, **F15**, and **D15**.

7. Copy the **range J21:J23** to the **ranges H21:H23**, **F21:F23**, and **D21:D23**.

8. Copy **cell H6** to **cells F6** and **D6**.

9. Enter the third and fourth quarter data:

	Quarter 4	Quarter 3
Cash Receipts from In-Store Customer Sales	125500	165000
Cash Receipts from Delivery Sales	11500	21500
Reduction in Accounts Receivable	200	0
Interest Received	620	700
Sale of Furniture	2650	0
Cash Disbursements for Merchandise Purchases	106300	120800
Cash Disbursements for Operating Expenses	44000	59000
Loan Payments (Principal)	0	0
Loan Payments (Interest)	0	0

10. Select **cell C6** and choose **View→Window→Split**.

11. Drag the vertical split bar to the left of **column A**.

12. Scroll so that **row 17** is the first visible row in both the top and bottom portions of the split window.

13. In the top portion of the window, type **124000** in **cell D17** and note that the change is also made in the bottom portion of the window.

14. Click **Undo** on the Quick Access toolbar and then choose **View→Window→Split** to remove the split.

Adjust Margins, Orientation, and Print Area

15. Choose **Page Layout→Page Setup→Margins→Narrow** and then choose **Orientation→ Landscape**.

16. Choose **File→Print** and review the preview.

17. Switch back to the **Cash Budget** tab; change the margins to **Normal** and set the orientation to **Portrait**.

18. Highlight the **range A1:J21** and choose **Page Layout→Page Setup→Print Area→ Set Print Area**.

19. Choose **Page Layout→Scale to Fit→Width ▼→1 Page**.

20. Choose **File→Print** and in the **Settings** section choose **Portrait Orientation→ Landscape Orientation**.

Apply Print Titles, Headings, and Gridlines

21. Switch back to the **Cash Budget** tab and choose **Page Layout→Scale to Fit→ Width ▼→Automatic**.

22. Highlight the **range A1:A3** and choose **Home→Alignment→Merge & Center**.

23. Select **cell E1** and choose **Page Layout→Page Setup→Breaks→Insert Page Break**. Repeat for **cells G1** and **I1**.

24. Replace the contents of **cell A3** with: `For Quarters Ending in 2017`

25. Highlight the **range A1:D3**, choose **Home→Alignment→Merge & Center ▼→ Merge Across**, and then center-align the content.

26. Choose **File→Print** and use the **Next Page** button to review all pages in the preview.

27. Switch back to the **Cash Budget** tab and choose **Page Layout→Page Setup→ Print Titles**.

28. Click in the **Rows to Repeat at Top** box and select **rows 1–3**. Click in the **Columns to Repeat at Left** box, click anywhere in **column A**, and then change the *D* to **B** and click **OK**.

29. Choose **File→Print** and use the **Next Page** button to review all pages in the preview.

30. Switch to the **Purchases Budget** tab; enter **439000** in **cell C5** and **22000** in **cell C6**.

31. In **cell C7**, type `=SUM(` and highlight the **range C5:C6**, and then type `)` and tap Enter .

32. Enter **17400** in **cell C8** and `=C7-C8` in **cell C9**.

33. Select the **Purchases Budget** and **Cash Budget** tabs, choose **Page Layout→ Sheet Options→Gridlines→Print Gridlines**, and choose **Page Layout→ Sheet Options→Headings→Print Headings**.

Use Goal Seek and Solver

34. Switch to the **CVP Analysis #1** tab.

35. Enter **120** in **cell F6**, **97** in **cell F7**, and **123625** in **cell D9**.

36. Enter `=$B$13*F6` in **cell D6**; copy that cell, click **cell D7**, and choose **Home→Clipboard→ Paste ▼→Formulas & Number Formatting**.

37. Enter `=D6-D7` in **cell D8** and then use **Paste ▼→Formulas** to copy that formula to **cell F8**.

38. Enter `=D9/B13` in **cell F9** and then choose **Home→Number→Accounting** in **cell F9**.

39. Enter `=D8-D9` in **cell D10** and then use **Paste ▼→Formulas** to copy that formula to **cell F10**.

40. Select **cell D10** and choose **Data→Forecast→What-if Analysis→Goal Seek**.

41. Change the **To Value** box to **0**, click in the **By Changing Cell** box, select **cell B13**, and click **OK** twice.

42. Right-click the **CVP Analysis #1** tab and choose **Move or Copy**, choose **(move to end)**, check the box for **Create a Copy**, and click **OK**.

43. Rename the **CVP Analysis #1 (2)** tab: `CVP Analysis #2`

44. Choose **Data→Forecast→What-if Analysis→Goal Seek**, ensure that the **Set Cell** entry is *D10*, and then set the **To Value** to **52000** and set the **By Changing Cell** box to **B13**; click **OK** twice.

45. Hold Ctrl and drag the **CVP Analysis #2** tab to the right to drop a copy of the worksheet to the right of all tabs and then rename the new tab: `CVP Analysis #3`

46. Select **cell D10** and then choose **Data→Analyze→Solver**; then click in the **By Changing Variable Cells** box, select **cell F6** and type a comma, select **cell F7** and type a comma, and select **cell D9**. Click the **Add** button.

47. Set up four constraints, one at a time, as indicated:

    Hint: Click Add to begin a new constraint and click OK after entering the details for each constraint.

Cell Reference		Constraint
Cell D9	>=	121000
Cell F6	<=	125
Cell F7	>=	95
Cell F8	<=	F6*23%

48. Click **Solve** and then click **OK** in the Solver Results dialog box.

49. Save and close your file.

Apply Your Skills

EA10-A1 Complete Budgets and a CVP Analysis for Dairy Producers, Inc.

In this exercise, you will create budgets and perform CVP analyses for Dairy Producers, Inc. You will first create a cash budget, adjusting settings to allow for efficient data examination. You will then create a purchases budget and adjust print settings. Lastly, you will perform CVP analyses using Goal Seek and Solver.

1. Open **EA10-A1-Budget** from your **Chapter 10** folder and save it as:
   EA10-A1-Budget-[YourName]
2. On the **Cash Budget** tab, enter **3200** as the beginning cash balance for the first quarter.
3. Enter the data for the four quarters:

	Quarter #4	Quarter #3	Quarter #2	Quarter #1
Cash Receipts from In-Store Customer Sales	$12,200	$11,300	$8,100	$14,200
Cash Receipts from Delivery Sales	$91,300	$71,800	$84,200	$81,600
Cash Receipts from Services Rendered	$700	$1,600	$2,300	$4,100
Interest Received	$650	$650	$600	$1,300
Sale of Machinery	$0	$4,000	$0	$0
Cash Disbursements for Merchandise Purchases	$64,200	$51,300	$55,400	$61,000
Cash Disbursements for Operating Expenses	$31,000	$36,900	$39,300	$34,200
Loan Payments (Principal)	$2,400	$2,400	$2,400	$2,400
Loan Payments (Interest)	$900	$900	$900	$900

4. Create formulas in the appropriate locations to summarize cash receipts, cash available, and cash disbursements.
5. Create formulas for the ending cash balances for Quarters 1–4 and for the beginning cash balances for Quarters 2–4.

Adjust Margins, Orientation, and Print Area

6. Apply **Narrow** margins and **Landscape** orientation and then switch to **Normal** margins and **Portrait** orientation.
7. Set the print area to display all data through the **Total Cash Receipts** row.
8. In Backstage view, scale the worksheet to **Fit All Columns on One Page** and set the orientation to **Landscape**.

Apply Print Titles, Headings, and Gridlines

9. Remove the scaling so the worksheet will print on multiple pages.

10. Insert vertical page breaks between each of the four quarters, taking care to adjust the three-line header at the top of the worksheet as necessary.

    Hint: Remove the merged-and-centered attributes in the header before adding page breaks.

11. Edit the header in **row 3** to: `For Quarters Ending in 2017`

12. Merge and center the three-line header at the top of the worksheet so that it does not extend beyond the fourth quarter data.

13. Set the worksheet so the three-line header at the top and the headers for **columns A–B** will print on every page.

14. Switch to the **Purchases Budget** tab and enter this data:

Budgeted Cost of Goods Sold	$237,000
Desired Ending Inventory	$20,000
Beginning Inventory	$25,100

15. Create formulas in the appropriate locations for total inventory required and required merchandise purchases.

16. Simultaneously apply gridlines and headings to every printed page on the **Cash Budget** and **Purchases Budget** tabs.

Use Goal Seek and Solver

17. Switch to the **CVP Analysis #1** tab and enter this data:

Sales Revenue Per Unit	$80
Variable Costs Per Unit	$58
Fixed Costs	$104,500

18. Create formulas in the appropriate locations for all remaining elements except Units Sold, which should remain blank.

19. Use **Goal Seek** to determine the breakeven unit sales.

20. Create a second **CVP Analysis** tab (named appropriately) and use **Goal Seek** to determine unit sales necessary to generate a net income of $18,500.

21. Create a third **CVP Analysis** tab (named appropriately) and use **Solver** to determine the maximum net income if all of the following apply: unit sales remain the same as those in the second CVP analysis, sales revenue per unit cannot exceed $82, variable costs per unit cannot fall below $55, fixed costs cannot fall below $104,500, and contribution margin as a percentage of sales revenue cannot exceed 32%.

22. Save and close your file.

EA10-A2 Complete Budgets and a CVP Analysis for Gary's Housewares

In this exercise, you will create budgets and perform CVP analyses for Gary's Housewares. You will first create a cash budget, adjusting settings to allow for efficient data examination. You will then create a purchases budget and adjust print settings. Lastly, you will perform CVP analyses using Goal Seek and Solver.

1. Open **EA10-A2-Budget** from your **Chapter 10** folder and save it as:
   EA10-A2-Budget-[YourName]

2. On the Cash Budget tab, enter **47200** as the beginning cash balance for the first quarter.

3. Enter the data for the four quarters:

	Quarter #4	Quarter #3	Quarter #2	Quarter #1
Cash Receipts from In-Store Customer Sales	$118,400	$156,000	$126,400	$172,000
Cash Receipts from Online Sales	$19,600	$33,200	$21,200	$24,600
Cash Receipts from Services Rendered	$8,000	$4,230	$3,800	$9,700
Reduction in Notes Receivable	$960	$1,550	$1,100	$1,400
Interest Received	$730	$850	$420	$650
Sale of Automobile	$0	$2,350	$0	$0
Cash Disbursements for Merchandise Purchases	$98,300	$127,300	$95,300	$107,400
Cash Disbursements for Operating Expenses	$73,600	$71,400	$69,100	$81,300
Loan Payments (Principal)	$2,600	$3,900	$3,900	$3,900

4. Create formulas in the appropriate locations to summarize cash receipts, cash available, and cash disbursements.

5. Create formulas for the ending cash balances for Quarters 1–4 and for the beginning cash balances for Quarters 2–4.

Adjust Margins, Orientation, and Print Area

6. Apply **Wide** margins and **Landscape** orientation and then switch to **Normal** margins and **Portrait** orientation.

7. Set the print area to display all data through the **Total Cash Receipts** row.

8. In Backstage view, scale the worksheet to **Fit All Columns on One Page** and set the orientation to **Landscape**.

Apply Print Titles, Headings, and Gridlines

9. Remove the scaling so the worksheet will print on multiple pages.

10. Insert vertical page breaks between each of the four quarters, taking care to adjust the three-line header at the top of the worksheet as necessary.

    Hint: Remove the merged-and-centered attributes in the header before adding page breaks.

11. Edit the header within **row 3** to: `For Quarters Ending in 2017`

12. Merge and center the three-line header at the top of the worksheet so that it does not extend beyond the fourth quarter data.

13. Set the worksheet so the three-line header at the top and the headers for **columns A–B** will print on every page.

14. Switch to the **Purchases Budget** tab and enter this data:

Budgeted Cost of Goods Sold	$420,000
Desired Ending Inventory	$35,000
Beginning Inventory	$26,700

15. Create formulas in the appropriate locations for total inventory required and required merchandise purchases.

16. Simultaneously apply gridlines and headings to every printed page on the **Cash Budget** and **Purchases Budget** tabs.

Use Goal Seek and Solver

17. Switch to the **CVP Analysis #1** tab and enter this data:

Sales Revenue Per Unit	$40
Variable Costs Per Unit	$31
Fixed Costs	$151,875

18. Create formulas in the appropriate locations for all remaining elements except Units Sold, which should remain blank.

19. Use **Goal Seek** to determine the breakeven unit sales.

20. Create a second **CVP Analysis** tab (named appropriately) and use **Goal Seek** to determine unit sales necessary to generate a net income of $72,000.

21. Create a third **CVP Analysis** tab (named appropriately) and use **Solver** to determine the maximum net income if all of the following apply: unit sales remain the same as those in the second CVP analysis, sales revenue per unit cannot exceed $43, variable costs per unit cannot fall below $28, fixed costs cannot fall below $150,000, and contribution margin as a percentage of sales revenue cannot exceed 34%.

22. If necessary, widen columns to display all Solver results.

23. Save and close your file.

Extend Your Skills

EA10-E1 Prepare Budgets and a CVP Analysis for Environmental Adaptations Co.

In this exercise, you will prepare cash and purchases budgets and CVP analyses for Environmental Adaptations Co. You will first create a cash budget, adjusting its appearance to facilitate data examination. You will then create a purchases budget and adjust print settings to ensure readability and ease of use. Lastly, you will use Goal Seek and Solver to create three CVP analyses.

Open **EA10-E1-Budget**. On the Cash Budget tab, create a cash budget based on a beginning cash balance of $10,400 and this data:

	Quarter #4	Quarter #3	Quarter #2	Quarter #1
Cash Receipts from In-Store Customer Sales	$153,000	$201,300	$172,000	$184,000
Cash Receipts from Delivery Sales	$14,000	$26,200	$13,500	$18,500
Reduction in Accounts Receivable	$200	$0	$1,000	$700
Interest Received	$800	$900	$900	$1,100
Sale of Furniture	$0	$0	$0	$3,200
Cash Disbursements for Merchandise Purchases	$129,600	$147,300	$122,600	$141,000
Cash Disbursements for Operating Expenses	$53,600	$72,000	$51,300	$68,100
Loan Payments (Principal)	$0	$3,600	$3,600	$3,600
Loan Payments (Interest)	$0	$850	$850	$850

Also enter the necessary formulas. Set up the budget to print with narrow margins and in Landscape orientation. Adjust the third line of the header to read **For Quarters Ended in 2017**. Insert page breaks such that data for each quarter appears on a separate page and use the Print Titles option to display the three-line header and the headers in columns A–B on every printed page. Set the print area to include only the cash data through row 15. Create a horizontal split that displays the itemized cash receipts directly above the itemized cash disbursements (only the split bar between them).

On the Purchases Budget tab, create a purchases budget based on this data:

Budgeted Cost of Goods Sold	$545,000
Desired Ending Inventory	$35,000
Beginning Inventory	$39,500

Also enter the necessary formulas. Simultaneously adjust the cash budget and purchases budget so they display headings and gridlines when printed.

On the CVP Analysis #1 tab, create a CVP analysis based on this data:

Sales Revenue	$50 per unit
Variable Costs	$32 per unit
Fixed Costs	$282,600

Also enter the necessary formulas but leave the Units Sold cell blank. Use Goal Seek to determine the breakeven number of units. Create a second CVP analysis tab and use Goal Seek to determine the required unit sales to achieve a net income of $8,500. Create a third CVP analysis tab that assumes unit sales equal to those calculated in the second CVP analysis. Assume that fixed costs cannot change, sales revenue per unit cannot exceed $54, variable costs per unit cannot fall below $30, and contribution margin as a percentage of sales revenue cannot exceed 40%. Name each CVP tab appropriately. Lastly, for each CVP analysis, freeze the three-line header at the top.

EA10-E2 Prepare Budgets and a CVP Analysis for KPF Industries

In this exercise, you will prepare cash and purchases budgets and CVP analyses for KPF Industries. You will first create a cash budget, adjusting its appearance to facilitate data examination. You will then create a purchases budget and adjust print settings to ensure readability and ease of use. Lastly, you will use Goal Seek and Solver to create three CVP analyses.

Open **EA10-E2-Budget**. On the Cash Budget tab, create a cash budget based on a beginning cash balance of $9,400 and this data:

	Quarter #4	Quarter #3	Quarter #2	Quarter #1
Cash Receipts from In-Store Customer Sales	$23,100	$28,600	$37,200	$31,300
Cash Receipts from Online Sales	$3,700	$6,300	$5,100	$4,200
Cash Receipts from Services Rendered	$1,550	$1,300	$1,200	$1,300
Sale of Fixed Assets	$850	$0	$0	$0
Cash Disbursements for Merchandise Purchases	$13,500	$21,600	$22,700	$23,200
Cash Disbursements for Operating Expenses	$15,000	$16,200	$18,500	$18,000
Loan Payments (Principal)	$0	$1,500	$1,500	$1,500
Loan Payments (Interest)	$0	$320	$320	$320

Also enter the necessary formulas. Set up the budget to print with wide margins and in Landscape orientation. Scale the printed worksheet so all columns fit on a single page. Set a print area to include only the cash data through row 14. Create a horizontal split that displays the itemized cash receipts directly above the itemized cash disbursements (only the split bar between them).

On the Purchases Budget tab, create a purchases budget based on this data:

Budgeted Cost of Goods Sold	$80,000
Desired Ending Inventory	$7,500
Beginning Inventory	$6,500

Also enter the necessary formulas. Simultaneously adjust the cash budget and purchases budget so they display headings and gridlines when printed.

On the CVP Analysis #1 tab, create a CVP analysis based on this data:

Sales Revenue	$100 per unit
Variable Costs	$77 per unit
Fixed Costs	$32,200

Also enter the necessary formulas but leave the Units Sold cell blank. Use Goal Seek to determine the breakeven number of units. Create a second CVP analysis tab and use Goal Seek to determine the required unit sales to achieve a net income of $11,300. Create a third CVP analysis tab that assumes unit sales equal to those calculated in the second CVP analysis. Assume that variable costs per unit cannot change, sales revenue per unit cannot exceed $103, fixed costs cannot fall below $31,500, and contribution margin as a percentage of sales revenue cannot exceed 25%. Name each CVP analysis tab appropriately. Lastly, for each CVP analysis, freeze the three-line header at the top.

EA10-E3 Prepare Budgets and a CVP Analysis for House of Electronics

In this exercise, you will prepare cash and purchases budgets and CVP analyses for House of Electronics. You will first create a cash budget, adjusting its appearance to facilitate data examination. You will then create a purchases budget and adjust print settings to ensure readability and ease of use. Lastly, you will use Goal Seek and Solver to create three CVP analyses.

Open **EA10-E3-Budget**. On the Cash Budget tab, create a cash budget based on a beginning cash balance of $23,200 and this data:

	Quarter #4	Quarter #3	Quarter #2	Quarter #1
Cash Receipts from In-Store Customer Sales	$12,400	$14,700	$16,300	$18,700
Cash Receipts from Online Sales	$15,300	$16,100	$21,000	$25,600
Cash Receipts from Services Rendered	$3,420	$2,950	$2,000	$3,900
Interest Received	$600	$510	$430	$720
Sale of Fixed Assets	$1,800	$0	$0	$0
Cash Disbursements for Merchandise Purchases	$16,000	$18,700	$19,600	$25,700
Cash Disbursements for Operating Expenses	$20,030	$21,900	$22,400	$23,200
Loan Payments (Principal)	$1,000	$1,000	$1,000	$1,000

Also enter the necessary formulas. Set up the budget to print with wide margins and in Landscape orientation. Scale the printed worksheet to 80% of its original size. Set a print area to include only the third and fourth quarters (if necessary, adjust the three-line header so it looks attractive when printed). Create a horizontal split that displays the itemized cash receipts directly above the itemized cash disbursements (only the split bar between them).

On the Purchases Budget tab, create a purchases budget based on this data:

Budgeted Cost of Goods Sold	$85,000
Desired Ending Inventory	$4,000
Beginning Inventory	$9,000

Also enter the necessary formulas. Simultaneously adjust the cash budget and purchases budget so they display headings and gridlines when printed.

On the CVP Analysis #1 tab, create a CVP analysis based on this data:

Sales Revenue	$50 per unit
Variable Costs	$32 per unit
Fixed Costs	$23,040

Also enter the necessary formulas but leave the Units Sold cell blank. Use Goal Seek to determine the breakeven number of units. Create a second CVP analysis tab and use Goal Seek to determine the required unit sales to achieve a net income of $3,500. Create a third CVP analysis tab that assumes unit sales equal to those calculated in the second CVP analysis. Assume that sales revenue per unit cannot change, variable costs per unit cannot fall below $30, fixed costs cannot fall below $22,000, and contribution margin as a percentage of sales revenue cannot exceed 39%. Name each CVP analysis tab appropriately. Lastly, for each CVP analysis, freeze the three-line header at the top.

Critical Thinking

EA10-C1 Discuss Optimal Viewing of Accounting-Related Worksheets

Depending on the business in question, budgets can be particularly lengthy. As a result, many of the features examined in this chapter—including Freeze Panes, Splitting, and Synchronous Scrolling—are particularly useful in the budgeting process. But budgets are not the only lengthy worksheets for which these features are beneficial.

Write a paragraph of at least four sentences in which you identify three types of accounting worksheets (other than budgets) that can be particularly long and for which these features would be useful. Write a second paragraph of at least six sentences to discuss how you would use these features to facilitate the use of your identified worksheets.

EA10-C2 Discuss What-If Analyses and Accounting-Related Worksheets

Estimates and projections are used extensively when completing the budgeting process and performing CVP analyses. While these are the primary areas in which accounting-related uncertainty must be examined, there are other instances where what-if analysis tools like Goal Seek and Solver can be beneficial.

Write a paragraph of at least five sentences in which you identify two circumstances for which the use of Goal Seek and/or Solver would be appropriate in an accounting-related worksheet. Write a second paragraph of at least five sentences to discuss how the use of these what-if analysis tools would provide more robust accounting data.

Self-Assessment Answer Key

Chapter 1: The Accounting Equation and Recording Journal Entries

Item	Answer	Page Number
1	True	4
2	False	4
3	True	5
4	True	8
5	False	10
6	False	10
7	False	13
8	False	16
9	True	17
10	True	18
11	D	4
12	B	5, 10
13	C	8
14	A	8, 10, 13
15	B	10
16	C	13
17	B	13
18	A	17
19	D	18
20	B	16

Chapter 2: Financial Statements

Item	Answer	Page Number
1	True	35
2	False	35
3	False	35
4	True	38
5	False	39
6	True	39
7	False	41
8	False	42
9	False	42
10	True	43
11	B	35
12	B	38
13	A	41
14	C	43
15	C	42
16	B	42
17	C	42
18	B	44
19	A	42
20	B	42

Chapter 3: Statement of Cash Flows

Item	Answer	Page Number
1	False	70
2	False	74–75
3	True	72
4	True	72
5	True	73
6	False	73–74
7	True	74
8	True	73
9	False	72
10	True	76
11	D	70
12	B	70
13	A	72
14	C	73
15	B	73
16	C	73
17	A	74
18	C	74–75
19	D	77
20	D	77

Chapter 4: Inventory Costing and Analysis

Item	Answer	Page Number
1	True	96
2	False	96
3	False	101
4	True	101
5	True	95
6	False	104
7	True	105
8	False	105
9	False	108
10	True	112
11	B	96
12	D	97
13	C	99
14	B	100
15	B	102
16	A	95
17	C	104
18	D	107
19	A	109
20	C	112

Chapter 5: Bank Reconciliation

Item	Answer	Page Number
1	False	131
2	True	131
3	True	131
4	False	129
5	False	134
6	True	135
7	False	137
8	True	138–139
9	True	141
10	False	141
11	B	129
12	D	130
13	A	130
14	C	131
15	D	134
16	A	135
17	C	138–139
18	D	138
19	B	141
20	A	141

Chapter 6: Depreciation Schedule

Item	Answer	Page Number
1	False	162
2	True	161
3	True	163
4	False	163
5	True	167
6	False	168
7	True	169
8	True	171
9	True	172
10	False	174
11	C	161
12	A	163
13	A	159
14	D	164
15	B	165
16	D	163
17	D	168
18	C	168
19	C	171
20	C	174

Chapter 7: Payroll Register

Item	Answer	Page Number
1	True	195
2	True	196
3	False	196
4	True	199
5	False	200
6	True	201
7	True	201
8	False	203
9	True	203
10	True	203
11	B	195
12	A	196
13	D	194
14	C	196
15	A	200
16	C	201
17	B	203
18	A	203
19	C	205
20	D	194

Chapter 8: Bond Amortization

Item	Answer	Page Number
1	True	228
2	False	230
3	False	230
4	False	229
5	True	234
6	True	235
7	False	235
8	True	237
9	False	236
10	True	239
11	D	230
12	B	229
13	D	230
14	C	230
15	A	233
16	A	237
17	C	234
18	D	239
19	A	238–239
20	D	241

Chapter 9: Financial Statement Analysis

Item	Answer	Page Number
1	True	262
2	True	264
3	False	266
4	True	267
5	False	270
6	False	271
7	True	271
8	True	273
9	False	275
10	True	276
11	C	262
12	B	264
13	A	265
14	D	265
15	C	271
16	A	273
17	B	273
18	C	275
19	C	275
20	D	275

Chapter 10: Budgeting and Cost Analysis

Item	Answer	Page Number
1	True	300
2	False	300
3	False	301–302
4	False	302
5	False	305
6	True	306
7	False	305
8	False	308
9	False	309
10	True	312
11	A	300
12	D	301
13	A	301
14	B	308
15	B	305–306
16	C	307
17	A	308
18	A	311
19	C	312
20	C	312

Glossary

absolute cell reference   A cell reference which, when its formula is moved, does not change

accelerated depreciation method   A depreciation method that results in more depreciation expense in the early years than in the later years

assets   Items of value within a business

balance sheet   A financial statement displaying asset, liability, and owner's equity accounts

bank reconciliation   A reconciliation designed to illustrate that the adjusted bank balance equals the adjusted book balance

benchmarks   Figures against which a business' financial performance can be measured

bond amortization   The spreading out of a bond discount or premium over the life of a bond

borders   Lines appearing on the edge of a cell

breakeven point   The level of sales necessary to generate total net income of $0, based on the estimated variable and fixed costs

budgeting   A process that is undertaken as part of the planning process for future periods

calculated columns   Columns within a table in which formulas are automatically copied when first entered

carrying value   Calculated as face value minus unamortized discount or plus unamortized premium

cash budget   A budget designed to estimate cash requirements for future periods.

circular reference   A formula that refers to its own cell or to another formula that refers to that cell

concatenate   A function that combines existing text within a single cell

contract interest rate   The rate that is attached to a bond and which is used to calculate interest payments

contribution margin   The unit selling price minus the unit variable cost

cost-volume-profit (cvp) analysis   An analysis that gauges the different income levels that can be expected based on the possible combinations of variable costs, fixed costs, and unit sales for a period

current ratio   A liquidity ratio: current assets / current liabilities

debt financing   Raising capital through borrowing money

debt ratio   A solvency ratio: total liabilities / total assets

debt-to-equity ratio   A solvency ratio: total liabilities / total equity

deposits in transit   A reconciling item representing deposits made near the end of a period that were not recorded by the bank until the subsequent period

depreciation   An estimate of the loss in value that an asset experiences during a period

direct method   A method for completing the operating activities section of the statement of cash flows that displays all sources and uses of cash that relate to the standard revenue-generating activities of the business

drag and drop   Dragging a cell's contents to a new location

effective interest rate   A rate that factors in the impact of compounding on the interest payment

equity financing   Raising capital through the issuance of stock

equity ratio   A solvency ratio: total equity / total assets

face value   Amount to be paid upon the maturity date of a bond

federal withholding tax   Tax withheld from an employee and remitted to the federal government

FIFO (first-in, first-out) method   A depreciation method under which the business assumes that the oldest goods added to inventory are sold to customers before any other goods.

fill color   Places a color within the background of a cell

financing activities   The third section within the statement of cash flows; displays activity related to long-term liabilities, stocks, bonds, and withdrawals

fixed assets   An asset expected to be held for over twelve months

flash fill   An automatic feature within Excel that can quickly populate a column with similar data types.

footers   Information that prints in the bottom margin of every page

format painter   An option allowing for the copying of text and number formats from one cell to another

function   A prewritten formula within Excel

Goal Seek   A data analysis tool that adjusts a single variable to arrive at a desired figure within a worksheet

gross pay   Total earnings for a period

headers   Information that prints in the top margin of every page

horizontal analysis   An analysis in which account balances are compared across time

importing   Bringing data from other application programs into Excel

income statement   A financial statement displaying revenues, expenses, and net income or loss

indirect method   A method for completing the operating activities section of the statement of cash flows; starts with net income and reconciles to include only those items that impacted the cash balance

investing activities   The second section within the statement of cash flows; displays purchases and sales of fixed assets

issue price   The price initially paid for a bond

journal entries   A visual display of a transaction

liabilities   The portion of assets owed to entities outside of the business

LIFO (last-in, first-out) method   A depreciation method under which the business assumes that the most recent goods added to inventory are sold to customers before any other goods

line charts   A chart that shows the progression of data over time

liquidity ratios   Ratios that indicate how quickly a company can convert assets to cash

long-term assets   *See* fixed assets

macro   A recorded set of mouse and keyboard actions that can be played back at any time

mandatory deductions   Amounts that employers are required by law to withhold from an employee's paycheck

margins   The space between the edge of the paper and the worksheet

market interest rate   *See* effective interest rate

maturity date   The date on which the bond's life ends

Medicare tax   Taxes withheld from employee earnings that are used to fund the Medicare system

mixed cell reference   A cell reference that contains a mixture of a relative reference and an absolute reference (one each for the row and column portion of the reference)

nested function   A function contained within another function

net pay   The final column in the payroll register in which the check amount is entered

note receivable   An amount owed to the company by an outside party

NSF check   Referred to as a non-sufficient funds check or an insufficient funds check, this is a reconciling item representing a rejected (bounced) check.

Office Clipboard   A temporary storage utility that allows multiple text and graphical items from an Office document or other program to be copied and pasted into another Office document

operating activities   The first section within the statement of cash flows. This section displays standard revenue-generating activities of the business

orientation   The direction of printing; either portrait or landscape

outstanding check   A reconciling item representing a check that has been written but has not yet been cashed

owner's equity   The portion of assets not owed to entities outside of the business and to which therefore the owners can lay claim

payroll register   Displays all earnings and deduction data for every employee within a single pay period

percentage method   A method for determining federal withholding tax under which taxes are calculated using tables published by the IRS

pie charts   A chart that is suitable when examining data that represent a portion of a whole

PivotCharts   A chart presenting data from a PivotTable

PivotTables   A data analysis tool that allows the user to summarize data in a variety of manners

plant assets   *See* fixed assets

profitability ratios   Ratios that provide insight into a company's ability to effectively generate income

profit margin   A profitability ratio: net income / revenue

purchases budget   A budget designed to estimate merchandise purchases given the current level of inventory and the expected demand over the coming period

Quick Analysis   A button that appears beside a table or worksheet data, from which various options (such as formatting and sparklines) can be selected

quick ratio   A liquidity ratio: (cash + short-term investments + accounts receivable) / current liabilities

quick styles   A style that is built into Excel

ratio analysis   An analysis in which the relationships between specific account balances are examined

relative cell reference   A cell reference that, when its formula is moved, maintains the same relative distance to the new formula

residual value   *See* salvage value

return on assets   A profitability ratio: net income / average total assets

right-dragging   Using the right mouse button to drag a cell's contents to a new location; a menu appears when the right mouse button is released

salvage value   The amount a company expects to receive for a fixed asset at the time of disposal

short-term asset   An asset expected to be held for fewer than twelve months

slicers   Menu frames displayed on a worksheet containing a PivotTable that include all filtering choices in one field

Social security tax   Taxes withheld from employee earnings that are used to fund the Social Security system

solvency ratios   Ratios that gauge a company's ability to meet long-term obligations

solver   A data analysis tool that can achieve a desired end within a worksheet by adjusting multiple variables

sparklines   Miniature charts that appear in a single worksheet cell

state income tax   Tax withheld from an employee and remitted to the applicable state government

statement of cash flows   A financial statement displaying sources and uses of cash

statement of owner's equity   A financial statement reconciling beginning and ending owner's equity

status bar   Displayed at the bottom of the Excel window, it includes formula results, zoom, permissions, macro recording, and more

structured references   References utilized within a calculated column of a table

transaction   A single event that has occurred within a business

useful life   The number of years a company expects to use a fixed asset

voluntary deductions Amounts that cannot be withheld from an employee's payroll check unless that employee authorizes the deduction

vertical analysis An analysis in which account balances within the same period are compared

wage-bracket method A method for determining federal withholding tax under which taxes are looked up with IRS tables

weighted average method A depreciation method that averages all inventory costs, resulting in Cost of Goods Sold and an Ending Inventory Balance that falls between those that would be calculated through the LIFO and FIFO methods

Index

A

A to Z sorting, 171
absolute cell references, 200–202
accelerated depreciation method, 159–160
accounting equation
  cell entries, 4
  data types, 4
  decimals, 5
  deleting entries, 4
  displaying, 23–24, 26
  elements, 3
  entering, 28
  figures, 6
  formatting changes, 5
  headers, 5–6
  negative numbers, 5
  number formats, 4
  replacing entries, 4
active cell, 3
addition operator, 70
aligning
  data for readability, 206–207
  entries, 41
  text, 39–41
amortization schedule, completing, 232–233, 246, 249, 252–255
arithmetic operators, 70
asset accounts, debits and credits, 7
assets
  accounting equation, 3
  fixed, 159

short-term, 159
useful life, 159
AutoComplete, 97
AutoFilter, using with PivotTables, 108
AutoSum, 96
AVERAGE function, 96, 107
axis titles, including in charts, 264–265

B

balance sheet
  creating, 46–48
  data entry, 59–60, 62
  explained, 34
  vertical analysis, 268–269
bank charges, 130
bank reconciliations
  benefits, 142
  creating, 132–133, 145–153
  overview, 129–130
benchmarks, 261
bold formatting, 208
bond amortization schedule
  benefits, 242
  completing, 241–242, 256–257
  creating, 245–255
  overview, 227–228
  protecting, 235–236
borders, applying, 43–44, 206, 208
breakeven point, 300
budgeting and cost analysis
  benefits, 315
  overview, 299–300

budgets
  completing, 318–328
  preparing, 329–332

C

capital accounts, debits and credits, 7
carrying value, 228
cash budget
  creating, 303–304
  defined, 299
cash flows, statement of, 69, 71, 75–80, 83–91
cell and range references, 70
cell comments
  adding to, 276
  deleting, 275
  formatting, 276
  inserting, 275, 277–278, 283–284, 286–287, 289, 291
cell contents, replacing, 76
cell entries
  aligning, 41
  completing, 4
  confirming, 4
  deleting, 4
  indenting, 42
  replacing, 4
cell formats, replacing, 77
cell ranges, printing, 306
cell references
  absolute, 200–202
  mixed, 201–202
  ranges, 70

relative, 72, 200

typing in formulas, 70

cells

comments, 275–278

merging, 42

modifying, 35

moving and copying, 10

protecting, 236–237, 247, 253, 255

Quick Styles, 135–137

unlocking in protected worksheets, 237–238

Center alignment, 41

charts. *See also* Quick Analysis

adjusting, 271–272

axis titles, 264–265

data source, 263

deleting, 266

formatting control, 265

inserting, 262

layouts, 272–273, 283, 286, 289, 291

line, 270–271

moving, 266

pie, 270–271

sizing, 266

source data, 267

sparklines, 273, 283, 286, 289, 291

styles, 283, 286, 289, 291

types, 263–264, 267, 282–283, 285–286, 288–290

circular references, 73–74

Clipboard, 8

column charts

axes, 270

changing, 271–272

creating, 184, 269

column width, modifying, 11

columns

adding and deleting, 165

adding to tables, 166–167

adjusting, 178–179, 181, 185

freezing, 300

hiding, 35–36

modifying, 34–35

selecting, 165–166

sorting, 171

specifying for printing, 308

in tables, 162

comments

adding to, 276

deleting, 275

formatting, 276

inserting, 275, 277–278, 283–284, 286–287, 289, 291

competitor's balances benchmark, 261

CONCATENATE function, 101–102

conditional formatting, 103–104, 137–139, 150. *See also* formatting

applying, 139–140, 147

highlighting, 208

presets, 137

rules, 138–139

contract interest rate, 227–228

contribution margin, 300

Copy command, 8, 11–13

copying

formulas, 74–75

and moving cells, 10

cost analysis. *See* budgeting and cost analysis

COUNT function, 96, 107

COUNT NUMBERS function, 96

credits, impact on account types, 7

current ratio, 262

Custom Filter command, 173

Cut command, 8, 11–13

CVP (cost-volume-profit) analysis, 300

completing, 318–328

creating, 313–315

preparing, 329–332

D

data analysis tools, 311–312

data and headers, highlighting, 208–209

data bars, applying, 104

data sets, separating, 206

data types, 4. *See also* external data

debits, impact on account types, 7

debt financing, 227

debt ratio, 262

debt-to-equity ratio, 262

decimals, 5

deductions in payroll register, 194

deleting

cell entries, 4

charts, 266

comments, 275

formatting elements, 268

modifying elements, 268

rows and columns, 165

source data, 267

tables, 166

types, 267

worksheets, 38

deposits in transit, 129

depreciation expense, 159–160

depreciation functions, 167––171, 179, 181–182, 185

depreciation schedules

benefits, 175

completing, 178–185

creating, 164–165

direct method, 69

disability insurance, 194

Dividends account, 33

division operator, 70

double-declining balance depreciation, 160–161

drag and drop

importing data, 131

moving and copying cells, 10

E

effective interest rate, 227–228

entries. *See* cell entries

equity financing, 227

equity ratio, 262

errors in bank reconciliations, 130

expense accounts, debits and credits, 7

expenses

entering, 36–37

financial statements, 33

exponentiation operator, 70

external data, importing, 130–132. *See also* data types

F

face value, 227
federal withholding tax, 193
FIFO (First In, First Out)
    method, 95
figures
  accounting equation, 6
  entering in accounting
    equation, 6
  formatting in accounting
    equation, 6
fill colors, applying, 44
filtering
  criteria and searches, 172–173
  customizing, 173
  PivotTables, 108–109
  tables, 179–180, 182, 185
financial functions, 228–233
financial statements
  analysis, 261–262, 279, 282–
    294
  benefits, 49
  creating, 52–64
  overview, 33–34
Find command, 76
fixed assets, 159
Flash Fill, 101
footers and headers, 141, 147, 150
Format Painter, 134, 146–147, 149
formatting. *See also* conditional
    formatting
  changes, 5
  comments, 276
  text with functions, 100–103
formulas. *See also* Goal Seek
  arithmetic operators, 70
  AutoComplete, 97
  cell and range references, 70
  copying, 74–75
  with structured references, 169
  typing cell references in, 70
freezing
  panes, 304
  rows and columns, 300
Function Arguments box, 98–99

functions
  AutoSum, 96
  depreciation, 167–171, 179,
    181–182, 185
  formatting text, 100–103
  inserting, 98–99
  inventory listing, 99
  nested, 102
  status bar, 97
  SUM formula, 96
  summarizing data, 99
  syntax, 97
future value argument, financial
    functions, 230
FV (Future Value) function,
    229–230

G

Get External Data commands,
    131–132
Goal Seek. *See also* formulas
  CVP (cost-volume-profit) analy-
    sis, 313–315
  and Solver, 323–324, 326, 328
  using, 320
gridlines
  applying, 322–323, 326, 328
  nonprinting, 309
  printing, 319–320
gross pay, 193
grouping operator, 70

H

headers
  accounting equation, 5–6
  and footers, 141, 147, 150
  highlighting data, 208–209
headings, printing, 309, 319–
    320, 322–323, 326, 328
hiding columns and rows, 35–36
highlights, 3, 208–209
HLOOKUP (Horizontal Lookup)
    function, 203–205
horizontal analysis
  completing, 268–269
  explained, 261

I

IF function, 195–197. *See also*
    nested IF function
importing external data, 130–132
income statement
  completing, 36–37
  data entry, 58–59, 61
  explained, 33
  horizontal analysis, 268–269
  modifying, 39–41, 45–46
income tax, state, 194
indenting cell entries, 42
indirect method, 69, 71
industry standards
    benchmark, 261
Insert Function option, 98–99
insufficient funds check, 130
interest rates, contract vs.
    effective, 227–228
inventory costing methods, 95,
    102–103, 114
inventory listings, editing,
    117–125
issue price, 227
italic formatting, 208

J

journal entries
  benefits, 20
  printing, 18–19
  recording, 7–8, 24–29

L

landscape orientation, 18, 306
Left alignment, 41
LEFT function, 100–101
liabilities, accounting equation, 3
liability accounts, debits and
    credits, 7
life of the bond, 227
LIFO (Last In, First Out)
    method, 95
line breaks, entering, 42–43
line charts, 270–271
liquidity ratios, 262

locking cells, 237
long text entries, 10
lookup functions and tables, 203–206

M

macros
 naming, 239
 recording, 239–242, 247–248, 250–251, 253, 255
 recording steps, 240
 running, 241, 247–248, 250–251, 253, 255
 saving in workbooks, 240
 security levels, 238–239
 storing, 240
mandatory deduction, 194
margins, setting, 305–308, 319, 322, 325, 327
maturity date, 227
MAX function, 96
Medicare tax, 194
merging cells, 42
MID function, 100–101
MIN function, 96
mixed cell references, 201–202
moving and copying, cells, 10
multiplication operator, 70

N

negative numbers, 5
nested functions, 102
nested IF function, 199–202. See also IF function
net income, 33
net pay, 193–194
non-sufficient funds check, 130
notes receivable, 129
NSF checks, 130
number formats, 4–5

O

OASDI, 194
Office Clipboard, 8
orientation
 adjusting, 319, 322, 325, 327
 explained, 306

modifying, 307–308
 portrait and landscape, 18
 rotation options, 39
outstanding checks, 129
owner's equity
 accounting equation, 3
 statement, 33, 39–41, 45–46, 59, 61–62

P

page orientation. See orientation
panes, freezing, 304
paper size, 306
password protection, 235
Paste command, 8, 11–13
Paste Options button, 9
payment argument, financial functions, 230
payroll register
 benefits, 210
 completing, 220–222
 creating, 213–219
 overview, 193–194
 populating, 197–198
percent operator, 70
percentage method, 193
periods argument, financial functions, 230
pie charts, 270–271
PivotCharts
 basing on PivotTables, 112–113
 creating and filtering, 111–112
PivotTables
 areas, 107
 creating, 109–111, 117–125
 examples, 105–106
 retaining, 112
 source data, 105
PMT (Payment) function, 228–230
portrait orientation, 18, 306
present value argument, financial functions, 230
presets, 137
print area, adjusting, 306–308, 319, 322, 325, 327
print settings, modifying, 309–311

printing
 and deleting tables, 166
 journal entries, 18–19
 setting options, 308–309
 tables, 166
 worksheets, 16–19, 305–307
prior performance benchmark, 261
profit margin, 262
profitability ratios, 262
protecting
 cells, 236–238, 247, 250, 253, 255
 workbook structure, 233–234
 workbooks and worksheets, 246–247, 250, 253, 255
 worksheets, 234–236, 250, 255
purchases budget
 completing, 309–311
 explained, 299
PV (Present Value) function, 229–230

Q

Quick Analysis, 174–175, 180, 182, 185. See also charts
Quick Layouts, using with charts, 272–273
quick ratio, 262
Quick Styles
 applying to cells, 135–137
 using, 146–147, 149
QuickBooks, importing data from, 131

R

range references, 70
ranges of cells, printing, 306
rate argument, financial functions, 230
ratio analysis, 262
ratios, calculating, 283–284, 286, 289, 291
readability of worksheets, 207–209
Redo command, 13–15
relative cell references, 72, 200
Replace feature, 76

replacing
cell contents, 76
cell entries, 4
cell formats, 77
residual value, 159
return on assets, 262
revenue accounts, debits and credits, 7
revenues, 33
Right alignment, 41
RIGHT function, 100–101
right-dragging, 8
rotating text, 39
ROUND function, 195
row height, modifying, 11
rows
adding and deleting, 165
adding to tables, 166–167
adjusting, 178–179, 181, 185
filtering, 172–173
freezing, 300
hiding, 35–36
modifying, 34–35
selecting, 165–166
in tables, 162

S

salvage value, 159
saving workbooks with macros, 240
scaling options, 307
sensitivity analysis, 72–73
Sheet Options, 308
short-term assets, 159
slicers, filtering PivotTables with, 108, 110–111
social security tax
calculating, 201–202
explained, 194
solvency ratios, 262
Solver, 312–315, 320, 323–324, 326, 328
sorting tables, 171, 173, 179–180, 182, 185
sparklines, 273–274, 283, 286, 289, 291
splitting worksheet window, 300–301, 304–305

state income tax, 194
statement
cash flows, 69, 71, 75–80, 83–91
owner's equity, 33, 39–41
status bar functions, 97
straight-line depreciation, 159
structured references, 167–169
styles. See Quick Styles
subtraction operator, 70
SUM function, 96, 107

T

tables
adding columns, 165–167
adding rows, 166–167
converting ranges, 161–162
creating, 161
deleting, 166
deleting columns, 165
features, 161
filtering, 179–180, 182, 185
formatting, 164
header row, 163
populating and formatting, 163
printing, 166
rows and columns, 162
selecting columns, 165–166
selecting rows, 165–166
sorting, 179–180, 182, 185
total row, 163
taxes, 194
templates, using, 49
text
extracting with functions, 100–101
formatting with functions, 100–103
rotating, 39
wrapping, 42–43
text entries, long, 10
text files, importing data from, 131–132
title rows, specifying, 308, 319–320, 322–323, 326, 328
transaction, defined, 6–7
Trust Center, accessing, 238

type argument, financial functions, 230

U

Undo command, 13–15
unlocking cells, 237–238
useful life of assets, 159
user changes, allowing, 235

V

vertical alignment, changing, 39–41
vertical analysis
completing, 268–269
explained, 261–262
VLOOKUP (Vertical Lookup) function, 203–206
voluntary deductions, 194

W

wage-bracket method, 193
weighted average method, 95
what-if analysis, 72–73
Withdrawals account, 7, 33
workbooks
creating, 5–6
protecting, 246–247, 250, 253, 255
protecting structure, 233–234
worksheet window, splitting, 300–301
worksheets
deleting, 38
enhancing, 208
freezing rows and columns, 300
managing, 38
navigating, 38
printing, 16–19, 305–307
protecting, 234–235, 246–247, 250, 253, 255
readability, 207–208
viewing in multiple windows, 301–302, 305
wrapping text, 42–43

Z

Z to A sorting, 171

NOTES

NOTES

NOTES

NOTES

NOTES

NOTES